THE COLLINS FIELD GUIDE TO THE
BIRDS
OF EAST AFRICA

THE COLLINS FIELD GUIDE TO THE

BIRDS

OF EAST AFRICA

John G. Williams

with over 660 species
illustrated in full colour by
Norman Arlott

Foreword by
Roger Tory Peterson

THE STEPHEN GREENE PRESS
Lexington, Massachusetts

TO PHILIPPA

First published in Great Britain in 1980 under the title A FIELD GUIDE TO
THE BIRDS OF EAST AFRICA by William Collins Sons & Co. Ltd.;
expanded from A FIELD GUIDE TO THE BIRDS OF EAST AND
CENTRAL AFRICA
Copyright © John Williams, 1963
First published in the United States of America in 1988 by
The Stephen Greene Press, Inc.
Distributed by Viking Penguin Inc., 40 West 23rd Street, New York, NY 10010

CIP data available
ISBN 0-8289-0661-0
Printed in Glasgow
by William Collins Sons & Co Ltd
set in Times Roman

Contents

5

CONTENTS

Colour plates

Foreword

Roger Tory Peterson

When I first set foot in East Africa in May, 1957, a pleasant, friendly man greeted me as I stepped from the ramp at the Nairobi airport. I had met him several years before in London at the British Museum, and it was then that he urged me to see for myself the bird wonders of East Africa.

Two reporters who also met the plane asked me whether my visit to Kenya meant that I was planning to do a Field Guide to the Birds of East Africa. I replied, 'Oh no! But the man who should do suoh a book is standing here beside me – John Williams.' Whether that was the moment when John Williams first conceived the idea of a Field Guide I do not know, but we soon talked earnestly of such a book. I urged him to feel free to use my well-known Field Guide system which had proved so practical in both Europe and North America, but I regretted that I could not paint the colour plates because of the overwhelming pressure of other commitments. However, John Williams had already tried his hand at painting the sunbirds, the *Nectariniidae*, a gorgeous galaxy of feathered gems, on which he is the world authority. He decided to undertake the drawings himself and estimated that it would take perhaps a year or two to bring such a work to completion. I knew better, for I had gone through the ordeal several times, and I gave him a minimum of four or five years which proved to be a more realistic estimate.

Africa, unlike that other great bird continent of the Southern Hemisphere, South America, has been blessed with a number of fine ornithological works with numerous illustrations, but most of them are heavy enough to be used as door stoppers. What was really needed was a pocket field guide – something that would give the traveller a dependable introduction to the species he was most likely to see. No man in all Africa was better qualified to tackle the project than John Williams, whose official position was Curator of Birds at Nairobi's Coryndon Museum. There is no question that he is the sharpest field observer I have encountered in that great continent with the possible exception of Jim Chapin, who during fifty years of his life collected in the forests of the Congo.

I vividly remember my first field trip with John Williams. Only a few hours after my arrival, we took the landrover over the Ngong hills and down to Lake Magadi near the Tanganyika border where we were joined by Sir Evelyn Baring then the Governor of Kenya, and himself a fine field ornithologist. Like other great field men I have known, John Williams was able to identify almost every bird, with amazing certainty, at the snap of a finger. He knew their identification tags, their 'field marks.' But here I was, thrown into a completely new avifauna. I could only say, when he ticked off another one, 'I'll take your word for it, old boy.' Our list for that week-end was well over 200 species. John Williams assures me that with a little planning a single 'big day' or 'century run' in East Africa could easily exceed 250 – more species than most active bird watchers see in a whole year in the British Isles or in the north-eastern United States.

In the past, Africa, to the traveller, meant the large game animals and primitive tribes. And the object of going on safari was to shoot. To-day shooting is being replaced by the more civilised sport of photographing – or just looking. The herds of big game are dwindling fast outside the parks and preserves. The once picturesque native peoples, except for the Masai and certain marginal groups, are now so westernised that they are as commonplace in their dress and activities as Europeans. The tourist, on the other hand, will find increasing pleasure in the spectacular bird life. People from temperate Europe and North America who are accustomed to the 'little brown jobs' will marvel at the iridescent sunbirds, bizarre hornbills, and gemlike bee-eaters, rollers and touracos. But half the fun is knowing what they are – to be able to put names to things.

John Williams has made it possible to put a name to most of the birds one will encounter, and I predict that the tourist offices will be swamped with requests about the birding spots of East and Central Africa. Already Lake Nakuru, ninety miles north of Nairobi in the Rift Valley is becoming a mecca for tourists from all parts of the world who are drawn by the spectacle of the flamingos. But the marabous, stilts, and waterfowl that populate the shore also merit attention, and so do the ground hornbills, secretary birds, emerald cuckoos and other fascinating birds that haunt the acacia groves. This field guide will give you their names.

ROGER TORY PETERSON, 1963

This foreword was originally written for the author's earlier book *A Field Guide to the Birds of East and Central Africa* which was greatly enlarged and newly illustrated to form the present volume.

Preface

This book is a Field Guide to the Birds of East Africa and its scope is epitomised in its title. The region specifically covered consists of Eritrea, Ethiopia, Somalia, Uganda, Kenya, Tanzania, Zanzibar and Pemba Islands, Mozambique, Malawi, Zambia and Zimbabwe. However, its value as a field reference work extends far beyond the political boundaries since distributions of all the species treated are given for the entire African Continent.

The greatest difficulty confronting an author of any book concerned with the birds of East Africa is one of selecting those species to be illustrated from a region with such a rich avifauna. To give an example of this superabundance, no fewer than 1,033 species of birds are known from the relatively small country of Kenya.

This volume has its origins in my *Field Guide to the Birds of East and Central Africa*, first published in 1963 and many times reprinted, which it now replaces. That guide concentrated upon the most common species of birds to be found in the vast region covered and those which drew attention by their spectacular appearance or loud calls. This new book greatly expands the coverage to include over 500 more species and entirely new artwork illustrates a much greater number of species depicting in full colour those which were originally shown in black and white. In the pages that follow 665 species are fully described and illustrated and the essential field characters of a further 633 species are enumerated in the text under the heading 'Allied Species'.

The data upon which this Field Guide is based have been compiled from many sources. They are drawn primarily from field-notes and specimens personally collected in all the regions covered; from information and specimens supplied by resident and visiting naturalists and from a study of all the available literature. I am especially indebted to Messrs P. A. Clancey, Tony Archer, Tim Barnley, Daphne Ball, Ivan Bampton, Steve Collins, Rob Glen, Tony Start and Alec Forbes-Watson for East African records; and to Messrs C. W. Benson, M. P. Stuart Irwin and Reay H. N. Smithers for data on relative abundance and distribution of certain species found in central Africa.

It is the author's pleasure to record his deep appreciation and gratitude to the many persons – too numerous to mention individually – who have assisted in so many ways, especially during his zoological field trips.

Norman Arlott would particularly like to thank Basil Parsons, Jack Block

11

and Robert Gillmor for their help and advice during the preparation of the illustrations.

The Unknown: There are still many places in eastern Africa which have never been explored zoologically. There can be no doubt that there still remain a small number of undescribed species of birds awaiting discovery. In the heart of the Impenetrable Forest of south-western Kigezi, Uganda, there exists a green turaco with very little red on the wings. This bird has never been collected, although seen by two ornithologists of repute besides the author. A very large all black swift has been observed on Marsabit Mountain in the Northern Frontier Province of Kenya; and a greyish, long-tailed bird with red or chestnut under tail-coverts has been glimpsed in the nearby Mathews Range.

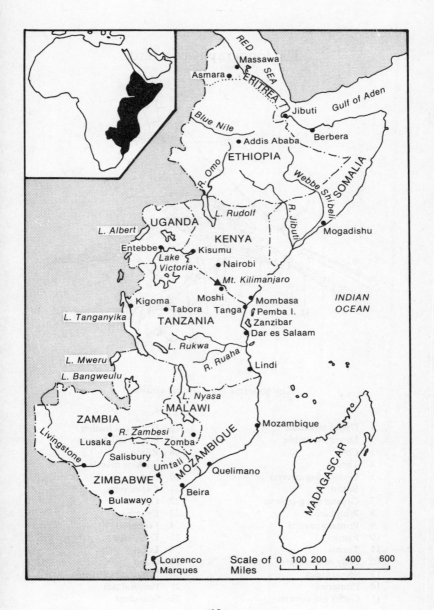

The topography of a bird

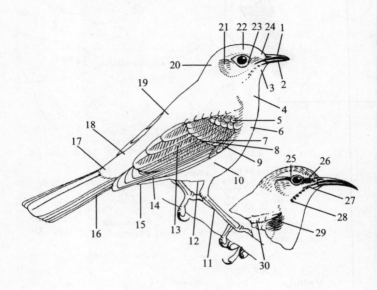

Key to terms used in this volume

1	Upper mandible	16	Outer tail feather
2	Lower mandible	17	Upper tail-coverts
3	Chin	18	Rump
4	Throat	19	Back or mantle
5	Lesser wing-coverts	20	Nape
6	Breast	21	Ear-coverts
7	Greater wing-coverts	22	Crown
8	Wingbar	23	Eye-ring
9	Primary coverts	24	Forehead
10	Flanks	25	Eye-stripe
11	Tarsus	26	Lores
12	Belly or abdomen	27	Gape
13	Secondaries	28	Moustachial stripe
14	Primaries	29	Pectoral tuft
15	Under tail-coverts	30	Scapulars

How to use this book

Visitors to Africa from Europe and America will find representatives of several bird families well-known in northern climes – birds of prey, ducks and geese, warblers, larks, pipits and wagtails, flycatchers and many others. Groups less familiar will include the ostrich, hamerkop, whale-headed stork, secretary bird, finfoot, jacanas, painted snipe, coucals, turacos, parrots, hornbills, wood-hoopoes, mousebirds, trogons, barbets, honey-guides, broadbills, pittas, babblers and chatterers, bulbuls, cuckoo-shrikes, drongos, helmet-shrikes, oxpeckers, white-eyes, sunbirds, weaver-birds and waxbills. The essential characters of these groups are enumerated in the text and illustrations.

In most instances it will be found possible to identify a given bird by referring to the illustrations and by noting the chief field characters as indicated in the captions to the plates. But however certain such identification may appear, it should still be confirmed by looking up the text, where closely allied species are listed and information given on distribution, habitat and habits.

Identification by Elimination: Identifying birds, at least in the early stages, is frequently a matter of elimination. In this process distribution and habitat play a major part. As an example, a large, black-looking sunbird found in Kenya at altitudes over 8,000 feet is almost certain to be the Tacazze Sunbird; below 7,000 feet it is equally likely to be the Bronze Sunbird.

Voice: As a general rule most birds are recognised by their visual characters; voice and song are of secondary importance, however valuable these may be in drawing attention to birds in the field. Nevertheless there are exceptions to this rule. Several cuckoos would be overlooked were it not for their loud and easily recognised calls, and among the cisticola warblers – a group of 'difficult' mainly brown birds – song and habitat have an important role in field recognition.

Written descriptions of birds' calls and song leave much to be desired, and there can be no doubt that the only satisfactory method of depicting voice is with the aid of bird recordings made in the field. Everyone interested in African bird-life owes a debt of gratitude to one of Africa's leading ornithologists, the late Mr M. E. W. North, for his work in this sphere. His first record, on which forty-two species of African birds may be heard, has been released by Cornell University.

Size: A bird's size is not easy to indicate in a species' description so that it means the same thing to everyone. The measurements given in the section 'Identification' indicate the average length of the bird from tip of bill to tip of longest tail feather. The following are a few comparative bird lengths which may be useful for those persons familiar with European or North American birds: European Willow Warbler 4½″; House Sparrow 5½″; European Song Thrush 9″; Wood Pigeon 16″; Rook 18″. Most of the American Wood Warblers measure between 4½ and 5½″; Cardinal 8½″; American Robin 9½″; and Blue Jay 11½″. In addition to size it is important to observe whether a bird is plump-looking like members of the thrush family or slim like the wagtails and bee-eaters.

Habits and Flight: A bird's field habits often provide good clues to its identity. A note should be made as to whether it perches in prominent positions and on vantage points such as telegraph poles and wires, like a stonechat, an augur buzzard or a fiscal shrike; or whether it is a skulker keeping to thick vegetation, like a boubou shrike or a cinnamon bracken warbler. Clues to identity may be found in characteristic habits, such as tail wagging in the wagtails and common sandpiper; or climbing about on branches in the manner of a tit, as is the habit of the red-headed malimbe and some other weavers. Modes of progression offer useful pointers. In the case of ground frequenting species the gait may be a hop or a walk. Among water birds the swimming level may be high in the water like a moorhen, or low like a diving duck, cormorant or darter. When taking off from water a bird may need to run along the surface before rising, like a moorhen, coot or diving duck; or spring clear in one jump like a surface feeding duck. The flight may be undulating as in the case of woodpeckers and honey-guides; rapid but erratic and given to changes of direction, typical of the sunbirds; or direct and fast as in the swifts. The wing-beats may be slow, as in the herons; or rapid as is the case with ducks and parrots. The bird may hover in the air like a kestrel, augur buzzard or pied kingfisher; or indulge in alternate glides on motionless wings and a period of rapid wingbeats, like the swifts.

Distinctive Plumage Patterns and Silhouettes: Aids to identification include pattern and colour contrasts of the entire plumage; the colour of the underparts, whether spotted, banded or immaculate, and the degree and extent of the spotting and banding; the presence or absence of a white rump patch, such as occurs in some species of sandpipers, swifts and wheatears; tail length and whether the outer tail feathers are white or not, and the extent of the white – important in nightjar recognition. The shape of the tail is often significant, whether it is forked and the degree of forking, or whether square, rounded or wedge-shaped, and whether central or outer tail feathers are greatly lengthened, as in many species of sunbirds, widow-birds, bee-eaters and rollers.

Wing patterns should always be noted, especially in the case of waders and ducks. Head markings, especially crown and eye stripes, are important in identifying many perching birds. Such stripes may be pale or dark, and situated on the crown, or above, through or below the eye. There may be pale or white feather rings around the eyes, as in the White-eyes and the White-eyed Slaty Flycatcher.

Subspecies: In treating the problem of subspecies it was essential to concentrate on the primary object of the Field Guide, the identification of bird species in the field. This rule has been relaxed only in those few cases where geographical races are so strikingly different that they may be recognised with certainty and ease. Examples are the various races of the yellow and blue-headed wagtail, and the black-breasted and green-breasted races of the beautiful sunbird. For the rest it is wiser to concentrate on species identification and to leave the vexed question of what constitutes a valid subspecies to the museum taxonomists.

Symbols: The symbols ♂ and ♀ indicate male and female respectively.

Adult ♂ and ♀ Ostrich

OSTRICH: Struthionidae

The largest living bird; flightless; two toes only on each foot.

OSTRICH *Struthio camelus*

Identification. 7–8ft, 2–2½m. Unmistakable; adult ♂ black and white; ♀ and immature greyish-brown. ♂ Somali race has neck and thighs blue-grey; in north African and Masai races the neck and thighs are flesh-pink.
Voice. Usually silent: breeding ♂♂ utter deep booming sound but this is seldom heard.
Distribution and Habitat. North African race, Sudan and north-eastern Ethiopia; Somali race, Somalia, eastern and southern Ethiopia and northern Kenya south to Voi. Masai race, southern Kenya and Tanzania. Although still common in eastern Africa, the ostrich is now extinct over much of its former range. Habitat, plains, open thorn-bush country and semi-desert. The Somali Ostrich is still common in northern Kenya and in the Meru National Park. The Masai Ostrich is found in Nairobi National Park, in Mara and on the Serengeti Plains, Tanzania.

GREBES: Podicipidae

Duck or teal-sized aquatic birds with slender pointed bills; tail-less appearance characteristic of family; expert divers; feet lobed, not webbed; sexes similar.

GREAT CRESTED GREBE *Podiceps cristatus*   **Plate 1**

Identification. 18–20in, 45–57cm. Adult with conspicuous chestnut and black frills on sides of head and a black tuft on each side of the crown; immature paler and lacks head frills and tufts. The other two grebes found in Africa are much smaller than this species.
Voice. Usually a silent bird but utters a low 'keek, keek, keek' during breeding season.
Distribution and Habitat. Local resident from Ethiopia southwards on both fresh and alkaline inland waters; sometimes on relatively small dams.

BLACK-NECKED GREBE   *Podiceps nigricollis*   **Plate 1**

Identification. 12in, 30cm. Adult dark above, white below with rufous along flanks; distinguished from Little Grebe by shape of crown, slender black neck, golden ear tufts and thin bill which appears to be slightly up-turned. Immature greyish and white without head plumes.
Voice. A slightly drawn-out 'tseeeep.'
Distribution and Habitat. An uncommon and local resident on both fresh-water and alkaline lakes. In many places spasmodic in its appearances and sometimes in numbers on lakes in the Rift Valley in Kenya.

LITTLE GREBE   *Podiceps ruficollis*   **Plate 1**

Identification. 10in, 25cm. Adult a small, dark grebe with chestnut-red face and throat patch and pale green gape. Immature brownish-grey, much paler and lacks chestnut on face and throat.
Voice. A loud and often prolonged trill.
Distribution and Habitat. A common resident throughout Africa in suitable localities. Occurs on fresh and brackish lakes, dams, ponds and slow-flowing rivers. Abundant on the Rift Valley lakes in East Africa.

PELICANS: Pelecanidae

Very large water birds with long, hook-tipped bills and a naked pouch suspended from the lower mandible and upper part of the throat. Sexes similar.

WHITE PELICAN   *Pelecanus onocrotalus*   **Plate 1**

Identification. 60–70in, 152–180cm. White except for black and grey flight feathers; in breeding plumage suffused salmon-pink. Immature pale buffish-brown, becoming whiter with successive moults. Pink-backed Pelican smaller and pale grey. White Pelicans are extremely gregarious, fishing in tightly packed flotillas, all the birds submerging their heads and necks at the same moment. They rest on shore in large groups and soar in thermal currents in flocks. The Pink-backed Pelican is a solitary fisher, catching fish with a heron-like striking action.
Voice. Generally silent except at nesting colonies when utters a guttural croaking.
Distribution and Habitat. Occurs commonly throughout Africa on large areas of inland water; uncommon on the coast. In East Africa vast numbers breed in the Rukwa swamps, southern Tanzania; also very abundant on Lake Nakuru in Kenya.

PINK-BACKED PELICAN   *Pelecanus rufescens*   **Plate 1**

Identification. 50–54in, 127–137cm. Adults pale grey with shaggy nape crest; the vinous-pink rump is conspicuous only in flight. Immature pale greyish-buff, best distinguished from immature White Pelican by smaller size. Less gregarious than its larger relative, large flocks being uncommon. Often associates with White Pelicans when resting.
Voice. Silent except at breeding colonies, when utters various croaking sounds.
Distribution and Habitat. Resident and local migrant on inland waters throughout Africa; uncommon on coast. In East Africa found on all the larger lakes, both alkaline and freshwater.

CORMORANTS: Phalacrocoracidae

Dark-plumaged, long-necked water birds with strong hook-tipped bills; small goose or duck-sized; swim and dive to capture food, mainly fish and frogs.

WHITE-NECKED CORMORANT   *Phalacrocorax carbo*   **Plate 1**

Identification. 36in, 91cm. The African race of the European Cormorant. Large blackish water-bird with white cheeks, foreneck and upper breast; eyes green. Immature has entire underparts white, darkening with successive moults. After swimming often perches with wings held half open, a characteristic attitude of cormorants and darters. Differs from Long-tailed Cormorant in larger size, relatively shorter tail and in adults white neck and chest.
Voice. Various guttural croaks uttered at the nest, otherwise silent birds.
Distribution and Habitat. Occurs commonly throughout eastern Africa, frequenting lakes, dams and larger rivers; less frequent on the coast. A gregarious breeder, nesting in colonies in trees, on rocky islands or in reed beds.

LONG-TAILED CORMORANT   *Phalacrocorax africanus*   **Plate 1**

Identification. 22–24in, 56–61cm. Distinguished from White-necked Cormorant by smaller size, entirely black underparts of adult, red eyes and relatively longer tail. Immature brownish-white below.
Voice. Normally silent but utters soft croaking at nest.
Distribution and Habitat. Common throughout Africa in suitable localities, on inland waters and less frequently on the coast.

Allied Species. The Socotran Cormorant *(Ph. nigrogularis)* is bronzy-black, intermediate in size between the White-necked and Long-tailed Cormorants. It is restricted to coasts of the Red Sea and the Gulf of Aden and is an entirely marine species.

DARTERS: Anhingidae

Large, long-necked, cormorant-like water birds with long tails. Differ from cormorants in having sharply-pointed, not hooked bills. Darters swim low in the water with only the head and neck showing, giving a good imitation of a snake swimming: hence the name 'snake-bird' often bestowed upon this species.

AFRICAN DARTER   *Anhinga rufa*   Plate 1

Identification. 38in, 96cm. Resembles a long-necked, long-tailed cormorant but has slender, pointed bill. The neck has a characteristic 'kink,' conspicuous both when bird is settled and in flight. Adult has a chestnut neck with a white stripe down each side; underparts black. Immature much paler with buffy-brown underparts.
Voice. Normally silent except for croaking sounds uttered at nest.
Distribution and Habitat. Occurs throughout Africa in suitable localities. Inhabits inland waters, favouring slow-flowing rivers and fresh and alkaline lakes. Common in East and Central Africa, especially on Kenya's Rift Valley lakes and lakes in western Uganda.

HERONS, EGRETS AND BITTERNS: Ardeidae

Tall, graceful wading birds with lax plumage. In flight the head is carried drawn back on the shoulders with the neck curved: cranes, storks and spoonbills fly with the neck extended. Many species are gregarious, nesting in mixed colonies often with other water birds.

LITTLE BITTERN   *Ixobrychus minutus*   Plate 2

Identification. 14in, 35cm. Adult ♂ greenish-black on crown and mantle, buff below; wing with a contrasting and conspicuous buffy-white wing-patch, specially noticeable in flight. Adult ♀ streaked dark brown and buff with a dark crown; wing-patch less conspicuous; immature similar but more streaked. Two races of Little Bittern occur in East and Central Africa, the nominate European race with a rather pale buffy neck and the African resident race, *I. m. payesii*, with the neck chestnut-buff.

Voice. A sharp 'kaaaa' when flushed from a reedbed, and various frog-like croaks.

Distribution and Habitat. The nominate European race is a winter visitor and passage migrant between October and March, most frequently encountered on spring migration. The African race is an uncommon and local bird throughout most of Africa. Both are skulkers in dense reed and papyrus beds where they are often overlooked.

DWARF BITTERN   *Ardeirallus sturmii*   Plate 2

Identification. 10in, 25cm. Adult, crown, neck and upperparts slate-grey; below buff streaked dark grey; immature similar but with buff edges to feathers of upperparts and more rufous-buff below. A skulker in dense waterside vegetation.

Voice. Utters a harsh croak when flushed.

Distribution and Habitat. Occurs throughout eastern and central Africa but very uncommon and not often seen. Occurs in reeds and papyrus beds fringing lakes and also in rank herbage along water courses in dry country. At least partly nocturnal and not infrequently picked up dead below telegraph wires with which they have collided.

NIGHT HERON *Nycticorax nycticorax*   Plate 2

Identification. 24in, 61cm. A thickset grey and white heron with crown and upperparts black; two long, slender white nape plumes; eye large, red. Immature pale brown with heavy buffish-white spots on upperparts and wing coverts; eye orange-brown. Mainly nocturnal, keeping to dense waterside cover during the day.

Voice. A loud harsh 'aaark' uttered at dusk while flying to feeding grounds.

Distribution and Habitat. Local resident and winter visitor to suitable localities throughout eastern and central Africa. Frequents marshes, swamps, lakes, rivers and coastal mangrove swamps where there is suitable cover to suit its nocturnal habits. Spends day in shelter of dense reed-beds, papyrus swamps or thickly foliaged trees near water. In Kenya it occurs commonly at Lakes Naivasha, Nakuru and Baringo, and several hundred pairs breed in the great heronry on the Tana River at Garsen.

WHITE-BACKED NIGHT HERON   *Nycticorax leuconotus* Plate 2

Identification. 24in, 61cm. Less thickset than the Night Heron. Upperparts dark brown with a concealed white streak down the back; crown and nape blackish with short dark plumes; neck and breast rufous-brown. Immature browner with whitish streaking and spots; lacks the white back streak. Widely distributed but rare in most places and not often seen; nocturnal.

Voice. A very harsh rasping croak.

Distribution and Habitat. Occurs from Ethiopia southwards but very uncommon except in the mangrove swamps on Pemba Island north of Zanzibar. Besides mangrove swamps it occurs in papyrus and reeds, and also along streams and rivers overhung with forest, such as occur in the Usambara Mts, north-eastern Tanzania. It is also reported to be not uncommon on the Barotse Plain, Zambia.

SQUACCO HERON *Ardeola ralloides* Plate 2

Identification. 18in, 46cm. A rather short-legged heron with deep vinous-buff upperparts and white wings; crown buff, streaked black; long crown plumes streaked black and white; below orange-buff. In non-breeding plumage the back is olive-brown with heavy streaking on neck and breast; immature similar to non-breeding dress. When settled bird appears to be uniformly coloured and its white wings are conspicuous only when it flies. In all plumages much darker than the Cattle Egret.

Voice. A short harsh croak, 'kaak,' but usually silent.

Distribution and Habitat. Resident and winter visitor throughout, locally common. Inhabits swamps, marshes and lakes, especially those with a thick cover of water plants.

Allied Species. The similar Madagascar Squacco Heron *(A. idae)* occurs in East and Central Africa as a non-breeding visitor. Its breeding plumage, rarely observed in East Africa, is white with a creamy tinge on crown and mantle; non-breeding plumage and immature resemble non-breeding Squacco Heron but may be distinguished by much heavier bill and broader, darker streaking on neck and chest. It occurs quite frequently on swamps in the Amboseli National Park in Kenya.

CATTLE EGRET *Ardeola ibis* Plate 2

Identification. 20in, 51cm. A relatively short-legged and thickset white heron with yellowish or flesh-coloured legs; bill yellow or dull orange. Breeding plumage white with orange-buff crown, chest and mantle; non-breeding and immature plumage entirely white. Often associated with big game and cattle, frequently away from water, catching insects disturbed by the animals; gregarious.

Voice. Various croaking sounds at nesting colonies, otherwise silent.

Distribution and Habitat. Distributed throughout Africa and common in East and Central Africa. Frequents swamps and marshes, pasture land and lake and river margins: usually associated with large mammals from elephants to cattle.

GREEN-BACKED HERON   *Butorides striatus*   Plate 2

Identification. 16in, 41cm. A small greyish heron with a blackish-green crown and mantle and paler grey underparts; brown streaks down centre of throat; secondaries and wing coverts edged greyish-brown. Immature paler and browner with whitish spotting on wing coverts; streaked dark brown below.
Voice. A guttural 'aaak' when flushed.
Distribution and Habitat. Widely distributed in eastern and central Africa but local and uncommon. It is a solitary bird found along wooded river banks, in swamps where there are fringing trees and in coastal mangrove swamps.
Allied Species. The Rufous-bellied Heron *(B. rufiventris)* is larger, 20in, 51cm, slate-grey with rufous wings and belly. It is an uncommon species frequenting swamps, marshes, dams and flood plains, more frequent in the south than the north of its range.

GREAT WHITE EGRET   *Egretta alba*   Plate 2

Identification. 34–36in, 89–92cm. Plumage entirely white at all ages; the largest of the African egrets, equal in size to a Black-headed Heron. Legs black; bill black, black and yellow or yellow. May be recognised by large size, entirely black legs and noticeably long bill. The Yellow-billed Egret is a smaller bird with a stumpy-looking yellow bill and relatively shorter legs; the Little Egret is still smaller with a black or black and grey bill, and black legs with contrasting yellow toes. The Cattle Egret in its all white non-breeding plumage has a yellow bill and yellowish legs.
Voice. A croaking 'arrk,' not unlike the call of the Black-headed Heron, but generally a silent bird.
Distribution and Habitat. A local resident throughout Africa in suitable localities. It inhabits swamps, borders of lakes, flooded areas and the sea coast. Many pairs breed in the great heron colony near Garsen on the Tana River, Kenya.

YELLOW-BILLED EGRET   *Egretta intermedia*   Plate 2

Identification. 26in, 66cm. Plumage entirely white; legs black except for small yellow area above tibia-tarsus joint (*not* a good field character); bill yellow. Smaller than the Great White Egret, but may be confused at a distance when

the stumpy-looking bill is a better field character than size. Little Egret is smaller and has yellow toes. Non-breeding Cattle Egret has yellowish legs.
Voice. Generally silent but sometimes utters a short 'kwark.'
Distribution and Habitat. Occurs locally throughout eastern and central Africa. Frequents swamps, margins of lakes, flooded areas and the coast.

LITTLE EGRET   *Egretta garzetta*   Plate 2

Identification. 22–24in, 56–61cm. Plumage entirely white except in the rare grey phase when the plumage is entirely pale grey or parti-coloured. Bill black merging to blue-grey towards base; legs black with conspicuous yellow toes. Combination of black or black and grey bill and yellow toes distinguish Little Egret from other egrets and non-breeding Cattle Egrets. The Reef Heron has a longer bill than a Little Egret and in its white plumage phase the bill is yellow or orange-yellow.
Voice. A short hoarse croak.
Distribution and Habitat. Common resident throughout Africa, locally very numerous. Inhabits marshes, swamps, shallow lakes, flood plains, mangrove swamps and the sea shore. The grey phase of the Little Egret has been recorded in coastal areas of Kenya and Tanzania and on Lake Baringo, Kenya Rift Valley.
Allied Species. The Reef Heron *(E. gularis)*, 25in, 62cm, has yellow toes like the Little Egret but is larger with a noticeably longer bill. There are two plumage phases, a dark grey phase and an all white, or white with some grey feathers. In the grey phase the species generally possesses a white throat and a black bill; in the white phase the bill is yellow in the race found in East Africa. It occurs mainly on the Kenya coast south into northern Tanzania; there are also records of the species on Lakes Turkana (Rudolf) and Nakuru in Kenya. The Black Heron *(E. ardesaica)*, 22in, 56cm, is very similar in size and proportions to the Little Egret and also has black legs and yellow toes; its entire plumage is slaty-black. This species is often called the umbrella bird on account of its habit of spreading the wings above the head whilst fishing. Local and uncommon in Kenya and further north, most frequent in coastal areas and at Lake Jipe on the Kenya-Tanzania border. Further south it is a much commoner bird.

GREY HERON   *Ardea cinerea*   Plate 2

Identification. 36–40in, 91–102cm. A large heron with grey upperparts, wings and tail; crown and neck white; a line of black streaks down front of neck; black band on each side of the head behind eye and black head crest. The similar Black-headed Heron has the crown and back of the neck black.

Immature differs from immature Black-headed Heron in having dark streaked, not unspotted buffish, white underparts.

Voice. A harsh loud 'raaark' when flushed; utters various croaking calls at the nest.

Distribution and Habitat. Resident and winter visitor throughout Africa on both inland waters and the coast. It is a much less common species than the Black-headed Heron and normally occurs near water whilst the Black-headed Heron is often found hunting in grassland.

BLACK-HEADED HERON *Ardea melanocephala* Plate 2

Identification. 38in, 96cm. A grey, white and black heron, slightly smaller than a Grey Heron from which it may be distinguished by its black crown and neck. Lack of rufous in the plumage distinguishes it from Goliath and Purple Herons. Immature has crown and neck grey.

Voice. A loud nasal 'kuark' and various croaking squawks at nest.

Distribution and Habitat. Resident throughout Africa in suitable areas and often common. Frequents pasture-land in addition to inland and coastal waters; its prey includes rodents and large insects.

GOLIATH HERON *Ardea goliath* Plate 2

Identification. 55–60in, 140–152cm. The largest African heron; its size, chestnut head, neck and underparts distinguish it from all other herons. Immature paler with greyish-white breast and belly. The Purple Heron is similar in plumage except for its black crown and neck markings but is much smaller. At a distance it may be distinguished by its black crown.

Voice. A loud deep 'arrrk.'

Distribution and Habitat. Resident in small numbers throughout East and Central Africa, found on both inland and coastal waters. Common on Lake Baringo, Kenya, nesting in a loose colony on Gibraltar Island.

PURPLE HERON *Ardea purpurea* Plate 2

Identification. 30–36in, 76–91cm. A medium-sized, rather slim grey and chestnut heron with a rufous neck in all plumages; crown black. Immature pale rufous, mottled on the mantle; below buff. Distinguished from the much larger Goliath Heron by black crown and black stripes on face and neck.

Voice. Usually silent, but sometimes utters a short 'aark' when flushed or when flying in to alight at nest. Utters various croaks when nesting.

Distribution and Habitat. Resident and winter visitor throughout East and Central Africa. Inhabits swamps and reed and papyrus beds bordering large lakes. It is common on lakes in the Kenya Rift Valley and on Lake Kyoga in Uganda.

WHALE-HEADED STORK: Balaenicipitidae

The Whale-headed Stork or Shoebill is the only species in the family Balaenicipitidae. It is a very large grey water bird, the size of a Marabou Stork, with a gigantic shoe-shaped bill.

WHALE-HEADED STORK   *Balaeniceps rex*   Plate 3

Identification. 60in, 152cm. Plumage entirely blue-grey; a huge boat or shoe-shaped bill and a tiny 'top-knot' crest. Not to be confused with any other species. The immature is similar but slightly browner.
Voice. Produces a chatter with its bill, in the same manner as a Marabou Stork.
Distribution and Habitat. A very local and uncommon resident in the heart of papyrus swamps in the Sudan, eastern Zaire, Uganda and the Bangweulu swamps in Zambia (rare). In Uganda its main centre of abundance is on Lake Kyoga; it also occurs in swamps around Lake Victoria and in the two western National Parks.

HAMERKOP: Scopidae

Another monotypic family. The Hamerkop is a brown water bird about the size of a Cattle Egret, having a superficial resemblance to both the Herons and the Storks. Flies with neck extended. It is remarkable for its gigantic nest, a stick structure with a side entrance hole, built in a tree fork near water. Feeds largely on frogs and tadpoles.

HAMERKOP   *Scopus umbretta*   Plate 2

Identification. 22–24in, 56–61cm. Entire plumage dusky brown with a thick square crest – the origin of the bird's name. Bill resembles that of heron but is hook-tipped. Immature similar to adult.
Voice. A series of shrill piping whistles; at times when several birds are present the noise is considerable.
Distribution and Habitat. Resident throughout Africa in suitable localities. Occurs on inland waters, favouring slowly running streams and rivers, lake margins and marshes. In Kenya it is common along the Athi River in the Nairobi National Park and in the Amboseli National Park.

STORKS: Ciconiidae

Large, long-legged, long-necked birds with usually straight bills: necks extended in flight, not drawn back as in the heron family.

ABDIM'S STORK   *Ciconia abdimii*   Plate 3

Identification. 32in, 81cm. A metallic-glossed black stork with a white belly and white lower back and rump. Bill deep green to carmine red at base; legs and feet dusky with pink joints. Immature similar but browner and duller. Black neck distinguishes species from Woolly-necked Stork; the larger European Black Stork has a black back and a red bill and legs.

Voice. Sometimes, when in flocks, utters a weak peeping call, but generally a silent bird.

Distribution and Habitat. Mainly a non-breeding visitor to East and Central Africa, nesting north of the equator, mainly in the Sudan. Spasmodic in its appearances, attracted by locust or grasshopper hatches. Gregarious. Often associates with flocks of European White Storks.

Allied Species. The European Black Stork *(C. nigra)*, 38in, 97cm, is glossed black with a white breast and belly; bill and feet red. Differs from Abdim's Stork in being larger and in having a black back and red bill and legs. It is a solitary species occurring as a very uncommon winter visitor in East Africa, but in Zambia and Rhodesia is a rare breeder. The European White Stork *(C. ciconia)*, 40in, 102cm, is a winter visitor and passage migrant to East and Central Africa, often in large concentrations. It is white except for its mainly black wings; bill and legs red. Its appearances tend to be spasmodic, dependent on presence of locusts and grasshoppers which form its main diet. Occurs on open plains, semi-desert country and cultivated or pasture-land.

WOOLLY-NECKED STORK   *Ciconia episcopus*   Plate 3

Identification. 34in, 86cm. A glossy black stork with metallic sheen on mantle and wing coverts, easily recognised by its white woolly neck and black crown patch. Immature similar but browner.

Voice. Usually silent, but reputed to utter harsh, raucous cry when nesting.

Distribution and Habitat. An uncommon species but with a wide range in eastern and central Africa. In East Africa most frequent on some of the Uganda lakes, the Mara River in southern Kenya and in coastal districts of Kenya and Tanzania. Local in Zambia and Rhodesia. Normally encountered singly or in pairs, along the margins of shallow lakes in inland localities and on old exposed coral reefs along the coast.

SADDLEBILL STORK *Ephippiorhynchus senegalensis* **Plate 3**

Identification. 66in, 168cm. Easily recognised by its large size, black and white plumage (the flight feathers are white) and its massive red and black bill with a yellow saddle across its base. Sexes similar but eye of ♂ brown, of ♀ yellow. Immature duller.
Voice. Silent except for bill chattering.
Distribution and Habitat. Widely distributed in Africa in small numbers except in extreme south and in Somalia. Frequents larger rivers, swamps, marshes and margins of inland waters. In East Africa most frequent in Uganda and Tanzania; widespread in central Africa but not common.

OPENBILL STORK *Anastomus lamelligerus* **Plate 3**

Identification. 36in, 91cm. Entirely blackish-brown in all plumages; bill long and stout, the cutting edges curving away from each other so that a wide gap is left when the bill is closed. This character is observed easily in the field.
Voice. Generally silent, but sometimes utters a weak croak when several birds are feeding together.
Distribution and Habitat. Local resident, sometimes in large concentrations, in suitable localities throughout Africa. It inhabits swamps and marshes, flooded areas and slowly flowing rivers. Distribution is governed by the presence of certain large water snails and bivalve molluscs which form its main diet. In East Africa it is common on lakes in Uganda and in southern Tanzania: several hundred pairs breed at the Tana River heronry at Garsen on the Tana River, Kenya.

MARABOU STORK *Leptoptilos crumeniferus* **Plate 3**

Identification. 60in, 152cm. A very large stork, grey above and with grey wings; white below with a white ruff at the base of its flesh-pink neck; adults develop a large air-filled pink pouch which hangs from the front of the neck and a reddish-pink fleshy growth at the back of the neck. Gregarious, often associated with vultures at carrion or lion kills.
Voice. Generally silent, except for bill rattling, but utters a variety of croaks and grunts at breeding colony.
Distribution and Habitat. Resident and local migrant throughout Africa in suitable areas, but rare in extreme south. It is mainly a scavenger, but also occurs near open water where it feeds on frogs, and it is also an important destroyer of locusts.

YELLOW-BILLED STORK *Ibis ibis*   **Plate 3**

Identification. 42in, 107cm. A pinkish-white stork with black wings, a bare red face and a slightly decurved orange-yellow bill. Adults in breeding plumage have carmine tips to the mantle and wing coverts. Immature duller and pale buffish-grey.
Voice. Silent, but utters various guttural calls at nesting colony.
Distribution and Habitat. Widespread through Africa in suitable habitats. Common in East Africa. Frequents inland waters and also found locally in coastal areas.

IBISES and SPOONBILLS: Threskiornithidae

Ibises are characterised by their relatively thin, decurved bills: spoonbills lose this character when the young bird develops the spatulate tip. Ibises and Spoonbills fly with the neck straight out, not tucked in like the herons.

SACRED IBIS *Threskiornis aethiopicus*   **Plate 3**

Identification. 30in, 76cm. White plumage, naked black head and neck, and purple-black plumes on lower back render identification easy. Immature lacks plumes and head and neck are covered with mottled black and white feathers.
Voice. Generally silent, but sometimes utters a harsh croak.
Distribution and Habitat. Resident throughout Ethiopian Region and common in East Africa. Frequents marshes, swamps, river banks, pasture and ploughed land and flood plains.

HADADA IBIS *Hagedashia hagedash*   **Plate 3**

Identification. 30in, 76cm. Entire plumage olive-grey, rather paler on under-parts, head and neck; metallic green wash on back and wing coverts, con-spicuous only under good viewing conditions.
Voice. One of Africa's best known bird sounds, a loud far-carrying 'har, har, har.'
Distribution and Habitat. Common resident throughout Africa in suitable habitats. Frequents swamps, marshes, flooded areas, rivers with treed banks, edges of lakes and pasture.
Allied Species. The Green Ibis *(Lampribis olivacea)* is a slightly larger bird than the Hadada Ibis from which it differs in having a lax mane-like crest. It occurs in mountain forest on Mt Kenya and the Aberdare Range in Kenya

and has been reported also in forest on Mt Kilimanjaro and the Usambara Mts in north-eastern Tanzania. It is a rare bird, rarely encountered and may be in part nocturnal. It is reputed to have a honking, goose-like call.

WATTLED IBIS   *Bostrychia carunculata*   Plate 3

Identification. 34in, 81cm. General colour dark grey with a lax nape crest and white wing-coverts; throat with a distinctive pendent wattle. Occurs in large flocks which stalk across grassland with almost military precision.
Voice. Various raucous calls, some of which are not unlike those of the Hadada Ibis.
Distribution and Habitat. Confined to the highlands of Ethiopia where it occurs on moorland grassland, swamps and ravines, where the flocks roost on cliffs. Extremely local but often common where found.

GLOSSY IBIS   *Plegadis falcinellus*   Plate 3

Identification. 24in, 61cm. Very dark-looking birds, at times appearing black in certain lights and at a distance: plumage dark blackish chestnut with purple, green and bronze metallic wash; head and neck paler, uniform chestnut. Immature and non-breeding birds lack the chestnut on head and neck which are dark with white flecks.
Voice. A harsh heron-like 'kaar' at nest colony.
Distribution and Habitat. Local resident in Africa, its numbers greatly augmented in winter by northern migrants. In East Africa it occurs on most of the inland lakes and swamps, but its numbers vary greatly from year to year. It breeds at Lake Naivasha, Kenya, in the Lake Rukwa area of southern Tanzania, and on the Kafue Flats in Zambia.

AFRICAN SPOONBILL   *Platalea alba*   Plate 3

Identification. 36in, 91cm. May be recognised by its long spatulate bill, bare red face and legs and all white plumage. Immature similar but pale brown tips to flight feathers and colours of soft parts duller. The European Spoonbill has a feathered face and black legs.
Voice. A double 'aark-ark' but normally silent.
Distribution and Habitat. Occurs locally in East and Central Africa, frequenting fresh water and brackish lakes, swamps, marshes and sandbars in rivers.
Allied Species. The European Spoonbill (*P. leucorodia*), 36in, 91cm, is a rare winter visitor to East Africa but breeds along the Red Sea and Somaliland coasts. It differs in having black legs and lacking the red face of the African bird.

FLAMINGOS: Phoenicopteridae

The Flamingos are a group of long-legged, long-necked birds which occur in large flocks on brackish lakes. Their bills are characteristic, flattened above with the tip bent down at an angle; plumage mainly pink and white.

GREATER FLAMINGO *Phoenicopterus ruber* Plate 3

Identification. 56in, 142cm. Plumage white with a pink wash; wing-coverts and axillaries bright coral-red; flight feathers black; bill pink with a black tip. Immature greyish-white with a pinkish-grey bill. A much larger and paler bird than the Lesser Flamingo, easily recognised by its pink bill.
Voice. A series of gruntings and murmurations, interspersed with goose-like honks.
Distribution and Habitat. Frequent on alkaline lakes in East Africa, especially those in the Rift Valley; uncommon southwards. Northern migrants occur spasmodically in coastal areas, when resident population is augmented by winter visitors between October and April.

LESSER FLAMINGO *Phoenicopterus minor* Plate 3

Identification. 40in, 101cm. Plumage deep pink, much darker and brighter than Greater Flamingo; bill dark carmine-red with black tip. Immature paler and greyer with little or no pink in plumage. A much smaller and more richly coloured species than Greater Flamingo; its dark carmine bill is a good field character.
Voice. Deep murmurations and honks.
Distribution and Habitat. Locally common on alkaline lakes in East and Central Africa, sometimes present in vast numbers on favoured lakes such as Nakuru and Elmenteita in Kenya. Very infrequent in coastal areas.

DUCKS and GEESE: Anatidae

The Ducks and Geese are an easily recognised group of birds, characterised by webbed feet and their bill structure with its nail-like tip and row of lamellae along the edges. Wing pattern in flight is an important field character.

FULVOUS TREE DUCK   *Dendrocygna bicolor*   **Plate 4**

Identification. 20in, 51cm. An erect, long-legged duck, tawny-rufous in colour with a number of cream stripes along the flanks; in flight white rump conspicuous. Flies with slow wing beats for a duck and legs extend beyond tail. Immature similar.
Voice. Loud, two-noted whistles.
Distribution and Habitat. Resident and local migrant from the Chad region and the Sudan and Ethiopia south to Natal. In East and Central Africa occurs locally on inland lakes and swamps; less common than the White-faced Tree Duck on the coast.

WHITE-FACED TREE DUCK   *Dendrocygna viduata*   **Plate 4**

Identification. 18in, 46cm. Both species of tree ducks, or whistling teal as they are often called, stand more erect than other ducks. The present species may be recognised in the field by the combination of white face and barred flanks.
Voice. A loud clear whistle, usually repeated several times.
Distribution and Habitat. Found locally throughout the Ethiopian Region. In East Africa its numbers and appearances in any given locality vary from year to year; it may be absent for several years and then turn up in abundance. Its numbers are more stable in Central Africa where it is common. It frequents inland lakes and marshes and the coast and islands off the coast.

EGYPTIAN GOOSE   *Alopochen aegyptiaca*   **Plate 4**

Identification. 24in, 61cm. Plumage brown to greyish-brown with contrasting white shoulders which are conspicuous in flight. Chestnut patch in centre of belly and chestnut patch around eye. Immature similar but duller and chestnut breast patch small or lacking. Occurs in pairs or small flocks. Often alights in trees.
Voice. A loud strident honking.
Distribution and Habitat. Resident throughout Ethiopian Region in suitable habitats. Frequents mainly inland waters, favouring lake margins, swamps and larger rivers.

BLUE-WINGED GOOSE   *Cyanochen cyanopterus*   **Plate 4**

Identification. 22in, 56cm. A brownish-grey goose with a small brent-goose-like bill and pale blue shoulders; primaries black, secondaries green. Immature similar but duller. The species has a remarkable carriage, both walking and standing with its chest thrust forwards and its head held above the back. Generally tame with little fear of man.

Voice. A soft melodious whistle and also a quack-like note.
Distribution and Habitat. Confined to the highland plateau of Ethiopia where it frequents the margins of lakes and rivers and grassy highland moorland. Generally in pairs but sometimes found in small flocks.

SPUR-WINGED GOOSE *Plectropterus gambensis* Plate 4

Identification. 30–36in, 76–91cm. Africa's largest waterfowl, the Spur-winged Goose has metallic glossed black upperparts and a white belly; bill dark flesh-red. ♀ smaller than ♂. Immature duller and browner.
Voice. Generally silent, but sometimes utters a whistle.
Distribution and Habitat. Resident and local migrant throughout Ethiopian Region: usually in small parties and often absent from apparently suitable haunts. In East Africa occurs on most of the Rift Valley lakes and is also common in western Uganda and in western Tanzania.

KNOB-BILLED DUCK *Sarkidiornis melanotos* Plate 4

Identification. ♂ 24in, 61cm, ♀ 20in, 51cm. A large black and white duck, the back and wings washed with metallic green and copper; the knob at base of the drake's bill is a good field character.
Voice. Generally a completely silent bird, but sometimes utters a creaking whistle.
Distribution and Habitat. Locally distributed in suitable areas throughout the Ethiopian Region; a local migrant in some localities. Occurs on inland waters including lakes, swamps, flooded land and large rivers. Frequently perches in trees. In East and Central Africa it is locally common, but numbers and appearances vary; usually present on Lake Naivasha in Kenya.

PYGMY GOOSE *Nettapus auritus* Plate 4

Identification. 13in, 33cm. Thickset, teal-sized waterfowl with greenish-black upperparts and bright rufous flanks; ♂ has a black-bordered green patch on sides of head and a bright orange-yellow bill; ♀ has greyish cheeks and a dull yellow bill. Immature similar to ♀. In all plumages white wing-bar conspicuous in flight.
Voice. A soft two or three note whistle, not often heard.
Distribution and Habitat. Resident, local but sometimes abundant over most of the Ethiopian Region. Occurs on fresh-water lakes and swamps where there is an abundant growth of water-lilies. In East Africa very common on Lake Kyoga, Uganda and in various localities in southern and western Tanzania; an uncommon bird in Kenya except on Lake Jipe near Taveta.

Common in central Africa on pools and lagoons with a plentiful aquatic vegetation.

AFRICAN BLACK DUCK *Anas sparsa* Plate 4

Identification. 19in, 48cm. A black-plumaged duck, slightly smaller than a mallard, with large white spots on the upperparts; white wing-bar which is conspicuous both when the bird is swimming and when on the wing. Normally occurs in pairs on streams and small rivers, flying to ponds and swamps at dusk.

Voice. A mallard-like quack.

Distribution and Habitat. In East and Central Africa very local and thinly distributed on wooded streams and rivers. In Kenya fairly numerous on the rivers which flow down Mt Kenya.

Allied Species. Hartlaub's Duck *(Pteronetta hartlaubii)*, 19in, 48cm, is another duck which frequents forested streams and rivers. It is dark chestnut with a black head and a pale blue shoulder patch, very conspicuous when the bird takes wing. In East Africa it occurs in the southern Sudan and probably in the Bwamba forest, western Uganda.

CAPE TEAL *Anas capensis* Plate 4

Identification. 14in, 35cm. A pale brownish and white duck with a bright pink bill and a pale crown; speculum emerald green, bordered above and below by a white stripe. A characteristic bird of alkaline and brackish lakes. It may be confused with the Redbilled Duck, but that species has a dark crown and a patch of orange-buff in the wings.

Voice. Usually a silent bird, but sometimes utters a short soft whistle; also reputed to quack.

Distribution and Habitat. Widespread in East Africa, locally common; less frequent further south. Occurs mainly on brackish or alkaline lakes; in Kenya it may be found on many of the Rift Valley lakes including Nakuru, Elmenteita, Magadi and Turkana.

Allied Species. The European Wigeon *(A. penelope)*, 18in, 46cm, may be recognised by its small goose-like bill, chestnut head with biscuit-buff crown and conspicuous white forewing; ♀ greyish-brown with a white belly. It is an uncommon winter visitor to East Africa. The Gadwall *(A. strepera)*, 20in, 51cm, is a brownish-grey duck with a chestnut and white speculum. It has been recorded on the Rift Valley lakes of Kenya and more frequently in Ethiopia. The well-known European Mallard *(A. platyrhynchos)* 23in, 58cm, is a very uncommon winter visitor to the highlands of Ethiopia and to the Sudan. The drake's combination of green head and white neck ring render it unmistakable.

YELLOW-BILLED DUCK *Anas undulata* **Plate 4**

Identification. 20in, 51cm. A dark greyish-brown duck with a conspicuous yellow bill; speculum green edged with narrow bands of black and white. Sexes similar and immature only slightly duller than adult.
Voice. A mallard-like quack.
Distribution and Habitat. Widespread in East and Central Africa, frequenting mainly fresh-water lakes, swamps and marshes. Usually encountered in small flocks or pairs.
Allied Species. The European Pintail *(A. acuta)*, ♂ 26in, 66cm, ♀ 22in, 56cm, may be recognised by its long tail (in the ♂) and long neck. It is a moderately common winter visitor to East Africa.

RED-BILLED DUCK *Anas erythrorhynchos* **Plate 4**

Identification. 15in, 38cm. Best identified by a combination of mainly red bill, blackish-brown cap which contrasts strongly with pale cheeks and the large pinkish-buff speculum which is very conspicuous in flight. The other red-billed duck with which it might be confused is the Cape Wigeon, but this species has no dark cap and the speculum is green bordered by two white stripes.
Voice. A weak whistle, but usually silent.
Distribution and Habitat. Widespread and common in East and Central Africa, frequenting almost any sort of surface water, fresh and alkaline. It often occurs in flooded areas after heavy rain.
Allied Species. The Garganey Teal *(A. querquedula)* 15in, 38cm, has a conspicuous pale blue-grey forewing, and in the ♂ a very conspicuous white stripe over the eye. It is a common winter visitor to East Africa, less frequent further south. The European Teal *(A. crecca)* 14in, 35cm, is an uncommon winter visitor to East Africa. It is darker than the Garganey and lacks the blue-grey shoulders of that species; ♂ with a chestnut and dark metallic green head. The European Shoveler *(A. clypeata)* 20in, 51cm, may be recognised in both sexes by its large spatulate bill. The drake is distinctively rufous, white and greenish-black: wing shoulders blue-grey. A common winter visitor to East Africa but very uncommon further south. Frequents both alkaline and freshwater lakes and swamps.

HOTTENTOT TEAL *Anas hottentota* **Plate 4**

Identification. 11in, 28cm. The smallest of the African ducks, dark brown in general coloration with a blackish-brown cap which contrasts with the buffy-white cheeks; sides of bill blue. Immature duller with less blue on bill. It is not unlike a very small Red-billed Duck at a distance, but is easily distinguished by its blue-sided bill. Wide white band in the wings, very conspicuous in flight.

Voice. A thin, reedy whistle; sometimes utters a low quack.

Distribution and Habitat. Occurs widely in East and Central Africa but is uncommon in the Sudan. Occurs on both fresh and brackish inland waters. In East Africa common on suitable waters where there is a growth of sedges and reeds.

AFRICAN POCHARD   *Aythya erythrophthalma*   Plate 4

Identification. 18in, 46cm. A uniformly-coloured, very dark-looking diving duck with a white patch in the wings during flight; bill pale grey. Drake may be mistaken for a drake Maccoa Duck at a distance but does not have that species' chestnut back, and the bill is pale grey not cobalt blue.

Voice. Normally a silent duck, but sometimes utters a brief quack when in flight.

Distribution and Habitat. A common bird in East and Central Africa; resident and local migrant. In East Africa its numbers increase from October onwards, the birds leaving again in early December. It occurs on both freshwater and alkaline lakes, especially where there is a good growth of papyrus and sedges.

Allied Species. The European Pochard *(A. ferina)*, 18in, 46cm, is an uncommon winter visitor to Ethiopia, the Sudan and Kenya. The drake may be recognised by its red head, pale grey back, blackish chest and white flanks; duck dark brown in front, mantle and flanks greyish. The White-eyed Pochard or Ferruginous Duck *(A. nyroca)*, 16in, 41cm, is a small edition of the African Pochard but is more chestnut and has a conspicuous white, not red, eye. It is a very uncommon winter visitor to East Africa. The Tufted Duck *(A. fuligula)*, 17in, 43cm, is another uncommon winter visitor to East Africa. The ♂ is black with white flanks, the ♀ brown with brownish-white flanks; both possess the characteristic drooping nape crest.

MACCOA DUCK   *Oxyura maccoa*   Plate 4

Identification. 17in, 43cm. A diving duck with back and flanks bright chestnut, head black and bill cobalt blue. Female drab brown, best recognised by her habit – shared by the ♂ – of swimming very low in the water with the tail cocked up almost at right angles. The African Pochard may be mistaken for the drake Maccoa but swims higher in the water and the drake's bill is blue-grey not bright cobalt blue.

Voice. Usually silent but drake in breeding season produces a variety of deep, far-carrying frog-like croaks and growls.

Distribution and Habitat. Resident East and South Africa, but everywhere uncommon. Occurs on inland lakes, both fresh-water and brackish, where there is an abundance of reeds, sedges or papyrus.

WHITE-BACKED DUCK *Thalassornis leuconotus* Plate 4

Identification. 16in, 41cm. A mottled dark brown and fulvous diving duck with a crescent-shaped white patch between the bill and the eye. Has a white back but this character is seen only when the bird is in flight away from the observer. It is a tame duck and like the Maccoa it is reluctant to fly.
Voice. Usually silent but sometimes utters a short whistle.
Distribution and Habitat. Local resident on inland waters, often small dams, where there is an abundance of aquatic vegetation. Local in East and Central Africa; in Kenya common on Lake Naivasha.

SECRETARY BIRD: Sagittariidae

The Secretary Bird, of which only one species is known, constitutes a very distinct family of the birds of prey. It is endemic to Africa. This large, long-legged, long-tailed grey bird with black 'plus-fours' is a great destroyer of noxious snakes and rodents.

SECRETARY BIRD *Sagittarius serpentarius* Plate 5

Identification. 40in, 101cm. A large pale grey, long-legged terrestrial bird of prey with black flight feathers and tibia; long central tail feathers. It is generally encountered singly or in pairs stalking across open country. Its conspicuous crest is often raised like a halo by the bird whilst hunting. Sexes similar; immature buffy-grey.
Voice. Generally silent, but in breeding season produces some remarkable croaks and even a lion-like cough.
Distribution and Habitat. Widely distributed but uncommon in East and Central Africa on open plains, bush country and farmlands. Feeds largely on snakes and other reptiles, rodents and large insects.

VULTURES, EAGLES, HAWKS and ALLIES: Accipitridae

Vultures are large or very large eagle-like birds with long wings, relatively short tails and small naked or down-covered heads. Usually observed soaring or at carrion. Eagles are medium-sized or large birds of prey with legs feathered to the toes, but Harrier Eagles have bare tarsi. In flight heads appear larger than vultures' heads. Buzzards resemble small eagles but have bare legs and much broader wings; all buzzards with the exception of the Mountain Buzzard perch frequently on telegraph poles. Kites have angular wings and are best distinguished by the more or less deeply forked tails and buoyant flight. Sparrow-Hawks and allies are smaller than buzzards and have short rounded wings and long tails. Harriers are slimly built hawks with long wings and long tails; flight buoyant. They hunt by quartering the ground from a few feet up.

RUPPELL'S VULTURE   *Gyps ruppellii*   Plate 5

Identification. 34in, 86cm. A large dark brown vulture with a dark back; feathers, especially of underparts and wing coverts, broadly edged with creamy-white, giving a scaly or spotted appearance. Immature pale, the feather margins wider than in adult. The adult White-backed Vulture has a conspicuous white rump and is uniformly coloured, not spotted. The immature is a very dark vulture with indistinct streaking on the underparts, much darker than the immature Ruppell's Vulture. The Lappet-faced Vulture is a much larger bird with a massive bill. For underside patterns in flight see illustrations.

Voice. Produces harsh squawks when squabbling over carrion.

Distribution and Habitat. Locally common in East Africa in open big game country and the vicinity of inland cliffs on which it nests. The species is common and nests on the cliffs of Hell's Gate, Naivasha, Kenya.

WHITE-BACKED VULTURE   *Gyps bengalensis*   Plate 5

Identification. 32in, 81cm. A large dark or pale brown vulture with a conspicuous white rump in flight; some examples, apparently very old birds, are pale creamy-brown. Immature very dark without white rump patch. Adults may be distinguished by uniform colour and white rump; immature much darker than Ruppell's Vulture. For underside patterns in flight see illustrations.

Voice. Harsh croaking squawks when at carrion.

Distribution and Habitat. Common in East Africa and the most frequently seen vulture in the National Parks; local in Central Africa. Soars above big game country; nests in forest or riverside trees, not on cliffs. Species previously known as *G. africanus*, but is now considered to be a race of the Indian *G. bengalensis*.

NUBIAN or LAPPET-FACED VULTURE
Torgos tracheliotus   **Plate 5**

Identification. 40in, 101cm. The largest of the African vultures with a massive bill; folds of naked skin on head and face purplish-grey. Immature similar but face lappets less developed and duller. For underside pattern in flight see illustrations.
Voice. Silent birds; utter a low squawk when fighting over carrion.
Distribution and Habitat. In East and Central Africa an uncommon resident, most frequent in the Kenya National Parks. Nests in isolated acacia trees. Like most of the vultures it is most frequent in big game country.
Allied Species. The Black Vulture *(A. monachus)*, 40in, 101cm, is a Palearctic species which wanders to the Sudan in the non-breeding season. It is a huge all black vulture with bare blue-grey skin on the head and neck. In flight it appears all black when viewed from below.

WHITE-HEADED VULTURE   *Trigonoceps occipitalis*   **Plate 5**

Identification. 32in, 81cm. This vulture differs from all others in having a striking white head, white secondaries (in the adult), a white belly and a red and blue bill. Immature recognised by its white belly, the secondaries being brown or particoloured and the head pale greyish-brown.
Voice. Silent except for hissing squeals when at carrion.
Distribution and Habitat. Occurs locally in East and Central Africa but nowhere numerous. In East Africa most frequent in the Kenya and Tanzania National Parks. Nests in isolated trees on open plains. Sometimes kills its own prey including francolins and monitor lizards.

HOODED VULTURE   *Necrosyrtes monachus*   **Plate 5**

Identification. 26in, 86cm. A small, entirely dark brown vulture with a rather short rounded tail and a thin weak bill; bare skin of face reddish pink. Immature similar but face skin whitish. Differs from immature Egyptian Vulture in having a rounded, not wedge-shaped tail.
Voice. A silent bird, no call recorded.
Distribution and Habitat. Widely distributed throughout the Ethiopian Region, found both on open plains and in big game country, and also in forested areas and cultivation. It is a common bird throughout the settled parts of Uganda, less common but far from rare in Kenya and Tanzania and widespread in Central Africa.

EGYPTIAN VULTURE   *Neophron percnopterus*   **Plate 5**

Identification. 26in, 66cm. A small mainly white vulture with a distinctive wedge-shaped white tail and black flight feathers; bare face yellow, bill slender. Immature dark brown and might be mistaken for the wider-winged Hooded Vulture but wedge-shaped tail distinctive. The Palmnut Vulture or Vulturine Fish Eagle is also largely white but its bare face is pink, the flight feathers are largely white and its white tail is crossed by a black band.

Voice. Silent birds; sometimes utter a hissing noise at carrion.

Distribution and Habitat. In East Africa widespread and locally common in Ethiopia and Somalia where it frequents the outskirts of settlements to feed on human excrement. In Kenya and Tanzania less frequent and encountered mainly around Masai encampments. It occurs in semi-desert country, the vicinity of inland cliffs upon which it breeds and in big game country.

Allied Species. The Palmnut Vulture or Vulturine Fish Eagle *(Gypohierax angolensis)*, 28in, 71cm, is a mainly white bird of prey with black scapulars and secondaries and a black band across its white tail; bare face pink, bill white. Immature wholly sooty or greyish-brown. It is associated with oil palms, eating the oily fruits, and also occurs in coastal areas where it feeds upon dead fish. Found throughout East and Central Africa where suitable conditions exist, but uncommon and very local. An exception is that on Pemba Island off the Tanzania coast it is a common bird.

LAMMERGEYER or BEARDED VULTURE
Gypaetus barbatus   **Plate 5**

Identification. 40in, 102cm. The Lammergeyer has a distinctive silhouette with long, narrow, angled wings and a long diamond-shaped tail. Upperparts, wings and tail dark grey with whitish shaft streaks; hind neck and underparts orange-rufous; head white with black band through eye terminating in a short bristly beard from the chin. Immature blackish-brown with variable pale streaking. Not gregarious and seldom visits animal carcasses until the vulture host has departed. Has the remarkable habit of dropping bones from a height to fracture them and eat the marrow.

Voice. Normally silent but sometimes utters a querulous whistle.

Distribution and Habit. Still a common species in the mountainous highlands of Ethiopia; rare in Kenya and northern Tanzania, where it frequents high inland cliffs. The most easily observed pair of Lammergeyers in Kenya are the pair which have made their home on the cliffs of Hell's Gate, a gorge near Lake Naivasha.

AFRICAN MARSH HARRIER   *Circus ranivorus*   Plate 7

Identification. 18–20in, 46–51cm. A dark or rufous-brown harrier without a white rump; adult male indistinctly streaked dark rufous on underparts. Adult male differs from the European Marsh Harrier in having tail and flight feathers barred black; female and immature are uniform dark brown without the creamy head and shoulder patches of the European bird.

Voice. A weak mewing cry, uttered by male when approaching nest.

Distribution and Habitat. Uncommon local resident in East and Central Africa. In East Africa it is most frequent in south-western Uganda, highland moorland and swamps in Kenya and in southern Tanzania. It occurs on open plains, wheatlands (in Kenya it often nests in the middle of a field of wheat), swamps, marshes and the margins of lakes.

Allied Species. Three species of European Harriers are winter visitors to East and Central Africa. The European Marsh Harrier *(C. aeruginosus)*, 19–22in, 48–56cm, is a brown harrier without a white rump; adult ♂ with grey tail and grey secondaries and black unbarred primaries; ♀ and immature lack grey in plumage and are uniformly brown with buff crown and shoulders. In Montagu's Harrier *(C. pygargus)*, 16–18in, 41–46cm, the ♂ is grey with a black wing bar, a grey throat and chest and rufous streaks on the belly; ♀ and immature brown with a white rump, not distinguishable in the field from ♀ of the Pallid Harrier. The ♂ Pallid Harrier *(C. macrourus)*, 17–19in, 43–48cm, is pale grey without a wing bar, underparts white without rufous streaking. All occur in open country, swamps, cultivation and moorland.

HARRIER HAWK or GYMNOGENE
Polyboroides radiatus   Plate 7

Identification. 24–27in, 61–68cm. A long-legged blue-grey hawk, not unlike a large edition of a chanting goshawk; tail long, wide and black, narrowly tipped white and with a broad white band; face bare, bright lemon yellow or pinkish-yellow; feathers of nape long, forming a lax crest; belly barred black and white. The immature may be dark brown, rufous or rufous-buff: birds in this plumage best identified by small head, lax crest and rather floppy flight. Sometimes seen raiding weaver-bird colonies, when it hangs by the legs, upside down, slowly flapping its wings while it robs the nests.

Voice. A drawn-out quavering whistle, often uttered in flight.

Distribution and Habitat. A local resident throughout most of the Ethiopian Region. In East Africa it is fairly numerous in the Kenya coastal forests and in western Uganda. It occurs in forest and wooded areas, park-like country, savannah woodland, especially in localities where there are baobab trees and in cultivated areas where the trees have not been felled. Sparsely distributed in Central Africa.

BATELEUR   *Terathopius ecaudatus*   Plate 6

Identification. 24in, 61cm. Identified in all plumages by its remarkably short tail. On the wing the adult is unmistakable, with contrasting black underparts and white undersides of wings; back and tail chestnut, rarely rufous-buff. Immature dark brown, sometimes with a distinctly paler head.

Voice. A sharp barking cry.

Distribution and Habitat. Widely distributed and common through East and Central Africa, especially in the Northern Frontier Province of Kenya. Generally seen on the wing, soaring high overhead – a habit which may well explain its continued abundance! Occurs in semi-desert and open country, bush and savannah woodland; less frequent in cultivated areas.

BLACK-CHESTED HARRIER EAGLE
Circaetus pectoralis   Plate 7

Identification. 27–28in, 68–71cm. The Harrier Eagles, and also the Bateleur, all have large, lax-feathered, owl-like heads and unfeathered legs. The Black-chested Harrier Eagle has dark grey upperparts and blackish throat and chest; remainder underparts and below wings immaculate white; tail with three whitish bands and a pale tip. Immature brown above with entirely pale rufous underparts, quite unlike the adult. In flight the unmarked white belly and wings distinguish this species from the adult Martial Eagle which has black spotting on belly and below wings. Some Augur Buzzards, when perched facing the observer, have a slight resemblance to a Black-chested Harrier Eagle, but may be distinguished by their bright yellow legs, not whitish, and their red tails.

Voice. Silent birds as a rule, but sometimes utter single or double shrill whistles.

Distribution and Habitat. A local resident in small numbers in East and Central Africa. It occurs in fairly open woodlands, cultivation, park-like country and semi-desert bush. In East Africa it is most frequent in the Rift Valley and in the northern parts of Kenya and Uganda. Feeds mainly upon snakes and lizards.

Allied Species. The Brown Harrier Eagle *(C. cinereus)*, 27in, 68cm, is entirely dark brown, quite different from the rusty-plumaged immature Black-chested Harrier Eagle. It may be distinguished from the immature Bateleur by its much longer tail. It is a local species in small numbers in East and Central Africa. In Kenya and Tanzania it favours savannah country where there are baobab trees. Two species of Banded Harrier Eagles occur but both are rare in East and Central Africa. The Banded Harrier Eagle *(C. cineras-cens)*, 24in, 61cm, is grey above and on the throat and chest; belly lightly barred black and white; conspicuous white band across the base of the tail and a black band across the middle of the tail. It favours riverine forest and trees growing around swamps. The Southern Banded Harrier Eagle *(C. fasciolatus)*, 24in, 61cm, lacks the white basal band on the tail which has three to five dark bands. It is a forest species, most frequent in Kenya coastal forests and forests in north-eastern Tanzania. Beaudouin's Harrier Eagle *(C. beaudouini)*, 27in, 69cm, is similar to the Black-chested Harrier Eagle but has brownish-grey diffused streaking on the throat and chest and sparse barring on the belly; above greyish. It could be mistaken for a Martial Eagle but has unfeathered legs. It is also closely related to the European Short-toed Eagle *(C. gallicus)*, a winter visitor to the Sudan and Ethiopia, but is much greyer and feathers of the belly have three narrow bars. It is a rare bird recorded from western Uganda and Kenya where it may be found near Lake Victoria and in the Mara Game Reserve.

GREAT SPARROWHAWK   *Accipiter melanoleucus*   Plate 6

Identification. 18–22in, 46–56cm. A very large sparrowhawk, about the size and build of the European Goshawk. Upperparts slaty-black, below white with a black patch on flanks above thighs. ♀ larger than ♂. In melanistic phase underparts black except for white throat. Immature brown above, below whitish, buff or rufous with heavy black streaks. Tail appears long in flight. Sometimes preys upon domestic poultry and pigeons.
Voice. A sharp, far-carrying 'keep-keep-keep,' uttered especially when nesting.
Distribution and Habitat. A local and uncommon resident in forests and wooded areas throughout much of the Ethiopian region. In East Africa most frequent in forests of the Kenya highlands.

AFRICAN GOSHAWK   *Accipiter tachiro*   Plate 8

Identification. 14–17in, 36–43cm. A medium-sized sparrowhawk, the ♀ much larger than the ♂. Upperparts dark slate-grey, below barred brown and white with a rufous wash; ♀ paler and less barred below than ♂. Immature dark or rufous-brown above, whitish below with heavy, drop-like dark spots. Lack of white rump distinguishes this species from Gabar Goshawk and Little Sparrowhawk. It is a much darker bird than the Shikra which has a pale blue-grey mantle; Ovampo Sparrowhawk is pale above and has white spots along shafts of tail feathers. An immature ♀ African Goshawk could be mistaken for an immature ♂ Great Sparrowhawk, but the African Goshawk has spotting of underparts heavier and more drop-like, not streaks.

Voice. A shrill 'wud, wud, wud, wud, wud' uttered by the bird either when perched or flying.

Distribution and Habitat. A local forest species in East and Central Africa; not uncommon in the highlands of Kenya in suitable forest country.

Allied Species. The Cuckoo Falcon *(Aviceda cuculoides)*, 17in, 43cm, is another forest hawk but more thickset with heavier rufous barring on belly and a short but conspicuous crest. In flight the Cuckoo Falcon has heavy, rather slow wing-beats; underside of wings mainly rufous whilst in African Goshawk under wing-coverts are white or buff with black markings.

SHIKRA   *Accipiter badius*   Plate 8

Identification. 11–13in, 28–33cm. A pale grey hawk without a white rump; underparts barred pale rufous or grey. Immature pale grey above with underparts blotched pale rufous. Lack of white rump distinguishes the Shikra from Little Sparrowhawk and Gabar Goshawk; the African Goshawk has slaty-black upperparts.

Voice. A high-pitched 'keek, ee, ee, keek.'

Distribution and Habitat. Resident throughout most of Africa except West African type rain forest and southern South Africa. Occurs in park-like country, semi-desert bush, acacia thickets, riverine and savannah woodland and in East Africa in coastal forest.

Allied Species. The Ovampo Sparrowhawk *(A. ovampensis)*, 12–14in, 30–35cm, resembles a Shikra and has underparts barred grey and white. The conspicuous white shaft spots on the central tail feathers are a good field character. It has a similar distribution and inhabits a similar habitat to the Shikra but is a much rarer bird. The Levant Sparrowhawk *(A. brevipes)*, 13–15in, 33–38cm, is a rare Palearctic winter visitor to the Sudan. It resembles the European Sparrowhawk but has grey not rufous cheeks and an orange-red eye. The European Sparrowhawk *(A. nisus)*, 11–15in, 28–38cm, is an uncommon winter visitor to Ethiopia and the Sudan, rarely further south. The ♂ has rufous not grey cheeks and rufous-barred underparts; ♀ darker and browner than Shikra with brown barring on underparts. The Rufous-breasted Sparrowhawk *(A. rufiventris)*, 12–14in, 31–36cm, is dark slaty-grey above with the underparts rufous, paler on the throat. It is a forest hawk most frequent in the highland forests of East Africa, rare in Central Africa.

LITTLE SPARROWHAWK   *Accipiter minullus*   **Plate 6**

Identification. 9–11in, 23–28cm. Above slate-grey with a distinct white rump; throat white, remainder underparts white narrowly barred grey and rufous. Immature brown above with white underparts, dark brown drop-like spots on breast and flanks. The Little Sparrow Hawk is a miniature edition of a ♂ African Goshawk except for its white rump. Adult ♂ Gabar Goshawk has a grey throat and chest; the Shikra lacks the white rump.
Voice. Silent woodland species; at nest sometimes utters a sharp 'kee, kee, kee, kee.'
Distribution and Habitat. A resident woodland and forest hawk throughout East and Central Africa, but everywhere uncommon and local.
Allied Species. The Western Little Sparrowhawk *(A. erythropus)*, 10–12in, 25–31cm, differs from the Little Sparrowhawk in having the chest and upper breast bright rufous. It occurs in the Bwamba Forest in western Uganda, west to Cameroons, south to Angola.

PALE CHANTING GOSHAWK   *Melierax poliopterus*   **Plate 8**

Identification. 19in, 48cm. A very upright-standing, long-legged grey hawk with a closely barred grey and white belly; legs bright orange-red, cere bright yellow; rump immaculate white. Immature brownish-grey above with broad brown streaking on the chest and rufous-brown barring on the belly, rump white as in the adult. The Dark Chanting Goshawk is darker grey, the rump is vermiculated black and white and the cere is orange-red not yellow.
Voice. A curious piping call, heard most often during nesting, which may be mistaken for the call of some species of small hornbill.
Distribution and Habitat. A resident in dry bush and acacia country in East Africa from Somalia, eastern Ethiopia and eastern Kenya south to central Tanzania. This is a well-known bird of the semi-desert bush areas of eastern and north-eastern Kenya; it is common in the Samburu country and near Lake Magadi.

DARK CHANTING GOSHAWK   *Melierax metabates*   **Plate 8**

Identification. 19in, 48cm. Very similar in general appearance to the Pale Chanting Goshawk but darker, the cere orange-red and the rump vermiculated black and white. The two Chanting Goshawks overlap in the area of Lake Baringo, Kenya but do not interbreed. Immature distinguished also by its barred rump.
Voice. A prolonged fluting chant but normally silent.
Distribution and Habitat. Ranges from western Ethiopia and the Sudan,

south through Uganda and western Kenya, south to Central Africa. Inhabits bush country, acacia woodland and savannah woodland. Not uncommon where it occurs.

GABAR GOSHAWK *Melierax gabar*   Plate 8

Identification. 12–15in, 31–38cm. A pale grey hawk with a white rump, grey throat and chest and grey and white barred belly. ♀ much larger than ♂. A melanistic phase is not uncommon, all sooty-black with grey bars in wings and tail. Immature has brown streaked chest and brown barred belly and flanks. A ♂ Gabar Goshawk could be mistaken for a ♀ Little Sparrowhawk but has the throat and chest uniform grey, not white. The African Goshawk and Shikra do not possess the white rump.

Voice. A high-pitched 'ki, ki, ki, ki, ki, ki.'

Distribution and Habitat. Occurs throughout the Ethiopian Region in suitable localities. It favours wooded and thornbush country, stands of acacias and park-like savannah. It is common and widespread in East Africa and Central Africa.

Allied Species. The Long-tailed Hawk *(Urotriorchis macrourus)*, 24–26in, 61–65cm, is a little-known forest treetop hawk rare in East Africa and known only from the Bwamba Forest, western Uganda. Elsewhere it ranges through the Congo forests to West Africa. It is grey above with a chestnut belly and a very long tail.

LIZARD BUZZARD *Kaupifalco monogrammicus*   Plate 7

Identification. 14–15in, 35–38cm. A thickset pale grey hawk with barred black and white belly and white throat with a conspicuous vertical black streak; rump white; cere and legs pinkish orange; tail black with a wide white bar. The Gabar Goshawk is not such a thickset hawk and has the throat grey without a black streak. Immature similar to adult. Hunts from a perch scanning the ground for lizards and large insects, its main food.

Voice. A clear ringing whistle, followed by a quick succession of notes 'chu, chu, chu, chu, chu, chu, chu.'

Distribution and Habitat. Widely distributed and locally common in East and Central Africa. Frequents open park-like country, cultivation, coconut plantations, woodland, edges of forests and areas where there are baobab trees.

GRASSHOPPER BUZZARD *Butastur rufipennis* **Plate 7**

Identification. 16–17in, 40–43cm. When perched the Grasshopper Buzzard resembles a large edition of a Kestrel; in flight it looks like a harrier with bright rufous wings but no white rump. In the north of its range it may be mistaken for a Fox Kestrel, but that bird is mainly rufous in colour and lacks the Grasshopper Buzzard's brownish-grey back. Upperparts brownish-grey; below buffy with short streaks; immature similar but more rufous in general colour.

Voice. A silent bird as a rule; sometimes utters a single plaintive whistle 'keeee.'

Distribution and Habitat. A breeding species in the Sudan, Ethiopia and Somalia: a non-breeding migrant southwards to dry areas of northern Uganda to eastern Kenya and north-eastern Tanzania between November and March. Occurs in acacia and semi-desert country. At times it is common during December and January in the Tsavo National Park, Kenya.

AUGUR BUZZARD *Buteo rufofuscus* **Plate 6**

Identification. 20–24in, 50–57cm. This is probably East Africa's most frequently seen bird of prey. Easily recognised by its slate-grey upperparts, chestnut-red tail and greyish-white and black barring on the secondaries. Underparts variable, entirely white, white with a black throat and chest or entirely black. Immature has underparts white, streaked or blotched with black, and the tail barred black and brown: immatures of the black phase are blackish-brown below, also with a barred tail. In flight the broad, mainly white wings and the chestnut tail are good field characters. The adult dark phase might be mistaken for a Bateleur but has a much longer tail.

Voice. A ringing, wild, far-carrying 'guang-guang.'

Distribution and Habitat. Common in the highlands of East Africa, much less frequent in Central Africa. Inhabits open moorland country, mountains, forest glades, inland cliffs, cultivation and baobab country. Often perches on telegraph poles and suchlike vantage points. A most valuable bird as it preys almost entirely upon rodents: the birds seen near chicken runs are not hunting the fowls but the rats and mice attracted by the chickens' food.

Allied Species. The slightly smaller Red-necked Buzzard *(B. auguralis)* 18–20in, 46–50cm, has dark greyish-brown upperparts washed with rufous on the back and crown; below, throat and chest dark brown and chestnut and sides of head and neck chestnut; belly white with heavy dark spots; tail chestnut with a black subterminal bar. Immature lacks the chestnut tail and underparts whitish, with heavy dark spots. Species breeds in the Sudan, Ethiopia and in north western Uganda. Inhabits wooded areas and more open country with large trees. The Mountain Buzzard *(B. oreophilus)*, 16–17in, 41–43cm, is without rufous in plumage; underparts with heavy dark spotting. It inhabits mountain forests locally in East Africa. The Steppe Buzzard *(B. buteo)*, 18in, 45cm, is a common winter visitor to East and Central Africa. Upperparts brown with variable rufous edgings to the feathers; underparts extremely variable, may be blotched or streaked or barred brown and rufous or entirely rufous. Tail rufous-brown, generally with many dark bars. Like the Augur Buzzard this species greatly favours telegraph poles as vantage points when hunting. The Mountain Buzzard hunts by soaring over forest, chameleons being its food. Another, but much rarer, visitor from the north is the Long-legged Buzzard *(Buteo rufinus)*, 24–26in, 61–66cm, a large pale rufous buzzard, rarely melanistic. Tail unbarred rufous in the adult. In flight looks very pale below, except for black wing patch, wing tips and dark thighs. Very uncommon winter visitor to East and Central Africa, most frequent northern Kenya and Karamoja, Uganda.

LONG-CRESTED EAGLE *Lophaetus occipitalis* Plate 6

Identification. 20–22in, 51–56cm. A blackish-brown eagle with a long, lax crest; legs feathered brownish-white. In flight pale bases of flight feathers form a whitish patch towards the end of each wing. Immature similar but crest shorter. Often seen perched on telegraph poles. The black phase of the Augur Buzzard has yellow unfeathered legs and lacks a crest.
Voice. Series of shrill whistles 'Kee, ee, ee, ee, ee, ee, ee.'
Distribution and Habitat. Common in many parts of East Africa, less frequent Central Africa. Occurs in open park-like country, wooded areas, the edges of forests and cultivation. It feeds almost entirely on rodents and other agricultural pests and is a most beneficial bird.

CROWNED EAGLE *Stephanoaetus coronatus* Plate 7

Identification. 32–36in, 81–92cm. A massive eagle, the size of a Martial but with a longer tail and more rounded wings; in silhouette looks like a gigantic sparrowhawk. Upperparts blackish, with a conspicuous rounded crest, like a halo, and underparts boldly blotched black, orange-rufous and white. Immature paler above and below whitish, washed with rufous on the chest; thighs and legs spotted black. In this plumage could be mistaken for a young Martial Eagle but that species has unspotted white legs and underparts.
Voice. A variety of musical whistles, rising and falling in pitch; often calls while flying.
Distribution and Habitat. Of wide distribution in the Ethiopian Region where there are forests and well-wooded areas, but everywhere very uncommon. It

is perhaps most frequent in the highland forests of Kenya and in Zaire. Its presence is usually governed by the presence of monkeys which form its main item of diet.

MARTIAL EAGLE *Polemaetus bellicosus* Plate 7

Identification. 30–34in, 76–86cm. A very large massive eagle, brownish-grey above and blackish on the throat; rest of underparts white with small dark spots; crest rounded, not always conspicuous. The adult Black-chested Harrier Eagle resembles this species but is smaller, has unfeathered legs, and breast and underside of wings are unspotted. Immature plumage resembles an immature Crowned Eagle, but this species is washed rufous on the chest and has black spotted legs and thighs.
Voice. Usually silent but sometimes utters a short gulping bark.
Distribution and Habitat. A bird of wide distribution in East and Central Africa. In East Africa it is most frequent in the National Parks such as Tsavo and Samburu. It inhabits savannah and semi-desert bush areas, along rivers with fringing forest and on open plains. It is usually encountered perched on top of an acacia or similar tree. It captures prey such as monkeys, hyrax, small antelopes and game birds.

AFRICAN HAWK EAGLE *Hieraaetus spilogaster* Plate 7

Identification. 24–28in, 61–71cm. A black and white eagle, larger than an Augur Buzzard; upperparts blackish with white feather bases showing through to a greater or lesser extent; underparts white with narrow black streaks on throat and breast. The adult Ayres' Hawk Eagle has heavy black drop-like spots on the underparts. The immature African Hawk Eagle is brown above and unspotted pale rufous-buff below; immature Ayres' Hawk Eagle has the rufous-buff concentrated on breast not over entire underparts, and has whitish tips to feathers of upperparts giving a speckled appearance. In flight the African Hawk Eagle has a black patch at wing joint otherwise underside of wings white; Ayres' Hawk Eagle has barred flight feathers and lacks the black patches below wings.
Voice. A loud yelping cry and a double or treble whistle.
Distribution and Habitat. A local and uncommon eagle in suitable localities throughout the Ethiopian Region. It frequents forested and savannah woodlands, baobab country and coastal forests, usually away from the haunts of humans. In East Africa it is most likely to be seen in the National Parks and in the coastal forests of Kenya and Tanzania.
Allied Species. Ayres' Hawk Eagle *(H. dubius)*, 20–24in, 51–61cm, has heavy drop-like spots on the underparts. It is a rare forest eagle in East and Central

Africa, most frequent in the Kenya highlands. It occurs in the forests around
Nairobi. Cassin's Hawk Eagle *(Hieraaetus africanus)*, 22in, 56cm, is black-
ish above, white below with a blackish flank patch and black axillaries. In
East Africa recorded from the Impenetrable-Kayonza forest, south-western
Uganda.

TAWNY EAGLE   *Aquila rapax*   **Plate 6**

Identification. 26–30in, 66–76cm. A uniformly brown eagle with a relatively
short rounded tail; plumage varies greatly from very dark brown (uncommon) to brown, rufous brown or even cream-coloured, a phase most frequent
in northern Kenya and Somalia. Immature usually paler than adult and
possesses two pale wing-bars in flight. The Steppe Eagle *(A. r. nipalensis)* is
now considered to be con-specific with the Tawny Eagle. Some examples are
not distinguishable with certainty in the field, but immature birds are rather
pale brown with an olive tinge, have conspicuous creamy wing-bars and a
white or whitish rump; the adults are blackish-brown, darker than most
Tawnys, with a golden nape patch. It is the sub-adult birds which are
often confused with adult Tawny Eagles. The Brown Harrier Eagle is easily
recognised by its large owl-like head and unfeathered whitish legs. Spotted
and Lesser Spotted Eagles have white or whitish rumps.
Voice. A raucous yelping cry.
Distribution and Habitat. Resident and local spasmodic migrant throughout
the Ethiopian Region outside the forest regions. The Steppe Eagle is a winter
visitor in varying numbers. Frequents cultivation, open and savannah bush
country and mountainous country; also common on open plains in big game
reserves. Associates with vultures and other carrion feeders at lion kills and
around camps but also hunts and kills for itself. Usually nests in trees.
Allied Species. The Spotted Eagle *(A. clanga)* 26–29in, 66–74cm, and the
Lesser Spotted Eagle *(A. pomarina)*, 24–26in, 61–66cm, are rare to uncommon (most frequent in Ethiopia) winter visitors to East Africa and are
difficult to identify. Adults are very dark purplish-brown, slightly paler
below, usually with some white on the upper tail-coverts. The immature
Spotted Eagle has many large white spots on upperparts and wings and a
noticeable white V at the base of the tail. The immature Lesser Spotted Eagle
is much less spotted and is sparsely marked with white at the base of the tail.
At close quarters its best character is a buff patch on the nape. The Imperial
Eagle *(A. heliaca)*, 31–33in, 78–84cm, is a brown eagle, more massive than a
Tawny, with more or less conspicuous white shoulder patches; nape and hind
neck paler than rest of plumage. A very uncommon winter visitor, but
frequent in Ethiopia and the Sudan.

VERREAUX'S EAGLE   *Aquila verreauxii*   Plate 7

Identification. 30–32in, 76–81cm. A large black eagle with centre of back and rump white; in flight whitish patch at base of flight feathers conspicuous; silhouette distinctive, see illustration. Immature dark with pale brown tips to feathers above and below. Species may be confused with certain Tawny Eagle plumages at this stage, but build, size and silhouette are distinctive.
Voice. A loud yelping cry, especially at nest.
Distribution and Habitat. An uncommon and very local eagle, resident in the Sudan, Ethiopia and Somalia south to Central Africa and South Africa. It is associated with rocky crags and inland cliffs upon which it breeds. It is most frequent in Ethiopia and in Kenya, where there are several pairs within a hundred miles radius of Nairobi.

WAHLBERG'S EAGLE   *Aquila wahlbergi*   Plate 7

Identification. 22in, 56cm. A small, rather narrow-winged brown eagle with a short pointed crest on the nape. A pale cream-coloured phase exists but is rare. In flight it might be mistaken for a Black Kite, but it has a long narrow unforked tail. At a distance, when size is not a good field character, it might be mistaken for a Tawny Eagle but its relatively long and narrow wings and long tail serve to identify it.
Voice. A two-noted whistle.
Distribution and Habitat. A local resident over most of the Ethiopian region. A resident in wooded or bush savannah and along lakes and rivers where there are trees. In East Africa it is commonest in the woodlands of Tanzania and locally frequent where it occurs in cultivated areas so long as there are plenty of trees. Widespread in Central Africa.
Allied Species. The European Booted Eagle *(Hieraeetus pennatus)*, 18–21in, 46–53cm, a species with two distinct plumage phases, is a small eagle with heavily feathered tarsi. Upperparts mottled dark brown, often with paler, reddish head; below either dark brown or whitish. In pale phase, in flight, dark primaries and secondaries contrast with white under wing coverts. Passage migrant and winter visitor to East Africa; relatively few records Central Africa.

AFRICAN FISH EAGLE   *Haliaeetus vocifer*   Plate 6

Identification. 30in, 76cm. Easily recognised by its distinctive colour pattern, white head, chest, back and tail; chestnut belly and shoulders and black wings. Immature duller with heavy black streaking on breast and some black on tail.

Voice. The far-carrying, wild, almost gull-like call is one of the characteristic sounds of the African wilds. When calling the bird throws its head backwards, even in flight.

Distribution and Habitat. Widely distributed and common through most of the Ethiopian Region; numerous in many places in East and Central Africa. Occurs in the vicinity of water – lakes, swamps, rivers, flooded areas, dams and the coast. It feeds largely on fish but will sometimes take large rodents and also waterbirds such as coots.

BLACK KITE   *Milvus migrans*   Plate 6

Identification. 21–23in, 53–58cm. Plumage brown to rusty-brown with a conspicuously forked tail; bill yellow. Immature similar but with pale streaking on underparts. The European race of the Black Kite, a common winter visitor, has a whitish-brown head and a black bill.

Voice. A high-pitched wavering call.

Distribution and Habitat. Resident and local migrant throughout East and Central Africa, frequenting savannah and open country, cultivated areas, towns, lakes and rivers and the coast. Often found in numbers when attracted by carrion or insect swarms. Often seen quartering roads for road kills. The European Black Kite is a winter visitor and passage migrant in East Africa; in Central Africa it appears mainly as a passage migrant.

Allied Species. The European Honey Buzzard *(Pernis apivorus)*, 20–23in, 51–58cm, is an uncommon winter visitor and passage migrant in East and Central Africa. It has a longer tail and narrower wings than the true buzzards. Its plumage is extremely variable; best field character is double dark bar across basal half of tail and black terminal band. It has a somewhat lethargic flight. Frequents wooded and forested areas and has the habit of robbing bees' and wasps' nests.

BLACK-SHOULDERED KITE   *Elanus caeruleus*   Plate 6

Identification. 13in, 33cm. A thickset, medium-sized hawk, pale grey above and white below, with a white, slightly forked tail and black shoulders. Immature darker above with white tips to feathers of mantle and wing-coverts; below with rusty wash on breast. Frequently hovers whilst hunting and settles on telegraph poles and wires. Often seen hunting at dusk and even when it is almost dark. When settled has the habit of slowly raising and lowering its tail.

Voice. Usually silent, but sometimes utters a clear piping whistle.

Distribution and Habitat. A common resident and local migrant in East and Central Africa; often congregates in numbers in areas where rodents are abundant. Inhabits savannah woodland and open grasslands, cultivation, margins of lakes and rivers and also mountain moorland.

Allied Species. The Bat Hawk *(Macheirhamphus alcinus)*, 16in, 40cm, is a remarkable hawk of crepuscular and nocturnal habits. In flight it has the silhouette of a Peregrine Falcon; it is dark brown with a little white on the throat and in the middle of the belly; eye very large and bright yellow; bill small and laterally compressed, gape huge like that of a nightjar. The bird appears at dusk and catches bats and late roosting swallows on the wing which it then proceeds to swallow whole. It is widely distributed in East and Central Africa but is everywhere rare. In East Africa the most likely localities are at Voi and Makindu in Kenya, and at the coast; the Bat Hawk is often recorded at dusk flying at or near Malindi.

SWALLOW-TAILED KITE *Chelictinia riocourii* Plate 6

Identification. 12in, 30cm. One of the most graceful birds of prey, almost tern-like in its appearance. Pale grey above, white below with a deeply-forked tail; black patch at angle of wing from below. Extremely buoyant in flight. Gregarious and nesting in acacia trees in colonies.

Voice. A soft mewing cry uttered at the nesting colony.

Distribution and Habitat. Occurs in the arid northern districts of Kenya and northern Uganda, to the Sudan, Ethiopia and Somalia. Appearances in the Northern Frontier Province and Turkana in Kenya vary greatly from year to year, but in some years it may be locally common. Feeds on rodents, lizards and large insects.

OSPREY *Pandion haliaetus* Plate 7

Identification. 20–23in, 51–58cm. Dark upperparts, contrasting white crown and mainly white underparts, long wings with black carpal patch, plus its habit of plunging feet first into the water to capture fish, render this an easy species to identify. Head slightly crested; legs blue-grey. Nearly always seen near water. Immature similar but with pale edges to feathers of upperparts.

Voice. Several barking calls, and also short whistles often uttered when two birds are competing over a single fish.

Distribution and Habitat. Resident in very small numbers in East Africa, breeding on islands or in old fish eagle's nests on Lake Naivasha in Kenya's Rift Valley and also on islands in Lake Turkana (Rudolf). Further north it is a common breeder on islands in the Red Sea. It is a fairly common winter visitor to East and Central Africa. Occurs near water – inland waterways, lakes and also the coast.

FALCONS: Falconidae

Falcons are characterised by their thickset build, sharply pointed wings and often extremely fast flight. They generally kill their prey by swooping on it at high speed.

PYGMY FALCON   *Poliohierax semitorquatus*   Plate 8

Identification. 7–8in, 18–20cm. A tiny white-breasted hawk with a distinctive shrike-like appearance when perched. This is very apparent when the bird alights on the top of an acacia tree, its favoured vantage point. The ♂ has a pale grey mantle, the ♀ a chestnut mantle. Immature similar to ♀ but duller.
Voice. A series of shrill notes 'ku, ku, ku, ku, ku, ku, ku, ku.'
Distribution and Habitat. A local resident in dry bush and savannah country in eastern and southern Africa, but not in Central Africa. It is locally common in the Northern Frontier Province of Kenya and in Turkana, Kenya. There it is often seen in the vicinity of buffalo weavers' nests, in which it lays its eggs.

LANNER   *Falco biarmicus*   Plate 8

Identification. 16–18in, 41–46cm. Upperparts pale grey with rufous or rufous-buff on crown and nape. Below pale buff with light black spotting, mainly on the flanks. The Peregrine is much darker, slate-grey above with greyish underparts with dusky barring. Immature Lanner browner above with heavy drop-like spots on underparts.
Voice. Shrill 'kre-kre-kre' at nesting sites.
Distribution and Habitat. Occurs locally throughout much of the Ethiopian Region, most frequent in the north of its range. In East Africa uncommon, most frequent in Northern Frontier Province and Turkana in Kenya. Usually found in vicinity of inland cliffs but visits more open country.
Allied Species. The Taita Falcon *(F. fasciinucha)*, 14–16in, 36–41cm, is a rare falcon confined to East and Central Africa, south to the Victoria Falls. Resembles a thickset small Lanner but with a relatively much shorter tail and pale, greyish-white rump. Grey above with rufous on nape, below deep rufous with sparse streaks. It is most frequent in south-western Ethiopia but is also seen in the Tsavo National Park and at Amboseli, Kenya. The Saker Falcon *(F. cherrug)*, 18in, 46cm, is like a large pale greyish-brown Peregrine with a whitish head, streaked underparts and bluish-white legs. It is an uncommon winter visitor to north-eastern Africa, rarely south to Kenya.

PEREGRINE   *Falco peregrinus*   **Plate 8**

Identification. 14–18in, 36–46cm. Two distinct races occur in Africa, a smaller, dark resident Peregrine, and a larger and paler Palearctic race which is a winter visitor and passage migrant. Upperparts and crown medium to dark slate-grey without rufous on crown or nape; heavy black moustache patches. Immature browner with spotted underparts. The adult Lanner is paler grey with much rufous on crown and nape.
Voice. A rapid, shrill 'kek, kek, kek, kek, kek,' usually uttered near nesting cliff.
Distribution and Habitat. Rare resident in suitable localities through East and Central Africa, more frequent in the north. Also winter visitor and passage migrant in varying numbers. Occurs in a variety of habitats, including open country and the vicinity of lakes, bush country, inland cliffs and cultivation.

AFRICAN HOBBY   *Falco cuvieri*   **Plate 8**

Identification. 11–12in, 28–31cm. Resembles a miniature Peregrine but upperparts much brighter blue-grey and dark rufous below; small chestnut patch on nape. When flying at a distance has the appearance of a large swift. Immature similar but feathers of upperparts with buff edgings. The European Hobby is paler above, buffy white below with rufous thighs; also rather larger. Taita Falcon has shorter tail and is very pale on the rump.
Voice. Shrill piping call notes, 'ke, ke, ke, ke, ke, ke, ke.'
Distribution and Habitat. Everywhere very uncommon and local in East and Central Africa. Frequents edges of forests, cultivation where there are isolated trees and also savannah country. Often crepuscular in its appearances.
Allied Species. The European Hobby *(F. subbuteo)*, 12–14in, 30–36cm, is a winter visitor and passage migrant to East and Central Africa. It is slightly larger and much paler than the African Hobby, the underparts being pale buff with black streaks and the thighs rufous. Eleonora's Falcon *(F. eleonorae)*, 15in, 38cm, resembles a very long-tailed European Hobby but with darker upperparts and rufous-buff below with heavier streaking; an all dark melanistic form also occurs. A very uncommon passage migrant, observed most frequently in Somalia and in central Tanzania; probably overlooked elsewhere.

RED-NECKED FALCON   *Falco chiquera*   **Plate 8**

Identification. 12–14in, 30–36cm. A thickset grey falcon with a conspicuous chestnut cap and nape and black and white barred belly. Seen from behind it might be mistaken for a ♂ Lanner but a view of the barred belly will identify it immediately. Immature browner above, buffy below with broken dark barring.

Voice. Shrill 'keep, keep, keep, keep.'

Distribution and Habitat. In East and Central Africa uncommon and local, most frequent in the southern Sudan and in northern Uganda where it is almost always associated with borassus palms, in which it nests. Also occurs in coconut plantations along the East African coast.

GREY KESTREL *Falco ardosiaceus* Plate 8

Identification. 14in, 36cm. An entirely grey kestrel with a conspicuous yellow face (bare skin around eyes and at base of bill). Flight feathers and rectrices barred dusky. Immature brownish, especially on underparts.

Voice. A harsh chatter, and sometimes, usually when nesting, a succession of shrill whistles.

Distribution and Habitat. In East Africa occurs in the Sudan and Ethiopia south to southern Tanzania; no records from Zambia. It frequents water courses where there are trees, wooded areas and cultivation. Crepuscular in its habits and feeds to some extent on bats. Nests in unoccupied hamerkops' nests and may often be seen perched near these. Everywhere local and uncommon.

Allied Species. The darker slate-grey or blackish-grey Sooty Falcon *(Falco concolor)*, 13–14in, 32–35cm, has the two central tail feathers protruding beyond the others and its flight and tail feathers are unbarred. It is a rare species in East Africa, nesting in the central Sudan and probably along the coasts of the Red Sea; elsewhere a non-breeding visitor and passage migrant.

DICKINSON's KESTREL *Falco dickinsoni* Plate 8

Identification. 13in, 32cm. This is another grey kestrel, distinguished from the Grey Kestrel by its blackish-grey back and contrasting greyish-white rump which is very conspicuous when the bird flies. Wings and tail feathers barred. Immature browner than adult.

Voice. Normally a silent bird, but sometimes utters a one or two note whistle.

Distribution and Habitat. Occurs locally in Tanzania, including Pemba Island, and in Central Africa. It is found mainly in Brachystegia woodland (Miombo) but will frequent almost any type of wooded area. Often seen perched on telegraph poles and dead trees; feeds largely upon insects.

KESTREL *Falco tinnunculus*   **Plate 8**

Identification. 13–14in, 33–36cm. The true kestrels are generally less thickset than other falcons and hunt their prey by hovering. The adult ♂ of the present species may be recognised by presence of black spots on its chestnut back; tail grey with a broad black subterminal bar. ♀ less brightly plumaged than ♂ and has a barred brown tail. African races of the kestrel are in general darker and usually have barred grey tails. The European Lesser Kestrel is smaller and the ♂ lacks black spotting on mantle; at close quarters its white not dark grey claws are distinctive. It may also be distinguished by its method of feeding, carrying its food to its mouth with one foot whilst the Kestrel holds its prey with two feet in the normal falcon manner. Both sexes of the Greater Kestrel may be distinguished by their barred flanks, creamy-white eyes and blue-grey, black-barred tail.

Voice. Normally silent but African races utter a shrill 'kee, kee, kee, kee, kee' at their nesting cliffs.

Distribution and Habitat. African resident races occur very locally in East and Central Africa, normally in the vicinity of inland cliffs. The European race is an abundant winter visitor and passage migrant in open country and cultivation outside forests.

Allied Species. The European Lesser Kestrel *(F. naumanni)*, 12in, 30cm, is also an abundant winter visitor and passage migrant; more gregarious than the Kestrel and normally encountered in flocks. Unspotted chestnut mantle in the ♂ and smaller size, gregarious habits and pale claws distinguish the species. It occurs throughout East and Central Africa in open areas. The Eastern Red-footed Falcon *(F. amurensis)*, 12in, 30cm, is sometimes found associated with flocks of Lesser Kestrels, but is uncommon in East Africa although in Central Africa it may be commoner than the Lesser Kestrel. It too is a winter visitor and passage migrant from the north. The ♂ is dark grey with a chestnut abdomen and thighs and white under wing-coverts; legs orange-red. ♀ has buff underparts streaked with black. The Western Red-footed Falcon *(Falco vespertinus)*, 12in, 30cm, is a much rarer winter visitor, in East Africa most frequently observed in the Sudan, but sometimes not uncommon in Central Africa. The ♂ differs in having the underside of the wings dark slate-grey, not white.

GREATER KESTREL *Falco rupicoloides*   **Plate 8**

Identification. 14in, 36cm. Resembles a ♀ European Kestrel at first sight but may be distinguished by its black-barred blue-grey rump and tail, barred mantle and barred flanks, and creamy-white eye. ♀♀ of European and Lesser Kestrels have barred brown tails and dark brown eyes.

Voice. A silent bird but at nest sometimes utters a weak kite-like whistle.
Distribution and Habitat. A local resident in Somalia, Ethiopia, south to Central Africa. Occurs in open bush country and semi-desert bush where there are scattered trees. Nests in trees while African races of the Kestrel are cliff nesters.

FOX KESTREL *Falco alopex* **Plate 8**

Identification. 15in, 38cm. Sexes alike. Entire plumage except black flight feathers coppery-chestnut with short black streaks on upperparts and breast; tail barred. Immature similar.
Voice. A shrill 'kee, kee, kee, kee.'
Distribution and Habitat. Occurs in the Sudan and Ethiopia, south to the Turkana district of north-western Kenya. Gregarious, nests in loose colonies on inland cliffs.

GAME BIRDS: Phasianidae

This family includes the quails, francolins, guineafowls and their allies. All are chicken-like terrestrial birds with moderate or short tails; sexes usually alike in African species.

COQUI FRANCOLIN *Francolinus coqui* **Plate 9**

Identification. 8–10in, 20–25cm. The term 'francolin' is reserved for those species with feathered throats; those species with bare unfeathered throats are called 'spurfowl.' The Coqui Francolin is a partridge-sized bird with outer tail feathers showing chestnut in flight; underparts barred black and white; legs dull yellow. ♀ with greyish-rufous upper breast. The underparts barring in this species is variable, in some races the barring is confined to the upper breast and flanks, in others it extends all over the belly.
Voice. A shrill 'qui-kit, qui-kit,' heard most often at dawn and in the evening.
Distribution and Habitat. A local resident throughout much of East and Central Africa. Frequents grasslands, savannah woodlands, Brachystegia woodland and hillsides where there is some bush cover.
Allied Species. Two forest francolins about the same size as the Coqui occur in the forests of Uganda and the southern Sudan. These are Nahan's Forest Francolin *(F. nahani)* and the Forest Francolin *(F. lathami)*. Both species have black underparts with conspicuous white spots. The former has the upperparts dark brown with black bases to the feathers, without white shaft streaks. The Forest Francolin has brown upperparts with distinct white shaft

streaks. Like other forest game birds these species are very shy and are best looked for on forest paths immediately after rain. Both occur in the Bwamba Forest, western Uganda.

RING-NECKED FRANCOLIN   *Francolinus streptophorus*   Plate 9

Identification. 10in, 25cm. A dark brown francolin with a ring of black and white barring encircling the neck; below buffy white with long, oval black markings on the flanks. ♀ similar but with upperparts barred pale brown.
Voice. Two soft notes followed by a piping trill.
Distribution and Habitat. An uncommon and local francolin found in Uganda, north-western Tanzania and the Mt Elgon area of Kenya. A skulker and easily overlooked, frequenting stony hillsides with sparse bush and grass.

CRESTED FRANCOLIN   *Francolinus sephaena*   Plate 9

Identification. 10–11in, 25–28cm. A bantam-sized francolin which usually carries its tail cocked up over its back. Above brown with distinctive white shaft streaks; below pale buff with mottling on the breast and triangular chestnut spots on sides of neck.
Voice. A very loud, far-carrying 'tee-dee-jee' uttered over and over again; birds especially noisy at dawn and dusk.
Distribution and Habitat. A resident, sometimes very common, in dry bush country in East Africa; less frequent in Central Africa. Frequents semi-desert bush, coastal thickets, and along water courses.

SHELLEY'S FRANCOLIN   *Francolinus shelleyi*   Plate 9

Identification. 11–12in, 28–31cm. A rather thickset francolin with a white throat, the chest blotched chestnut and the belly mottled black and white; creamy-white shaft streaks on upperparts; outer tail feathers black in flight; flight feathers grey with some rufous at base. The similar Redwing Francolin has mainly rufous flight feathers.
Voice. A shrill 'tee, ji, ji, ji, ji, ji, ji.'
Distribution and Habitat. Occurs locally in Kenya and south-western Uganda, south through Tanzania to Central Africa where locally common. Lives in grasslands, light woodlands and mixed areas of bush and grass.

REDWING FRANCOLIN   *Francolinus levaillantii*   Plate 9

Identification. 12–13in, 31–33cm. This is a small chicken-sized francolin, mainly rufous-buff with reddish flight feathers and a conspicuous rufous patch on the hindneck; chest deep rufous. Shelley's Francolin differs in having a black and white mottled belly. The Montane Francolin has round black spots on the rufous chest.

Voice. A shrill 'kee-el-de-we' repeated frequently.

Distribution and Habitat. A local and uncommon francolin ranging from western Kenya and Uganda south to Zambia and Malawi. A highland bird, in East Africa most frequent in the western highlands and the Cherengani range; in Central Africa on the Nyika Plateau, Malawi and Balovale and Mankoya districts, Zambia.

MONTANE FRANCOLIN   *Francolinus psilolaemus*   Plate 9

Identification. 12–13in, 31–33cm. Related to the Redwing Francolin and like that species has much rich chestnut on the wings and a rufous hind-neck patch; its belly is buff, mottled with chestnut and black. It may be distinguished by its rufous upper chest band which is heavily marked with round black spots.

Voice. Relatively silent birds, but around dusk before roosting frequently utter a three or four note strident grating call.

Distribution and Habitat. Confined to mountain grasslands, alpine moorlands and rocky outcrops in the highlands of Ethiopia and Kenya where it is found on Mt Kenya, the Aberdare Mts, the Mau and Mt Elgon.

HILDEBRANDT'S FRANCOLIN   *Francolinus hildebrandti*   Plate 9

Identification. 14–15in, 35–38cm. Sexes unlike. ♂ with white underparts heavily blotched with black; the ♀ pale coffee colour on the underparts. This is a chicken-sized francolin with dark finely-vermiculated upperparts and red legs. When pairs or family parties are encountered the striking difference in plumage between the sexes is a good field character.

Voice. A three note, loud 'kok, kok, kok' repeated over and over again, often very rapidly. Calls mainly at dawn and dusk.

Distribution and Habitat. A very local and generally uncommon species in hilly country in East Africa. Occurs in Kenya and southwards to Zambia. It frequents well-wooded hill country, scrub covered hillsides and sometimes on hillsides where the only cover is a little grass and rocks. In Kenya it is most frequent in the Loita Hills.

Allied Species. Clapperton's Francolin *(F. clappertoni)*, 14in, 35cm, occurs in the Sudan, northern Uganda and the Mt Elgon area, western Kenya. It is dark in colour without pale shaft streaks on upperparts; on the wing it shows a pale buff wing patch, very like the wing patch of the Yellow-necked Spurfowl.

HEUGLIN'S FRANCOLIN *Francolinus icterorhynchus* **Plate 9**

Identification. 11–12in, 28–31cm. A medium-sized rather dark francolin with dusky upperparts; below pale buff with black mottling on the chest and black spots on the belly; ♂ possesses two spurs on each leg. Often observed perched on top of termite hills in savannah woodland.
Voice. A shrill three note call, uttered usually at dusk.
Distribution and Habitat. Local resident in the southern Sudan and northern Uganda. It is most frequent in savannah woodlands of north-western Uganda in areas where there are many termite hills. It perches freely on these termite hills and in trees.

JACKSON'S FRANCOLIN *Francolinus jacksoni* **Plate 9**

Identification. 13–15in, 33–38cm. ♂ larger than ♀ but plumages alike. A rich brown francolin with white margined chestnut neck and belly, throat white; legs and bill red. This is a mountain forest bird confined to Kenya. It may be recognised by the combination of red bill and legs, and chestnut underparts. The Scaly Francolin which occurs alongside Jackson's Francolin has red legs, but its plumage is mainly dark greyish-brown without chestnut.
Voice. Birds call loudly at dusk, prior to roosting in bamboo clumps and forest trees; call, a harsh 'grrr, grrr, grrr.'
Distribution and Habitat. Confined to mountain forest on Mt Kenya, the Aberdare Mts, the Kinangop plateau, the Mau forest and the Cherengani Mts, Kenya. In parts of the Aberdare forest the species is abundant. Mountain forest, mixed forest and bamboo are the bird's normal habitat.
Allied Species. The Handsome Francolin *(Francolinus nobilis)*, 13–14in, 33–36cm, of the Ruwenzori and Kivu mountain forests, western Uganda and Zaire is similar to Jackson's Francolin but with a rich purplish-chestnut back and grey crown; below the feathers chestnut edged with grey; throat greyish-white. It occurs in bamboo and mountain forest and is very shy and seldom observed. The Chestnut-naped Francolin *(Francolinus castaneicollis)*, 14–15in, 36–38cm, is another large francolin with a white throat and a great deal of chestnut red in the plumage and with red bill and legs. It differs from Jackson's Francolin by its buffy-white belly. It is confined to mountain areas in Ethiopia and Somalia where there is plenty of cover.

SCALY FRANCOLIN *Francolinus squamatus* **Plate 9**

Identification. 10–12in, 25–31cm. A dark, uniform coloured francolin with conspicuous red legs. Plumage above and below brown broadly streaked darker brown. A well-known forest species called 'redleg' by Kenya sportsmen.

Voice. A rapid, guttural 'kew-koo-wah, kew-koo-wah.'
Distribution and Habitat. A resident in forest and thick bush in the vicinity of forest from the Sudan and Ethiopia south to north-eastern Zambia. Although common in many parts of the Kenya highlands and northern Tanzania it is a local bird, absent from many apparently suitable localities. Its presence is betrayed by the birds' noisy calls towards dusk. After rain this and other species of forest-haunting francolins may be seen on forest paths.

RED-NECKED SPURFOWL   *Francolinus afer*   Plate 9

Identification. 13–14in, 33–36cm. This is a very variable species which may have the underparts vermiculated grey and white, with or without chestnut streaks, or the belly feathers may be black, edged with greyish-white. All races have greyish-brown upperparts with dark shaft stripes, a bare red throat and red legs. The Grey-breasted Spurfowl has a bare orange throat, chestnut-margined feathers above and below and a grey chest with dark shaft stripes. Swainson's Spurfowl has a red bare throat but blackish-brown legs.
Voice. A loud, shrill 'kraaek, kraaek' uttered from thick cover, either early in the morning or just before the birds take up their roosts at dusk.
Distribution and Habitat. A resident in wooded districts in East, Central and Southern Africa. In East and Central Africa black-breasted races occur in coastal districts of Kenya south to eastern Zambia, Malawi and southwards. Races with grey underparts, with or without chestnut streaks, occur in western Kenya, Uganda and southwards through Tanzania. Species occurs in wooded and savannah grasslands, park-like country and hillsides where there is plenty of cover. In many parts of its range it is a shy and retiring bird which would often be overlooked were it not for its noisy call.
Allied Species. The Grey-breasted Spurfowl *(Francolinus rufopictus)*, 14–15in, 36–38cm, has a very restricted distribution in acacia woodland on the Serengeti plains and around Lake Eyasi, northern Tanzania. It has a bare orange-pink throat and chestnut-red streaking above and below; chest grey. Swainson's Spurfowl *(Francolinus swainsoni)*, 13–14in, 33–36cm, occurs widely in Central Africa. It resembles one of the grey-breasted races of the Red-necked Spurfowl but has blackish not red legs. It occurs in woodland and neglected cultivation.

YELLOW-NECKED SPURFOWL   *Francolinus leucoscepus* Plate 9

Identification. 13–14in, 33–36cm. A greyish-brown spurfowl with underparts buffy streaked darker brown; throat conspicuously bare, bright yellow to orange red at base; bird stands high on its legs. In flight shows pale wing patches.

Voice. A loud, grating 'graark, grak, grak,' especially vocal in the early morning and towards dusk.

Distribution and Habitat. This is the commonest francolin throughout its range in East Africa, in north-eastern Uganda, Kenya and northern Tanzania. Frequents open bush country, margins of forests, woodland and dry bush country.

HARLEQUIN QUAIL *Coturnix delegorguei* Plate 9

Identification. 6½in, 16–17cm. ♂ easily recognised by mainly black underparts and black and white throat markings. ♀ has pale rufous-grey underparts without spots, streaks or barring. This is the commonest of the African quails and in East and Central Africa is subject to extensive irregular migrations, when it may become extremely abundant locally in open grasslands.

Voice. A four note whistle, 'pleet, pleet – pleet, pleet.'

Distribution and Habitat. Widely distributed resident and local migrant throughout Ethiopian Region, except West African forest areas. Frequents open grasslands where its presence may be detected by its plaintive call-notes. Occurs from sea level up to 8,000ft, 2440m, and over. In seasons of good rains it is very common on the Athi Plains near Nairobi, Kenya.

Allied Species. The European Quail *(Coturnix coturnix)*, 7in, 18cm, occurs as a passage migrant and winter visitor to the Sudan, Ethiopia, northern Uganda and northern Kenya. This bird and its African race, the Cape Quail, differ from the ♀ Harlequin Quail in having a brown or chestnut throat patch (♂♂) or spotted chest and flanks (♀♀). The Cape Quail is a local resident from Ethiopia southwards to South Africa. It is a highlands species, usually found at over 7000ft, 2140m, in East Africa, Malawi and Zambia.

BLUE QUAIL *Coturnix chinensis* Plate 9

Identification. 5in, 13cm. ♂ identified by its bright slate-blue underparts, slate back, chestnut wing coverts and white throat markings. ♀ rufous-brown with chest and flanks barred with black. Immature similar to ♀.

Voice. Normally silent but sometimes utters a weak flute-like whistle.

Distribution and Habitat. Local and very uncommon in East Africa, more frequent in Central Africa where relatively frequent in Zambia and Malawi. Inhabits damp grasslands, neglected cultivation and open plains. To some extent a local migrant.

Allied Species. The Stone Partridge *(Ptilopachus petrosus)*, 10in, 25–26cm, is a small dark brown game bird mottled with pale buff with a creamy-white belly. Best identified by its characteristic habits: occurs on small rocky hills in small parties; when walking holds its tail cocked up over its back like a tiny bantam fowl. Legs red. Its call is a shrill peeping 'weet, weet, weet, weet' and is especially noisy at dusk. It occurs in the southern Sudan, Ethiopia, northern Uganda and north-western Kenya.

HELMETED GUINEAFOWL *Numida meleagris* Plate 9

Identification. 20–22in, 51–56cm. General colour slate-grey, spotted all over with round white spots; head and neck sparsely feathered with a bony horn protruding from crown; blue and red or all blue wattles at base of bill. The Tufted Guineafowl which has a tuft of nasal bristles at the base of the bill is now considered to be conspecific. Gregarious outside breeding season.
Voice. A loud cackling call, repeated frequently.
Distribution and Habitat. Locally common through most of East and Central Africa in bush country, arid thornbush areas, neglected cultivation, open park-like country and savannah woodlands.

CRESTED GUINEAFOWL *Guttera edouardi* Plate 9

Identification. 18–22in, 46–56cm. A chicken-sized guineafowl, black covered with round bluish-white spots; lower half of neck purplish-black unspotted; crown without helmet, crested with long curling black feathers; neck and face bare, cobalt blue and red. The closely allied Kenya Crested Guineafowl has the lower neck blue spotted, not unspotted purplish-black.
Voice. A harsh 'churrr, tuk, tuk, tuk'; also soft clucking notes.
Distribution and Habitat. Occurs in southern Sudan, Uganda and western Kenya south to Central Africa and southwards. Inhabits rain forest, riverine forest, deciduous thickets and dense scrub. Local and often overlooked.

KENYA CRESTED GUINEAFOWL *Guttera pucherani* Plate 9

Identification. 18–22in, 46–56cm. Plumage black with bluish-white spots above and below; upper neck and face bare, cobalt blue and red; crown with curly black crest. The closely related Crested Guineafowl has the feathers at the base of the neck purplish-black without spots.
Voice. Similar to Crested Guineafowl calls, harsh guttural 'tuks' and softer clucking notes.
Distribution and Habitat. A very local and decreasing resident in forested and thickly wooded areas in southern Somalia, Kenya east of the Rift Valley, north-eastern Tanzania and Zanzibar. The birds from the Jombeni mountains, Kenya, are larger than Kenya coastal specimens. Species shy and seldom seen unless heavy rain has driven them to the relative dryness of forest paths and tracks. Most frequent in the Sokoke-Arabuku Forest, Kenya coast.

VULTURINE GUINEAFOWL *Acryllium vulturinum* **Plate 9**

Identification. 23–24in, 58–61cm. A most handsome long-tailed guineafowl with feathers of upper mantle and chest elongated and striped white, black and blue; breast bright cobalt blue; head and neck bare, slate-grey, with patch of downy chestnut feathers on nape; head small for the bird's size, imparting a vulturine appearance. Gregarious, normally occurs in flocks.

Voice. A series of loud, shrill cackles and a loud "kak, kak, kak, kak, kak, kak, kak.'

Distribution and Habitat. A local resident in dry thornbush country, semi-desert areas and dry forest in Somalia, eastern Ethiopia, eastern Kenya and north-eastern Tanzania. Numbers fluctuate greatly, species at times very uncommon; in other more favourable years it may be abundant.

BUTTON QUAILS: Turnicidae

Button Quails superficially resemble the true Quails but differ in lacking a hind toe. They occur in areas of tall grass and when flushed rise at one's feet; dropping into the grass again a short distance away, they are very difficult to flush a second time.

BUTTON QUAIL *Turnix sylvatica* **Plate 9**

Identification. 5½in, 14cm. In general appearance resembles a small buff-coloured quail or a round-winged lark. Seldom observed except when flushed at one's feet. The Black-rumped Button Quail differs in having a distinct blackish rump in flight. The Quail Plover has a curious jerky flight and black and white wings.

Voice. A rather frog-like 'whoo, whoo, whoo,' very difficult to locate in grassy plains.

Distribution and Habitat. A local resident, sometimes common, throughout suitable areas of Ethiopian Region. Common in many parts of East and Central Africa. Frequents bush country where there is abundant grass cover, in old neglected cultivation, in sisal cultivation and savannah bush where there is long grass. In many places at least partially migratory and its numbers in any locality may vary greatly.

Allied Species. The Black-rumped Button Quail *(T. nana)*, 5in, 13cm, occurs in western Kenya, Uganda, Tanzania and southwards. It is less common than the Button Quail except perhaps in parts of Zambia where it occurs around the edges of dambos where the Button Quail is not found. In flight its dark rump is conspicuous. The Quail Plover *(Ortyxelos meiffrenii)*, 4½in, 12cm, is a tiny lark-like bird with noticeable black and white wings. It is found only in areas where the silvery 'Heskanit' grass grows. It is most frequent in the Sudan but also occurs in northern Uganda and very locally in northern and eastern Kenya.

CRANES: Balearicidae

The Cranes are large, stately terrestrial birds, superficially resembling storks, from which they differ externally in having the nostrils in a long groove, and the hind toe short. The various species inhabit open country, cultivation and marshes. Voices loud, trumpet or goose-like. Long neck and legs extended in flight. Gregarious outside breeding season.

CROWNED CRANE   *Balearica regulorum*   **Plate 10**

Identification. 40in, 102cm. Upperparts slate-grey, paler on neck and underparts; wings appear mainly white in flight with black primaries and chestnut secondaries; forehead with a black, velvety cushion with a conspicuous tuft of straw-coloured, bristle-like feathers on the crown; bare cheeks and neck wattles white and red. Sexes similar; immature brownish with broad pale edgings to feathers. The Crowned Crane can be mistaken only for the closely related Sudan Crowned Crane, which is a little smaller with a blackish neck.
Voice. A loud, drawn-out honking call 'ah, aahow, ah, aahow,' which has been likened to the honking of Canadian geese. Calls often uttered in flight.
Distribution and Habitat. A local resident, common in Kenya and Uganda, southwards to Central Africa. Occurs on open plains, marshes, swamps and cultivated land; gregarious unless nesting.
Allied Species. The Sudan Crowned Crane *(B. pavonina)*, 36in, 92cm, has a blackish-grey neck. It occurs in the Sudan, Ethiopia and northern Uganda. The Wattled Crane *(Bugeranus carunculatus)*, 50in, 126cm, is pale grey with a white neck and two white-feathered pendant wattles from chin. It occurs in two isolated populations, one in the highlands of Ethiopia, the other in southern Tanzania (Rukwa) and Central Africa where it is commoner than the Crowned Crane. Favoured localities for the species are the Kafue Flats and the Bangweulu swamps in Zambia. The European Crane *(Grus grus)*, 45in, 114cm, and the Demoiselle Crane *(Anthropoides virgo)*, 38in, 96cm, occur as winter visitors to the Sudan and northern Ethiopia. The former is grey with a black face and foreneck and a white stripe from cheeks down sides of neck; red patch on crown. The Demoiselle Crane is grey with conspicuous white ear tufts and black foreneck and chest.

CRAKES, RAILS and COOTS: Rallidae

The Rails and their allies are generally marsh or water-haunting birds with rounded wings and apparently weak flight with legs dangling. Toes long and slender; tails short and often carried cocked up. Crakes have relatively short and thick bills; rails have longer slender bills; moorhens and coots have heavy thickset bodies and small heads and often swim.

BLACK CRAKE   *Limnocorax flavirostra*   **Plate 10**

Identification. 8in, 20cm. Plumage entirely slaty-black with contrasting apple-green bill and bright pink legs. Less skulking than most crakes and rails and often seen feeding among water-lily leaves at the edge of reed and papyrus beds.

Voice. A trilling 'r-r-r-r-r-r-r-r, yok' and various clucking sounds. It is possible to mistake the trill of a Little Grebe for the call of a Black Crake.

Distribution and Habitat. Occurs throughout the Ethiopian Region where a combination of water and fringing vegetation exists. It is common in East and Central Africa. In the Amboseli National Park, Kenya, these crakes have become very tame and may be observed at close quarters without being disturbed.

Allied Species. The Kaffir Rail *(Rallus caerulescens)* is a local but widespread resident in rank vegetation in permanent swamps in East and Central Africa, but is shy and difficult to observe. It is 11in, 28cm, in length with a slender bill; upperparts dark brown, flanks barred black and white. The European Corn Crake *(Crex crex)*, 10½in, 27cm, is a passage migrant and winter visitor to East and Central Africa, found in dry open grasslands. Seldom observed unless flushed at one's feet. Plumage buff-brown with blackish streaks on underparts; throat greyish. Rufous wings conspicuous in flight. In East Africa mainly a passage migrant and many records are of birds which have killed themselves by flying into telegraph wires. The African Crake *(Crex egregia)*, 10in, 25cm, has dark olive and black upperparts and black and white barred flanks and belly. It is a resident, locally migratory, throughout East and Central Africa. Occurs both in rank grass in dry areas and in rank vegetation near water. It is a shy bird and its presence is usually indicated by its call, a high-pitched chittering trill. Rouget's Rail *(Rallus rougetii)*, 11in, 28cm, is a species confined to the moorlands and marshes of the highlands of Ethiopia. It is uniformly coloured, above dark olive-brown, below rufous-brown with white under tail coverts. The Grey-throated Rail *(Canirallus oculeus)*, 12in, 31cm, has distinctive white-spotted flight feathers, olive-brown above, chestnut on the neck and underparts. A forest species keeping to dense cover; in East Africa known only from the Bwamba Forest, western Uganda.

STRIPED CRAKE *Porzana marginalis*   Plate 10

Identification. 7in, 18cm. An olive-brown crake with feathers of upperparts edged white, imparting a striped appearance; below grey.
Voice. A deep 'grrrrr' like a snore; also utters a rapid churring call resembling a tree-frog's croaks.
Distribution and Habitat. An extremely uncommon species but with a wide distribution in Africa, most frequent in the Balovale district in Zambia. An intra-African migrant which frequents seasonally flooded grasslands, swamps and marshes. Many records are of birds which have flown into lighted windows and telegraph wires whilst migrating at night.
Allied Species. The Nkulengu Rail *(Himantornis haematopus)*, 17in, 43cm, is a brown, grey and black forest species with red eyes and red legs. It is known only from the Bwamba Forest, western Uganda in East Africa. It produces a loud, far-carrying snore-like sound. Baillon's Crake *(Porzana pusilla)*, 7in, 18cm, has rufous-brown upperparts with white streaks on mantle and wing coverts and black and white barring on flanks; below grey. The nominate European race has been recorded from Somalia as a winter visitor; the African race is widespread in East and Central Africa but is rare or overlooked due to its skulking habits. It inhabits swamps, marshes and flooded grasslands. Two other European crakes are winter visitors in small numbers, the Little Crake *(Porzana parva)*, 7½in, 19cm, similar to Baillon's Crake but lacks white streaking on wing-coverts and flanks very lightly barred with white, and the Spotted Crake *(Porzana porzana)*, 9in, 23cm, which may be distinguished by its white spotted underparts. The Little Crake occurs in the Sudan, northern Uganda and Ethiopia; the Spotted Crake widespread in East and Central Africa but is most uncommon and generally overlooked.

WHITE-SPOTTED CRAKE *Sarothrura pulchra*   Plate 10

Identification. 5½in, 14cm. The Sarothrura group of crakes, or Flufftails as they are sometimes called, are difficult to observe and identify in the field. Some species frequent marshes and grasslands; others are forest dwellers. Their presence is usually indicated by their calls. The present species, which is typical of the group, has in the ♂ the head, neck, chest and tail rich chestnut; the rest of the plumage is black with white spots. The ♀ is barred black and buff above and below.
Voice. A bell-like note, repeated over and over again: 'goong-goong-goong.'
Distribution and Habitat. Occurs locally in the Sudan, Uganda, western

Kenya and south to north western Zambia. It is a bird of swampy forests where it would be overlooked were it not for its call. It is common in many of the Uganda forests but is not often seen.

Allied Species. The White-winged Crake *(Sarothrura ayresi)*, 5in, 13cm, differs in having a white secondaries patch, conspicuous when the bird flies. It occurs in marshes in the Ethiopian highlands. The Buff-spotted Crake *(Sarothrura elegans)*, 5½in, 14cm, differs from the White-spotted Crake in having the upperparts spotted buff not white; ♀ brown above with small spots of black and buff. This is a bird of grasslands and thickets, widespread but everywhere very uncommon in East and Central Africa. The Red-chested Crake *(Sarothrura rufa)*, 5½in, 14cm, has the head, neck, chest and upper mantle chestnut; rest of plumage black streaked and spotted with white. ♀ black above, brownish on head and neck, feathers spotted, barred and edged buff; below buff, barred brown on chest and flanks. Widespread but extremely local East and Central Africa, frequenting wet grasslands and marshes; call quail-like but more rapid. The Chestnut-headed Crake *(Sarothrura lugens)*, 5½in, 14cm, has head, nape and sides of face chestnut; rest upperparts black with white streaks; throat white, chest and belly streaked black and white. ♀ black above with brown head, streaked white on upper mantle, lower mantle and rump white spotted; below white with brown markings on chest and flanks. Occurs in grassy marshes in western Tanzania. Boehm's Crake *(Sarothrura bohmi)*, 5½in, 14cm, has head and neck chestnut merging to black with white streaks on rest upperparts; below, breast and flanks white with black streaks. ♀ sooty black with white flecks and barring; below white, barred dark brown. A bird of short grassy marshes and flooded grasslands found in Uganda, western Kenya and south to Malawi and Zambia; very uncommon and local. Chestnut-tailed Crake *(Sarothrura lineata)*, 5½in, 14cm, has the head, neck, back and tail chestnut; throat whitish; rest of plumage black with white streaks. ♀ mottled brown and black, including the head and tail. Occurs in marshes and wet moorland grassland at high altitudes. Found in the south-eastern Sudan, western Kenya and southwards to Malawi. Not uncommon in montane swamps on the Aberdare Mts, Kenya.

MOORHEN   *Gallinula chloropus*   Plate 10

Identification. 13in, 33cm. A thickset, blackish-slate bird of aquatic habits with a red frontal shield and a red bill with a yellow tip; white streaks along flanks and white feathers under tail; legs green. Jerks tail while walking or swimming. Immature paler and browner often with whitish on face and throat. The Lesser Moorhen is smaller and paler and has the bill mainly yellow.

Voice. Liquid croaking sounds and a harsh 'kr-aa-rk.'

Distribution and Habitat. Common through most of the Ethiopian Region, inhabiting swamps, marshes, lakes, rivers, ponds, streams and dams.

LESSER MOORHEN   *Gallinula angulata*   Plate 10

Identification. 10in, 25cm. Main distinctions from Moorhen are its mainly yellow bill and much smaller size. A more skulking species than the Moorhen, locally an intra-African migrant and at least partly nocturnal.

Voice. Various soft clucking sounds.

Distribution and Habitat. Occurs locally in East and Central Africa, frequenting overgrown pools near forest, dams with plenty of aquatic vegetation and flooded grasslands. Shy and skulking, most frequently encountered in the early morning and at dusk.

PURPLE GALLINULE   *Porphyrio porphyrio*   Plate 10

Identification. 18in, 46cm. Larger than a coot with long bright pink legs and a red head-shield and bill; back deep green merging to bright purple-blue on wings, head and underparts; face and throat washed bright blue; white feathers below tail. Immature dusky bluish-grey with horn-coloured legs. Climbs among reeds and papyrus beds in water; shy. In flight dangling red legs very conspicuous. The Red-knobbed Coot is slaty-black with white frontal shield and bill and grey legs. The Moorhen is much smaller with white flank streaks and green legs.

Voice. A hoarse grunting call and various clucking notes.

Distribution and Habitat. Resident and local migrant in many parts of East and Central Africa, but not a common bird. Frequents dense swamps and papyrus and reed beds, especially where there is an abundant growth of water-lilies, the buds of which it eats.

ALLEN'S GALLINULE   *Porphyrio alleni*   Plate 10

Identification. 10in, 25cm. Back and wings green, below purplish-blue, darker on the head; head-shield greenish-white; bill and legs dusky red. Immature browner with rufous-brown underparts.

Voice. A deep croak 'grrrrrr' and soft clucking sounds.

Distribution and Habitat. Local and uncommon in East and Central Africa, but shy and retiring and often overlooked. Inhabits swamps, flooded grasslands, and rank grass and other vegetation at the margins of marshes and lakes.

RED-KNOBBED COOT *Fulica cristata* **Plate 10**

Identification. 16in, 41cm. A large thickset waterbird, blackish-slate all over with a white frontal shield and bill. In breeding dress has two dark red knobs at the base of the frontal shield. Normally gregarious. Immature similar but with a whitish throat. The European Coot lacks the two red knobs at the base of the bill. Flight laboured and weak with legs dangling. Swims well and has characteristic habit of bobbing the head whilst swimming. Dives for most of its food.
Voice. A harsh, deep-sounding 'kwork' and various other grunting calls.
Distribution and Habitat. Resident and local migrant in East and Central Africa; common on Rift Valley lakes in East Africa. Frequents lakes and swamps and dams where there is an abundance of aquatic vegetation and reed and papyrus beds.
Allied Species. The European Coot *(F. atra)*, 15in, 38cm, is a winter visitor in small numbers to the Sudan and Ethiopia, south to northern Kenya. It lacks the red knobs at the base of the frontal shield and has an ill-defined whitish wingbar in flight.

FINFOOTS: Heliornithidae

The Finfoots are aquatic swimming birds with a superficial resemblance to grebes or small cormorants. They possess a long tail of stiff feathers and bright orange-red legs and feet. They frequent densely-wooded streams and rivers where there is an abundance of cover overhanging the water.

AFRICAN FINFOOT *Podica senegalensis* **Plate 10**

Identification. 18–21in, 46–53cm. A duck-sized aquatic bird with brown upperparts, a long stiff tail and orange-red legs; the bill is also reddish at base. ♂ larger than ♀ and has the neck slate-grey with an ill-defined whitish stripe down the sides. The ♀ and immature have the front of the neck whitish. Species swims low in the water: ♀ and young resemble immature Great Crested Grebe until orange legs and long tail are observed.
Voice. Usually silent, but sometimes utters a weak 'keeee.'
Distribution and Habitat. Local resident in suitable localities in East and Central Africa. Occurs mainly on perennial rivers and streams with thickly-wooded banks and vegetation overhanging the water. In Kenya also occurs in coastal creeks where there is a thick cover of mangroves.

BUSTARDS: Otididae

Large or very large terrestrial birds with three-toed feet and long necks; mainly buff with dark vermiculations. Frequent open plains, dry bush country and semi-desert. Gait a stately walk. Behaviour varies, sometimes very shy, running or crouching at the first sign of danger; at other times completely fearless of humans. Flight powerful with slow deliberate wing-beats.

KORI BUSTARD *Ardeotis kori*   Plate 10

Identification. 30–40in, 76–101cm. ♂ larger than ♀. Upperparts and neck vermiculated black and greyish-buff; the head crested. Feathers of neck very lax giving the effect of a thick-necked bird. Best identified by large size, lack of chestnut at back of neck and lax neck feathers. The Arabian Bustard has much finer vermiculations on the neck and the wing coverts are tipped white, not black and white. Jackson's Bustard is smaller and has the back of the neck bright reddish-chestnut.

Voice. Less vocal than many other bustards, but at times utters a far carrying 'kah, kah, kah.'

Distribution and Habitat. A local resident in the south-eastern Sudan, Ethiopia, Somalia, Uganda, Kenya and Tanzania. Occurs in open plains country, open dry bush and semi-desert areas. Most frequent in Kenya where widespread and common in the Northern Frontier Province. ♂ has a remarkable display; standing erect it inflates its neck like a balloon, then raises its tail so that it lies along its back.

Allied Species. The Arabian Bustard *(A. arabs)*, 29–35in, 74–90cm, has ♂ larger than ♀. Browner on upperparts than Kori Bustard, wing-coverts tipped white and neck vermiculations very fine. It occurs in the Sudan, Ethiopia, Somalia and rarely in northern Kenya and Uganda. Denham's or Jackson's Bustard *(Neotis denhami)*, 30in, 76cm, has the back of the neck bright rufous. It occurs in the Sudan and Ethiopia, south to Zambia; very local and uncommon; a species which is decreasing for unknown reasons. Heuglin's Bustard *(N. heuglinii)*, 30in, 76cm, has the crown, sides of face and chin black in the ♂. ♀ has the sides of the face mixed black and white. It occurs in semi-desert country in eastern Ethiopia, Somalia and northern Kenya. Common in Dida-Galgalla desert, Kenya.

BUFF-CRESTED BUSTARD *Eupodotis ruficrista*   Plate 10

Identification. 21in, 53cm. The Buff-crested Bustard is a relatively small species with black underparts in both ♂ and ♀ and a drooping pinkish-buff crest. The ♂ has a remarkable display flight, flying straight up into the air then stalling and descending to the ground like a pricked balloon with the wings held at an angle.

Voice. A long drawn-out whistle.

Distribution and Habitat. Occurs in dry bush country and open woodlands through East and Central Africa. It is locally common in the arid bush of the Northern Frontier Province, Kenya.

Allied Species. The Little Brown Bustard *(Heterotetrax humilis)*, 18in, 45cm, is the smallest African bustard, the size of a Yellow-necked Francolin with buff upperparts and a white belly. It is now a rare bird found locally in arid bush country in northern Somalia.

WHITE-BELLIED BUSTARD   *Eupodotis senegalensis*   Plate 10

Identification. 24in, 61cm. A white-breasted bustard with a very conspicuous blue-grey neck; ♂ with inverted black V-mark on throat. Upperparts finely vermiculated orange-buff and black. The ♀ Buff-crested Bustard has a white chest but is black on the belly and under tail coverts. ♀ ♀ of Black-bellied and Hartlaub's Bustards have whitish or pale buff underparts with black markings on the chest, but lack all trace of the blue-grey on the neck.

Voice. A very loud, far-carrying 'oo-warka, oo-warka.'

Distribution and Habitat. Local resident in the Sudan, Ethiopia, Somalia, eastern Uganda and Kenya, south through central and eastern Tanzania to Zambia where it is uncommon. Occurs on open plains, semi-desert bush and open woodland.

BLACK-BELLIED BUSTARD   *Eupodotis melanogaster*   Plate 10

Identification. 24in, 61cm. Underparts of ♂ black, of ♀ pale buff with black vermiculations on chest. ♂ rump and tail deep buff vermiculated and barred dark brown, appearing buffy-brown in flight. ♂ Hartlaub's Bustard differs in having the rump and tail black and the ♀ with heavy black chevrons on chest.

Voice. A single note 'mm-wark.'

Distribution and Habitat. A local resident in East and Central Africa, frequenting open plains, grasslands, light savannah woodlands and bush. Species has decreased in numbers in recent years. On the grassy plains of eastern Kenya it is now much less common than Hartlaub's Bustard; previously the Black-bellied was the commoner species.

Allied Species. Hartlaub's Bustard *(E. hartlaubii)*, 24in, 61cm, has a black rump and tail in the ♂, and heavy black chevrons on the chest in the ♀. It ranges from eastern Sudan, Ethiopia, northern Somalia, Uganda, Kenya south to central Tanzania. It occurs in open grasslands, mixed bush and grass and open woodland savannah, and in East Africa is most frequent in the eastern Kenya Highlands and the Mt Marsabit area of northern Kenya.

JACANAS or LILY-TROTTERS: Jacanidae

The Jacanas or Lily-trotters are curious long-legged water birds, somewhat resembling rails or plovers, with very long toes. Their enormous feet enable them to walk and feed on waterlily leaves and floating aquatic vegetation. Their nests are sodden platforms of water-weeds and their eggs are remarkable for their very high gloss.

AFRICAN JACANA   *Actophilornis africanus*   **Plate 12**

Identification. 9–11in, 23–28cm. A bright chestnut, plover-like bird with a large bluish-white head shield, nearly always seen walking about on floating aquatic vegetation. At close quarters the bluish-white bill and shield are conspicuous. The Lesser Jacana is much smaller than the African Jacana and has no head shield and little chestnut in plumage.
Voice. A series of chittering call-notes.
Distribution and Habitat. Widely distributed and often common in suitable localities over much of East and Central Africa. Occurs on open waters where there is an abundance of aquatic floating vegetation, especially water-lilies.

LESSER JACANA   *Microparra capensis*   **Plate 12**

Identification. 6in, 15cm. This is a sandpiper-sized water-bird, mainly grey and white with purplish-black patch on the back of the base of the neck and a little chestnut on the crown; white patch in wings conspicuous in flight. It has the same range as the African Jacana but is much rarer; small size, white wing patch and lack of frontal shield are best field characters.
Voice. A sharp 'kruup.'
Distribution and Habitat. Occurs widely in East and Central Africa, local and uncommon in East Africa but commoner in Zambia. More skulking than larger relative, inhabiting areas of grass in flooded pans, dams, swamps and marshes.

STONE CURLEWS or THICKNEES: Burhinidae

The Stone Curlews or Thicknees (also called Dikkops) are a group of medium-sized sandy or grey-coloured plover-like birds with large heads and very large yellow eyes; mainly nocturnal in habits and some species often seen on roads at night. Legs long and hind toe absent.

SPOTTED STONE CURLEW *Burhinus capensis* Plate 11

Identification. 17in, 43cm. Upperparts sandy-rufous with black mottling giving the impression of heavy spotting; below pale buff to white on belly with black streaks on throat and chest. The European Stone Curlew and the Senegal Stone Curlew are streaked above, not spotted. The greyer Water Dikkop is finely vermiculated black and grey above with dark streaks.
Voice. A far-carrying curlew-like whistle, usually uttered after dark.
Distribution and Habitat. A widespread but local resident in East and Central Africa. Frequents open bush and lightly wooded areas, dry rocky riverbeds and broken ground. During the day usually observed resting in the shade of acacia bushes, more active at dusk and at night. Frequents roads at night and many are killed by motor vehicles.
Allied Species. The European Stone Curlew *(B. oedicnemus)*, 16in, 41cm, is tawny or greyish-tawny above with heavy black streaking; two white wing bars. It is a winter visitor to East Africa, south to northern Kenya and Uganda. The Senegal Stone Curlew *(B. senegalensis)*, 15in, 38cm, is also streaked above but has only one white wing bar which can be seen only when the bird is in flight. This species is resident in northern Kenya and Uganda and northwards and frequents both dry bush and sand bars along rivers. The Water Dikkop *(B. vermiculatus)*, 14½in, 37cm, is greyer than the other species. It is found along rivers and the shores of lakes throughout Uganda, Kenya, Tanzania and Central Africa; very common on the Tana River, Kenya.

PLOVERS: Charadriidae

The Plovers are small or medium-sized birds of the wading-bird type although some species occur on dry plains. They are more thickset than the sandpipers and allies, with thicker-looking necks and relatively larger heads.

LONG-TOED LAPWING *Vanellus crassirostris* Plate 11

Identification. 12in, 31cm. A distinctive long-legged plover with the habits of a lily-trotter, generally observed on floating aquatic vegetation. Face, front half of crown, throat and upper breast white; remainder of breast and belly black; abdomen and under tail-coverts white; a great deal of white in the wings, conspicuous in flight. Bill carmine-red with black tip; legs deep maroon red.

Voice. A loud metallic 'tik – tik – tik – tik.'

Distribution and Habitat. A local resident from the southern Sudan, Uganda and Kenya, southwards to Malawi and Zambia. It frequents lakes and swamps where there is an abundance of floating vegetation, but in some localities, for example at Entebbe, Uganda and the Kafue Flats, Zambia, it may be seen on the shores of rivers and lakes. It is numerous and tame in the Amboseli National Park, Kenya.

BLACKSMITH PLOVER   *Vanellus armatus*   **Plate 11**

Identification. 11in, 28cm. A conspicuous species with contrasting black, white and grey plumage. The crown is white, there is a black patch on the mantle and the cheeks and underparts are black. Immature duller with buff edgings to feathers of upperparts.

Voice. A loud 'tik, tik, tik, tik' call, resembling two pieces of metal being knocked together.

Distribution and Habitat. Locally common from southern Kenya to Central Africa. Occurs on the shores of both fresh and alkaline lakes, swamps and rivers and also on cultivated land such as ploughed fields.

SPUR-WINGED PLOVER   *Vanellus spinosus*   **Plate 11**

Identification. 10½in, 27cm. A striking black, white and greyish-brown plover. Differs from the closely allied Blacksmith Plover in having the back entirely pale greyish-brown without a black patch and the crown black, not white. Wings and tail strongly patterned black and white. Like the Blacksmith Plover has a small spur on bend of wing but this is not normally visible in the field.

Voice. Usually silent unless disturbed on nesting ground, when they have a loud and shrill 'yak, yak, yak' call.

Distribution and Habitat. Resident in the Sudan, Ethiopia and Somalia, south to Uganda and Kenya. It frequents the vicinity of water and marshes, preferring areas of short grass. It occurs alongside the Blacksmith Plover in southern Kenya.

BLACKHEAD PLOVER   *Vanellus tectus*   **Plate 11**

Identification. 10in, 25cm. This is a rather small dry-country plover with pale greyish-brown upperparts, a black crown with an upturned crest and underparts white but cheeks, neck and a streak down middle of breast black; a

small red wattle in front of each eye. Bill red with black tip, legs maroon red.
Voice. A shrill, two or three note whistle, heard usually at dusk or at night.
Distribution and Habitat. Resident in arid thorn-bush country from the Sudan, Ethiopia and Somalia to Kenya. Species largely nocturnal and when encountered during the day is usually seen in pairs or small parties in the shade of acacia trees. Partial to grassy airstrips where these exist. In Kenya it is common north of Garissa and in the vicinity of Lake Baringo in the Rift Valley.

WHITE-HEADED PLOVER   *Vanellus albiceps*   Plate 11

Identification. 11in, 28cm. This species is remarkable for the long pendent yellow wattles in front of eyes; plumage brown and white with a white crown and black shoulders. Wings with long spurs. Immature similar but duller.
Voice. A very noisy plover, uttering a rapid 'tak, tak, tak, tak, tak, tak.'
Distribution and Habitat. Very local and uncommon south-western Sudan, northern Uganda and western Tanzania, more frequent Central Africa. This is a bird of sandbanks in the larger rivers such as the Zambesi, Sabi and Limpopo. In Tanzania it occurs along the margins of lakes and swamps but is uncommon.

SENEGAL PLOVER   *Vanellus lugubris*   Plate 11

Identification. 10in, 25cm. This is a long-legged rather small grasslands plover with greyish-brown upperparts and chest and a conspicuous white patch on the forehead. It resembles the larger highlands species, the Black-winged Plover, but may be distinguished by its relatively longer legs and on the wing by its white secondaries patch and its black and white under wing-coverts; the Black-winged Plover has white under wing-coverts.
Voice. A most melodious two to four note whistle.
Distribution and Habitat. Locally distributed in suitable areas in East and Central Africa. It is normally found in localities below 5,000ft, 1,530m, whilst its near relative the Black-winged Plover usually frequents areas over 6,000ft, 1,830m. The Senegal Plover is attracted by recently burned-over grasslands and to bush areas which are being cleared and burned for cultivation. In East Africa it is often common in cleared patches of bush along the Kenya coast and the open grasslands of the Mara Game Reserve. In Uganda it is common in the Ruwenzori National Park.

BLACK-WINGED PLOVER   *Vanellus melanopterus*   Plate 11

Identification. 11in, 28cm. Upperparts greyish-brown becoming grey on neck and head; forehead white; chin white, merging to grey on the throat and black on the upper breast; remainder underparts white, under wing-coverts white. From the smaller Senegal Plover it may be distinguished by its white under wing-coverts which are conspicuous in flight and when the bird raises its wings on alighting.

Voice. Usual call a loud 'cee-chee-chee-reek,' quite unlike the plaintive whistle of the Senegal Plover. Often very noisy when its breeding grounds are invaded.

Distribution and Habitat. This is a highlands species found usually above 7,000ft, 2,140m. It ranges from the eastern Sudan and Ethiopia to Kenya and northern Tanzania. It is an abundant species on the Kinangop Plateau in Kenya.

CROWNED PLOVER   *Vanellus coronatus*   Plate 11

Identification. 11in, 28cm. Upperparts uniform pale greyish-brown; top of head black with a white ring on crown; below, chin white merging to pale brown on breast, margined black; abdomen white; bill red with black tip, legs red.

Voice. A noisy scolding whistle, repeated frequently.

Distribution and Habitat. A locally common resident throughout East and Central Africa, also occurs in Angola and South Africa. It inhabits short grassy plains, open bush country, semi-desert areas, grassy airstrips and cultivation.

Allied Species. The Bronze-winged or Violet-tipped Courser *(Rhinoptilus chalcopterus)*, 11in, 28cm, has a superficial resemblance to a Crowned Plover. It may be identified by its more upright stance and the blackish-brown patch on the chin and below the eyes. It is nocturnal in its habits and if seen by day is usually resting in the shade of some bush or small tree. Any bird seen on the road at night which looks like a Crowned Plover is likely to be the Violet-tipped Courser.

WATTLED PLOVER   *Vanellus senegallus*   Plate 11

Identification. 13in, 33cm. A large long-legged plover with pale olive-brown plumage, a black chin and black streaked throat, a white forehead and a conspicuous red and yellow wattle in front of the eyes; bill greenish-yellow with black tip, legs yellow.

Voice. A shrill 'peek-peek.'

Distribution and Habitat. In East Africa the Wattled Plover is a local resident in the southern Sudan, Uganda and western Kenya and Tanzania south to the Zambezi River. It frequents open grassy areas generally adjacent to water.

BROWN-CHESTED WATTLED PLOVER
Vanellus superciliosus   **Plate 11**

Identification. 10in, 25cm. In general appearance not unlike a Senegal Plover. Front half of the crown tawny-rufous, the hinder half black; a small yellow wattle in front of the eye; upperparts, throat and chest grey with a chestnut band across the lower breast, more developed in the ♂ than the ♀.
Voice. Various shrill whistles.
Distribution and Habitat. A rare and little-known species which has been recorded on grassy plains, often in company with the Senegal Plover, in Uganda, western Kenya and northern Tanzania.

SPOT-BREASTED PLOVER   *Vanellus melanocephalus*   **Plate 11**

Identification. 12in, 30cm. Upperparts ashy-brown with a slight greenish wash; crown black with a short crest; below, throat and neck black and chest streaked black; remainder underparts white; tail white with black sub-terminal bar; legs yellow.
Voice. Reputed to have a call like that of the European Lapwing.
Distribution and Habitat. Confined to the highlands of northern and central Ethiopia. Frequents the margins of high altitude swamps and marshes and short grassy moorland where there is water. Local and uncommon.
Allied Species. The Grey Plover *(Pluvialis squatarola)*, 11–12in, 28–31cm, is a common winter visitor and passage migrant in East Africa, less frequent in Central Africa. In spring plumage black below and mottled silvery-white and black above. Winter and immature birds have upperparts more uniform greyish-brown and white below; black axillaries conspicuous in flight in all plumages. Its voice is distinctive, a drawn-out 'tlee-oo-ee.' Commonest on coastal mudflats, but also found on inland waters in smaller numbers. Birds in full breeding plumage may be seen on the Kenya coast between April and early May. The Lesser Golden Plover *(P. dominica)*, 10in, 25cm, is a very uncommon winter visitor to the Sudan, Ethiopia and Somalia. It occurs on short grassy areas and plains. In breeding dress the upperparts are mottled yellow and black; below mainly black. In winter the back is mottled yellow and blackish but underparts are greyish white; axillaries greyish-buff. Occurs in flocks.

KITTLITZ'S PLOVER   *Charadrius pecuarius*   **Plate 11**

Identification. 5½in, 14cm. Dusky grey-brown upperparts with blackish shoulders; white forehead band prolonged above the eyes round the back of the neck to form a white collar; black band behind white forehead and black streak through eye; below white, richly washed orange buff on chest and belly. Immature mottled above and whitish below.

Voice. A clear plaintive whistle.

Distribution and Habitat. Resident in suitable places through East and Central Africa. It occurs on sand or mud flats at the coast and also on inland waters. It is often found in small flocks on grassy flats along the margins of inland lakes and is usually tame and without fear of man.

Allied Species. The White-fronted Sand Plover *(C. marginatus)*, 5½in, 14cm, occurs as a breeding bird on sandy parts of the East African coast and sandbanks of the larger lakes and rivers in Central Africa. It is pale tawny above with a white forehead; below white with rufous wash on chest and upper breast. The Ringed Plover *(C. hiaticula)*, 7½in, 19cm, is a common winter visitor to East Africa, rarer in Central Africa. Its black and white forehead bands, broad black band through eye and black chest band are distinctive; white wing bar conspicuous in flight; bill orange with black tip; legs orange-yellow. Immatures have a dusky breast band, often not complete in front and less black on head. The similar Little Ringed Plover *(C. dubius)*, 6in, 15cm, has no white wing-bar and its legs are pinkish-flesh, not yellow or orange. It is a winter visitor to East Africa, mainly on inland waters. The Kentish Plover *(C. alexandrinus)*, 6½in, 16cm, is a resident on the coast of the Red Sea and Somalia, rare southwards. It is similar to a Ringed Plover but the black chest band is incomplete and the hind half of the crown is pale tawny.

THREE-BANDED PLOVER   *Charadrius tricollaris*   **Plate 11**

Identification. 7in, 18cm. In general appearance not unlike a slim Ringed Plover but with two black bands across the breast, not one. Upperparts dark olive-brown with a white forehead and a white stripe above and behind the eye; eyelids red; bill orange-red with a black tip; legs coral pink. Immature has back feathers edged buff and two black chest bands incomplete.

Voice. A plaintive 'wik, wik' usually uttered when flushed.

Distribution and Habitat. Widespread resident in East and Central Africa on lake shores, dams, streams, rivers and rain pools. Uncommon on the coast but does occur at times along edge of tidal pools and lagoons.

Allied Species. Forbes' Plover *(C. forbesi)* is a rare species recorded from western Uganda, western Tanzania and Zambia. It is a little larger than the Three-banded Plover, 8in, 20cm, and the forehead is olive-brown, not white.

CHESTNUT-BANDED SAND PLOVER
Charadrius venustus **Plate 11**

Identification. 6in, 15cm. Pale buffy-grey above with a white band across primaries which is conspicuous in flight; forehead white followed by narrow black and pale chestnut bands; below white with a narrow pale chestnut band across chest. ♀ lacks the black band on forehead; immature similar but with buff edges on feathers of back and wings.

Voice. A double 'tsk, tsk,' softer than Three-banded Plover's call.

Distribution and Habitat. A very local species known from Lake Magadi in southern Kenya and Lakes Manyara and Natron and smaller alkaline lakes in northern Tanzania. In East Africa confined to brackish or alkaline lakes.

Allied Species. The Mongolian Sand Plover *(C. mongolus)*, 8in, 20cm, and the Great Sand Plover *(C. leschenaultii)*, 10in, 25cm, are both abundant winter visitors to the East African coast but are uncommon inland; very few records of either species in Central Africa. In winter both are pale greyish plovers with white underparts and a greyish patch on each side of the chest; best recognised on bill characters, the Mongolian Plover having a short stubby bill, the Great Sand Plover a much larger bill. In spring plumage the Mongolian Plover has a broad pale chestnut chest band, the Great Sand Plover a relatively narrow band. The Caspian Plover *(C. asiaticus)*, 8in, 20cm, has a broad chestnut band across the chest, edged by black, in the ♂; in the ♀ chest band mottled grey. Somewhat similar to Mongolian Plover but inhabits open grassy plains, not tidal flats. A winter visitor to East and Central Africa; normally in flocks.

AVOCET *Recurvirostra avosetta* **Plate 11**

Identification. 17in, 43cm. Contrasting black and white plumage, thin black upturned bill and blue-grey legs enable this species to be identified with ease. Immature with brownish dark markings not black. During flight legs extend beyond tail. Wades in shallow water and feeds gracefully with a side to side scything motion of its bill; sometimes swims, especially when a hatch of aquatic insects is in progress. In East Africa sometimes seen in very large flocks, hundreds and occasionally even thousands strong.

Voice. A loud 'kleep' or 'kloop,' uttered whilst on the wing.

Distribution and Habitat. Winter visitor and also resident, breeding in small numbers in East and Central Africa. Avocets frequent both fresh and alkaline lakes, exposed mud-flats, estuaries and sand banks. In East Africa sometimes abundant in winter on lakes Naivasha, Elmenteita and Nakuru and a regular breeder at Lake Magadi.

Allied Species. The European Oyster-Catcher *(Haemantopus ostralegus)*, 17in, 43cm, is an uncommon winter visitor to the coast of Kenya and

Tanzania. Its black and white plumage, orange bill and pink legs make it unmistakable.

BLACK-WINGED STILT   *Himantopus himantopus*   Plate 11

Identification. 15in, 38cm. Unmistakable: in flight very long pink legs trail 5–6in, 12–15cm, beyond tail. Plumage black and white, or in the case of immature and sub-adult birds, black, white and grey. Black undersides of sharply pointed wings conspicuous in flight.
Voice. A shrill, yelping 'kyip, kyip, kyip.'
Distribution and Habitat. Uncommon local resident and abundant winter visitor in East Africa; less common in Central Africa. Frequents fresh and brackish inland waters; uncommon on coast. In Kenya numerous on lakes Naivasha, Magadi, Nakuru and Elmenteita.

CRAB PLOVER   *Dromas ardeola*   Plate 11

Identification. 14in, 35cm. A thickset black and white wader with a large head, heavy bill and blue-grey legs. Immature grey above, not black. At a distance when flying the general black and white plumage and trailing blue legs can give the impression that the bird is an avocet, but at closer quarters the two cannot be confused.
Voice. A musical yelping call uttered on the wing, somewhat similar to that of an oyster-catcher.
Distribution and Habitat. Breeds on islands in the Red Sea off Somalia. A non-breeding visitor to the Kenya and Tanzania coasts. Frequents sand and mud flats. It is usually present in numbers at Mida Creek on the Kenya coast.

PAINTED SNIPE: Rostratulidae

This very distinctive bird combines the field appearance of a snipe and a rail. When flushed from thick sedges at the edge of water its slow flight, rounded buff-spotted wings and dangling legs give a very rail-like impression. It is further remarkable in that the ♀ is more brightly coloured than the ♂ and it is the ♀ who initiates courtship and the ♂ who incubates and hatches the young.

PAINTED SNIPE   *Rostratula benghalensis*   Plate 12

Identification. 10–11in, 25–28cm. When flushed dangling legs and rounded wings (with large round buff spots) present an appearance nearer rails than snipe. ♀ larger and more brightly coloured with chestnut on back of neck and throat; white ring around eye, extending as a streak behind eye, conspicuous when bird observed on the ground. Bill slightly down-curved and reddish-brown in colour. ♂ much paler and greyer.

Voice. Normally silent birds even when flushed, but reputed to utter a guttural croak and a short trill.

Distribution and Habitat. Found locally in East and Central Africa but nowhere really common. Frequents swamps, and sedge-lined margins of lakes and marshes; also areas where there are mudflats overgrown with marsh grass. Often overlooked unless flushed.

SNIPE, SANDPIPERS and ALLIES: Scolopacidae

A group of numerous small to medium-sized wading birds with long legs, slender bills and pointed and angular wings. In many species the summer (breeding) and winter plumages differ greatly. Most of the members of this Family occurring in East and Central Africa are non-breeding visitors only, their chief breeding grounds being in Arctic or sub-Arctic regions. Many species highly gregarious in winter quarters in Africa.

AFRICAN SNIPE   *Gallinago nigripennis*   **Plate 12**

Identification. 11in, 28cm. Difficult to distinguish from the European Common Snipe in the field, but upperparts are darker and tail feathers are much narrower, mainly white without chestnut patches; it also has a slower more direct flight than the European bird. The Great Snipe is a heavier looking bird with a relatively short bill and conspicuous white spots on the wing-coverts. In the hand the African Snipe may be recognised by its white belly and tail of 16 feathers, the outer ones being narrow and mainly white.

Voice. Usually a silent bird, sometimes uttering a rasping 'tssp' when flushed. In the breeding season it utters a constantly repeated 'chok, chok, chok, chok.' In diving flight during courtship display produces a vibrating drumming sound.

Distribution and Habitat. Resident, local and largely confined to higher altitudes from Ethiopia southwards through Kenya and Uganda to South Africa. Occurs in swamps, marshy alpine moorlands, edges of lakes and flooded areas.

Allied Species. The European Common Snipe *(G. gallinago)*, 10½in, 27cm, is a winter visitor in varying numbers to East Africa; rare in Central Africa. Like the African Snipe it has a white belly; tail feathers broad, 14–16, marked with rufous and grey patches. The Great Snipe *(G. media)*, 11in, 28cm, is a winter visitor and passage migrant to East Africa, more frequent in Central Africa. It is larger in body but has a shorter bill than the African and Common Snipe; its underparts are more or less barred, not pure white. The Jack Snipe *(Lymnocrytes minima)*, 7½in, 19cm, occurs spasmodically in East Africa, usually in small numbers. It is small and may be recognised by the absence of a buff central stripe on the crown. Usually solitary and flushes silently; flight slow, normally of short duration. Other Palearctic waders which are winter visitors to East Africa include the following well-known species: Curlew Sandpiper *(Calidris ferruginea)*, Little Stint *(C. minuta)*, Temminck's Stint *(C. temminckii)*, Dunlin *(C. alpina)* rare, Knot *(C. canutus)* rare, Sanderling *(C. alba)*, Broad-billed Sandpiper *(Limicola falcinellus)*, Ruff *(Philomachus pugnax)*, Black-tailed Godwit *(Limosa limosa)*, Bar-tailed Godwit *(L. lapponica)*, Turnstone *(Arenaria interpres)*, Terek Sandpiper *(Tringa cinereus)*, Common Sandpiper *(T. hypoleucos)*, Greenshank *(T. nebularia)*, Redshank *(T. totanus)*, Spotted Redshank *(T. erythropus)*, Marsh Sandpiper *(T. stagnatilis)*, Green Sandpiper *(T. ochropus)*, Wood Sandpiper *(T. glareola)*, Whimbrel *(Numenius phaeopus)* and Curlew *(N. arquata)*.

COURSERS and PRATINCOLES: Glareolidae

The Coursers and Pratincoles are small or medium-sized birds allied to the Plovers with relatively short arched bills. In the Coursers the hind toe is absent and the birds resemble small, long-legged plovers. Pratincoles have short legs and possess a hind toe; their field appearance is somewhat tern-like and like terns they are found near water, while coursers inhabit arid areas and grassland.

TEMMINCK'S COURSER   *Cursorius temminckii*   Plate 12

Identification. 8in, 20cm. A small rufous-buff plover-like bird with a black patch on the abdomen. Immature with buff ends to feathers of upperparts giving a speckled appearance. Often found on grasslands which have been burned recently. The Cream-coloured Courser is larger and paler and has whitish underparts without a black patch. The Two-banded Courser has two black bands across the breast. Heuglin's Courser has a chestnut V at the base of the throat, followed by a chestnut breast band. The much larger Violet-tipped (Bronze-winged) Courser resmbles a Crowned Plover but may be distinguished by the blackish-brown patches on the throat and below the eyes.

Voice. A metallic piping call usually uttered as the bird takes wing; otherwise silent.

Distribution and Habitat. Locally common in East and Central Africa but subject to local movements. It frequents short grass areas such as open plains and aerodromes, and is attracted to such places after a grass fire.

Allied Species. The Cream-coloured Courser *(C. cursor)*, 9in, 23cm, is a resident in Ethiopia, Somalia and south to central Kenya. It occurs in arid, semi-desert country. The Violet-tipped Courser *(Rhinoptilus chalcopterus)*, 12in, 30cm, is similar in general appearance to a Crowned Plover but has a more upright stance and the blackish patches on the throat and below the eyes distinguish it. It is mainly nocturnal and is often seen on roads at night. It is a very local resident in East and Central Africa, often spasmodic in its appearances. It is most frequent in Zambia where it is not uncommon on roads passing through Brachystegia and mopane woodland.

TWO-BANDED COURSER *Hemerodromus africanus* Plate 12

Identification. 8in, 20cm. Mottled black and buff above, pale buff below with two conspicuous black bands across the chest. Immature similar but paler and greyer.

Voice. A weak piping call.

Distribution and Habitat. An uncommon and local species found in eastern Ethiopia, Somalia, Kenya and the northern half of Tanzania. Frequents semi-desert plains and open bush.

HEUGLIN'S COURSER *Hemerodromus cinctus* Plate 12

Identification. 10in, 25cm. Upperparts brown with heavy sandy-buff streaking; white stripe over eye and upper tail coverts white; underparts buffy-white with a chestnut V on lower neck, blackish streaks below the V and a chestnut band across breast. Immature similar. Mainly nocturnal.

Voice. A piping 'wik o wik, wik o wik, wik o wik,' not unlike some nightjar's call.

Distribution and Habitat. Occurs locally from southern Sudan, Ethiopia and Somalia south to central Tanzania and Zambia. Inhabits semi-desert bush country and in the south mopane woodland.

EGYPTIAN PLOVER *Pluvianus aegyptius* Plate 12

Identification. 8in, 20cm. A short-legged plover-like bird with crown, back and band on chest black; white stripe above eye to nape; chest and belly creamy buff; wings grey. This strikingly patterned bird is the well-known 'crocodile bird' of the writings of Herodotus, but present day observations of it entering a crocodile's mouth to pick food from between the reptile's teeth are lacking.

Voice. A weak, sand plover type of call 'teep, teep, teep.'

Distribution and Habitat. Occurs very locally in the southern Sudan, Ethiopia and northern Uganda. Found on sandbars in rivers and lakes. As a rule found in pairs or family parties; often tame and fearless of man.

PRATINCOLE   *Glareola pratincola*   **Plate 12**

Identification. 10in, 25cm. A tern-like brown bird with a long forked tail, white rump and sealing-wax red base to the bill; legs black and short; throat warm buff with narrow black border. Immature duller and has breast band of narrow dusky streaks. Flight erratic and tern-like; chestnut under wings conspicuous in flight. The Madagascar Pratincole lacks the black collar around throat and has much shorter outer tail feathers. The White-collared Pratincole is a smaller bird with a white collar round back of neck. Gregarious and may often be seen hawking insects like huge swallows over or near water.

Voice. Noisy in flight, birds in flocks keeping up a harsh, rather tern-like 'keeyak' or a rapid chattering call.

Distribution and Habitat. Locally common in East and Central Africa. Frequents lakes and other inland waters but uncommon on coast. Much subject to local movements and in Sudan and Ethiopia, and perhaps further south, numbers augmented during winter months by visitors from Europe. Nearly always in flocks.

Allied Species. The Black-winged Pratincole *(G. nordmanni)* differs only in having under wing-coverts and axillaries black not chestnut. Recorded only in Sudan and Ethiopia, rare. The much shorter-tailed Madagascar Pratincole *(G. ocularis)*, 9½in, 24cm, occurs as a non-breeding visitor to coastal districts of East Africa, mainly along the Kenya coast between Mombasa and Lamu where in some years it may be observed in large flocks. Distinguished from the Pratincole by its lack of the thin black collar round throat. The White-collared Pratincole *(Galachrysia nuchalis)*, 8in, 20cm, also lacks the black throat collar, but has a white collar round back of neck. It is a very local little bird associated with rocks on lakes and rivers in East and Central Africa. It may be seen on rocks off Entebbe, Uganda, and on the Zambezi in Central Africa.

GULLS and TERNS: Laridae

The Gulls and Terns are medium-sized or larger swimming birds. Gulls are more robust and wider-winged than the Terns with slightly hooked bills; tails usually square or rounded; gregarious. Terns are more slender and graceful than gulls and usually have forked tails; also gregarious.

GREY-HEADED GULL *Larus cirrocephalus*   Plate 12

Identification. 16in, 40cm. This is a medium-sized white and pale grey gull with a conspicuous grey head; red bill and legs; primaries black with white tips. Immature mottled pale brownish-grey above and on head. Winter plumaged Black-headed Gulls have the primaries mainly black with a longitudinal white streak.
Voice. Normally silent except at nesting colonies when utter series of loud cackling calls.
Distribution and Habitat. Locally common on inland waters in East and Central Africa. This is mainly an inhabitant of inland lakes but in East Africa it sometimes occurs on the coast in the non-breeding season.
Allied Species. The European Lesser Black-backed Gull *(L. fuscus)*, 22in, 56cm, is an uncommon winter visitor to East and Central Africa, most frequent on inland waters. The adult has blackish-grey upperparts and yellow legs; the immature is mottled brown and has pale brown legs. The Black-headed Gull *(L. ridibundus)*, 15in, 38cm, occurs in winter in East Africa where it is most frequent on the coast. In non-breeding plumage it may be recognised by its black primaries and white forewing, black only at the tip. In summer plumage with a chocolate-brown head. Other Palearctic gulls which occur in winter in northern East Africa are Herring Gull *(L. argentatus)*, Slender-billed Gull *(L. genei)*, Great Black-headed Gull *(L. ichthyaetus)*, Little Gull *(L. minutus)*.

SOOTY GULL *Larus hemprichii*   Plate 12

Identification. 17–18in, 43–46cm. This is the common gull along the East African coast. Above dark greyish-brown on mantle, head and throat; hind neck with a white collar; below brownish on chest and flanks, rest white; bill green with black and red tip; legs dusky olive. The much rarer White-eyed Gull is smaller with a blackish head, a white eye-ring and a red, black-tipped bill.
Voice. A ringing mewing call but birds usually silent.
Distribution and Habitat. Resident and visitor to the coast of the Red Sea and

East Africa. A common species in harbours along the East African coast and at Aden. Nests on offshore islands. The birds often compete with kites for garbage thrown overboard from ships in port.

WHITE-EYED GULL   *Larus leucophthalmus*   Plate 12

Identification. 16in, 41cm. Similar to the Sooty Gull but with blackish head, white ring around eye, and red bill with a black tip; legs yellow; white on hind neck and chest. Immature may be distinguished from immature Sooty Gull by dusky red bill.

Voice. Various mewing calls, similar to those of Sooty Gull.

Distribution and Habitat. Resident on the coasts of the Red Sea and northern Somalia, nesting on islands off the Somalia coast; a rare visitor further south.

WHISKERED TERN   *Chlidonias hybrida*   Plate 12

Identification. 10in, 25cm. In breeding plumage rather dark grey with a black cap; a conspicuous white cheek stripe; under wing-coverts white; bill and feet red. Winter plumages and immature similar to White-winged Black Tern but slightly larger and heavier looking with more extensive dark markings behind eye and on nape.

Voice. Various rasping notes but usually silent except at nesting colony.

Distribution and Habitat. This is a local resident on inland waters in East and Central Africa, its numbers augmented by winter visitors from the north. Occurs on both fresh and alkaline lakes; in Kenya common on Lakes Naivasha and Nakuru in the Rift Valley.

WHITE-WINGED BLACK TERN   *Chlidonias leucoptera*   Plate 12

Identification. 9½in, 24cm. Distinctive in summer plumage with contrasting black body plumage and mainly white wings and tail. Whiskered Tern has grey body plumage, a black cap and white streak on cheeks and sides of neck. In non-breeding dress similar to Whiskered Tern but has less black on nape and behind eye.

Voice. Silent birds, but sometimes utter a 'kerrr' flock call.

Distribution and Habitat. Common winter visitor and passage migrant in East and Central Africa and an uncommon and very local resident in Kenya and Tanzania, and perhaps elsewhere. Occurs on both fresh and alkaline lakes and rare on the coast except on migration. Often in loose flocks; flies backwards and forwards over the water, dipping frequently to pick off insects on the surface.

Allied Species. The Black Tern *(C. niger)*, 9½in, 24cm, occurs as a winter visitor to the Sudan but is rare further south. It is greyish-black with white under wing-coverts in summer, and in winter dress may be distinguished by black patch on each side of the breast. The Little Tern *(Sterna albifrons)*, 9in, 23cm, is a winter visitor and passage migrant in East Africa on both inland and coastal waters. It is pale grey above with a black cap and white forehead; bill yellow with black tip, feet yellow. The Gull-billed Tern *(Gelochelidon nilotica)*, 15in, 38cm, is thickset with pale grey upperparts and a stout black bill. Crown black in summer plumage, white with indistinct grey streaks in winter. Common winter visitor and passage migrant to East Africa. It is possible the species nests in East Africa, perhaps in the Lake Rudolf (Turkana) region where it is common and in full plumage in summer. The Caspian Tern *(Hydroprogne tschegrave)*, 21in, 53cm, occurs along the East African coast and also on inland waters; rare in Zambia. It occurs in breeding dress throughout the summer on Lake Rudolf (Turkana), Kenya, but nesting has not been confirmed. This very large tern has a heavy bright orange-red bill; cap black in summer, heavily streaked black in winter. The Lesser Crested Tern *(Sterna bengalensis)*, 14in, 36cm, and the slightly larger Swift Tern *(S. bergii)*, 19in, 48cm, both occur on the East African coast. The former has an orange-yellow bill, the latter a lemon-yellow bill. Both often associate at rest with Sooty Gulls. The White-cheeked Tern *(S. repressa)*, 13in, 33cm, is a marine species which nests on islands off the East African coast. It is medium grey, including the underparts, with a black cap and a broad white streak below the eye to the nape; bill black to dusky red towards base; tail strongly forked and outer tail feathers long and slender. The Roseate Tern *(S. dougallii)*, 15in, 38cm, which also nests on offshore islands in East Africa has rosy-white underparts, whiter appearance and long white tail streamers. The European Common Tern *(S. hirundo)*, 14in, 35cm, is a spasmodic visitor along the East African coast. It is paler grey than the White-cheeked Tern and white below. Other marine terns which sometimes turn up along the East African coast are the Noddy *(Anous stolidus)*, 16in, 40cm, which is sooty-brown above and below with a grey cap, the Sooty Tern *(Sterna fuscata)*, 16in, 40cm, blackish-brown above with a white forehead and underparts and the Bridled Tern *(S. anaethetus)*, 14in, 35cm, a similar species which may be distinguished by its white collar across the hind neck.

AFRICAN SKIMMER   *Rhynchops flavirostris*   **Plate 12**

Identification. 14in, 35cm. The African Skimmer is a tern-like bird with dark brown upperparts and white below; wings very long; bill of remarkable structure, red with a yellow tip; it is compressed to a thin vertical blade and the lower mandible projects forwards nearly 1in, 2.5cm, in front of the upper mandible. When feeding the skimmer flies over the water surface ploughing the water with the projecting lower mandible. This characteristic ploughing of the water and the bill shape are good field characters. The species is usually gregarious.

Voice. A loud harsh tern-like call 'kreeep.'

Distribution and Habitat. Local resident and partial migrant in East and Central Africa, south to the Zambezi River. In Kenya common on Lake Rudolf (Turkana) where colonies nest on Central Island and at Ferguson's Gulf.

SANDGROUSE: Pteroclididae

Sandgrouse are a family of thickset, pigeon-like terrestrial birds: wings long and pointed, flight rapid. Legs short, feathered to base of toes. Most species are gregarious and inhabit arid regions; they come to drink at water in early morning or late evening, according to species.

CHESTNUT-BELLIED SANDGROUSE
Pterocles exustus   **Plate 13**

Identification. 12in, 30cm. Sexes unlike; ♂ with upperparts sandy-brown; narrow black band across chest; ♀ streaked and barred buff and brown. Both ♂ and ♀ have long narrow, needle pointed central tail feathers. White tips to inner flight feathers form a conspicuous white bar when bird is in flight. Species gregarious and flights to water in early morning.

Voice. A guttural clucking which sounds rather like 'guttar, guttar, guttar, guttar, guttar, guttar.'

Distribution and Habitat. Resident in the Sudan, Ethiopia and Somalia south to northern Tanzania. This is the commonest sandgrouse in most parts of Kenya and northern Tanzania. It inhabits semi-desert bush country, arid plains and open thornbush.

Allied Species. The Spotted Sandgrouse *(Pterocles senegallus)*, occurs in the Sudan, Ethiopia and northern Somalia. It also possesses long central tail feathers. Both sexes may be distinguished from the Chestnut-bellied Sandgrouse in having bright orange-buff throats and in the ♂ the lack of a black chest band.

BLACK-FACED SANDGROUSE   *Pterocles decoratus*   **Plate 13**

Identification. 11in, 28cm. Central tail feathers not elongated; black pattern on face and throat (♂) and broad white band across chest are good field characters. This is a rather small, stumpy-looking sandgrouse; less gregarious than other species, but does form flocks when flighting to water in the early morning and often associated with Chestnut-bellied Sandgrouse.

Voice. A series of chuckling whistles of three notes 'chucker, chucker, chucker.' Also utters a series of short notes.

Distribution and Habitat. Resident through Somalia and eastern Ethiopia through Kenya to central Tanzania. Inhabits dry thorn-bush areas and semi-desert scrub. Locally common in the Tsavo National Park, Kenya.

Allied Species. Lichtenstein's Sandgrouse *(P. lichtensteinii)*, 11in, 28cm, is found in semi-desert in the Sudan, Ethiopia, Somalia, northern Uganda and north-western Kenya. It is similar to the Black-faced Sandgrouse but may be distinguished by its black-spotted neck and in the ♂ the lack of a black throat patch. The Four-banded Sandgrouse *(P. quadricinctus)*, 11in, 28cm, has a deep buff unspotted neck and buff, chestnut, white and black bands across the chest in the ♂, a white throat and orange buff neck and chest in the ♀. It occurs in the Sudan, southern Ethiopia, northern Uganda and north-western Kenya. Both it and Lichtenstein's Sandgrouse flight to water at dusk, even arriving after dark. The Double-banded Sandgrouse *(P. bicinctus)*, 10in, 25cm, has two distinct narrow bands, white and black, across the chest in the ♂, and both sexes have black and white barred bellies. It occurs in dry woodlands in Zambia and Malawi.

YELLOW-THROATED SANDGROUSE
Pterocles gutturalis   **Plate 13**

Identification. 13in, 33cm. Tail feathers not elongated. This is the largest of the East African sandgrouse. Both sexes may be recognised by their conspicuous yellowish-buff throats and large size.

Voice. Guttural calls 'guttar, guttar, guttar,' not unlike calls of Chestnut-bellied Sandgrouse but louder and harsher.

Distribution and Habitat. Local resident and partial intra-African migrant in Ethiopia southwards to Central Africa. This species frequents open grassy plains, such as the Athi Plains in Kenya and the Serengeti Plains in northern Tanzania, but sometimes seen in open acacia country. Flights to drink in early mornings, often in large flocks. Often spasmodic in its appearances in many localities in East Africa; in some years abundant, in others absent.

DOVES and PIGEONS: Columbidae

Medium-sized, plump birds with small rounded heads and the base of the bill swollen; flight rapid. Many species have characteristic deep cooing calls. The terms 'dove' and 'pigeon' are used loosely to indicate size, the smaller species being called doves, the larger pigeons.

SPECKLED PIGEON *Columba guinea* **Plate 13**

Identification. 16in, 41cm. Easily recognised by its vinous chestnut back, unspotted grey underparts, white-spotted wing-coverts and, in flight, its conspicuous pale grey rump. The Olive Pigeon has the underparts purplish-grey with white spots and the bill and legs are yellow; the Speckled Pigeon has a black bill and red legs.
Voice. A series of deep guttural double coos.
Distribution and Habitat. Widespread resident in East Africa. Inhabits open country, acacia woodland, cultivated areas and rocky hillsides and cliffs. In several places breeds in human habitations like a domestic pigeon.
Allied Species. The Somaliland Pigeon *(Columba olivae)*, 15in, 38cm, is lavender-grey with crown and nape pinkish-brown; hind neck iridescent brown. It is a very uncommon cliff-dwelling species restricted to northern Somalia.

OLIVE PIGEON *Columba arquatrix* **Plate 13**

Identification. 15in, 38cm. A large, very dark-looking pigeon with white-spotted underparts and bright yellow bill and legs. The similar but much rarer White-naped Pigeon has the back of the head white, not grey, and the bill and feet red, not yellow.
Voice. A deep rolling series of notes ending in a cooo.
Distribution and Habitat. A common species in many parts of East and Central Africa. Unlike the Speckled Pigeon it is a forest species in both highland and lower altitude forest: it also occurs in acacia woodlands and is attracted to wheat fields.

WHITE-NAPED PIGEON *Columba albinucha* **Plate 13**

Identification. 14in, 36cm. Similar in general appearance to the Olive Pigeon but easily distinguished by its conspicuous white nape patch and pinkish-red bill and feet.
Voice. A deep, quavering double coo, followed by other cooing notes.
Distribution and Habitat. An extremely rare pigeon with a restricted distribution in Zaire and adjacent areas in western Uganda. It is most frequent in the Bwamba Forest on the western side of the Ruwenzori mountains. It can usually be seen at the Mongiro hot springs which it visits to drink.
Allied Species. The White-collared Pigeon *(C. albitorques)*, 14in, 36cm, is uniform blackish slate with a white collar across the back of the nape and neck from ear to ear. This is a little-known bird inhabiting remote cliffs and gorges in northern and central Ethiopia.

AFEP PIGEON *Columba unicincta* **Plate 13**

Identification. 14in, 36cm. An all-grey pigeon with pale grey edgings to feathers of the mantle imparting a scaly appearance; below grey, washed pink in the ♂, under tail-coverts white; tail with a whitish band.
Voice. A soft, long drawn out cooo.
Distribution and Habitat. A forest pigeon known from the southern Sudan, western and central Uganda, western Kenya, western Tanzania and Zambia. A rather shy bird which would often be overlooked were it not for its distinctive call. It may be seen in fruiting fig trees.

BRONZE-NAPED PIGEON *Columba delegorguei* **Plate 13**

Identification. 13in, 33cm. A dark grey forest pigeon; ♂ has a broad white patch on the base of the hindneck; ♀ without this white patch but with a pale rufous head and greenish-rufous on the hindneck. It is a shy and elusive species, often overlooked.
Voice. A distinctive 'coo-co-coo, coo, coo, coo, coo.'
Distribution and Habitat. Ranges from the southern Sudan south through Uganda and Kenya to Tanzania and Malawi. Inhabits mountain forests; uncommon and local. In East Africa it is perhaps most frequent in the forests of Mt Kenya. Its flight is swift and direct.

DUSKY TURTLE DOVE *Streptopelia lugens* **Plate 13**

Identification. 11in, 28cm. Also called Pink-breasted Dove. A medium-sized dark grey dove with a chestnut patch on the side of each wing and a black patch on each side of the neck.
Voice. A deep four-note 'coo, coo, coo, coo.'
Distribution and Habitat. This is a high altitude species, found in or near forested areas. It occurs in the Sudan and Ethiopia southwards through Uganda and Kenya to Malawi and Zambia. In East Africa it is a common species on the South Kinangop, the Aberdare Mts and around Nairobi, Kenya.

RED-EYED DOVE *Streptopelia semitorquata* **Plate 13**

Identification. 12in, 30cm. This is the largest of the brownish-grey doves with a black collar on the hindneck. It may be recognised by its size, conspicuous pale grey forehead and deep vinous-pink underparts. In the smaller Mourning Dove and Ring-necked Dove the underparts are much paler and greyer. The Dusky Turtle Dove may be distinguished by its chestnut wing patches and black neck patches – not a black collar.

Voice. Its call notes are characteristic, a deep 'coo coo, co co, co co.'

Distribution and Habitat. A common resident in East and Central Africa where it occurs in wooded and forested areas and gardens often in the vicinity of water. In Kenya it is a well-known garden bird; it is a common dove in Nairobi.

MOURNING DOVE *Streptopelia decipiens* Plate 13

Identification. 11in, 28cm. A rather pale grey dove with a pink flush over the underparts; basal half of the outer tail feathers black; black collar on hind neck; bare skin around eyes carmine; iris pinkish-white. The similar but smaller, greyer Ring-necked Dove has a very dark brown eye and has a quite different call.

Voice. A deep growling 'garoow' followed sometimes by shorter notes.

Distribution and Habitat. Occurs locally in acacia woodland in East and Central Africa, especially stands of acacias along rivers. Its pale eye and distinctive call are good field characters.

RING-NECKED DOVE *Streptopelia capicola* Plate 13

Identification. 10in, 25cm. A grey dove with a black collar on the hindneck, the grey below merging to white on the belly; eye very dark brown. This is a paler and smaller bird than the Red-eyed Dove from which it may also be distinguished by its white belly. The closely related Mourning Dove is paler and pinker, has a whitish eye and quite a different call.

Voice. A distinctive 'Cooo, coco, cooo, coco.'

Distribution and Habitat. A common resident over much of East and Central Africa in a variety of habitats. It frequents acacia woodland, semi-desert bush, thornbush country, various types of savannah woodland, cultivation and gardens. In Kenya it is especially abundant in the Northern Frontier Province, where it congregates in very large flocks at water-holes during the dry weather.

Allied Species. The White-winged Dove *(S. reichenowi)*, 10in, 25cm, is an extremely local bird confined to acacia woodland near water on the border of north-eastern Kenya and southern Somalia. It resembles the Ring-necked Dove except for large white wing patches. The Vinaceous Dove *(S. vinacea)*, 10in, 25cm, may be distinguished from other ring-necked doves by its pink forehead; undersides of wings slate-grey. It occurs in the Sudan and Ethiopia and in northern and western Uganda; inhabits savannah woodland and bush and cultivation where there are trees.

LAUGHING DOVE   *Streptopelia senegalensis*   **Plate 13**

Identification. 9½in, 24cm. A small dove with rusty upperparts, much blue-grey in the wings but no black collar on hindneck. Bases of feathers on foreneck black giving a mottled appearance; chest pink merging to white on abdomen; much white on tail; eyes dark brown.
Voice. A five note call 'oh-cook, cook -oou, oou,' distinctive when heard.
Distribution and Habitat. Occurs throughout most of the Ethiopian Region and often common. In Central Africa less abundant than in East Africa, but often common where it does occur. Inhabits thornbush and acacia wood-land, cultivation and gardens, generally below 7,000ft, 2,140m.

LEMON DOVE   *Aplopelia larvata*   **Plate 13**

Identification. 10in, 25cm. A thickset dark-backed dove with vinous-rufous underparts; forehead, sides of face and throat whitish. The immature has rusty edgings to the feathers of upperparts.
Voice. A silent bird which sometimes utters a low 'cooo.'
Distribution and Habitat. Widely distributed in forests from southern Sudan southwards to the Zambesi River. A shy and secretive bird which is often overlooked. Feeds largely on the ground. Most likely to be seen towards evening when it has the habit of walking along paths and tracks through forest.

NAMAQUA DOVE   *Oena capensis*   **Plate 13**

Identification. 8½in, 21cm. A very small dove with a long tail; sexes unalike. ♂ with black face, throat and chest; upperparts greyish-brown, greyer on the crown; belly white. ♀ lacks black on face, throat and chest. In flight wings show much cinnamon-rufous. Immature like ♀ but with rufous, black and white spotted upperparts. The long graduated tail ensures easy identification.
Voice. Normally silent; utters a weak 'koo, koo' when breeding.
Distribution and Habitat. Common resident in East and Central Africa. Frequents arid and semi-desert bush country, acacia stands, especially in sandy areas, and open dry woodlands.

TAMBOURINE DOVE   *Turtur tympanistria*   **Plate 13**

Identification. 9in, 23cm. Sexes unalike. ♂ dark brown above with a white forehead and eyestripe; underparts white; in the ♀ the forehead and eyestripe are grey and the throat, breast and flanks are also pale grey. Immature spotted on upperparts.

Voice. A series of drawn-out coos, diminishing in intensity.
Distribution and Habitat. Widely distributed in East and Central Africa. Inhabits forest and wooded areas and cultivation in or alongside forest; feeds mainly on the ground; flight swift and direct.

EMERALD-SPOTTED WOOD DOVE
Turtur chalcospilos   **Plate 13**

Identification. 8in, 20cm. A small dove with much cinnamon-rufous in the wings in flight. Upperparts dull brown with large metallic green wing spots; below vinous-pink, paler on belly; bill red with a black tip. The similar Blue-spotted Wood Dove has dark metallic blue wing spots and a red bill with a yellow tip.
Voice. A series of protracted coos, with pauses between each at first, gradually becoming quicker without pauses.
Distribution and Habitat. Locally common throughout much of East and Central Africa. Occurs in bush country, savannah woodland, woodland where there is thick undercover and in coastal scrub.
Allied Species. The Blue-spotted Wood Dove *(T. afer)*, 8in, 20cm, resembles the Emerald-spotted Wood Dove but is darker, with a red-tipped yellow bill and dark blue metallic spots on the wings. Inhabits dense woodland and forested areas locally in East and Central Africa. The Black-billed Wood Dove *(T. abyssinicus)*, 8in, 20cm, may be distinguished from the Blue-spotted Wood Dove by its paler plumage and slaty-black bill. It occurs in the Sudan, Ethiopia, northern Uganda and extreme north-western Kenya. It inhabits savannah woodland and bush country.

GREEN PIGEON   *Treron australis*   **Plate 13**

Identification. 12in, 30cm. A thickset, apple-green pigeon with coral-red cere and feet; bill greyish-white. Tail may be green or grey; a pale grey broad collar on hind-neck. Bruce's Green Pigeon differs in having the breast and abdomen bright yellow, not green.
Voice. A harsh croaking call, 'ka-roo-ka,' not at all a call one would normally associate with a pigeon.
Distribution and Habitat. Local resident East and Central Africa in wooded and savannah areas, open country where there are fig trees. The presence of birds in fruiting fig trees is often not suspected until the unmistakable call is heard, so well does their plumage blend with the foliage.
Allied Species. Bruce's Green Pigeon *(T. waalia)*, 12in, 30cm, differs in having a bright yellow breast and abdomen. It occurs in the Sudan, Ethiopia, northern Uganda and northern Kenya, in relatively arid regions especially along dry water-courses where there are fig trees.

PARROTS: Psittacidae

This is a group of vividly coloured birds with large heads and powerfully hooked bills. First and fourth toes are directed backwards; flight rapid and direct with short wing-beats. Many species are noisy uttering loud squawking and screeching calls.

RED-FRONTED PARROT *Poicephalus gulielmi* Plate 16

Identification. 12in, 30cm. Also called Red-headed Parrot, a most misleading name as the red plumage is confined to the forehead and a patch on the shoulders and edge of wings; plumage otherwise bright green with a yellowish-green rump. Immature lacks red on the forehead. In the field appears as a large dark green parrot with a pale rump; the red forehead is not always conspicuous.

Voice. A series of typical parrot squawks.

Distribution and Habitat. Local resident in highland forest of Kenya and northern Tanzania. This is the parrot one often sees flying over forest on Mt Kenya and Mt Kilimanjaro.

Allied Species. The well-known Grey Parrot *(Psittacus erithacus)*, 12in, 30cm, all grey with a contrasting scarlet tail, occurs throughout Uganda, the southern Sudan, western Kenya and western Tanzania. It is found, usually in flocks, in the tops of forest trees. The birds are common in the forests around Entebbe and on the Sesse Islands in Lake Victoria. The Brown-necked Parrot *(Poicephalus robustus)*, 13in, 33cm, resembles a larger edition of the Red-fronted Parrot but with a silvery-looking head and dull red frontal patch; bill larger. It occurs in Tanzania, Malawi and Zambia southwards but is everywhere uncommon. It occurs in open woodland, riverine forest and stands of baobab trees.

ORANGE-BELLIED PARROT *Poicephalus rufiventris* Plate 16

Identification. 10in, 25cm. A characteristic parrot of dry bush areas, especially where there are baobab trees. The bright orange-red breast of the adult ♂ is very conspicuous in the field and renders identification easy. The ♀ is less brightly coloured and may have the underparts green, or green with an orange wash. She is best identified by the associated ♂. The species is almost always seen in pairs or family groups. Immature birds resemble the adult ♀.

Voice. A shrill screeching call whilst in flight.

Distribution and Habitat. Locally not uncommon Ethiopia and Somalia southwards through Kenya to northern Tanzania. It frequents dry bush country and thornbush and is very partial to baobab trees.

BROWN PARROT *Poicephalus meyeri*   Plate 16

Identification. 10in, 25cm. This is an ash-brown parrot, more or less tinged with green, with a yellow band across the crown and a blue or green rump; underparts green. The somewhat similar Brown-headed Parrot has no yellow on the crown. The Yellow-fronted Parrot of Ethiopia has the crown and cheeks yellow.

Voice. A series of harsh parrot-type squawks.

Distribution and Habitat. Widespread and often common in East and Central Africa, but distribution patchy and birds often absent from apparently suitable localities.

Allied Species. The Brown-headed Parrot *(P. cryptoxanthus)*, 10in, 25cm, is all green with a greyish-brown head; no yellow on crown. In East Africa mainly a coastal bird found in mangroves along the Kenya coast; it also occurs in Tanzania and Malawi south to the Zambesi. In Malawi it occurs in acacia woodland. The rare and little-known Niam-Niam Parrot *(P. crassus)*, 11in, 28cm, which occurs in the south-western Sudan is very similar but has the greyish-brown of the head extended on to the chest; eye red. The Yellow-fronted Parrot *(P. flavifrons)*, 10in, 25cm, is another green parrot but with bright yellow crown and cheeks. It is known only from northern and central Ethiopia. The Rose-ringed Parrakeet *(Psittacula krameri)*, 14in, 36cm, is a long-tailed parrot, yellowish-green with a bluish-grey nape, a dull red half collar and a black throat. The ♀ lacks the black throat. It occurs in the southern Sudan and northern Uganda, in open savannah woodland and stands of acacia. A small billed race is also found in northern districts of Ethiopia and Somalia.

RED-HEADED LOVEBIRD *Agapornis pullaria*   Plate 16

Identification. 5in, 13cm. Plumage bright green with forehead and throat bright red; rump blue; tail tomato red with subterminal black bar and green tips, central tail feathers green; bill red. ♀ similar but red on head and throat paler and less extensive. Under wing coverts in ♂ black, in ♀ green.

Voice. A sustained twittering call 'si, si, si, si, si, si' uttered both in flight and when settled.

Distribution and Habitat. A local and generally uncommon species in western Ethiopia, the southern Sudan, Uganda and north-western Tanzania. Occurs in savannah woodland, forest margins, scrub covered hillsides and cultivation.

Allied Species. The Black-winged Lovebird *(Agapornis taranta)*, 5½in, 14cm, is confined to the highlands of Ethiopia in juniper forest and cultivation near the forest. It is a bright green species with a red forehead in the ♂; tail green with a black subterminal bar.

FISCHER'S LOVEBIRD *Agapornis fischeri* Plate 16

Identification. 5½in, 14cm. General colour green with forehead, cheeks and throat orange, merging to dull yellowish on crown, hindneck and chest; undersides of wings green. The Red-headed Lovebird has a redder head and the undersides of the wings in the ♂ are black. Lilian's Lovebird has the throat and chest tomato red.
Voice. High-pitched twittering calls and whistles.
Distribution and Habitat. A local resident confined to northern Tanzania; species introduced to southern Kenya at Lake Naivasha and at the coast. Occurs in flocks in open grasslands, acacia woodland, dry bush country especially where there are baobab trees and in cultivation. In some areas it does some damage to grain crops.
Allied Species. Lilian's Lovebird *(A. lilianae)*, 5½in, 14cm, occurs in Central Africa. It is similar to Fischer's Lovebird but has a green rump uniform with the mantle whilst Fischer's Lovebird has a blue rump; throat and chest tomato red.

YELLOW-COLLARED LOVEBIRD
Agapornis personata Plate 16

Identification. 6in, 15cm. A green lovebird with a blackish-brown head and a wide yellow band across the chest and extending over the hindneck to form a collar on neck and mantle.
Voice. Sustained twittering calls.
Distribution and Habitat. Local resident in various parts of Tanzania from the Arusha area and the Serengeti Plains to Lake Rukwa. It frequents open bush and grasslands and open woodland where there are baobab trees and millet cultivation. Like Fischer's Lovebird it is usually encountered in flocks.

BLACK-COLLARED LOVEBIRD
Agapornis swinderniana Plate 16

Identification. 5in, 13cm. A green lovebird with a black and orange collar on the hindneck; rump blue; tail red at base, a black subterminal band and green tips; below yellowish-green with an orange wash on the chest.

Voice. Subdued twittering calls, softer and less sustained than other love-birds.

Distribution and Habitat. A West African and Zaire species which just enters the East African area in the Bwamba forest in western Uganda. It is a rain forest species which feeds mainly upon fig seeds.

TURACOS: Musophagidae

The Turacos, Louries or Plantain-eaters, as they are variously called, are a group of medium or large-sized arboreal birds confined to Africa. The forest species are remarkable for their brightly coloured plumage and long tails; many species possess rich crimson-red flight feathers. Most have loud harsh calls.

LIVINGSTONE'S TURACO   *Tauraco livingstonii*   **Plate 15**

Identification. 16in, 41cm. Plumage mainly green, including tail; crown with a well-marked, white-tipped green crest; flight feathers mainly crimson-red; tail blackish with a strong green gloss. Schalow's Turaco has a violet-purple glossed tail and a longer more attenuated crest; the Black-billed Turaco has a much shorter and rounded crest and a black, not red, bill. Fischer's Turaco also has a short crest but hindneck is bright crimson-red.

Voice. A loud, far-carrying 'kaar, kaar, kaar, kaar – kaar' which is repeated frequently.

Distribution and Habitat. Local resident from central Tanzania south to Malawi and southwards. Its place is taken in Zambia by the closely related Schalow's Turaco. This is the common turaco of southern Tanzania and Malawi in the thicker forest areas: its loud calls are one of the characteristic sounds of the forests.

Allied Species. Two species of turacos have their main distribution in Ethiopia, the White-cheeked Turaco *(T. leucotis)*, 16in, 41cm, and Prince Ruspoli's Turaco *(T. ruspolii)*, 16in, 41cm. The former is green with a rounded navy-blue crest and a white patch on the cheeks and ear-coverts; flight feathers crimson-red; belly grey; tail blue-black. Two races occur, the nominate with the nape feathers tipped white, and the other in south-eastern Ethiopia and adjacent areas of Somalia which has the nape tipped dull crimson. Both inhabit woodland and forested country. Prince Ruspoli's Turaco is a rare bird found in juniper forest in southern Ethiopia from Lake Abaya to Boran. It is similar to the White-cheeked Turaco but has forehead and front part of crest greenish-grey; rest of crest rosy red with broad white tips followed by a tuft of red feathers on the nape.

SCHALOW'S TURACO *Tauraco schalowi* **Plate 15**

Identification. 16in, 41cm. Sometimes considered as con-specific with Livingstone's Turaco from which it differs by its longer and more attenuated crest and a violet-purple, not green-glossed tail.
Voice. Similar harsh 'kaaar, kaaar, kaaar' calls to Livingstone's Turaco.
Distribution and Habitat. Occurs locally from south-western Kenya southwards through western Tanzania to Zambia. It also inhabits wooded and forested localities.

BLACK-BILLED TURACO *Tauraco schuttii* **Plate 15**

Identification. 16in, 41cm. Similar to Livingstone's Turaco but with a short rounded, white-tipped crest and a black, not red, bill.
Voice. A far-reaching 'kaaw, kaaw, kaaw, kaaw' call.
Distribution and Habitat. Local resident forests and savannah woodland near forest in the southern Sudan, Uganda and western Kenya.

FISCHER'S TURACO *Tauraco fischeri* **Plate 15**

Identification. 16in, 41cm. This is another mainly green turaco, with a short thick crest and a bright blood-red patch on the nape and hindneck; flight feathers mainly crimson.
Voice. A far-reaching, croaking 'kaw, kaw, kaw, kaw' but less vocal than many other species of turacos.
Distribution and Habitat. Local resident in forested and wooded areas along the Kenya and Tanzania coast, from the Tana River to Tanga and the Usambara Mts; also resident on Zanzibar Island. Common in the Shimba Hills National Park, Kenya.

HARTLAUB'S TURACO *Tauraco hartlaubi* **Plate 15**

Identification. 16in, 41cm. This is the common forest turaco of the Kenya Highlands. Plumage mainly green and purplish-black; crest dark bluish-black; a round white patch above and in front of eye and a white streak below the eye. It draws attention to its presence by its loud croaking calls.
Voice. A high-pitched croaking call 'kaw, kaw, kaw, kaw, kaw' repeated frequently.
Distribution and Habitat. Resident in highland forest of Kenya and north-eastern Tanzania. It is common in the forests around Nairobi, Kenya.

VIOLET-CRESTED TURACO *Tauraco porphyreolophus* **Plate 15**

Identification. 16in, 41cm. Head with thick, violet-black crest, no white patches on face. Upperparts blue-grey merging to green on mantle; throat and breast grass green to pale grey on abdomen; flight feathers mainly crimson. This is a savannah woodlands turaco with conspicuous blue-grey on upperparts and with crimson-red flight feathers. Hartlaub's Turaco has no pale blue-grey on upperparts, possesses white head markings and inhabits forests.
Voice. A far-carrying gobbling call 'kurru, kurru, kurru' repeated over and over again.
Distribution and Habitat. A local resident from southern Kenya southwards through Tanzania to Central Africa. Frequents a variety of habitats including rain forest fringes, savannah woodlands and wooded water courses.

WHITE-CRESTED TURACO *Tauraco leucolophus* **Plate 15**

Identification. 15in, 38cm. A violet-blue turaco with a green breast and conspicuous pure white crest, cheeks and throat; forehead blue-black; bill pale yellow, large. Its mainly white head distinguishes this species from all other turacos; its red flight feathers are conspicuous in flight.
Voice. The call starts with a deep 'aaah' as if the bird were drawing in its breath, followed by a guttural croaking 'garrr, garrr, garrr, garrr.'
Distribution and Habitat. Inhabits more open areas than most turacos such as riverine forest and woodland and scrub strips along dry watercourses where there are fig trees. It ranges from the southern Sudan, Uganda to western Kenya. It is numerous on the lower slopes of Mt Elgon, western Kenya and in the Soroti district, Uganda.

RUWENZORI TURACO *Tauraco johnstoni* **Plate 15**

Identification. 16in, 41cm. A red-winged green and blue turaco with a deep red patch on the hind neck and a red patch in the centre of the chest. Bare yellow skin around the eye in the nominate Ruwenzori race, but skin around the eye feathered in the race found in south-western Uganda.
Voice. A guttural 'kow-kow-kow-kow.'
Distribution and Habitat. In East Africa occurs in mountain forest on the Ruwenzori Mts, western Uganda, and in the Impenetrable Forest and forested slopes of the Birunga Volcanoes of south-western Uganda. Inhabits mountain forests over 7,000ft, 2,134m.

ROSS'S TURACO　*Musophaga rossae*　**Plate 15**

Identification. 20in, 51cm. A large violet-black turaco with crimson flight feathers, a square crimson crest and a very conspicuous orange-yellow bare face and bill.

Voice. A great variety of croaking and cackling calls. Birds usually found in loose parties and often very noisy.

Distribution and Habitat. Local resident in southern Sudan, Uganda and western Kenya and western Tanzania south to northern Zambia. Frequents forested areas of various types, savannah woodland, wooded water-courses and in Zambia recorded in deciduous thickets.

GREAT BLUE TURACO　*Corythaeola cristata*　**Plate 15**

Identification. 28–30in, 71–76cm. This is the finest and largest of the turacos. Upperparts and throat verditer-blue, breast pale apple green, abdomen chestnut; no red in wings; tail very long, pale greenish-yellow with a wide black terminal band; head with rounded black crest; bill orange-red and yellow. This tree-top species frequently fans and closes its tail, rendering itself most conspicuous.

Voice. A series of loud croaking 'kok, kok, kok, kok, kok' calls terminating in a series of bubbling croaks.

Distribution and Habitat. A West African species which extends eastwards to the southern Sudan, Uganda and western Kenya. It is a forest species, most frequent in the great Zaire forests. It also occurs in strips of riverine forest and sometimes into savannah woodland near forest margins.

EASTERN GREY PLANTAIN-EATER　*Crinifer zonurus*　**Plate 15**

Identification. 20in, 51cm. A large brownish-grey turaco with a white belly and long tail with a terminal black band; no red in wings but shows a white bar in flight; nape and hind neck feathers long with whitish tips imparting a mane-like effect.

Voice. Very noisy birds, uttering a variety of loud cackling or laughing call notes.

Distribution and Habitat. Locally common resident in Sudan, Ethiopia, Uganda, western Kenya and Tanzania. Inhabits savannah woodlands, cultivation where there are trees and riverine vegetation. Usually in small noisy parties.

WHITE-BELLIED GO-AWAY-BIRD *Corythaixoides leucogaster*
Plate 15

Identification. 20in, 51cm. This is a grey, black and white dry country turaco without red in the wings. It is a very noticeable bird with its long tail, pronounced crest and white belly; black tips to wing coverts, forming black bars across the wings.

Voice. A very loud and penetrating sheep-like bleating call 'gaarr, warrrr' which has been rendered 'go awayaaaa' – hence the bird's common name.

Distribution and Habitat. A local resident, often common, from the southern Sudan and central Ethiopia and Somalia, south through Uganda, Kenya and the northern half of Tanzania. Inhabits dry thorn-bush country and belts of acacia woodland and riverine acacias.

Allied Species. The Common Go-Away-Bird *(C. concolor)*, 19in, 48cm, is an entirely grey bird with a pronounced crest and long tail. It occurs from southern Tanzania south through Malawi and Zambia to South Africa, in dry woodlands.

BARE-FACED GO-AWAY-BIRD *Corythaixoides personata*
Plate 15

Identification. 20in, 51cm. A pale greyish-backed, white-breasted turaco without red in the wings, with a bare black face; greenish patch in the middle of the chest; head crested and tail long. The bare black face is a good field character.

Voice. A series of deep bleating calls, and wild ringing chuckles.

Distribution and Habitat. Widely distributed and locally common in central and southern Ethiopia, Uganda, western and southern Kenya, Tanzania and Zambia. Inhabits savannah woodlands, park-like country, open bush especially where there are euphorbia and fig trees and in riverine forest.

CUCKOOS and COUCALS: Cuculidae

The Cuckoos are medium-sized, slim birds with long tails; one of their chief external characters is that their first and fourth toes are directed backwards. Most species are parasitic in their breeding habits, laying their eggs in the nests of foster parents. However, the Coucals and Green Coucal or Yellowbill *(Centropus* and *Ceuthmochares)* build their own nests and rear their own young.

RED-CHESTED CUCKOO   *Cuculus solitarius*   **Plate 14**

Identification. 12in, 31cm. A dark blue-grey cuckoo with a rusty-brown patch on throat and upper breast; chin grey; underparts barred buffy-white and black. Immature blackish with dark throat and black and white barred belly. A shy tree-top species, far oftener heard than seen.

Voice. A distinctive, rather shrill call of three notes 'wip, wip, weeooo.' Often calls immediately before rains break and known locally as the 'rain-bird' – its call being rendered 'it will rain.'

Distribution and Habitat. A resident and intra-African migrant through most of the Ethiopian Region. Common in East and Central Africa. It frequents a variety of habitats where there are trees from open park-like country, woodlands, forest and bush to cultivation and gardens.

Allied Species. The Black Cuckoo *(C. clamosus)*, 12in, 31cm, looks like a melanistic edition of a Red-chested Cuckoo, with blackish underparts, often with some indistinct barring on the chest. It has a distinctive and mournful call, a descending, long-drawn-out 'too, too, toooooo.' It occurs throughout East and Central Africa. It is partial to stands of acacia trees, riverine forest and coastal scrub. The Great Spotted Cuckoo *(C. glandarius)* is a scarce resident in East and Central Africa and also a Palearctic winter visitor and passage migrant. Length 16in, 41cm, greyish-brown above boldly spotted with white; head crested; chest and belly white; tail long and graduated with white tips. Immature with crown black and primaries chestnut. The well-known European Cuckoo *(C. canorus)*, 13in, 33cm, is a common winter visitor and passage migrant. The African Cuckoo *(C. gularis)* may be distinguished from the European bird by a conspicuous yellow base to bill and complete white bars, not spots, across tail. Occurs locally in East and Central Africa. The Lesser Cuckoo *(C. poliocephalus)* is much smaller, 10in, 26cm, and occurs as a migrant in Zambia, Tanzania and eastern Kenya. The Black and White Cuckoo *(C. jacobinus)*, 13in, 33cm, is a crested species with black upperparts and a short white wing-bar which is noticeable in flight; underparts variable, white, greyish or washed buff in immature birds. Levaillant's Cuckoo *(C. levaillantii)*, 14in, 36cm, is similar but may be distinguished by its whitish underparts and heavy black streaking on throat and chest. A melanistic phase also occurs which can be recognised in the field only on size. Both occur locally in East and Central Africa. The Thick-billed Cuckoo *(Pachycoccyx audeberti)*, 14in, 36cm, is a large-billed, long-tailed cuckoo, dark grey above, white below; tail white-tipped. Everywhere very uncommon, usually in Brachystegia woodland and often associated with wood-hoopoes and helmet shrikes.

EMERALD CUCKOO · *Chrysococcyx cupreus* · **Plate 14**

Identification. 9in, 23cm. Although the ♂ is one of the most brightly coloured birds in Africa and the species is widespread, the Emerald Cuckoo is far oftener heard than seen. The ♂ is brilliant metallic green all over, including wings and tail, except for the lower breast and belly which are bright canary yellow. The ♀ has the upperparts metallic green with rufous bars and the underparts are white, barred dark metallic green. It is much darker below than the allied Didric and Klaas' Cuckoos.

Voice. A loud clear whistle, 'choo, choo – too, wee,' which can be rendered as 'Hello Georgie.'

Distribution and Habitat. Resident and intra-African migrant throughout most of East and Central Africa. Although mainly a forest tree-top bird it occurs also in scrub, acacia woodlands and coastal thickets. It is not an easy bird to observe and its presence is usually revealed only when the ♂ is calling: at other times it is easily overlooked.

DIDRIC CUCKOO · *Chrysococcyx caprius* · **Plate 14**

Identification. 7½in, 19cm. A metallic green cuckoo with mainly white underparts; above metallic green with coppery gloss; tail mainly blackish with round white spots on the outer feathers. ♀ more heavily washed rufous-copper above and mottled rufous on underparts. Klaas' Cuckoo is smaller and greener and has white outer tail feathers with a few black markings. The Didric Cuckoo is parasitic upon weaver-birds and it is most in evidence where weaver colonies exist.

Voice. A plaintive whistle 'dee, dee, dee, DEE, dric.'

Distribution and Habitat. Common resident and partial intra-African migrant throughout. In East Africa it occurs throughout the year but in Central Africa it is present mainly between October and April. In East Africa its most frequent habitat is thornbush and acacias and in dry highland forest. In Central Africa it occurs in most types of woodland and has also been recorded from papyrus swamps.

KLAAS' CUCKOO · *Chrysococcyx klaas* · **Plate 14**

Identification. 6½in, 16cm. A small bright green cuckoo with very white underparts and a patch of green on each side of the chest; outer tail feathers white with a few black markings. The Didric Cuckoo has black outer tail feathers spotted with white. The ♀ Klaas' Cuckoo is bronze-brown above with some green bars; underparts washed buff with sparse dark brown barring. Immature similar but more heavily barred green above.

Voice. A series of plaintive two or three note whistles, repeated slowly at intervals, 'twee-teu' or 'too-hee-tee.'

Distribution and Habitat. A common resident and partial intra-African migrant, in East Africa and Malawi present throughout the year, in Zambia and southwards most records are between October and April. Frequents a variety of habitats from forests and forest margins, woodland, bush country and acacia stands to coastal thickets. It is often much in evidence in fruiting fig trees. Its white outer tail feathers are conspicuous in flight and if the green colour of the plumage is not seen clearly the bird can be mistaken for a honeyguide.

Allied Species. The Yellow-throated Green Cuckoo *(Chrysococcyx flavigularis)*, 7in, 18cm, is bronzy-green above; throat with broad yellow streak bordered with green; breast and belly barred green and pale brown. ♀ has sides of face and underparts pale brown, barred dark green. A West African forest species, in East Africa known only from the Bwamba Forest, western Uganda.

WHITE-BROWED COUCAL   *Centropus superciliosus*   Plate 14

Identification. 16in, 41cm. Coucals are heavily built, rather clumsy looking birds with an awkward floundering flight when flushed out of cover. One's impression is a mainly chestnut-plumaged bird with a long broad tail. The present species may be recognised by a wide whitish stripe over the eye and in having the crown and hindneck earth-brown, the latter streaked creamy-white. Eye ruby-red, conspicuous at close quarters.

Voice. A very distinctive bubbling call, which has been likened to water being poured out of a bottle, and which has given rise to a common name for this species – 'water-bottle bird.'

Distribution and Habitat. A locally common resident in East and Central Africa. Inhabits grassy bush country, areas of rank undergrowth, coastal scrub and similar thick cover. Uncommon in thickets of papyrus and other swamp vegetation inhabited by the Blue-headed and Black Coucals.

Allied Species. The Blue-headed Coucal *(C. monachus)*, 18in, 46cm, has a dark chestnut back and a shiny navy-blue crown and nape. It occurs in thick cover near or over water in East Africa. The Black Coucal *(C. grillii)*, 15in, 38cm, is also confined to swamps and marshes, uncommon in East Africa but locally common in Central Africa. ♂ in breeding plumage oily-black, ♀ and non-breeding ♂ streaked tawny and black. The black ♂♂ are conspicuous sitting on some vantage perch over the swamp vegetation.

SENEGAL COUCAL   *Centropus senegalensis*   **Plate 14**

Identification. 16in, 41cm. A black-crowned coucal with rufous back and wings, a blackish tail and buffy-white underparts. Differs from the Blue-headed Coucal in smaller size and dead black, not iridescent blue-black crown.

Voice. Bubbling flute-like notes similar to call of White-browed Coucal.

Distribution and Habitat. Local resident southern Sudan, Ethiopia and northern Somalia, south to northern Uganda and extreme western Kenya. Inhabits bush and thick cover mainly in savannah woodlands but often in sugar-cane cultivation.

Allied Species. The Green Coucal or Yellowbill *(Ceuthmochares aereus)*, 13in, 33cm, is a slim greenish-grey coucal with a long broad tail and a conspicuous yellow bill. Instead of living in undergrowth it is a skulker amongst creepers and dense foliage of forest trees and is often overlooked unless one hears its distinctive calls. These are a series of harsh clicking notes culminating in a devilish chuckling scream; it also utters a querulous 'oo – weee,' not unlike a kite's call note. It is local and uncommon in East and Central Africa.

OWLS: Strigidae

Mainly nocturnal birds of prey characterised by large heads, rather flattened faces and conspicuous facial discs, and forward facing eyes. Plumage soft and downy and flight noiseless; ear-tufts present in many species: hooked bills and powerful claws.

AFRICAN BARN OWL   *Tyto alba*   **Plate 20**

Identification. 13in, 33cm. A golden-buff owl profusely mottled grey and speckled white; facial disc distinctive, heart-shaped; no ear tufts; underparts white with some dark brown spotting on chest and flanks; legs long.

Voice. A wavering, wild shriek. At nesting place produces subdued snoring noise and bill snapping.

Distribution and Habitat. Uncommon local resident in East and Central Africa. Often associated with human habitations, making its home in lofts and immediately below roofs. Nocturnal; feeds almost entirely upon rats and mice.

Allied Species. The Cape Grass Owl *(T. capensis)*, 13in, 33cm, may be distinguished from the Barn Owl by its blackish-brown upperparts, which may or may not be peppered with white. This is a very uncommon bird in East and Central Africa which frequents open moorland and extensive marshes, usually at high altitudes. Like the Barn Owl it is nocturnal and also preys upon small rodents. In Kenya it is most frequently encountered on the moorlands of Mt Kenya and the Aberdare Mts, the South Kinangop plateau and marshes in the highlands of western Kenya.

AFRICAN MARSH OWL   *Asio capensis*   Plate 20

Identification. 14in, 36cm. Short ear tufts present. Often starts hunting, quartering the ground in a harrier-like manner, before dusk. This bird is a dark brown and buff edition of the European Short-eared Owl which is an uncommon winter visitor to northern parts of East Africa. Upperparts rather dark brown with slight buff mottling; below whitish, heavily mottled dull brown and buff.
Voice. Sometimes produces a hoarse croaking note, but generally a silent bird.
Distribution and Habitat. Local resident East and Central Africa. Frequents open moorlands, grasslands, swamps and marshes.
Allied Species. The Abyssinian Long-eared Owl *(A. abyssinicus)*, 18in, 46cm, resembles a larger edition of the European Long-eared Owl and has the same upright stance. Sooty-brown with some buff markings; below blotched and barred dark brown and white on a buff ground; ear-tufts well developed. A rare and little-known owl recorded from the highlands of Ethiopia, Mt Kenya in Kenya and the Ruwenzori mountains in western Uganda.

AFRICAN WOOD OWL   *Ciccaba woodfordi*   Not illustrated

Identification. 13in, 33cm. A forest or woodland owl resembling a smaller edition of the European Tawny Owl; no ear tufts. Above dark chocolate-brown with white markings on the scapulars; below barred and mottled dark brown and white. Roosts by day in thick foliage; often overlooked unless its presence is indicated by small birds mobbing it.
Voice. A sustained hooting, 'Hoo, hoo, hu – hoo, hu, hu, hu.'
Distribution and Habitat. Local resident East and Central Africa in forests and woodland; occurs from sea-level to over 8,000ft, 2,440m.

VERREAUX'S EAGLE OWL   *Bubo lacteus*   Plate 20

Identification. 24–26in, 61–66cm. Ear tufts present; general colour finely vermiculated brownish-grey; underparts without heavy spotting; facial disc whitish with a black band on each side. This owl is sometimes encountered in the daytime sleeping in some thickly foliaged acacia tree, often near water; its whitish face edged by black on each side is a good field character.

Voice. A mournful 'hu, hu, hu, hu, hu, hu, hu' in ascending scale.

Distribution and Habitat. Locally common in many parts of East and Central Africa. It frequents wooded water courses, acacia and Brachystegia woodlands and bush and savannah country. In Kenya it is more than usually common in the Amboseli National Park and the Samburu Game Reserve.

Allied Species. Pel's Fishing Owl *(Scotopelia peli)*, 25–30in, 64–76cm, inhabits wooded and forested water-courses where there is thick cover; feeds on fish. Head large and plumage lax, bright rufous-buff barred and spotted with dark brown. It is a rare bird in East Africa, most frequent on the Tana and Mara rivers in Kenya, but commoner and more widespread along the larger rivers and swamps of Central Africa.

SPOTTED EAGLE OWL *Bubo africanus* **Plate 20**

Identification. 20in, 51cm. A thickset, rather pale owl with ear-tufts; upperparts greyish-brown, vermiculated and mottled greyish-white and with rounded white spots; below whitish with irregular brown barring and heavy brown spotting on the breast. Verreaux's Eagle Owl is larger, finely vermiculated grey all over and lacks the heavy dark spots on underparts.

Voice. A low mournful hooting and also calls very like those of a stone curlew.

Distribution and Habitat. Locally common in East and Central Africa. Frequents dry bush country, rocky slopes, bush-clad ravines and savannah woodland. Often seen on roads after dark and many are killed by motor vehicles.

Allied Species. Mackinder's Eagle Owl *(B. capensis)*, 22in, 56cm, is a thickset eagle owl mottled orange-buff, dark brown and white with conspicuous ear-tufts and fiery-orange eyes. The Spotted Eagle Owl has no orange-buff in the plumage and its eyes are dark brown or pale yellow. This is an uncommon species found in the highlands of Ethiopia, Kenya and the Nyika plateau Malawi and Zambia. Inhabits rocky cliffs and escarpments but also occurs in more open country, often near water. The Nduk Eagle Owl *(B. vosseleri)*, 22in, 56cm, is known only from mountain forest in the Usambara Mts northeastern Tanzania. It is mainly tawny, barred and blotched with blackish-brown. The closely related Fraser's Eagle Owl *(B. poensis)*, 20in, 51cm, is dark rufous above, paler rufous below, narrowly barred all over with dark brown; ear tufts conspicuous; facial disc rimmed with black. In East Africa it has been recorded in forests in south-western Uganda.

PEARL-SPOTTED OWLET   *Glaucidium perlatum*   **Plate 20**

Identification. 8in, 20cm. Distinguished by lack of ear-tufts and relatively long white-spotted tail; underparts white with heavy dark brown streaks. Species more frequently observed during the daytime than most owls and its whereabouts is often indicated by the presence of small birds engaged in mobbing.

Voice. A distinctive, low but far-carrying 'we-ooo, we-ooo,' not unlike the call of a water dikkop.

Distribution and Habitat. Locally common in many parts of East and Central Africa. Occurs in dry bush country, savannah woodlands, acacia stands and riverine vegetation.

Allied Species. The Red-chested Owlet *(G. tephronotum)*, 8in, 20cm, has umber-brown upperparts, a white collar on the hindneck and rufous-brown chest and flanks. It is known from the Kakamega Forest and Mt Elgon in western Kenya and the forests of western Uganda. The Barred Owlet *(G. capense)*, 9in, 23cm, differs from the Pearl-spotted Owlet in having the breast barred rich brown, not streaked. It occurs in bush and wooded country, often along rivers, in eastern Kenya, Tanzania and Central Africa; uncommon. Pale desert races of the Little Owl *(Athene noctua)*, 10in, 25cm, occur in the Sudan, northern Ethiopia and Somalia. They resemble a larger, paler edition of the Pearl-spotted Owlet but with a shorter tail. They live in holes in termite hills.

AFRICAN SCOPS OWL   *Otus scops*   **Plate 20**

Identification. 7in, 18cm. This tiny owl may be recognised by the combination of very small size and well-developed ear tufts. Plumage finely vermiculated pale grey, or rarely rufous, with heavier brown and white markings; black and white markings on breast. The Pearl-spotted Owlet is larger, lacks ear tufts and has a longer tail, and the underparts are white with brown streaks, not vermiculated. The European Scops Owl is a winter visitor to East Africa.

Voice. The call of the African Scops Owl is one of the characteristic sounds of the African night, a soft two note 'kee-oo' run together to sound as one note.

Distribution and Habitat. Common in many parts of East and Central Africa, frequenting bush country, acacia belts along dry river beds, savannah woodland and localities where there are baobab trees.

Allied Species. The White-faced Scops Owl *(O. leucotis)*, 10½in, 27cm, has a conspicuous white facial disc bordered black on each side, long black-tipped ear tufts and brilliant orange eyes; below whitish with rather narrow dark streaks. This is a local species in East and Central Africa; it occurs in woodland and bush and acacia country. Its call is distinctive, a rather dove-like 'cuc-coo.' The Pemba Scops Owl *(O. rutila)*, 8in, 20cm, is russet-brown with black streaks on the head and white spots along the edge of the scapulars; below finely vermiculated grey and russet-brown with a few short streaks. It is confined to Pemba Island, north of Zanzibar off the East African coast. The Sokoke Scops Owl *(O. irenae)*, is a recently discovered species known only from the Sokoke-Arabuku Forest, Kenya coast. Length 6½in, 16½cm, vermiculated grey and white with large white scapular spots; below vermiculated grey with a few drop-like spots on the chest. It has a call similar to that of a tinker-bird, a series of 'tonk, tonk, tonk, tonk, tonk.'

NIGHTJARS: Caprimulgidae

These are nocturnal insectivorous birds with small weak bills but huge gapes, large eyes, tiny feet and long wings. Plumage of 'dead-leaf' pattern which gives excellent camouflage when the bird is resting during the day.

NUBIAN NIGHTJAR   *Caprimulgus nubicus*   **Plate 20**

Identification. 8½in, 22cm. General colour mottled pale golden-buff and pale grey; indistinct rufous collar on hindneck; first four primaries with white spots; apical third of two pairs outer tail feathers white. ♀ lacks white in wings and tips of tail feathers are buff. Best recognised by its pale coloration.
Voice. A liquid 'chucker, chucker, chucker, chucker.'
Distribution and Habitat. Local, sometimes relatively common in the Sudan, Ethiopia and Somalia south to southern Kenya. It inhabits arid bush country and semi-desert areas.
Allied Species. The European Nightjar *(C. europaeus)*, 10–11in, 25–28cm, is a common winter visitor and passage migrant in East Africa, less frequent in Central Africa. Best recognised by black streaks in middle of back, white tips to the two outer pairs of tail feathers, white spots (buff in ♀) to three outer flight feathers and lack of a rufous collar on hindneck. The Fiery-necked Nightjar *(C. pectoralis)*, 9½in, 24cm, is warm vinous-brown with bold black and buff markings, a broad rufous collar on hindneck and rufous extending to sides of neck; apical third of outer tail feathers white. It has a beautiful liquid call, 'too, dee – he, he, heeer,' repeated slowly over and over again. It occurs locally in Uganda, Tanzania and Central Africa along roads through forest, open woodland and thick bush country.

ABYSSINIAN NIGHTJAR   *Caprimulgus poliocephalus*   **Plate 20**

Identification. 9½in, 24cm. Best field characters for this species are very dusky plumage and white two outer pairs of tail feathers. These tail feathers have dusky outer webs but when the bird is in flight they appear entirely white. Rufous collar on hindneck.

Voice. A plaintive, drawn-out 'pee, ooo, wee,' not unlike the call of a grey plover.

Distribution and Habitat. Local resident and partial migrant south-eastern Sudan and Ethiopia south through highland areas Uganda and Kenya to Tanzania and the Nyika Plateau Malawi and Zambia. Normally occurs in areas over 5,000ft, 1,530m. Inhabits forest edges, bush, woodland and cultivated areas.

Allied Species. The Dusky Nightjar *(C. fraenatus)*, 10in, 25cm, is a dusky nightjar boldly mottled blackish-brown and with orange-buff spots on back and wing coverts and a rufous collar on hindneck. It differs from the Abyssinian Nightjar in having broad white tips to the outer tail feathers; in ♀ Dusky Nightjar tail tips are greyish. Local resident in East Africa south to Tanzania. The White-tailed Nightjar *(C. natalensis)*, 9½in, 24cm, has the apical half of the tail feathers white and the upperparts handsomely mottled orange-buff and black. It is a species associated with water, found near swamps, marshes and streams. It is a local resident and partial migrant in western Kenya and Uganda south to Zambia. The Plain Nightjar *(C. inornatus)*, 9in, 23cm, has rather a small head and slim appearance; upperparts grey or buffy-grey without conspicuous spots. Best field characters are lack of white patch on throat and reduction or absence of white spots on primaries; outer tail feathers broadly tipped white or grey in ♀. It occurs locally in East Africa in arid areas. The Star-spotted Nightjar *(C. stellatus)*, 9in, 23cm, is large-headed, grey or rufous-grey with small black and buff star-shaped spots on crown and scapulars. It occurs in dry bush country of Ethiopia and northern Somalia south to northern Kenya; everywhere very uncommon.

DONALDSON-SMITH'S NIGHTJAR
Caprimulgus donaldsoni **Plate 20**

Identification. 7in, 18cm. This species is so much smaller than other species that size is its best field character. It is rich rufous, more rarely grey, in general colour with dark brown and cream markings; bright rufous collar on hindneck; wing coverts and breast spotted creamy-white; two outer pairs of tail feathers with broad white tips and white spots on four outer flight feathers.

Voice. A series of short churring calls.

Distribution and Habitat. Resident Ethiopia and Somalia south through Kenya to north-eastern Tanzania. A bird of bush and arid bush country, locally common in parts of eastern and northern Kenya.

Allied Species. The Freckled Nightjar *(C. tristigma)*, 11in, 28cm, is a large, heavily built nightjar with a noticeably large head; it is associated with rocky outcrops. It is dark and uniformly-coloured without the cream-coloured spots and markings on upperparts characteristic of most nightjars. White patch on throat and tail tipped white. It occurs locally in suitable habitats in East and Central Africa. Bates' Forest Nightjar *(C. batesi)*, 11½in, 29cm, is another large and dark nightjar but with more buff spotting which is found in West African type rain forest. In East Africa it is known only from the Bwamba Forest, western Uganda.

MOZAMBIQUE NIGHTJAR   *Caprimulgus clarus*   Plate 20

Identification. 11in, 28cm. This nightjar is boldly spotted cream on wing coverts and upperparts and has large white spots on the flight feathers; tail long and strongly graduated, the central feathers projecting ½–1in, 12–25mm, beyond others; outer web of two pairs outer tail feathers white.
Voice. An even, rather slow 'tok, tok, tok, tok, tok.'
Distribution and Habitat. Occurs in Ethiopia and Somalia, south through Kenya to northern Tanzania. Frequents arid and semi-arid bush country and often concentrated along rivers and near swamps and marshes. Perhaps the commonest nightjar to be found in Kenya.
Allied Species. The Long-tailed Nightjar *(C. climacurus)*, 11½–17in, 29–43cm, is very similar to the Mozambique Nightjar but has a much longer tail in the ♂, the central feathers protruding up to 6in, 18cm, beyond the others. Ranges from the Sudan south through northern and western Uganda, in bush and savannah woodland; call a prolonged soft churr. The Gaboon Nightjar *(C. fossii)*, 10in, 25cm, also resembles the Mozambique Nightjar but its tail is not graduated, but square or sometimes even slightly forked. It has a clucking call. Ranges from Uganda and western Kenya south to Central Africa.

STANDARD-WINGED NIGHTJAR   *Macrodipteryx longipennis*
Plate 20

Identification. 9in, 23cm. The adult ♂ is remarkable in having the shaft of the ninth primary elongated about 12 inches and terminating with a very broad flag-like web. In flight the standards can be mistaken for two small birds or moths flying above and behind the nightjar! The ♀ lacks the standards but both sexes may be distinguished by having no white spots on the flight feathers.
Voice. A shrill continuous churring.
Distribution and Habitat. Occurs as a breeding visitor from February to May in the southern Sudan, Ethiopia, northern Uganda and northern Kenya: in non-breeding season birds move northwards to northern Ethiopia and the central Sudan. Occurs in open grasslands, bush and savannah woodlands often near water.

PENNANT-WINGED NIGHTJAR   *Macrodipteryx vexillarius*
Plate 20

Identification. 12in, 30cm. Adult ♂ possesses remarkable ninth primary feathers which are elongated to over twice the total length of the bird; these feathers are white with some brown on the outer web towards the base. The ♀ lacks these plumes. Upperparts mottled and spotted dark brown and buff; conspicuous rufous collar on hind neck; below mottled on breast but abdomen white. Combination of large size and white belly are the best field characters if pennant wing feathers absent.
Voice. On its breeding grounds has a high-pitched piping call, but generally a silent bird for a nightjar.
Distribution and Habitat. Non-breeding visitor to southern Sudan, Uganda and Kenya between February and August, migrating southwards to breeding grounds in southern Tanzania and Central Africa in August and September. Locally common, especially in Zambia where it frequents woodlands and stony hillsides. Often settles on roadways and many are killed by motor vehicles.

SWIFTS: Apodidae

In general appearance swallow-like but may be distinguished by the formation of their wings which are more slender and scythe-like, their short tails and their manner of flight which is rapid and direct, often gliding considerable distances without flapping wings. Skeletally quite distinct from swallows, having flat skulls and a foot structure in which all four toes point forwards.

ALPINE SWIFT   *Apus melba*   **Plate 21**

Identification. 8½in, 22cm. A very large brown and white swift with a wingspan of 21in, 53cm; easily recognised by its white underparts and brown chest band.
Voice. A loud trill.
Distribution and Habitat. In East Africa breeds on cliffs on Mt Kenya and the Ruwenzori Mts, western Uganda. Elsewhere a non-breeding visitor. In the Kenya Highlands it is to be seen flying low in the wake of thunderstorms.

MOTTLED SWIFT   *Apus aequatorialis*   **Plate 21**

Identification. 9in, 23cm. The largest East African swift, dark brown with pale edgings to the feathers of the underparts imparting a scaly or mottled appearance; ill-defined whitish chin patch.

Voice. Loud trilling whistles uttered by the birds as they fly around nesting cliffs; sound of wings noticeable.

Distribution and Habitat. Local in many parts of East and Central Africa. Associated with cliffs and breeds in colonies in rockface crevices. In Kenya large colonies of Mottled Swifts nest in the cliffs of Hell's Gate gorge near Lake Naivasha.

NYANZA SWIFT   *Apus niansae*   **Plate 21**

Identification. 6in, 15cm. Plumage sooty brown with whitish throat; tail rather short, forked. The Black Roughwing Swallow is black with a very long forked tail and has a characteristic swallow flight. Horus and White-rumped Swifts have white rumps. The European Swift and Mouse-coloured Swift are larger; both are difficult to distinguish in the field, but are not associated with inland cliffs as is the Nyanza Swift.

Voice. A typical swift-type screech at nesting cliffs.

Distribution and Habitat. Resident in Ethiopia, Kenya and northern Tanzania. Aerial, may occur anywhere but especially over high ground. Swifts, including this species, are often in evidence in the vicinity of storm clouds. Breeds in colonies in crevices of high inland cliffs; in Kenya there are colonies in the cliffs of Hell's Gate gorge, Lake Naivasha, where they nest alongside Mottled Swifts.

Allied Species. The European Swift *(A. apus)*, 6½in, 16½cm, is blackish brown with a whitish throat; a winter visitor and passage migrant in East and Central Africa. The African Swift *(A. barbatus)*, 7in, 18cm, is very similar but has a slightly whiter throat and narrow whitish margins to feathers of underparts. It occurs mainly in highland forest areas of East and Central Africa and nests singly in holes and crevices in large forest trees such as junipers. The Mouse-coloured or Pallid Swift *(A. pallidus)*, 6½in, 16½cm, is very like the European Swift but a little paler in colour. It has been recorded as a non-breeding visitor to East Africa.

SCARCE SWIFT   *Apus myoptilus*   **Plate 21**

Identification. 6½in, 16½cm. An entirely brown swift with a slightly paler greyish-white throat; tail forked and outer tail feathers elongated and attenuated. In flight the tail is often kept closed, when the two long outer tail feathers project behind the bird like a spike. Flight very rapid and wing beats fast for a swift.

Voice. Usually silent; call unrecorded.

Distribution and Habitat. Extremely uncommon and local in East and Central Africa. In Kenya recorded from Mt Kenya and the Aberdare Mts, from the Cherengani Mts and Mt Elgon in western Kenya; in Uganda it occurs on the Ruwenzori range and in south-western Kigezi. This is a highlands species which flies high, seen only when thunder-storms or cloud force them to fly lower than usual.

LITTLE SWIFT *Apus affinis*   Plate 21

Identification. 5in, 13cm. A black swift with a square, not forked, tail, a white rump and a white patch on the chin. The Horus and White-rumped Swifts have forked tails.
Voice. A shrill, sharp twittering call, usually when flying in flocks around nesting sites.
Distribution and Habitat. Local resident and partial migrant through East and Central Africa. Aerial, associated with buildings in towns and country, bridges and cliffs. Gregarious, often in large flocks; breeds in colonies.

WHITE-RUMPED SWIFT *Apus caffer*   Plate 21

Identification. 5½in, 14cm. A slimly built black swift with a sharply contrasting white rump and white throat patch; tail deeply forked and the outer pairs of tail feathers long and slender. The Horus Swift also has a white rump and a white throat but has the tail less deeply forked and the outer tail feathers are broad, not attenuated.
Voice. Low twittering call, less shrill than most swifts.
Distribution and Habitat. Locally common in East and Central Africa; a partial migrant in some areas. When breeding it takes over the mud nests of swallows, unlike the Horus Swift which nests in tunnels in earth banks and the Little Swift which builds its nests of airborne debris. Occurs in the vicinity of nesting swallows and often over inland swamps and lakes.

HORUS SWIFT *Apus horus*   Plate 21

Identification. 6in, 15cm. A thickset black swift with a white rump, forked tail and white on the throat extending on to the chest and forehead; tail not so deeply forked as White-rumped Swift and outer pairs of tail feathers broad, not attenuated.
Voice. A shrill, twittering scream, usually when in flocks at nesting colony.
Distribution and Habitat. Local resident and partial migrant from the Sudan and Ethiopia southwards to Central Africa and South Africa. Breeds in colonies in holes excavated in earth or sandy banks of rivers or cliffs. Aerial, often seen over water and in the wake of thunderstorms.

PALM SWIFT *Cypsiurus parvus*   **Plate 21**

Identification. 5in, 13cm. A very slim swift with slender wings; tail deeply forked and outer pairs of tail feathers attenuated. Pale greyish-brown, indistinctly paler on throat. Slim build and greyish-brown plumage render it easy to identify.

Voice. A very high-pitched twittering call uttered on the wing.

Distribution and Habitat. Locally common in East and Central Africa in suitable habitats where palms exist. Associated with various kinds of palms – coconut palm, borassus and dom palms in which it nests. It is especially common along the East African coast and in Malawi.

SABINE'S SPINETAIL *Chaetura sabini*   **Plate 21**

Identification. 4½in, 11½cm. A glossy blue-black swift with a white rump and white upper tail coverts which reach almost to the tip of the tail; underparts, throat and chest blue-black, breast, belly and under tail coverts white.

Voice. A high pitched call similar to that of a Palm Swift.

Distribution and Habitat. This is a rare West African and Congo forest swift, in East Africa known from the Kakamega Forest, western Kenya, and the Budongo and Bwamba Forests in western Uganda. It flies high over the tree-tops and is attracted low only when termites or some other food supply is on the wing near ground level.

MOTTLED-THROATED SPINETAIL
Telacanthura ussheri   **Plate 21**

Identification. 5½in, 14cm. In general appearance resembles a longer tailed Little Swift, with a white mottled throat and chest and a small white patch on the belly. Tips of tail feathers spiny.

Voice. Usually silent but sometimes utters a rather rasping twitter when flying near nesting site.

Distribution and Habitat. Local and uncommon in East and Central Africa; often associated with baobab trees, nesting inside hollow trees.

BOEHM'S SPINETAIL *Neafrapus boehmi*   **Plate 21**

Identification. 4in, 10cm. A very small species of spinetail with a very short tail; wings strongly angled and flight bat-like. Plumage blackish with a white rump, and white breast and abdomen.

Voice. Not recorded.

Distribution and Habitat. Like the Mottled-throated Spinetail often found in the vicinity of baobab trees in which it nests. It is a very uncommon and local species known from Kenya and Tanzania south to Malawi and Zambia and southwards.

CASSIN'S SPINETAIL *Chaetura cassini* **Plate 21**

Identification. 6in, 15cm. Not unlike a large edition of Boehm's Spinetail and like that species tail very short; wings notched and flight erratic and bat-like. Narrow white band across rump and white belly. A forest species which normally flies high but visits forest pools for drinking.
Voice. Not recorded.
Distribution and Habitat. In East Africa known only from the Budongo Forest and other forested areas in western Uganda. Uncommon and little-known.

MOUSEBIRDS or COLIES: Coliidae

The Mousebirds are a family endemic to Africa. Among their characters they are able to move the outer toes backwards or forwards; claws strong and hooked, adapted for climbing branches; plumage hair-like and lax; tail long and slender, graduated, composed of ten stiff feathers; bill thick and rather finch-like; usually found in small flocks or family parties. Their habit of climbing and running about amongst branches with their long tails pointed downwards gives them a very rodent-like appearance.

SPECKLED MOUSEBIRD *Colius striatus* **Plate 14**

Identification. 13in, 33cm. Upperparts brown; head slightly crested; sides of face greyish-white; chin and throat dusky, the feathers with pale tips giving a speckled appearance; remainder underparts tawny with brown barring on breast. In flight the bird reminds one of a tiny cock pheasant with a long brown tail.
Voice. A series of short twittering call notes and a harsher single or double 'tsssk.'
Distribution and Habitat. Resident, locally common, in East and Central Africa. Inhabits forested and wooded areas, dense scrub, and cultivation and gardens. Occurs in small parties. At times destructive to growing vegetables and fruit trees.
Allied Species. The White-headed Mousebird *(C. leucocephalus)*, 12in, 31cm, is a dry country species found in southern Somalia, Kenya and northern Tanzania. It may be distinguished from the Speckled Mousebird by its barred upperparts and white crown and crest.

BLUE-NAPED MOUSEBIRD *Colius macrourus*   **Plate 14**

Identification. 14in, 36cm. General colour greenish ash-grey; tail feathers very long and slender; head crested; turquoise-blue patch on nape; base of bill and bare face deep carmine-red. Uniform colour and blue nape patch distinguish this species.

Voice. A loud clear whistle 'peeeeee, peeeeeeeeee.'

Distribution and Habitat. Ranges from the Sudan, Ethiopia and Somalia through Uganda and Kenya to Tanzania. This is a bird of bush and arid bush country, normally found in small parties.

Allied Species. The Red-faced Mousebird *(Colius indicus)*, 13in, 33cm, differs from the Blue-naped Mousebird in being more greenish-grey above and in lacking the blue nape patch. It occurs in bush country from southern Tanzania south through Zambia and Malawi to the Zambesi River.

TROGONS: Trogonidae

The Trogons are medium-sized forest birds with long broad tails, soft plumage, brilliantly green above, vivid red on the belly; their first and second toes turned backwards. Although so brightly coloured they are easily overlooked as they remain motionless when settled.

NARINA'S TROGON *Apaloderma narina*   **Plate 16**

Identification. 12in, 30cm. Upperparts, head, throat and upper breast brilliant shining green; remainder underparts scarlet-red; inner secondaries and median wing-coverts finely vermiculated black and grey; tail dark bluish-green with outer three pairs tail feathers white. The ♀ has the throat and upper breast brown, merging to greyish-pink on chest; belly scarlet. One's first indication of a trogon is a flash of vivid green and scarlet as the bird moves from perch to perch, but when motionless, in spite of its bright colours, it is not easy to see against a background of green foliage. Birds usually single or in pairs; sometimes they are members of mixed arboreal bird parties. The Bar-tailed Trogon is smaller and darker and has the outer tail feathers barred black and white.

Voice. A rather dove-like, soft 'coo, coo' repeated over and over again. The ♂ raises and lowers the tail as it calls and this movement often gives away the bird's whereabouts.

Distribution and Habitat. Locally distributed in forested or thickly wooded areas throughout most of Africa. In East Africa occurs in rain forest, riverine forest, coastal bush and woodland and dry highland forest. In Central Africa occurs in most suitable habitats, sometimes in Brachystegia and mopane woodland.

BAR-TAILED TROGON *Apaloderma vittatum* **Plate 16**

Identification. 11in, 28cm. Smaller than Narina's Trogon and darker with the head and throat bluish-black washed with bronzy-green; chest violet and green; breast and belly deep scarlet; tail bluish-black, the three outer pairs of feathers barred black and white. ♀ has the head, throat and chest brown, otherwise similar to the ♂.
Voice. A series of clear double whistles 'klu, klu.'
Distribution and Habitat. Occurs in damp mountain forests in East Africa, Zambia and Malawi. Much less common than Narina's Trogon.

KINGFISHERS: Alcedinidae

The Kingfishers are a distinct family of small or medium-sized birds most of which are brightly coloured. Not all species prey upon fish: some feed largely upon large insects and lizards and occur in localities far from water.

GIANT KINGFISHER *Ceryle maxima* **Plate 16**

Identification. 16in, 41cm. Head crested; upperparts slate-grey finely speckled with white; below chestnut and white with black spotting or streaking; bill massive, black. ♂ has the throat and breast chestnut and the abdomen white; the ♀ has the throat and upper breast white with black markings and the lower breast and abdomen chestnut. Immature has the neck and chest mixed black and chestnut. This is the largest African kingfisher; very large size and chestnut on underparts render it a conspicuous and easily recognised species.
Voice. A loud raucous 'y, aark' or several harsh 'kee-ak, kee, ak-kee, ak' calls; also a sustained chattering call.
Distribution and Habitat. A widely distributed but very local resident throughout Ethiopian Region in small numbers. It is associated chiefly with rivers and streams where there is a fringe of trees. Occurs also on dams and lakes where these have wooded banks. In East Africa it is most frequent on mountain streams in forest. It occurs singly or in pairs. Fresh-water crabs form an important item of diet.

PIED KINGFISHER *Ceryle rudis*   Plate 17

Identification. 10in, 25cm. Head crested; plumage entirely black and white and tail relatively long; upperparts spotted and barred black and white; below white with two (♂) or one (♀) incomplete black bands.
Voice. A sharp 'keek, keek.'
Distribution and Habitat. Local resident, often common, throughout Ethiopian Region in suitable localities, except in northern Somalia. It occurs both on inland waters and on the coast. When hunting often hovers over the water in search of its prey. It is very common in Uganda where it is often seen perched on telegraph wires over water.

HALF-COLLARED KINGFISHER *Alcedo semitorquata* Plate 17

Identification. 6½in, 16½cm. A cobalt-blue kingfisher with a cinnamon breast and a blue patch on each side of the foreneck; bill black. The closely related Shining-blue Kingfisher is bright ultramarine blue above and bright chestnut below.
Voice. A shrill pipe, but bird usually silent.
Distribution and Habitat. Ranges from Ethiopia south through Kenya and Tanzania to Central Africa. An uncommon and extremely local species. Frequents streams in forest or woodland, and rivers where there is abundant vegetation along the banks.

SHINING-BLUE KINGFISHER *Alcedo quadribrachys* Plate 17

Identification. 6½–7in, 16½–18cm. An ultramarine-blue kingfisher with bright chestnut-red underparts; bill black. The similar Half-collared Kingfisher is much paler, cobalt-blue above and cinnamon below.
Voice. A shrill peeping call.
Distribution and Habitat. A Zaire forest species found in western and southwestern Uganda, western Kenya, western Tanzania and Zambia. Inhabits thickly-wooded and forested streams, rivers and lakes.

MALACHITE KINGFISHER *Alcedo cristata*   Plate 17

Identification. 5½in, 14cm. Head crested, crown feathers pale cobalt-blue barred with black; upperparts bright ultramarine blue; throat white, cheeks and underparts rufous. The Malachite Kingfisher may be recognised by its elongated crest feathers which contrast with the colour of the mantle. The Pygmy Kingfisher may be recognised in lacking a prominent crest and its crown feathers are deep ultramarine, the same colour as its back. Immature

Malachite Kingfishers have blackish bills; the bill in the adult is red.

Voice. A sharp but not very loud 'teep, teep' uttered usually when the bird flies.

Distribution and Habitat. Locally common in East and Central Africa with exception of northern Somalia. Frequents permanent inland water where there is fringing vegetation; feeds largely upon small fish and dragonfly larvae.

Allied Species. The White-breasted Kingfisher *(A. leucogaster)*, 5in, 13cm, is a small ultramarine-blue species with a dusky red bill; below, throat and belly white; band across chest and flanks bright fiery-chestnut. It inhabits swamp forest and streams in dense forest. In East Africa it is known from several forests in Uganda and there is a single record for the species from north-western Zambia.

PYGMY KINGFISHER   *Ispidina picta*   Plate 17

Identification. 4½in, 11½cm. Lacks conspicuous crest; crown and upperparts ultramarine-blue, crown barred black; sides of head and hindneck orange-rufous with lilac wash; throat white, remainder underparts orange-rufous; bill red. Lack of conspicuous head crest and general darker appearance distinguish this species from the Malachite Kingfisher.

Voice. A thin squeaky peep.

Distribution and Habitat. Local resident most of East and Central Africa. This is essentially a forest or woodland kingfisher and it is often found far from water in East African coastal bush. Its main diet consists of crickets and other insects. It does, however, also occur along wooded streams and dams where it will prey upon fish fry.

DWARF KINGFISHER   *Myioceyx lecontei*   Plate 17

Identification. 4in, 10cm. Upperparts dark ultramarine-blue; crown chestnut; forehead black; below rufous; bill flattened and squared at tip, red. The Pygmy Kingfisher differs in having a barred black and ultramarine-blue crown and the bill is not specially flattened or square tipped.

Voice. A weak but high-pitched peep.

Distribution and Habitat. In East Africa known from western Uganda where it inhabits dense forest, not always near water. Feeds largely upon crickets.

WOODLAND KINGFISHER   *Halcyon senegalensis*   Plate 17

Identification. 8in, 20cm. A medium-sized kingfisher with a very conspicuous bill which has the mandible black and the maxilla red. Upperparts greenish-blue, head greyish; below whitish to pale grey on breast; wings and wing coverts black and bright blue.

Voice. A harsh, high-pitched trilling whistle 'kee, rrrraaaah,' repeated frequently.

Distribution and Habitat. Local resident in East and Central Africa, but absent from eastern districts of Kenya and Tanzania. It is a very common and widespread bird in Uganda. It frequents savannah country and open woodlands and the margins of forests.

MANGROVE KINGFISHER   *Halcyon senegaloides*   Plate 17

Identification. 8in, 20cm. A thickset greenish-blue kingfisher, greyer on the head; underparts whitish to pale grey on breast; bill entirely red. The similar Woodland Kingfisher has a black and red bill.

Voice. A series of harsh drawn-out notes.

Distribution and Habitat. Confined to coastal districts of Kenya and Tanzania. Frequents mangrove swamps, coastal bush, open woodland and gardens.

BLUE-BREASTED KINGFISHER   *Halcyon malimbicus*   Plate 17

Identification. 10in, 25cm. Resembles a large edition of the Woodland Kingfisher but wide breast band vivid pale blue; bill black and red.

Voice. A very vocal kingfisher producing a wide range of loud, ringing whistles, followed by slower notes 'keeoo, keeoo, keeoo, keeoo.'

Distribution and Habitat. Found locally in Uganda and western Tanzania south to north-western Zambia. It is common in the Budongo Forest, western Uganda. This is a forest kingfisher, often found some distance from water.

CHOCOLATE-BACKED KINGFISHER   *Halcyon badius*   Plate 17

Identification. 8in, 20cm. Easily recognised by its deep chocolate-rufous head, back and wing-coverts; below white with a creamy-white tinge on chest; blue wing bar and blue and black tail; bill dusky red.

Voice. Produces a series of relatively slow, descending whistles.

Distribution and Habitat. A West African species found in some of the forests of central and western Uganda. Not uncommon in Budongo Forest, western Uganda. Usually seen perched above forest trails or above surface water in forest. Feeds upon frogs, lizards and large insects.

STRIPED KINGFISHER   *Halcyon chelicuti*   **Plate 17**

Identification. 6½in, 16½cm. This is one of the less brightly coloured king-fishers. Upperparts pale greyish-brown with a pale greenish-blue rump, conspicuous only when the bird is in flight. Underparts white or buffy-white, streaked dusky on breast and flanks; bill blackish, tinged red at base.
Voice. A very loud shrill trill, frequently uttered especially at dusk.
Distribution and Habitat. Common and widespread through most of East and Central Africa, but not in forest. Occurs in woodland savannah, culti-vated areas and in Brachystegia and mopane woodland. A dry country kingfisher which feeds upon lizards and large insects.

BROWN-HOODED KINGFISHER   *Halcyon albiventris*   **Plate 17**

Identification. 8–8½in, 20–22cm. A thickset, black-backed kingfisher with a greyish-brown or pale brown head, buff-tinged flanks (sometimes buff on chest) and an all-red bill. The rather similar Mangrove Kingfisher differs in having a blue-grey back.
Voice. A shrill piping call.
Distribution and Habitat. Ranges from southern Somalia south through Kenya and Tanzania to Central Africa. Local and uncommon. Inhabits wooded and savannah country often in the vicinity of rivers. Feeds largely upon insects.

GREY-HEADED KINGFISHER   *Halcyon leucocephala*   **Plate 17**

Identification. 8in, 20cm. Upperparts black with contrasting bright cobalt blue wing feathers, rump and tail; head and nape very pale grey or brownish-grey, to whitish on throat and breast; abdomen deep chestnut; bill red. This is a dry country kingfisher which feeds upon lizards and large insects. The blue of the wings and tail are very conspicuous when the bird flies. Often found in open woodland along rivers.
Voice. A weak, chattering 'ji, ji, ji-jeeee.'
Distribution and Habitat. Common locally in East and Central Africa. Fre-quents wooded areas, acacia country and dry semi-desert bush.

BEE-EATERS: Meropidae

Bee-eaters are medium-sized, slim birds of brilliant plumage; bills long and slightly decurved; legs short and wings sharply pointed; very graceful fliers. Named bee-eaters on account of their diet, made up largely of bees, wasps and hornets which the birds swallow with impunity.

MADAGASCAR BEE-EATER *Merops superciliosus* Plate 18

Identification. 11–11½in, 28–29cm. A dull green bee-eater with long central tail feathers; crown dull olive-brown; white forehead and cheek streaks; chestnut on throat; rest of underparts pale green. A much duller and browner looking bird than the Blue-cheeked Bee-eater and dark crown conspicuous in field.

Voice. A distinctive, liquid 'pruuk' not unlike that of the European Bee-eater.

Distribution and Habitat. Resident and intra-African migrant. Breeds in coastal districts of Kenya and Tanzania and occurs in East and Central Africa as an uncommon visitor. Inhabits open bush country and savannah woodlands; often roosts in mangrove swamps alongside Carmine Bee-eater.

Allied Species. The Blue-cheeked Bee-eater *(M. persicus)*, 12in, 30cm, is a winter visitor and passage migrant to East and Central Africa. It is sometimes considered to be conspecific with the Madagascar Bee-eater. It is bright green with long central tail feathers; top of head green with a bluish wash; forehead and cheeks, above and below black eye streak, blue; chin yellow to chestnut on throat. It is more often found in the vicinity of water than the Madagascar Bee-eater. The European Bee-eater *(M. apiaster)*, 11in, 28cm, is another winter visitor and passage migrant. It has yellowish-chestnut upperparts, darker on the crown; forehead white; throat yellow bordered black; breast and belly greenish-blue.

CARMINE BEE-EATER *Merops nubicus* Plate 18

Identification. 14–15in, 36–38cm. Central tail feathers very elongated; head and throat dark greenish-blue; upperparts and belly bright carmine red; rump pale cobalt-blue; wings and tail deep carmine red. This brilliant carmine-red bee-eater with its contrasting dark head is easy to recognise. Gregarious, often in large flocks, especially at roosts, and also breeds in large colonies. The Southern Carmine Bee-eater has the throat carmine-pink like the rest of the underparts.

Voice. A rather metallic, double call-note 'took, took.'

Distribution and Habitat. Resident and partial intra-African migrant from the Sudan, Ethiopia and Somalia south to northern Uganda, north-western and eastern Kenya and north-eastern Tanzania. The species is common along the Kenya coast between November and the end of March. It frequents coastal bush, savannah country and arid bush country. Numbers often concentrate around grass fires. This bee-eater has developed a special method of hunting its prey in some localities, especially in Turkana, north-western Kenya. There it is often seen using sheep and goats as animated perches, and it also perches on the back of Kori Bustards for the same purpose.

Allied Species. The Southern Carmine Bee-eater *(M. nubicoides)*, 15in, 38cm, is an even more beautiful bird than the northern species, from which it differs in having the throat as well as the rest of the underparts bright carmine pink. It is an intra-African migrant, moving between South Africa and the southern half of eastern Tanzania and to south-western Lake Victoria. In the northern part of its range it appears in April, moving southwards in September. In Zambia there are records of the species throughout the year; it breeds between September and November; in Malawi nesting takes place between August and November. The Little Green Bee-eater *(M. orientalis)*, 9in, 23cm, is golden-green with greatly elongated central tail feathers; black stripe through eye and black band across lower neck. It is a local and uncommon species in the Sudan, north-western Uganda and northern Ethiopia. Inhabits open savannah woodland and bush country.

WHITE-THROATED BEE-EATER *Merops albicollis* Plate 18

Identification. 11in, 28cm. Central tail feathers extremely long and slender, projecting 4in, 5cm, beyond others. Upperparts pale green, merging to blue on rump; crown blackish, forehead and eye-streak white; below, chin white, followed by a broad black band across throat; breast and flanks pale green to white on abdomen. In flight wings appear pale cinnamon. Its very long central tail feathers, black throat band and cinnamon wings are good field characters.

Voice. A series of soft, double twittering notes.

Distribution and Habitat. Resident and partial migrant in the Sudan, Ethiopia and Somalia south through Uganda and Kenya to central Tanzania. In East Africa mainly a passage migrant October to May, but some birds breed in Uganda and probably Kenya and Tanzania also. Frequents a variety of habitats, from forest margins to semi-desert bush country, acacia stands and savannah woodland.

BOEHM'S BEE-EATER *Merops boehmi* Plate 18

Identification. 9in, 23cm. A medium-sized green bee-eater with very long central tail feathers which are slightly spatulate at the tips; crown and throat rufous-brown; blue streak below black eye-stripe.

Voice. A soft liquid trill and single 'tssp' notes.

Distribution and Habitat. An uncommon and non-gregarious species found in southern half of Tanzania and in Central Africa. Frequents bush and woodland along streams and open woodland.

CINNAMON-CHESTED BEE-EATER
Merops oreobates   **Plate 18**
Identification. 8½in, 22cm. Central tail feathers not elongated, tail square; upperparts bright green; below, throat yellow bordered by a black throat band; breast deep cinnamon chestnut. The Blue-breasted Bee-eater is smaller and has cinnamon-chestnut confined to area immediately below blue-black throat band; also habitat is quite different.
Voice. A sharp three note 'tee-see-seep.'
Distribution and Habitat. Ranges from the southern Sudan to Ethiopia, Uganda, Kenya and northern and western Tanzania. Occurs usually in localities above 4,000ft, 1,220m. Inhabits woodlands, forests and margins of forest; often seen along roads through forest; almost always perched high off the ground on branches of trees. The Blue-breasted Bee-eater inhabits mixed grassland and bush, rarely perching in trees.

BLUE-BREASTED BEE-EATER *Merops variegatus*   **Plate 18**

Identification. 72in, 18cm. Central tail feathers not elongated, tail square. Smaller than the Cinnamon-chested Bee-eater; above bright green, throat yellow with a broad blue and black chest-band; white patch below black eye stripe conspicuous; cinnamon-chestnut below chest-band to pale greenish-buff on belly.
Voice. Loud sharp 'teeep,' similar to call of Little Bee-eater.
Distribution and Habitat. Uncommon and local in southern Sudan and Ethiopia, south through Uganda and extreme western Kenya and north-western Tanzania and Zambia. Its usual habitat is in tall grasslands or mixed grasslands and bush. The birds commonly settle on thick grass stems.

LITTLE BEE-EATER *Merops pusillus*   **Plate 18**

Identification. 6in, 15cm. Central tail feathers not elongated, tail square. A very small green bee-eater with a yellow throat, a blue-black neck patch and a conspicuous black eye-stripe. Perches near to the ground on small bushes and even grass stems. The Blue-breasted Bee-eater is larger, the throat patch below the yellow throat is deep blue, and there is a conspicuous white patch below the black eye-streak.
Voice. Usually silent, but sometimes utters a single or double squeaky 'teeep' or 'tee, tsp.'
Distribution and Habitat. Resident and partial migrant through most of East and Central Africa. Favours a variety of habitats including coastal bush, light woodland, open plains with scattered small bushes, waterside vegetation and the edges of swamps and marshes.

SOMALI BEE-EATER *Merops revoilii* Plate 18

Identification. 6½in, 16½cm. A pale green, square-tailed bee-eater with a pale cinnamon-buff breast; throat white; rump pale silvery blue, conspicuous when bird flies.

Voice. A brief, clear trill of three to five notes.

Distribution and Habitat. Local and uncommon in eastern Ethiopia and Somalia south to northern and eastern Kenya. Inhabits fairly open arid bush country; perches on bushes, usually near the ground.

WHITE-FRONTED BEE-EATER *Merops bullockoides* Plate 18

Identification. 9in, 23cm. Tail square, central feathers not elongated. Upperparts green to cinnamon on nape, hoary-white on forehead; below, throat bright red, breast and abdomen cinnamon-buff; upper and under tail coverts ultramarine blue, conspicuous in flight.

Voice. A shrill, nasal 'waark, aark' or 'waaru.'

Distribution and Habitat. A very local resident, but not uncommon where it does occur, from central Kenya to South Africa. In East Africa it is most frequent in the Rift Valley near Lakes Naivasha and Nakuru, Kenya, and in the highlands near Iringa, Tanzania. Locally common in Central Africa. It occurs in bush country and in cultivation near water in Kenya, and in scrub and on hillsides in Tanzania.

RED-THROATED BEE-EATER *Merops bulocki* Plate 18

Identification. 8½in, 22cm. A bright green, square-tailed species with a brilliant red throat; rufous on hind neck and belly. Differs from the larger White-fronted Bee-eater in having green, not frosted-white, crown.

Voice. Clear liquid trill.

Distribution and Habitat. Ranges through the southern Sudan and western Ethiopia south to northern Uganda. Inhabits open grassland savannah; partial to the banks of larger rivers and to deep eroded gullies.

BLUE-HEADED BEE-EATER *Merops mulleri* Plate 18

Identification. 7½in, 19cm. A square-tailed bee-eater with a deep chestnut back; crown and nape ultramarine blue merging to cobalt blue and white on forehead; chin with a bright scarlet streak; lower throat blue-black to deep blue on rest of underparts and tail.

Voice. A weak 'tsssssp.'

Distribution and Habitat. A very uncommon and local bird in East Africa known only from the Kakamega Forest, western Kenya. Records from Uganda need confirmation. A forest species inhabiting glades in dense forest, perching on dead branches.

BLACK BEE-EATER *Merops gularis* Plate 18

Identification. 7½in, 19cm. A square-tailed black bee-eater with a vivid scarlet throat; lower back, rump and heavy spots on underparts bright cobalt blue.
Voice. A sustained clear liquid trill, interspersed with sharp high pitched 'tssssps.'
Distribution and Habitat. A West African and Zaire species which ranges to the forests of western Uganda. Inhabits forests, usually found in the vicinity of forest swamps and streams rather than in glades.

SWALLOW-TAILED BEE-EATER *Merops hirundineus* Plate 18

Identification. 8½in, 22cm. Tail deeply forked; above and below golden-green with a bright orange-yellow throat and a blue band across base of the throat; upper and under tail-coverts blue. Species easily recognised by conspicuous forked tail.
Voice. A shrill, far-carrying 'chiree, chiree' repeated again and again.
Distribution and Habitat. Local resident in southern Sudan, south-western Ethiopia and south through western Uganda and western Tanzania to Central Africa where fairly common in Malawi but more sparsely distributed in Zambia and southwards. It occurs in savannah woodland, acacia country and Brachystegia woodland.

ROLLERS: Coraciidae

The Rollers are thickset, large-headed, medium-sized birds of bright plumage. Most species occur singly or in pairs unless migrating, when they form loose flocks. They are usually observed perched on some vantage point, such as a telegraph pole, dead branch or termite hill, whence they scan the ground for large insects and lizards which form their diet.

LILAC-BREASTED ROLLER *Coracias caudata* Plate 16

Identification. 16in, 41cm, with tail streamers. Upperparts tawny-brown or greenish-brown; rump and wing coverts ultramarine blue; throat and breast rich lilac; remainder underparts greenish-blue. In the Somali race of this roller, which also occurs in north-eastern Kenya, the lilac is reduced, being confined to a patch on the throat and foreneck. Species easily recognised by combination of lilac chest and long tail streamers. Often seen perched on telegraph poles and wires. In some lights wings show brilliant blue and black in flight.

Voice. A series of harsh chattering notes.

Distribution and Habitat. Local resident and partial intra-African migrant ranging from Somalia and Ethiopia through East and Central Africa. It occurs in woodlands, open bush country especially where there are isolated trees to serve as vantage points, and even on open plains if there are telegraph poles or fences on which it can perch.

Allied Species. The Racquet-tailed Roller *(C. spatulata)*, 16in, 41cm, with tail streamers, may be recognised by its greenish-blue underparts and spatulate-tipped tail streamers. It occurs in Brachystegia and mopane woodlands in southern Tanzania, Malawi, Zambia and southwards.

ABYSSINIAN ROLLER   *Coracias abyssinica*   Plate 16

Identification. 18in, 46cm. Plumage bright azure blue with a pale chestnut back; outer pair of tail feathers greatly lengthened to form long streamers.

Voice. Harsh, querulous 'kar, aaark' and similar calls.

Distribution and Habitat. Locally common in the southern Sudan, Ethiopia, northern Uganda and north-western Kenya. Occurs in open country, savannah woodland and bush country, nearly always where there are large termite hills in which it nests.

Allied Species. The European Roller *(C. garrulus)*, 12in, 31cm, is a common winter visitor and passage migrant in East Africa, less plentiful in Central Africa. It is similar to the Abyssinian Roller in general colour and pattern but lacks the long tail streamers and is slightly duller. It passes through eastern Kenya in very large concentrations during March and early April. Inhabits open woodland and bush country and cultivated areas. Often perches on telegraph poles and wires.

RUFOUS-CROWNED ROLLER   *Coracias naevia*   Plate 16

Identification. 13in, 33cm. This is a large and thickset species which lacks tail streamers; above olive-grey, rufous on crown and a white patch on nape; underparts rufous-brown with narrow white streaks; wings and tail blackish with a deep purple-blue gloss, conspicuous when the bird flies.

Voice. Call less harsh than most other rollers, a querulous 'kaak, kaak.'

Distribution and Habitat. Local but widespread resident and partial intra-African migrant in East and Central Africa. It occurs in wooded areas, bush country where there are scattered trees and in cultivated country. Single birds are the rule, but small parties occur when food supply (grasshoppers) is unusually plentiful.

Allied Species. The Broad-billed Roller *(Eurystomus glaucurus)*, 10in, 25cm, is a rather small thickset roller, bright vinous-chestnut and with a conspicuous yellow bill; wings blackish with a bright purplish-blue gloss noticeable in flight. Partly crepuscular in its habits, indulging in flights above tree-top level at dusk. Its call is a loud cackling chatter. It is a local resident and migrant over East and Central Africa and occurs in wooded areas, riverine forest and coastal forests. The closely related Blue-throated Roller *(E. gularis)*, 10in, 25cm, may be distinguished by its conspicuous blue throat patch and forked tail. It is a West African species which occurs in the forests of south-westen Sudan and western Uganda. Like the Broad-billed Roller it favours trees with dead branches which afford lookout posts. The Blue-bellied Roller *(Coracias cyanogaster)*, 14in, 41cm, has a distinctive colour pattern; head, neck and breast pale pinkish-grey; back black; belly deep blue; wings ultramarine with band of pale blue; tail greenish-blue, forked. Inhabits savannah woodlands in southern Sudan and north-western Uganda.

HOOPOES: Upupidae

The Hoopoes are a small group of medium-sized birds of unmistakable appearance. Plumage boldly barred pinkish-rufous, white and black, with a conspicuous crest of erectile feathers. Feed largely on the ground; ant-lion larvae are an important item of diet.

AFRICAN HOOPOE   *Upupa epops africana*   Plate 14

Identification. 11in, 28cm. Plumage bright pinkish-rufous barred black and white on upperparts; wings and tail black barred white except for primaries which are all black; long black-tipped erectile crest; bill slightly curved. Flight rather butterfly-like, slowish and undulating. European and Senegal Hoopoes differ in having a white bar across the primaries.

Voice. A low, penetrating 'hoo-hoo, hoo-hoo, hoo-hoo, hoo, hoo, hoo' which might be mistaken for the call of a dove when first heard.

Distribution and Habitat. Local resident in East and Central Africa. Occurs in bush country, savannah woodland and stands of acacia.

Allied Species. The European and Senegal Hoopoes *(U. epops)*, 11in, 28cm, which are races of the same species, may be distinguished by the white bar across the flight feathers; in the African Hoopoe the primaries are black. The European Hoopoe is a winter visitor and passage migrant in East Africa, south to southern Tanzania and Malawi; the Senegal Hoopoe is a resident in western Kenya, northern Uganda and southern Sudan.

WOOD HOOPOES and SCIMITARBILLS: Phoeniculidae

The Wood Hoopoes and Scimitarbills are medium-sized, slender birds with long graduated tails; plumage black with green, blue or purple gloss; bills long and more or less decurved. Arboreal, usually in small parties except the smaller Scimitarbills; noisy birds keeping up a constant chatter.

GREEN WOOD HOOPOE   *Phoeniculus purpureus*   Plate 14

Identification. 15–16in, 38–41cm. A slender black bird, highly glossed green above and below, with a long graduated tail, a slightly curved red bill and red legs; a white bar across wing feathers and white tips to tail feathers except central pair. Occurs in noisy family parties, climbing over tree trunks and branches and exploring cracks for insects. The Violet Wood Hoopoe is similar but is glossed with purple and violet.
Voice. A series of harsh chattering notes.
Distribution and Habitat. Locally common in East and Central Africa. Frequents various types of woodlands especially acacias.
Allied Species. The Violet Wood Hoopoe *(Ph. damarensis)*, 15in, 38cm, is very similar to the Green Wood Hoopoe, differing mainly in having the upperparts and belly glossed with violet or purple; green on throat. Occurs in stands of riverine acacias in bush country in southern Ethiopia and in Kenya. The White-headed Wood Hoopoe *(Ph. bollei)*, 14–15in, 36–38cm, has black body plumage glossed with green; wings and tail glossed purplish-blue; head white; no white markings on wings and tail. A forest species found in the southern Sudan, Uganda and western and central Kenya. The Forest Wood Hoopoe *(Ph. castaneiceps)*, 11in, 28cm, differs from the White-headed Wood Hoopoe in its smaller size and blackish bill and feet. It is found in the southern Sudan and in Uganda. The head may be either white or blackish glossed green. The Black-billed Wood Hoopoe *(Ph. somaliensis)*, 15in, 38cm, is similar to the Violet Wood Hoopoe but has a blackish bill and dusky red feet. It is found in eastern Ethiopia and Somalia south to north-eastern Kenya. The Black Wood Hoopoe *(Ph. aterrimus)*, 9in, 23cm, is a violet-black species with a white bar across the flight feathers, a dull yellow bill and blackish feet. It occurs in savannah and acacia woodland in the southern Sudan, south-western Ethiopia and northern Uganda.

AFRICAN SCIMITARBILL   *Phoeniculus cyanomelas*   Plate 14

Identification. 11in, 28cm. The Scimitarbills differ from the wood hoopoes in their very slender, greatly curved bills. The present species has the bill and legs black; plumage black glossed purple with a white bar across flight feathers and white tips to some of the tail feathers.
Voice. A low whistle 'hooee, hooee, hooee.'
Distribution and Habitat. Local resident in East and Central Africa in open woodland, savannah and bush country.

ABYSSINIAN SCIMITARBILL   *Phoeniculus minor*   Plate 14

Identification. 9in, 23cm. Plumage black, glossed purplish-blue on upper-parts; wings and tail black with violet wash, no white spots; bill strongly decurved, orange-red with a dusky tip; feet black.
Voice. Normally silent but sometimes utters a brief trill.
Distribution and Habitat. Local resident in southern Sudan, Ethiopia, Somalia, Uganda, Kenya to southern Tanzania. Inhabits dry bush country and belts of acacias along dry water courses.

HORNBILLS: Bucerotidae

The Hornbills are a very distinctive group of birds of medium or large size characterised by their large curved bills which often possess casque-like structures on the culmens. The Family has remarkable breeding habits, the female in most cases being imprisoned during incubation, plastered up in the nesting hole with mud and animal droppings brought by the male, leaving only a narrow slit through which she is fed by her mate.

GREY HORNBILL   *Tockus nasutus*   Plate 19

Identification. 18–20in, 46–51cm. General colour pale tawny-brown; head pale grey with white stripe each side of crown; breast and abdomen white; wing coverts edged whitish-buff. Bill in ♂ black with ivory-coloured stripe at base upper mandible; ♀ has dark reddish bill with ivory-white basal half to upper mandible. The Pale-billed Hornbill is distinguished by its pale dull yellowish bill.
Voice. A two note piping whistle 'phee-hoo' repeated rather slowly over and over again.
Distribution and Habitat. Locally common through East and Central Africa. This is a bush country species, usually seen in pairs or small family parties. In

Central Africa it inhabits open acacia woodland and Brachystegia woodland.
Allied Species. The Pale-billed Hornbill *(T. pallidirostris)*, 18in, 46cm, occurs in dry bush and wooded areas, including Brachystegia, from Tanzania to Malawi and Zambia and southwards. It may be distinguished from the very similar Grey Hornbill by its pale creamy-yellow bill.

RED-BILLED HORNBILL *Tockus erythrorhynchus* Plate 19

Identification. 17–18in, 43–46cm. Upperparts brownish-black with a white line down back; wing coverts spotted white; underparts white; tail, central feathers black, rest black and white except outermost which are white; bill dull red, dusky at base of lower mandible, rather slender and down-curved. The Yellow-billed Hornbill has bill rich yellow; the Crowned Hornbill has a dull red bill but upperparts and wings are black without white spots; Jackson's Hornbill has an ivory-tipped red bill in the ♂, a black bill in the ♀. Von der Decken's Hornbill is similar but has no white spots on the wings.
Voice. A continuous 'wot, wot, wot, wot, wot, wot, wot, wot, wot.'
Distribution and Habitat. A common resident in East and Central Africa frequenting dry bush country, open acacia woodland, riverine woodland and in Central Africa mopane woodland. It is one of the characteristic birds of the dry districts of Kenya and its call a common sound in the bush.

VON DER DECKEN'S HORNBILL *Tockus deckeni* Plate 19

Identification. 17–20in, 43–51cm. A white-breasted species with black wings without white spots; bill in ♂ bright red with terminal third ivory-white; ♀ smaller than ♂ and with an entirely black bill. The species may be recognised on a combination of wing and bill characters. Jackson's Hornbill has the same bill characters but has wing coverts white spotted.
Voice. A monotonous piping whistle, not unlike that of the Red-billed Hornbill – 'wek, wek, wek, wek, wek, wek, wek, wek, wek.'
Distribution and Habitat. Locally common from central Ethiopia and southern Somalia south to central Tanzania. Inhabits dry bush country and open acacia woodland.
Allied Species. Jackson's Hornbill *(T. jacksoni)*, 17–20in, 43–51cm, closely resembles Von der Decken's Hornbill but may be distinguished by its white-spotted wing-coverts. It ranges from the southern Sudan and central Ethiopia to northern Uganda and western Kenya. Inhabits bush country and woodland.

YELLOW-BILLED HORNBILL   *Tockus flavirostris*   **Plate 19**

Identification. 18–21in, 46–53cm. A white breasted hornbill with white spotted black wings and a deep orange-yellow bill. The combination of bill and wing characters render identification easy.

Voice. A yelping, piping note 'ke, ke, ke, ke, ke, ke, ke' repeated over and over again.

Distribution and Habitat. Local resident Ethiopia and Somalia south through Kenya and north-eastern Uganda to northern Tanzania; also occurs in Zambia and Malawi south to South Africa. It is a dry bush country bird in East Africa; in Central Africa it is found in acacia and mopane woodland.

HEMPRICH'S HORNBILL   *Tockus hemprichii*   **Plate 19**

Identification. 22–23in, 56–59cm. In general appearance blackish-grey with a white belly and white edgings to wing coverts and scapulars; bill dusky red, long and rather slender; tail, outer pair feathers blackish, next two pairs white, central tail feathers black. Differs from the commoner Crowned Hornbill in lacking white streaks on side of head and nape, and in having two pairs tail feathers wholly white.

Voice. A two or three note piping call.

Distribution and Habitat. Local and uncommon resident south-eastern Sudan, Ethiopia, Somalia, northern Uganda and western Kenya. Nearly always associated with rocky broken country and inland cliffs in which it nests. In Kenya not uncommon in Lake Baringo district.

CROWNED HORNBILL   *Tockus alboterminatus*   **Plate 19**

Identification. 19–20in, 48–51cm. Upperparts, wings and tail blackish-brown; white tips to tail feathers; breast and abdomen white; bill dusky red. The species may be distinguished by its dark plumage and dull red bill.

Voice. A thin piping whistle, quite unlike the calls of related hornbills.

Distribution and Habitat. Local resident through most of East and Central Africa. It frequents dry highland forest, woodlands and wooded river banks and rain forest.

Allied Species. The Pied Hornbill *(T. fasciatus)*, 19in, 48cm, is a West African forest hornbill which occurs eastwards to the southern Sudan and western Uganda. It resembles the Crowned Hornbill but may be recognised by its ivory-white bill with a reddish tip. Two other Zaire forest hornbills known from forests of western Uganda are the Red-billed Dwarf Hornbill *(T. camurus)*, 14in, 36cm, pale brown with a white belly, a bright red bill and a double white wing-bar; and the Black Dwarf Hornbill *(T. hartlaubi)*, 14in,

36cm, with black upperparts, a white streak from above eye to nape, and a red and black bill; below grey on throat to whitish on belly.

WHITE-CRESTED HORNBILL
Tropicranus albocristatus **Plate 19**

Identification. 26in, 66cm, tail 17in, 43cm. A black hornbill with an unmistakable long, graduated, white-tipped black tail; forehead to nape white, the feathers long and lax forming a crest; white tips to greater wing coverts forming a wing-bar.
Voice. A plaintive 'oo-oo-oo-oo-ah,' soft but far-carrying; also reputed to utter chicken-like squawks.
Distribution and Habitat. Another West African forest hornbill which extends eastwards to the Bwamba Forest, western Uganda. Arboreal and often associated with troops of colobus monkeys, preying upon insects disturbed by the animals.

WATTLED BLACK HORNBILL *Ceratogymna atrata* **Plate 19**

Identification. ♂ 32in, 81cm; ♀ 30in, 76cm. A large black hornbill with broad white tips to the tail feathers; bill with a high-pointed casque; bright cobalt blue neck wattles; ♀ differs in having a rufous-brown head and neck.
Voice. A loud nasal squawk and drawn-out whistles.
Distribution and Habitat. This is yet another West African hornbill which occurs in the Bwamba forest, western Uganda. The species inhabits rain forest and is much attracted to fruiting fig trees. It attracts attention by the loud swishing noise made by its wings in flight.

WHITE-TAILED HORNBILL *Bycanistes sharpii* **Plate 19**

Identification. 22–24in, 56–61cm. A relatively small black and white hornbill with an ivory-white bill with blackish patch on side; a low casque present in ♂. Plumage black on back and chest; large white wing-patch; rump, breast and abdomen white; tail, central pair of feathers black, rest white. Small size and white outer tail feathers best field characters.
Voice. A shrill, high-pitched 'keep, keep, keep, keep' and more guttural 'ark, ark, ark' noises.
Distribution and Habitat. A West African and Zaire species which extends eastwards to the Bwamba forest, western Uganda, where it is not uncommon. A forest hornbill most in evidence when figs and other trees are in fruit.
Allied Species. The White-thighed Hornbill *(B. albotibialis)*, 27–28in, 68–71cm, is a large black and white species best distinguished by its tail

pattern – entirely white with a black band across the centre; bill greyish-white and casque, in ♂, decurved and pointed; breast black, lower abdomen and thighs white. Still another West African species, recorded from forests of western Uganda, especially Bwamba and Budongo. Inhabits tree-tops, most noticeable when fig trees are fruiting.

TRUMPETER HORNBILL   *Bycanistes bucinator*   Plate 19

Identification. 24–26in, 61–66cm. This is one of the commoner large black and white hornbills with, in the ♂, well-developed casques on their bills. It may be distinguished from the Black and White-casqued Hornbill and the Silvery-cheeked Hornbill by its white breast and abdomen. In the other two species the breast is black and only the lower abdomen is white.

Voice. An assortment of loud harsh braying cries and a grunting call.

Distribution and Habitat. Local resident from southern Somalia, through Kenya and Tanzania to Zambia, Malawi and Rhodesia. Frequents thickly wooded and forest country, coastal scrub and riverine forest. It is common in the forests of the Kenya coast and is the black and white hornbill which is conspicuous in the mist forest at the Victoria Falls.

BLACK AND WHITE-CASQUED HORNBILL
Bycanistes subcylindricus   Plate 19

Identification. 27–30in, 69–76cm. The Black and White-casqued Hornbill may be recognised by the black and white casque and by its white secondaries, which form a large white wing patch, conspicuous both when the bird is settled and on the wing. The Silvery-cheeked Hornbill has an entirely dull whitish casque and its secondaries are black. The Trumpeter Hornbill is smaller and has the breast and abdomen white; its casque is flattish and dusky.

Voice. A great variety of very raucous calls 'raaak, raaak, raaak, raaak, raaak' and loud single notes such as 'raaaaak.'

Distribution and Habitat. Locally common in the southern Sudan, Uganda, western Kenya and north-western Tanzania. This is a true forest hornbill, local, but common where it occurs. In Uganda it is numerous in most of the large forests and it is also common in the Kakamega Forest, western Kenya.

SILVERY-CHEEKED HORNBILL   *Bycanistes brevis*   Plate 19

Identification. 26–29in, 66–74cm. The Silvery-cheeked Hornbill may be distinguished from the Trumpeter and Black and White-casqued Hornbills by its entirely black wings and dull white casque in the ♂. The ♀ has a less developed casque which is horn coloured like the remainder of the bill; it is best recognised by its entirely black wings.

Voice. Similar calls to those of the Black and White-casqued Hornbill, a series of loud raucous brayings and grunts.

Distribution and Habitat. Local resident from southern Ethiopia and southern Somalia south through eastern Kenya and Tanzania to Malawi. This is mainly a forest species, especially numerous in Kenya coastal forests and bush and in the mountain forests of north-eastern Tanzania. Like its near relatives it draws attention to its whereabouts by its loud calls.

GROUND HORNBILL *Bucorvus leadbeateri* Plate 19

Identification. 42in, 107cm. This species and the closely related Abyssinian Ground Hornbill are the largest of the African Hornbills; both are largely terrestrial. General plumage black with white flight feathers which are noticeable only when the bird flies. Skin of face and throat unfeathered, bright red; in ♀ throat skin red or bluish-grey. Usually encountered in pairs or family parties walking over the ground. In the distance they have a distinct resemblance to domestic turkeys.

Voice. A succession of deep lion-like grunts.

Distribution and Habitat. Very local resident in Kenya, Uganda (except in northern districts) Tanzania and Central Africa. It frequents open country, sparse woodland and in Zambia along the edges of dambos. In Kenya it is most frequent in the Rift Valley and in the Mara River area.

ABYSSINIAN GROUND HORNBILL
Bucorvus abyssinicus Plate 19

Identification. 42in, 107cm. Very similar to the Ground Hornbill but distinguished by its curious casque which is truncated and open in front; in the Ground Hornbill the casque is closed. Bare skin of face and neck mainly blue-grey or red and grey.

Voice. Deep far-carrying grunting sounds.

Distribution and Habitat. A local species found in the southern Sudan, Ethiopia, northern Somalia, northern Kenya and northern Uganda, where it is common in some areas.

BARBETS: Capitonidae

The Barbets are related to the woodpeckers and like those birds have the first and fourth toes directed backwards; thickset birds with large heads and short heavy bills; extremely variable plumage characters. Mainly fruit eaters and are often numerous in fruiting fig trees and other fruit-bearing trees and bushes.

DOUBLE-TOOTHED BARBET   *Lybius bidentatus*   Plate 22

Identification. 9in, 23cm. A large barbet, black above, with a deep crimson throat and breast; fan-shaped white patch on flanks; large ivory-coloured bill. Much attracted to fruiting fig trees. The larger Black-breasted Barbet also has an ivory bill but in this species the throat and upper breast are black, not crimson.

Voice. A rather wood hoopoe-like 'cheks, cheeeks' but often a silent bird for a barbet.

Distribution and Habitat. Local resident and probably partial migrant in search of fruiting trees. Occurs in southern Sudan and Ethiopia south to Uganda, western Kenya and north-western Tanzania. Inhabits lightly forested areas, savannah woodlands and park-like country where there are scattered fig trees. In Kenya common in the Kitale and Mt Elgon area.

Allied Species. The Black-breasted Barbet *(L. rolleti)*, 11in, 28cm, occurs in the southern Sudan and in north-western Uganda. It is an even larger species than the Double-toothed Barbet, with an ivory bill, black throat and breast and crimson belly; a tuft of black hair-like feathers on the chin. Also attracted to fruiting fig trees.

BLACK-BILLED BARBET   *Lybius guifsobalito*   Plate 22

Identification. 6in, 15cm. A black barbet with a red crown, face and throat; bill black; wing feathers with yellow edgings. The closely related Red-faced Barbet *(L. rubrifacies)* has no red on the crown or throat and the bill is greyish-white.

Voice. A loud metallic 'awk, awk, awk.'

Distribution and Habitat. A local resident in southern Sudan, Ethiopia, Uganda and western Kenya. Inhabits savannah woodlands, cultivation where there are fig trees and bush country.

RED-FACED BARBET   *Lybius rubrifacies*   Plate 22

Identification. 6in, 15cm. A black barbet with a red face and a pale greyish-white bill; wing feathers with yellow edgings. Lack of red on crown and throat distinguishes it from the Black-billed Barbet.

Voice. A low nasal 'yak' repeated several times.

Distribution and Habitat. A very uncommon species found only in south-western Uganda and north-western Tanzania. Inhabits savannah woodland and park-like country, especially where there are fig and euphorbia trees.

BLACK-COLLARED BARBET *Lybius torquatus*   Plate 22

Identification. 6in, 15cm. Upperparts finely vermiculated brown and grey; crown, face and foreneck scarlet; a black band across breast; belly pale yellowish. The combination of red face, black chest band and yellowish belly renders this species easy to identify. Often seen in pairs on the topmost branches of dead or leafless trees.

Voice. A loud, three or four note whistle, repeated several times, 'kor, kooroo – kor, kooroo.'

Distribution and Habitat. Local resident, at times common, from Zaire eastwards to Kenya, south through Tanzania to Malawi and Zambia. In Kenya most frequent in coastal forests, including Brachystegia woodlands. Otherwise frequents savannah woodlands, riverine forest and cultivation where there are fig and other fruit-bearing trees.

BROWN-BREASTED BARBET *Lybius melanopterus*   Plate 22

Identification. 6½in, 16½cm. A brown barbet with a red head and a wide pale brown band across the chest; belly white; bill ivory-white with slight blue tinge; wings and tail black. Its red head, pale bill, brown chest and white belly are characteristic.

Voice. A harsh, nasal 'aark, aark.'

Distribution and Habitat. A very local species which ranges from Somalia south through eastern Kenya and Tanzania to Malawi. It frequents open savannah woodlands, riverine forest and thick coastal scrub. It is most common in eastern Kenya where it is partial to fig trees growing along rivers such as the Tana.

BLACK-BACKED BARBET *Lybius minor*   Plate 22

Identification. 6in, 15cm. Upperparts black with a white V on the back; forehead red; below white merging to bright salmon-pink on abdomen; bill whitish.

Voice. A penetrating but not very loud 'tonk, tonk.'

Distribution and Habitat. A very uncommon and local species found in south-western Tanzania, Malawi and Zambia. Frequents edges of forests, riverine forest, thickets and rich woodland. Most frequent in the south of its range.

WHITE-HEADED BARBET   *Lybius leucocephalus*   **Plate 22**

Identification. 6–6½in, 15–16½cm, is a variable black and white barbet with a white head; several very distinct races have been described with a dark belly and dark tail, with a white tail or with underparts white and tail white. Best recognised by its white head and blackish bill.

Voice. A metallic call of two syllables; also loud 'teks.'

Distribution and Habitat. Ranges from the southern Sudan southwards through Uganda, Kenya and Tanzania to Zambia. It is a bird of savannah woodlands or cultivation where there are fig trees.

Allied Species. Vieillot's Barbet *(L. vieilloti)*, 6in, 15cm, is a striking yellow barbet with red forehead and cheeks; below yellow, speckled and blotched with red. It occurs in savannah woodland in the central and southern Sudan to northern Ethiopia; local and uncommon. The Banded Barbet *(L. undatus)*, 6in, 15cm, is a species confined to Ethiopia. Forehead red; head, neck and throat blue-black with a white stripe behind eye; mantle, rump and wing-coverts blackish with white spots; underparts yellowish-white barred with black. Occurs in woodland at medium and high altitudes.

SPOTTED-FLANKED BARBET
Tricholaema lacrymosum   **Plate 22**

Identification. 5in, 13cm. Crown, mantle and throat blue-black with a white stripe above the eye and another from the bill running along side of neck; breast and abdomen yellowish-white with drop-like black spots along flanks.

Voice. A series of metallic clinking notes.

Distribution and Habitat. Local resident, sometimes common, in the southern Sudan, Uganda, Kenya and Tanzania. Occurs mainly in acacia woodland and scrub.

Allied Species. The Brown-throated Barbet *(T. melanocephalum)*, 5in, 13cm, is a dry bush country species found in the Sudan, Ethiopia, Somalia, Kenya and Tanzania. Upperparts brown streaked yellow on back and rump and flight feathers edged yellow; throat brown (or black) with rest of underparts white with a few brown or red tipped feathers in the centre of the breast. The Hairy-breasted Barbet *(T. flavipunctatum)*, is a larger, 6½in, 16½cm, thickset species, with dark upperparts thickly spotted with yellow and with two conspicuous white stripes on the face, above and below the eye; underparts yellowish-green, streaked and spotted black and with the terminations of the breast feathers long and hair-like. It is a rain forest species recorded from the south-western Sudan, Uganda and the Kakamega Forest in Kenya.

RED-FRONTED BARBET   *Tricholaema diadematum*   **Plate 22**

Identification. 5in, 13cm. Upperparts blackish-brown with yellow streaks and yellow edging to feathers of wings and tail; forehead bright red; yellow stripe above eye; below yellowish-white, more or less spotted with brown.
Voice. A plaintive, rather drawn-out 'twa, twa, twa, twa' or a harsh double note 'ki, waa.'
Distribution and Habitat. Locally common resident southern Sudan and southern Ethiopia, Uganda, Kenya and northern half Tanzania. The species inhabits acacia woodland, scrub and dry bush country.

GREY-THROATED BARBET   *Gymnobucco bonapartei*   **Plate 22**

Identification. 7in, 18cm. Whole bird dusky brown except head and neck which are ashy-grey; two bristle tufts (like tufts from a toothbrush) at base of bill around nostrils. These bristle tufts, and the bird's white eye, are conspicuous in the field and render this species easy to identify.
Voice. A long-drawn-out 'hooooo' or 'chooooo,' difficult to locate unless the bird is perched in a dead tree. When feeding it is usually completely silent, its presence indicated by falling figs.
Distribution and Habitat. Local resident in forest areas in the southern Sudan, Uganda and western Kenya.
Allied Species. Whyte's Barbet *(Buccanodon whytii)*, 6in, 15cm, occurs locally in wooded areas and Brachystegia woodland in southern Tanzania and in Central Africa. It is brown, blackish on the hind crown and chest; forehead and curved band below eye pale greenish-yellow; flight feathers edged with white.

WHITE-EARED BARBET   *Gymnobucco leucotis*   **Plate 22**

Identification. 6in, 15cm. This is a blackish-looking barbet with a white belly and a conspicuous white streak down each side of the neck; rump white, noticeable when the bird flies away from the observer.
Voice. A three note 'ko, ko, ko' and a short shrill trill.
Distribution and Habitat. An evergreen forest species found locally in Kenya, Tanzania, Malawi, Rhodesia and Angola. In East Africa the species is common in forest on the Chyulu Hills, south-eastern Kenya and on Mt Kilimanjaro, Tanzania.
Allied Species. The Green Barbet *(Buccanodon olivaceum)*, 6in, 15cm, is a uniformly-coloured dark olive-green species with a dusky head. It occurs in coastal forests of Kenya, eastern Tanzania and in Malawi.

YELLOW-SPOTTED BARBET   *Buccanodon duchaillui*   **Plate 22**

Identification. 6in, 15cm. Upperparts black, heavily spotted yellow; crown deep crimson; underparts mottled black and yellow.
Voice. A deep, far-carrying trill.
Distribution and Habitat. An uncommon and very local barbet in western and southern Uganda and western Kenya. Inhabits forest tree-tops and is easily overlooked until one can recognise its call. Much attracted to fruiting fig trees.

MOUSTACHED GREEN TINKERBIRD
Pogoniulus leucomystax   **Plate 22**

Identification. 3½in, 9cm. General colour olive-green, slightly more greyish on underparts; a whitish stripe from base of bill down sides of neck. This tiny barbet is a tree-top haunter and difficult to observe, but is sometimes seen at clumps of Loranthus (a parasitic mistletoe) the berries of which form an important item of diet. The whitish moustache stripe is fairly conspicuous through glasses.
Voice. A monotonous 'tink, tink, tink, tink' repeated over and over again; also utters a shrill trill.
Distribution and Habitat. A local but sometimes common resident in mountain forest from central Kenya south to Malawi and eastern Zambia. In East Africa it is most numerous in the forests of the western highlands around Molo, Kenya.
Allied Species. The Green Tinkerbird *(P. simplex)*, 3in, 8cm, is found in the coastal forests of Kenya, south through eastern Tanzania to southern Malawi. It differs from the Moustached Green Tinkerbird in lacking the whitish moustache stripe. The Western Green Tinkerbird *(P. coryphaea)*, 3½in, 9cm, is a West African species which reaches western Uganda forests; it is black above with a broad yellow streak from the crown to the rump; wing feathers edged yellow; underparts grey. The Speckled Tinkerbird *(P. scolopaceus)*, 4in, 10cm, is another West African species which occurs in the forests of Uganda and western Kenya. Upperparts brown speckled with yellow; below mottled greenish-yellow and brown. It has the habit of creeping about branches of high forest trees in the manner of a woodpecker.

RED-FRONTED TINKERBIRD   *Pogoniulus pusillus*   **Plate 22**

Identification. 3½in, 9cm. Upperparts blackish, heavily streaked pale yellow or white; rump yellow; forehead bright scarlet; below pale greenish-buff. This is a common dry-country bird; its red forehead is conspicuous in the field. The

Red-fronted Barbet, which occurs alongside this species, is a much larger bird with a heavy bill.

Voice. A shrill, slow trill.

Distribution and Habitat. Local resident, often common, from Ethiopia and Somalia south to the northern half of Tanzania. In western Kenya and Uganda and southwards its place is taken by the Yellow-fronted Tinkerbird. The Red-fronted Tinkerbird occurs in bush and acacia woodland; it is often numerous in acacia woodland along rivers and wadis.

Allied Species. The Yellow-fronted Tinkerbird *(P. chrysoconus)*, 3½in, 9cm, differs mainly in having the forehead yellow. It occurs in the southern Sudan, Uganda, western Kenya, western and southern Tanzania and in Central Africa. Inhabits savannah woodland, scrub and bush and in Central Africa Brachystegia woodland.

GOLDEN-RUMPED TINKERBIRD
Pogoniulus bilineatus   **Plate 22**

Identification. 4in, 10cm. Upperparts glossy black with a bright golden-yellow rump; conspicuous white stripes above and below eye; black moustache stripe; underparts pale grey to pale greenish on belly. The Yellow-throated Tinkerbird has yellow stripes above and below eye and the throat is yellow.

Voice. A monotonous 'tink' uttered again and again with an interval of a few seconds between notes.

Distribution and Habitat. A local resident in forests from Uganda and Kenya south to Natal, South Africa. It occurs in rain forest, highland dry forest, coastal woodland and scrub and evergreen forest.

Allied Species. The Yellow-throated Tinkerbird *(P. subsulphureus)*, 4in, 10cm, occurs in western and central Uganda in forests. Its facial stripes are yellow, not white, and it has a yellow chin. The Red-rumped Tinkerbird *(P. atroflavus)*, 5in, 13cm, looks like a large edition of the Golden-rumped Tinkerbird but with a scarlet, not yellow, rump patch. It is known from the Bwamba Forest, western Uganda. The Lemon-rumped Tinkerbird *(P. leucolaima)*, 4in, 10cm, may be conspecific with the Golden-rumped Tinkerbird from which it differs mainly in having a lemon-yellow rump. It occurs in Uganda, western Kenya and western Tanzania in forest and woodland.

YELLOW-BILLED BARBET *Trachylaemus purpuratus*   **Plate 22**

Identification. 9in, 23cm. A rather long-tailed forest treetops barbet, shiny black above; forehead and throat greyish with deep crimson tips to the feathers; belly mottled yellow and black; bare face and bill yellow, conspicuous in field.

Voice. A deep frog-like croaking, followed by sharp clinking notes.

Distribution and Habitat. Local and uncommon forest bird in the southern Sudan, Uganda, western Kenya and north-western Tanzania. Very elusive until its call notes are recognised.

LEVAILLANT'S BARBET *Trachyphonus vaillantii* Plate 22

Identification. 8½in, 22cm. This is one of the several brightly coloured 'ground barbets' which occur in bush country and woodland and which are associated with termite hills into which they burrow to nest. The present species has a short black crest, a black nape and mantle; head and throat bright yellow heavily mottled with crimson; a white-spotted black band across chest; remainder of underparts bright yellow with scarlet streaks on breast. The Red and Yellow Barbet has white-spotted upperparts and no red streaks on the breast.

Voice. A curious churring, trilling song which has been likened to that of a nightjar; also utters a clinking call.

Distribution and Habitat. Local resident Tanzania, south through Malawi and Zambia to South Africa. It is a bird of bush country and dry woodlands where there are thickets, dead trees and termite hills.

RED AND YELLOW BARBET
Trachyphonus erythrocephalus Plate 22

Identification. 9in, 23cm. Another brightly coloured 'ground barbet.' This is a striking yellow and red bird with upperparts, wings and tail black, heavily spotted with round white spots. At first sight it may give the impression of a gaudily coloured woodpecker and like a woodpecker it has an undulating flight. The underparts are bright pale yellow, washed with orange on the chest, with a narrow white-spotted black band across the upper breast; the ♂ has a black streak down the centre of the throat.

Voice. A loud and unmistakable 'toogel-de-doogle' repeated over and over, often by several birds in chorus.

Distribution and Habitat. A local resident Ethiopia, Somalia, Kenya and north-eastern Tanzania. Frequents semi-arid bush country and open thornbush areas, favouring localities where there are termite hills in which it breeds. It is widely distributed and common in many parts of the Northern Frontier Province of Kenya.

Allied Species. The Yellow-breasted Barbet *(T. margaritatus)*, 8in, 20cm, differs from Red and Yellow Barbet in having the sides of the head, throat and breast lemon-yellow with a black patch at base of neck; narrow breast-band mottled red, black and white. ♀ has no black neck patch. Occurs in the Sudan, Ethiopia and Somalia in arid bush country.

D'ARNAUD'S BARBET   *Trachyphonus darnaudii*   Plate 22

Identification. 6½in, 16½cm. Upperparts brown with whitish spots on back, wings and tail; crown black spotted with yellow; sides of face yellow, spotted black; underparts pale sulphur-yellow spotted with black on the throat and breast. Some races have the crown completely black and extensive black on throat and chest. It is possible that some of the populations of this barbet should be classified as full species rather than races.

Voice. Birds call in chorus, two or more facing one another and uttering a loud four or five note song 'doo, do, dee, dok' over and over again.

Distribution and Habitat. Local resident, sometimes very common, from the southern Sudan, southern Ethiopia and Somalia, southwards through Uganda and Kenya to south-western Tanzania. Mainly a bird of dry bush country and open thornbush country. Nests at the bottom of a hole excavated in flat ground. The species is especially common in the Lake Baringo area, Kenya.

HONEYGUIDES: Indicatoridae

A family of rather small birds, 4–8in, 10–20cm long, of sombre brown, olive, grey and white plumage. All species have a considerable amount of white in their three outer pairs of tail feathers, a conspicuous field character when the birds are in flight. They are parasitic in their nesting habits, laying their eggs in the nests of birds such as bee-eaters, barbets and woodpeckers. Honeyguides feed largely upon bees' wax and bee larvae and are often encountered near native bee-hives hung in trees. They can be attracted by nailing lumps of bees' comb to tree trunks. The Greater Honeyguide has developed a most remarkable habit of guiding human beings to the nests of wild bees in order to feed upon the honeycomb and grubs when the nest is chopped out.

GREATER or BLACK-THROATED HONEYGUIDE
Indicator indicator   Plate 23

Identification. 8in, 20cm. Upperparts greyish-brown, below dusky-white; throat black in adult ♂; yellow patch on shoulders not usually observed in field; bill of adult bright pink; outer three pairs of tail feathers mainly white, conspicuous in flight. Species remarkable in having a distinct immature

plumage in which white underparts are washed with orange-buff on neck and chest. Best identified by size, pink bill of adult and black throat of adult ♂.
Voice. A very distinct two note call 'weet-eer' repeated every few seconds. Birds have special calling places where they sit at intervals for weeks on end. When trying to draw attention to a bees' nest the birds have an excited chattering call 'ke, ke, ke, ke, ke, ke, ke, ke, ke.'
Distribution and Habitat. A widespread resident, but not common, in East and Central Africa. Occurs in a variety of habitats, including margins of rain forest, in highland dry forest, cultivation where there are trees, arid thorn-bush and acacia woodland.

LESSER HONEYGUIDE   *Indicator minor*   **Plate 23**

Identification. 5½in, 14cm. Upperparts dull olive-green, below pale grey to whitish on belly; bill short and stumpy; three outer pairs of tail feathers mainly white which are very conspicuous when the bird flies.
Voice. A continuous, monotonous 'pew, pew, pew' with an occasional interval.
Distribution and Habitat. A common and widespread species through most of East and Central Africa. Occurs in a variety of habitats from forest, savannah woodland and cultivation to acacia woodland and bush country. Often overlooked as it is conspicuous only in flight when attention is aroused by its white tail feathers.

THICK-BILLED HONEYGUIDE   *Indicator conirostris*   **Plate 23**

Identification. 6in, 15cm. A honeyguide with bright olive-green upperparts with darker streaks on mantle and wings; below grey, darker than in Lesser Honeyguide, with blackish streaks sometimes present on throat; bill noticeably thick and heavy.
Voice. A rather sharp 'tssp-tssp.'
Distribution and Habitat. A very local and uncommon honeyguide known from Uganda and western Kenya, where recorded from Mt Elgon and the Kakamega Forest. Inhabits forests; sometimes observed at wild bees' nests.
Allied Species. Most remarkable of the honeyguides is the Lyre-tailed Honeyguide *(Melichneutes robustus)*, 8in, 20cm, which has the inner tail feathers black and curved outwards giving the tail a lyrate shape; short outer rectrices white. The bird has a remarkable aerial display, undulating and spiraling high above the forest then curving downwards to land in the tree-tops. During this descent it produces a nasal tooting and a sound similar to that of a snipe in aerial display. It is known in East Africa only from the Bwamba forest, western Uganda. The Least Honeyguide *(Indicator exilis)*, 4½in, 11cm, is another forest species which occurs in Uganda, western Kenya and

southwards to north-western Zambia. In appearance it is a miniature of the Thick-billed Honeyguide. Even smaller is Chapin's Least Honeyguide *(I. pumilio)*, 4in, 10cm, with a dark malar stripe and medium grey underparts with faint dusky streaking; a forest species known in the forests of Uganda and Kakamega in Kenya. A third forest species, known from western Uganda, is Willcock's Honeyguide *(I. willcocksi)*, 4½in, 11cm, which is best distinguished by its lack of a malar stripe and in having the grey underparts washed with green. Two very small honeyguides found in bush and acacia country are the Pallid Honeyguide *(I. meliphilus)*, 4in, 10cm, also without a malar stripe and with very pale greyish underparts; it occurs in Kenya, Tanzania and Zambia. The second species the Narok Honeyguide *(I. narokensis)*, 3½in, 9cm, also lacks a malar stripe and has pale underparts with a trace of dusky streaking; it occurs in bush country of both western and eastern Kenya.

SPOTTED HONEYGUIDE *Indicator maculatus* Not illustrated

Identification. 7½in, 19cm. An olive-green honeyguide with round yellowish-green spots over chest to belly. Immature birds have underparts streaked not spotted.

Voice. A curious mewing call, just like the sound produced by a small kitten.

Distribution and Habitat. A West African species found in a few forests in western Uganda. Inhabits dense rain forest where it usually keeps to the high tree-tops.

Allied Species. The Scaly-throated Honeyguide *(I. variegatus)*, 7½in, 19cm, is more greyish above than the Spotted Honeyguide and may be distinguished by the scaly appearance of the throat and chest. It occurs in acacia woodland and in riverine woodland in East and Central Africa: local and uncommon.

(Plate 23) Wahlberg's Honeyguide *(Prodotiscus regulus)*, 4in, 10cm. Three members of the genus *P.* occur in East Africa; all have the bill slender and pointed. The present species is greyish-brown to whitish on the abdomen; three outer pairs of tail feathers mainly white. The field appearance suggests a Dusky Flycatcher with much white in the tail. The other two species are both green-backed. Cassin's Honeyguide *(P. insignis)*, 3½in, 9cm, with bright green upperparts and dark grey underparts occurs in western Kenya and Uganda in forests. The Zambezi Honeyguide *(P. zambesiae)*, 3½in, 9cm, is dull olive above with pale grey underparts. It occurs in woodland areas from eastern Kenya south to Zambia. The very rare Zenker's Honeyguide *(Melignomon zenkeri)*, 5in, 13cm, is also slender-billed; dull olive-brown, paler below; also with white in the outer tail feathers. In general appearance it looks like a small greenbul. It has been recorded once in the Bwamba Forest, western Uganda.

WOODPECKERS: Picidae

This is a family of chisel-billed, wood-boring birds with powerful feet (two toes directed forwards, two backwards) and stiff tails which act as props in climbing tree trunks and branches; flight undulating. Woodpeckers nest in holes which they excavate in trees.

RED-BREASTED WRYNECK   *Jynx ruficollis*   Plate 23

Identification. 6in, 15cm. This is a woodpecker-like bird but lacks the pointed stiff tail feathers of the true woodpeckers, its rectrices being soft and rounded. General pattern nightjar-like, brownish-grey marbled, speckled and vermiculated with white and dark brown; blackish line down centre of crown and mantle; throat and upper breast deep chestnut-brown.
Voice. A sharp 'kee, kee, kee, kee, kee' not unlike the call of a kestrel.
Distribution and Habitat. Local and uncommon in East Africa south to Malawi and Zambia where it is rare. It frequents dead timber and stands of acacia woodland and in silhouette looks remarkably like a weaver-bird.
Allied Species. The European Wryneck *(J. torquilla)*, 5½in, 14cm, is an uncommon winter visitor to east Africa as far south as northern Tanzania. It is smaller and lacks the rufous chest of the African bird.

NUBIAN WOODPECKER   *Campethera nubica*   Plate 23

Identification. 7in, 18cm. Upperparts olive-grey, spotted and indistinctly banded yellowish; crown and nape scarlet, the ♀ with crown black with white spots; below creamy-white with round black spots on breast and flanks; ♂ with red malar stripe, ♀ with black stripe; shafts of tail feathers yellowish. The red on the head and the golden tail are conspicuous in the field. The Golden-tailed Woodpecker is greener above with black streaks on underparts, not round spots.
Voice. A loud and far-carrying 'cing, cing, cing, cing,' almost a metallic yaffling call, difficult to describe in words but not easily forgotten when once heard.
Distribution and Habitat. Local resident from the Sudan, Ethiopia and Somalia south through Uganda and Kenya to northern Tanzania. A bird of open bush and acacia woodland, often common.
Allied Species. Bennett's Woodpecker *(C. bennettii)*, 8in, 20cm, is greenish above with dark and pale barring; underparts yellowish-white with black spots; crown red in ♂; the ♀ has a white spotted black crown and a red nape, chocolate malar stripe and chocolate throat patch. This is an uncommon

woodpecker found in woodland and savannah bush in Tanzania, Malawi, Zambia and southwards. The Spotted-throated Woodpecker *(C. scripto-ricauda)*, 7in, 18cm, is another ladder-backed greenish woodpecker with spotted underparts, closely resembling a Nubian Woodpecker from which it may be distinguished by its black spotted throat. It is found in Brachystegia woodland in the Morogoro district, Tanzania. Another rare Tanzania woodpecker is Stierling's Woodpecker *(C. stierlingi)*, 6in, 15cm, with uniform olive-brown upperparts and a black nape patch; crown of ♂ red, ♀ olive-brown; underparts greenish-white streaked and barred with black. It occurs in south-western Tanzania.

GOLDEN-TAILED WOODPECKER
Campethera abingoni   **Plate 23**

Identification. 7in, 18cm. Similar to Nubian Woodpecker but differs in having black streaks not round spots on the underparts.
Voice. A sustained laughing call 'waa, waa, waa, waa.'
Distribution and Habitat. Ranges from southern Sudan and southern Somalia southwards through eastern and south-western Kenya through Tanzania to Central Africa. Inhabits woodland, especially Brachystegia and coastal woodland. Rather uncommon and local.

LITTLE SPOTTED WOODPECKER
Campethera cailliautii   **Plate 23**

Identification. 6½in, 16½cm. Bright green upperparts, spotted with yellowish-white; crown scarlet in ♂, in ♀ crown black with white spots, nape scarlet; below yellowish white spotted with black.
Voice. A high-pitched 'tee, tee, tee, tee.'
Distribution and Habitat. Of wide distribution in southern Uganda, southern Kenya and Tanzania to Central Africa. Inhabits woodlands, savannah country and in coastal districts often seen in coconut plantations.
Allied Species. The Fine-spotted Woodpecker *(C. punctuligera)*, 7in, 18cm, is similar to a Nubian Woodpecker in general appearance but has much finer spotting above and below. It is a rare species known from the Bahr-el-Ghazel area of the Sudan. The Golden-backed Woodpecker *(C. abyssinicus)*, 6in, 15cm, is bright golden-green on the mantle and bright red on the rump and upper tail coverts; below whitish with short dark streaks; ♂ has the crown red, ♀ greyish-brown. Another rare woodpecker known only from the highlands of Ethiopia.

FINE-BANDED WOODPECKER
Campethera taeniolaema **Plate 23**

Identification. 7in, 18cm. Upperparts bright olive-green; crown and nape crimson (crown white-spotted in ♂); underparts pale yellow, closely barred olive-green. It may be distinguished by its unbarred green mantle and closely barred underparts.

Voice. Usually a silent bird, but sometimes utters a series of typical woodpecker 'yaffling' notes.

Distribution and Habitat. A bird of highland forest known from the southern Sudan, Uganda, western and central Kenya and northern Tanzania. It is usually seen on dead trees on the edge of forest and in forest clearings. It is most frequent in the forests of the western highlands of Kenya around Molo.

Allied Species. The closely related Green-backed Woodpecker *(C. permista)*, 6in, 15cm, is known from the forests of the southern Sudan, western Uganda and south-western Ethiopia. It may be recognised by its black-spotted, not barred, face and greenish underparts barred with black.

BROWN-EARED WOODPECKER   *Campethera caroli*   **Plate 23**

Identification. 7½in, 19cm. Upperparts golden-olive without markings; crown dark olive with crimson streaks in the ♂; below olive with dense round yellowish-white spots; ear-coverts and band down side of neck maroon-brown.

Voice. A silent bird; no call recorded.

Distribution and Habitat. A local forest species known from the southern Sudan, Uganda, western Kenya and north-western Tanzania. A rain forest woodpecker which usually keeps high in the tree-tops.

BUFF-SPOTTED WOODPECKER   *Campethera nivosa*   **Plate 23**

Identification. 5½in, 14cm. A bright olive-green woodpecker without markings on back; crown of male brown with a red band on the nape; ♀ lacks red on crown and nape; below, throat yellowish-white with olive streaks, breast and belly olive with round yellowish spots.

Voice. Mainly silent but sometimes utters a soft, metallic 'ting, ting, ting.'

Distribution and Habitat. An uncommon species in East Africa, recorded from the southern Sudan, Uganda and from the Kakamega Forest, western Kenya. Inhabits forest, where it may be found both in the tree-tops and in heavy undergrowth near the ground.

CARDINAL WOODPECKER   *Dendropicos fuscescens*   Plate 23

Identification. 5in, 13cm. A small woodpecker with the upperparts barred blackish-brown and yellowish; forehead brown; crown and nape scarlet in ♂, dark brown in ♀; below dusky or greenish white, streaked blackish on breast and flanks. This is the commonest and most widespread of the small woodpeckers, distinguished by its laddered back and streaked underparts.
Voice. A rather brief trilling call.
Distribution and Habitat. Resident, often common, through East and Central Africa; occurs also in West and South Africa. Frequents a great variety of country from arid bush to woodlands and forests. Often found in pairs and as members of mixed bird parties.
Allied Species. The Uganda Spotted Woodpecker *(D. poecilolaemus)*, 5in, 13cm, resembles a pale Cardinal Woodpecker but may be distinguished by having the neck and chest finely speckled black, not streaked. It occurs in the southern Sudan, Uganda and western Kenya. The uncommon Brown-backed Woodpecker *(Ipophilus obsoletus)*, 5in, 13cm, occurs locally in East Africa, south to northern Tanzania. It favours country where there are many isolated fig trees. It may be distinguished from the Cardinal Woodpecker in having the mantle plain ash-brown, not laddered, and the fore half of the crown brown with red on the hind crown in the ♂ only. The Gabon Woodpecker *(D. gabonensis)*, 5½in, 14cm, has bright olive-green upperparts, yellow below with heavy black streaking; crown and nape scarlet in the ♂, dark brown in the ♀. It is a West African forest species known in East Africa only from the Bwamba Forest, western Uganda.

GREY WOODPECKER   *Mesopicos goertae*   Plate 23

Identification. 7in, 18cm. Head and underparts grey, often with a red streak down centre of belly; crown scarlet in ♂, grey in ♀; mantle golden-green, unbarred, with a contrasting red rump and upper tail coverts. Lack of barring or streaking and combination of grey head and belly, golden-green back and red rump render this species easy to identify.
Voice. A three note, metallic 'yaffle.'
Distribution and Habitat. Occurs from West Africa eastwards to Ethiopia, southwards through Uganda and Kenya to northern Tanzania. Inhabits open woodlands, cultivated areas where there are trees and acacia woodland. It is a common species in the Kenya Highlands.

OLIVE WOODPECKER   *Mesopicos griseocephalus*   Plate 23

Identification. 7–7½in, 18–19cm. General colour golden olive-green, unmarked above and below, with a grey head; upper tail coverts and streak in centre of belly deep wine-red; crown of ♂ streaked deep crimson, ♀ crown grey. The related Grey Woodpecker has the breast grey, not olive-green, and ♂ has bright red crown.

Voice. A churring call, 'chi-r-r-r-ee.'

Distribution and Habitat. A local and uncommon woodpecker found at altitudes over 6,000ft, 1,830m, in western Uganda, the highlands of Tanzania and Zambia and Malawi. A mountain forest bird found both in the tree-tops and near the ground.

YELLOW-CRESTED WOODPECKER
Mesopicos xantholophus   **Plate 23**

Identification. 8½in, 22cm. A large rather thickset woodpecker; uniform dark olive mantle; crown black, streaked especially towards the nape with yellow in ♂; underparts dark olive with round whitish spots; chin white.

Voice. A shrill churring 'pirit,' often repeated several times; but generally a silent bird.

Distribution and Habitat. A local and uncommon resident in the southern Sudan, Uganda and the Kakamega Forest, western Kenya. Inhabits forests where it keeps mainly to the tree-tops.

Allied Species. Elliot's Woodpecker *(M. elliotii)*, 6½in, 16½cm, is a slim woodpecker with a bright green back and the front half of the crown black; hind crown and nape scarlet in ♂, black in ♀; underparts pale greenish yellow with black streaks. A rain forest woodpecker recorded in western Uganda, where it is most frequent in the Bwamba Forest and the Mpanga Forest near Fort Portal.

BEARDED WOODPECKER *Thripias namaquus*   **Plate 23**

Identification. 9in, 23cm. A large, dusky-looking woodpecker with a conspicuous red nape patch in ♂, black in ♀. Upperparts dusky olive-brown, barred and spotted white; black streak on each side of throat; centre of throat white; rest of underparts finely barred and mottled olive-grey or blackish and white.

Voice. A series of loud, harsh 'yaffling' calls.

Distribution and Habitat. Widely distributed and locally common in East and Central Africa. Frequents highland forest areas, woodlands and especially acacia woodlands. In Central Africa occurs chiefly in acacia and drier woodlands, less frequent in Brachystegia woodlands.

Allied Species. The African Peculet *(Verreauxia africana)*, 3in, 8cm, is a diminutive species in East Africa known from the Bwamba Forest, Uganda.

Upperparts golden-olive, below grey; bare skin around eye maroon-red; ♂ has red-brown frontal patch. Species lives in forest undergrowth within a few feet of the ground. Its tiny size and bare red skin around eye renders identification easy.

BROADBILLS: Eurylaimidae

This is mainly an Asiatic Family with a few species in Africa. They are flycatcher-like in their general appearance and may be recognised by their large and very broad bills.

AFRICAN BROADBILL   *Smithornis capensis*   Plate 23

Identification. 5in, 13cm. Upperparts brown or olive-brown, streaked black; crown black in ♂, grey in ♀; feathers of lower back and rump with white bases, sometimes puffed out, at other times hidden by the scapular feathers; underparts creamy-white, streaked black on chest and flanks; bill very large and broad, black above, pink below. Bird usually sits on a horizontal branch or vine, from which it makes remarkable circular flights around its perch, displaying as it does so the white on its back and rump.

Voice. A strange high-pitched, vibrating sound, almost like a klaxon horn – 'rrrrrrrrrrrrrrrrrrrrrr' produced either during the bird's circular flight or while it is at rest.

Distribution and Habitat. Locally distributed in small numbers from West Africa eastwards to Uganda and Kenya, south through Tanzania to Central Africa and South Africa. Frequents forested areas, bamboo forest and dense forest and scrub along rivers.

Allied Species. The Red-sided Broadbill *(S. rufolateralis)*, 4½in, 11½cm, may be recognised by rufous patches on each side of the chest. It is a West African forest species which extends eastwards to the forests of western Uganda. Grauer's Green Broadbill *(Pseudocalyptomena graueri)*, 4½in, 11½cm, is known in East Africa only in the Impenetrable-Kayonza forests of south-western Kigezi, Uganda. It is bright green with a pale blue face, throat and chest and a black line above the eye; crown greenish-buff with black spots. This, one of the rarest birds in Africa, occurs in bamboo and mixed bamboo and montane forest.

PITTAS: Pittidae

A group of brilliantly coloured forest birds of thrush size; legs long, tails very short; terrestrial; very shy and seldom observed alive in the wild state.

AFRICAN PITTA *Pitta angolensis* **Plate 23**

Identification. 7in, 18cm. A plump thrush-sized bird with dark green upperparts; crown black with a broad olive-buff stripe on each side; rump and spots on wing coverts brilliant pale verditer blue; throat pale pink, breast buff; abdomen and under tail-coverts deep carmine-red. Owing to its retiring habits this is a bird not often seen. Usually the most one sees is a fleeting glimpse as it is disturbed from the forest floor, when the impression is of a dark bird with a good deal of bright pale blue and carmine red.

Voice. A deep short trill, followed by a sharp flap of the wings.

Distribution and Habitat. Occurs as a breeding bird in central Tanzania south to the Zambesi river and Transvaal. In non-breeding season migrates by night to Zaire, northern Tanzania, Kenya and Uganda. Migrating birds sometimes attracted by lights and consequently picked up in various unlikely places. Inhabits forest areas and very dense scrub.

Allied Species. The Green-breasted Pitta *(P. reichenowi)*, 6½in, 16½cm, differs in having a green breast and a black patch on the throat. It is a West African forest species which extends into Uganda, where it is most frequent in the Budongo Forest.

LARKS: Alaudidae

A group of ground-living song birds: often gregarious in non-breeding season. Hind claw often elongated and more or less straight. Build usually heavier and bills more robust than pipits and wagtails which are also terrestrial in their habits.

RUFOUS-NAPED LARK *Mirafra africana* **Plate 24**

Identification. 6–7in, 15–18cm. Rufous or greyish-brown above with very distinct black centres to the feathers; nape more or less rufous but in Kenya highlands race *athi* rufous absent; wings large and rounded, mainly rufous, conspicuous in flight; below buff with black markings on chest; tail relatively short for size of the bird. The Red-winged Bush Lark is larger, has a longer tail, and habitually perches on the tops of small bushes.

Voice. Song uttered from post, termite hill or small bush; a clear whistle of four or five notes 'cee-wee-wee, cheee, weee' repeated over and over again.

Distribution and Habitat. The Sudan, south through Kenya and Uganda to Central Africa and South Africa. Locally common in many places especially Kenya and Uganda. Occurs in open plains and grassy bush country.

Allied Species. The Collared Lark *(M. collaris)*, 5in, 13cm, is a bright rufous lark with white streaking and edging to feathers of upperparts; underparts

Continued after colour plates on page 256

The Colour Plates

Plate 1 GREBES, PELICANS, CORMORANTS AND DARTER

1 WHITE PELICAN *Pelecanus onocrotalus*
Plumage white or pinkish-white; immature brownish-white.

2 PINK-BACKED PELICAN *Pelecanus rufescens*
Smaller than White Pelican; plumage pale grey with pink rump; drooping crest.

3 LONG-TAILED CORMORANT *Phalacrocorax africanus*
Relatively small; plumage all black with long tail; immature whitish below.

4 AFRICAN DARTER *Anhinga rufa*
Long pointed bill, not hooked at tip; conspicuous white neck stripe; immature much paler and lacks white neck stripe; whitish below.

5 WHITE-NECKED CORMORANT *Phalacrocorax carbo*
5a. Tail relatively short, larger than Long-tailed Cormorant; foreneck white.
5b. Immature white below.

6 BLACK-NECKED GREBE *Podiceps nigricollis*
Medium size; golden ear tufts; slender black neck and slender up-tilted bill.

7 LITTLE GREBE *Podiceps ruficollis*
7a. Small size; chestnut face and throat.
7b. Immature greyer and lacks chestnut on face and throat.

8 GREAT CRESTED GREBE *Podiceps cristatus*
8a, 8b. Large size; chestnut and black head frills and black crown tufts, lacking in immature.

Plate 2   HERONS AND HAMERKOP

1 NIGHT HERON *Nycticorax nycticorax*   page 23
   1a. Black crown and back, white breast.
   1b. Immature brown with whitish spots on back and wings.

2 WHITE-BACKED NIGHT HERON   23
   Nycticorax leuconotus
   Rufous neck and breast; white streak down back conspicuous in flight.

3 LITTLE BITTERN *Ixobrychus minutus*   22
   Very small; ♂ has black back and buff-white wing patch. ♀ and
   immature brown above, streaked below.

4 DWARF BITTERN *Ardeirallus sturmii*   23
   Very small; slate-grey upperparts; below buff heavily streaked slate-
   grey.

5 SQUACCO HERON *Ardeola ralloides*   24
   Small; back and chest orange-buff; all white wings conspicuous only in
   flight; immature darker and browner, striped breast.

6 GREEN-BACKED HERON *Butorides striatus*   25
   Small; greenish-black crown and back; grey underparts; immature
   paler with whitish spots on wing coverts.

7 GREAT WHITE EGRET *Egretta alba*   25
   Large; white; black legs and toes; bill yellow or black.

8 LITTLE EGRET *Egretta garzetta*   26
   Small; white, black legs, yellow toes; black bill.

9 YELLOW-BILLED EGRET *Egretta intermedia*   25
   Medium size; white; black legs and toes; stumpy yellow bill.

10 CATTLE EGRET *Ardeola ibis*   24
   Small; crown, back and chest orange-buff; bill and legs yellowish or
   flesh-coloured; non-breeding and immature all white.

11 HAMERKOP *Scopus umbretta*   28
   Small; entirely dark brown; characteristic crest shape; bill hook-tipped.

12 GOLIATH HERON *Ardea goliath*   27
   Very large; rufous crown, neck and underparts; immature paler,
   greyish-white below.

13 BLACK-HEADED HERON *Ardea melanocephala*   27
   Large; grey; black crown and hindneck.

14 GREY HERON *Ardea cinerea*   26
   Large; grey; white crown.

15 PURPLE HERON *Ardea purpurea*   27
   15a. Medium size, slender; dark with rufous neck; dark crown.
   15b. Immature paler and sandier.

2

Plate 3   STORKS, IBISES AND FLAMINGOS

1   WATTLED IBIS *Bostrychia carunculata*   page 32
Lax crest; white wing patch.

2   SACRED IBIS *Threskiornis aethiopicus*   31
Adult with naked black head and neck; immature has neck and head
feathered, white with black spots.

3   HADADA IBIS *Hagedashia hagedash*   31
Brownish-grey; mantle and wings washed metallic green; distinctive
'hah, dah, dah' call.

4   GLOSSY IBIS *Plegadis falcinellus*   32
Slim build; dark chestnut with metallic gloss; often appears blackish in
field; immature duller, less chestnut.

5   YELLOW-BILLED STORK *Ibis ibis*   31
Pinkish-white with black wings and tail, bare red face and yellow bill.
Immature greyish-white and black.

6   AFRICAN SPOONBILL *Platalea alba*   32
Spatulate bill; bare reddish-pink face and legs.

7   LESSER FLAMINGO *Phoenicopterus minor*   33
Smaller; plumage flushed deep pink; bill deep carmine-red. Immature
pale grey.

8   ABDIM'S STORK *Ciconia abdimii*   29
Medium size; black and white, glossed bronze on back and wings;
rump white. Black Stork is larger with black rump and red bill and legs.

9   WOOLLY-NECKED STORK *Ciconia episcopus*   29
Woolly white neck and contrasting dark body.

10   GREATER FLAMINGO *Phoenicopterus ruber*   33
Larger; white or pinkish-white in contrast to red wings; bill flesh-pink.
Immature greyish-white.

11   MARABOU STORK *Leptoptilos crumeniferus*   30
Large; bare head and heavy bill; neck pouch conspicuous when in-
flated.

12   SADDLEBILL STORK *Ephippiorhynchus senegalensis*   30
Large; black, red and yellow bill; white flight feathers; immature duller
and greyer.

13   WHALE-HEADED STORK *Balaeniceps rex*   28
Very large; entirely slate-grey plumage; huge bill.

14   OPENBILL STORK *Anastomus lamelligerus*   30
All black plumage and open bill.

Plate 4   DUCKS AND GEESE

1 **CAPE TEAL** *Anas capensis*   page 36
1a, 1b. Pale head; pink bill; double white wing bar in flight.

2 **PYGMY GOOSE** *Nettapus auritus*   35
2a, 2b. Small; chestnut flanks; ♂ has green head patch and orange
bill; ♀ lacks green on head and has dusky yellow bill.

3 **MACCOA DUCK** *Oxyura maccoa*   38
3a, 3b. ♂ chestnut and black; blue bill; ♀ dull plumaged; bill grey.
Swims low in water, often with tail cocked up.

4 **AFRICAN POCHARD** *Aythya erythrophthalma*   38
4a, 4b. Dark plumage; pale grey bill; white wing bar.

5 **RED-BILLED DUCK** *Anas erythrorhynchos*   37
5a, 5b. Blackish cap; red bill.

6 **HOTTENTOT TEAL** *Anas hottentota*   37
6a, 6b. Black cap; sides of bill blue.

7 **YELLOW-BILLED DUCK** *Anas undulata*   37
7a, 7b. Sides of bill bright yellow.

8 **WHITE-BACKED DUCK** *Thalassornis leuconotus*   39
8a, 8b. Mottled rufous-brown and black; white back in flight.

9 **AFRICAN BLACK DUCK** *Anas sparsa*   36
9a, 9b. Frequents rivers and streams; dark plumage with white spots
on upperparts.

10 **BLUE-WINGED GOOSE** *Cyanochen cyanopterus*   34
Hunched stance with head drawn back; blue shoulders.

11 **KNOB-BILLED DUCK** *Sarkidiornis melanotos*   35
♂ with large fleshy knob at base of bill; ♀ smaller and lacks knob.

12 **SPURWING GOOSE** *Plectopterus gambensis*   35
Very large; black above with metallic sheen; flesh-red bill.

13 **EGYPTIAN GOOSE** *Alopochen aegyptiaca*   34
Contrasting white shoulders specially noticeable in flight; chestnut
breast spot.

14 **WHITE-FACED TREE DUCK** *Dendrocygna viduata*   34
White face; black and white barred flanks.

15 **FULVOUS TREE DUCK** *Dendrocygna bicolor*   34
Creamy-white flank stripes; white rump in flight.

Plate 6   **BIRDS OF PREY (1)**

Plate 7   **BIRDS OF PREY (2)**

1 **VERREAUX'S EAGLE** *Aquila verreauxii*   page 53
   1a, 1b. Black with contrasting white back and rump patches; yellow
   cere; distinctive flight silhouette; immature mottled brown.

2 **MARTIAL EAGLE** *Polemaetus bellicosus*   51
   Black spotted breast. Immature whitish below; legs and thighs unspotted.

3 **CROWNED EAGLE** *Stephanoaetus coronatus*   50
   Underparts blotched black, rufous and white; immature whitish below;
   black spotted legs and thighs.

4 **OSPREY** *Pandion haliaetus*   55
   Long wings; white below, mottled brown on chest; dark head pattern.

5 **AFRICAN MARSH HARRIER** *Circus ranivorus*   43
   Barred tail and primaries; head and shoulders dark brown, not buff.

6 **WAHLBERG'S EAGLE** *Aquila wahlbergi*   53
   Brown; relatively narrow wings and long square-ended tail; small nape
   crest.

7 **HARRIER HAWK** *Polyboroides radiatus*   43
   Blackish tail with white band; long legs; barred underparts.

8 **LIZARD BUZZARD** *Kaupifalco monogrammicus*   48
   Black throat streak; white rump; grey chest, barred belly.

9 **GRASSHOPPER BUZZARD** *Butastur rufipennis*   49
   Wings largely rufous; rump dark; when perched resembles giant
   kestrel.

10 **AFRICAN HAWK EAGLE** *Hieraaetus spilogaster*   51
    Feathered legs; underparts white with narrow black streaks; immature
    pale rufous below.

11 **BLACK-CHESTED HARRIER EAGLE**   44
    Circaetus pectoralis
    Large, lax-feathered head; bare legs; unspotted white breast; immature
    pale rufous-buff below.

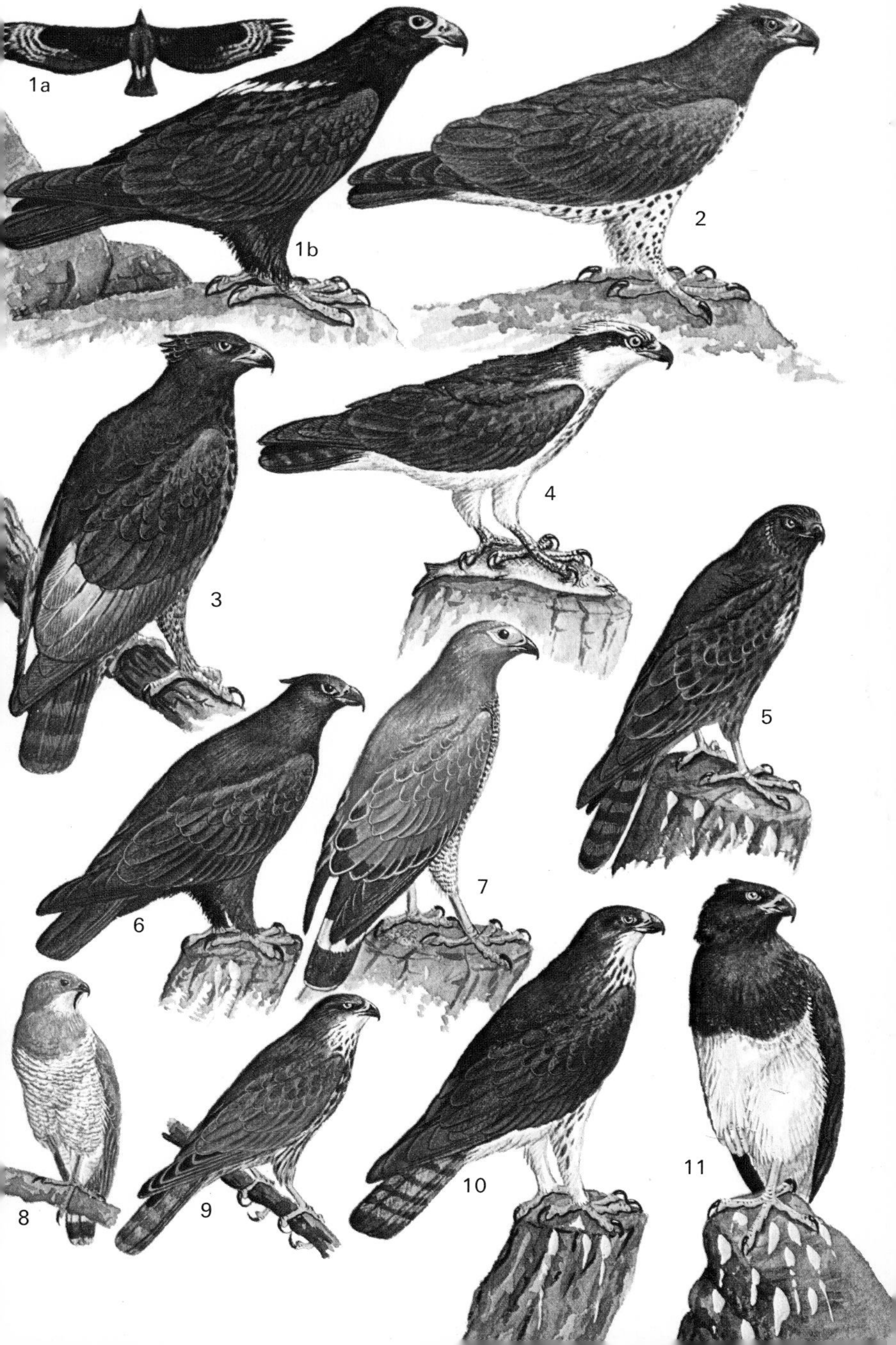
1a
1b
2
3
4
5
6
7
8
9
10
11

Plate 8   **BIRDS OF PREY (3)**

1 **PYGMY FALCON**   *Poliohierax semitorquatus*   page 56
   Small size; when perched has a shrike-like appearance; ♂ has grey
   back; ♀ has a rufous-brown back.
2 **DARK CHANTING GOSHAWK**   *Melierax metabates*   47
   Barred grey rump; orange-red cere; immature dark grey-brown with
   dark streaks on chest and brown barring on breast.
3 **PALE CHANTING GOSHAWK**   *Melierax poliopterus*   47
   White rump; yellow cere; orange-red legs; immature brown with
   streaked chest; rufous barring on breast.
4 **GABAR GOSHAWK**   *Melierax gabar*   48
   White rump; lightly barred underparts; banded tail; immature has
   chest streaked with brown.
5 **AFRICAN GOSHAWK**   *Accipiter tachiro*   45
   Slate-grey upperparts; rump dark; immature whitish below with dark
   spots.
6 **SHIKRA**   *Accipiter badius*   46
   Pale grey upperparts, including rump; central tail feathers unmarked
   grey; immature also pale grey above, below blotched pale rufous.
7 **RED-NECKED FALCON**   *Falco chiquera*   57
   Associated with palms; chestnut cap and neck; barred belly.
8 **AFRICAN HOBBY**   *Falco cuvieri*   57
   Very sharply-pointed wings; dark blue-grey upperparts; dark rufous
   below.
9 **PEREGRINE**   *Falco peregrinus*   57
   Crown, nape and back dark slate-grey; no rufous-buff nape patch;
   immature browner and dark streaked below.
10 **LANNER**   *Falco biarmicus*   56
   Rufous-buff nape patch; back pale grey; immature pale brown,
   streaked below.
11 **KESTREL**   *Falco tinnunculus*   59
   Chestnut back spotted with black; ♀ head rufous, not grey; tail barred
   black and brown.
12 **GREATER KESTREL**   *Falco rupicoloides*   59
   Sexes similar; tail barred black and blue-grey; eyes creamy-white.
13 **FOX KESTREL**   *Falco alopex*   60
   Sexes similar; entirely foxy-brown; tail strongly barred.
14 **GREY KESTREL**   *Falco ardosiaceus*   58
   Largely crepuscular; uniform grey plumage; yellow skin around eyes.
15 **DICKINSON'S KESTREL**   *Falco dickinsoni*   58
   Grey plumage with contrasting pale rump; strongly barred tail.

8

Plate 9   GAME BIRDS AND BUTTON QUAIL

1 **SCALY FRANCOLIN** *Francolinus squamatus*   page 63
Uniformly dark plumaged; red bill and legs; forest and thick bush.

2 **SHELLEY'S FRANCOLIN** *Francolinus shelleyi*   61
Belly mottled black and white; no rufous hindneck patch.

3 **CRESTED FRANCOLIN** *Francolinus sephaena*   61
Chestnut neck spots; white streaks on upperparts; often carries tail
cocked up.

4 **COQUI FRANCOLIN** *Francolinus coqui*   60
Underparts barred black and white; legs yellowish.

5 **RING-NECKED FRANCOLIN** *Francolinus streptophorus*   61
Ring of black and white barring around neck; flanks heavily spotted.

6 **REDWING FRANCOLIN** *Francolinus levaillantii*   61
Rufous patch on hindneck; rufous-buff on belly.

7 **HILDEBRANDT'S FRANCOLIN** *Francolinus hildebrandti*   62
Sexes dissimilar; ♂ white below with heavy black spotting; ♀ rufous-
buff below, unspotted.

8 **HEUGLIN'S FRANCOLIN** *Francolinus icterorhynchus*   63
Dusky upperparts; below creamy white spotted black; ♂ possesses two
spurs on each leg.

9 **JACKSON'S FRANCOLIN** *Francolinus jacksoni*   63
Red bill and legs; heavy chestnut streaks on underparts; inhabits
mountain forest.

10 **MONTANE FRANCOLIN** *Francolinus psilolaemus*   62
Round black spots on chest.

11 **HARLEQUIN QUAIL** *Coturnix delegorguei*   65
♂ has distinctive black and white throat markings and black belly. ♀
has uniform buffy-white underparts and lacks black throat markings.

12 **YELLOW-NECKED SPURFOWL**   64
Francolinus leucoscepus
Bare yellow throat; underparts buffy-white, streaked brown.

13 **RED-NECKED SPURFOWL** *Francolinus afer*   64
13a, 13b. Bare red throat and red legs; very variable species, some
races have white streaked black underparts, others with grey and
white vermiculated underparts.

14 **BLUE QUAIL** *Cotornix chinensis*   65
Very small; bright slate-blue underparts; ♀ has chest and flanks barred
with black; no slate-blue.

15 **BUTTON QUAIL** *Turnix sylvatica*   67
Very small; lacks hind toe; rump same colour as rest of upperparts.

16 **KENYA CRESTED GUINEAFOWL** *Guttera pucherani*   66
Lax black crest; blue-spotted neck feathers.

17 **CRESTED GUINEAFOWL** *Guttera edouardi*   66
Lax black crest; neck feathers unspotted purplish-black.

18 **VULTURINE GUINEAFOWL** *Acryllium vulturinum*   67
Upper mantle and chest feathers long and slender, striped blue, black
and white; breast cobalt-blue.

19 **HELMETED GUINEAFOWL** *Numida meleagris*   66
Conspicuous bony helmet; bare face and throat mainly blue.

9

Plate 10   CRANE, CRAKES AND RAILS, FINFOOT AND BUSTARDS

Plate 11   **STONE CURLEW, PLOVERS,**
AVOCET AND STILT

1 **SPUR-WINGED PLOVER** *Vanellus spinosus*   page 78
   Back entirely greyish-brown; crown black.

2 **KITTLITZ'S PLOVER** *Charadrius pecuarius*   82
   White eye-stripe and collar; buff underparts.

3 **THREE-BANDED PLOVER** *Charadrius tricollaris*   82
   Two black bands across breast.

4 **CHESTNUT-BANDED SAND PLOVER** *Charadrius venustus*   83
   Narrow pale chestnut band across chest.

5 **BLACKHEAD PLOVER** *Vanellus tectus*   78
   Black crown and crest; white throat; red eye wattle.

6 **BLACKSMITH PLOVER** *Vanellus armatus*   78
   White crown; black patch on back.

7 **BLACK-WINGED PLOVER** *Vanellus melanopterus*   80
   Broad black chest band; under wing-coverts white.

8 **SENEGAL PLOVER** *Vanellus lugubris*   79
   Narrow black chest band; under wing-coverts black and white.

9 **SPOT-BREASTED PLOVER** *Vanellus melanocephalus*   81
   Crest, crown and throat black; chest streaked black.

10 **BLACK-WINGED STILT** *Himantopus himantopus*   84
   Very long pink legs; black and white plumage; straight slender bill.
   Immature birds much greyer than adults.

11 **CROWNED PLOVER** *Vanellus coronatus*   80
   White ring on crown; legs red; bill red with black tip.

12 **BROWN-CHESTED WATTLED PLOVER**   81
   Vanellus superciliosus
   Chestnut band across breast, more extensive in ♂; forehead tawny-
   rufous; small yellow eye wattle.

13 **CRAB PLOVER** *Dromas ardeola*   84
   Black and white plumage, blue-grey legs and heavy bill.

14 **WATTLED PLOVER** *Vanellus senegallus*   80
   Red and yellow eye wattle; yellow legs.

15 **WHITE-HEADED PLOVER** *Vanellus albiceps*   79
   White crown; long drooping yellow wattles.

16 **AVOCET** *Recurvirostra avosetta*   83
   Upturned bill; black and white plumage; blue-grey legs.

17 **LONG-TOED LAPWING** *Vanellus crassirostris*   77
   White front; red and black bill. Walks on floating aquatic vegetation
   like a lily-trotter.

18 **SPOTTED STONE CURLEW** *Burhinus capensis*   77
   Heavily spotted underparts; largely nocturnal, often on roads at night.

Plate 12   JACANAS, SNIPE, GULLS AND TERNS

Plate 13   SANDGROUSE AND PIGEONS

13

Plate 14 CUCKOOS, MOUSEBIRDS, HOOPOE AND WOOD HOOPOES

1 EMERALD CUCKOO *Chrysococcyx cupreus*   page 108
Brilliant green plumage and yellow breast; ♀ barred below.

2 RED-CHESTED CUCKOO *Cuculus solitarius*   107
Distinct rufous throat; distinctive call of three notes, 'wip, wip, weeoo'.
Immature dark with blackish throat.

3 WHITE-BROWED COUCAL *Centropus superciliosus*   109
Chestnut wings, long black tail and pale stripe above eye; flight weak
and floundering.

4 KLAAS' CUCKOO *Chrysococcyx klaas*   108
Vivid green and white with green chest patches; outer tail feathers
mainly white.

5 SENEGAL COUCAL *Centropus senegalensis*   110
Dull black crown without metallic sheen.

6 DIDRIC CUCKOO *Chrysococcyx caprius*   108
Upperparts coppery-green; tail dark with white spots. ♀ barred below.

7 AFRICAN HOOPOE *Upupa epops africana*   134
Distinctive crest; primaries black without white bar.

8 GREEN WOOD HOOPOE *Phoeniculus purpureus*   135
Red bill and legs; white in wings and tail.

9 BLUE-NAPED MOUSEBIRD *Colius macrourus*   122
Gregarious; long slender tail; blue patch on nape.

10 SPECKLED MOUSEBIRD *Colius striatus*   121
Gregarious; long thick tail; crested; speckled chest.

11 AFRICAN SCIMITARBILL *Phoeniculus cyanomelas*   136
Black bill and feet; white spots on tail and wings.

12 ABYSSINIAN SCIMITARBILL *Phoeniculus minor*   136
No white markings on wings or tail; bill orange-red.

14

Plate 15   **TURACOS**

15

Plate 16   **PARROTS, TROGONS, GIANT KINGFISHER AND ROLLERS**

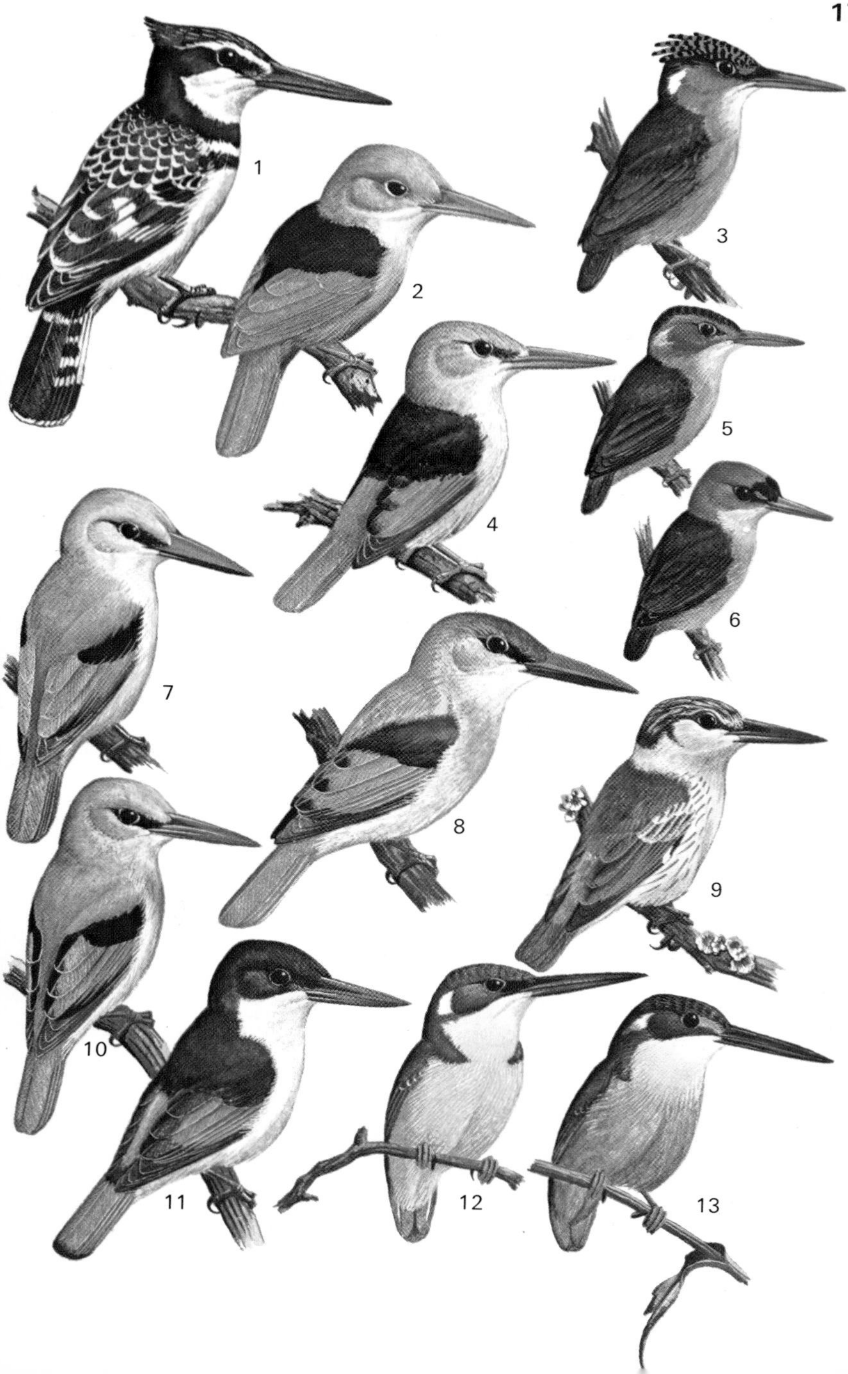
1
2
3
4
5
6
7
8
9
10
11
12
13

Plate 18 **BEE-EATERS**

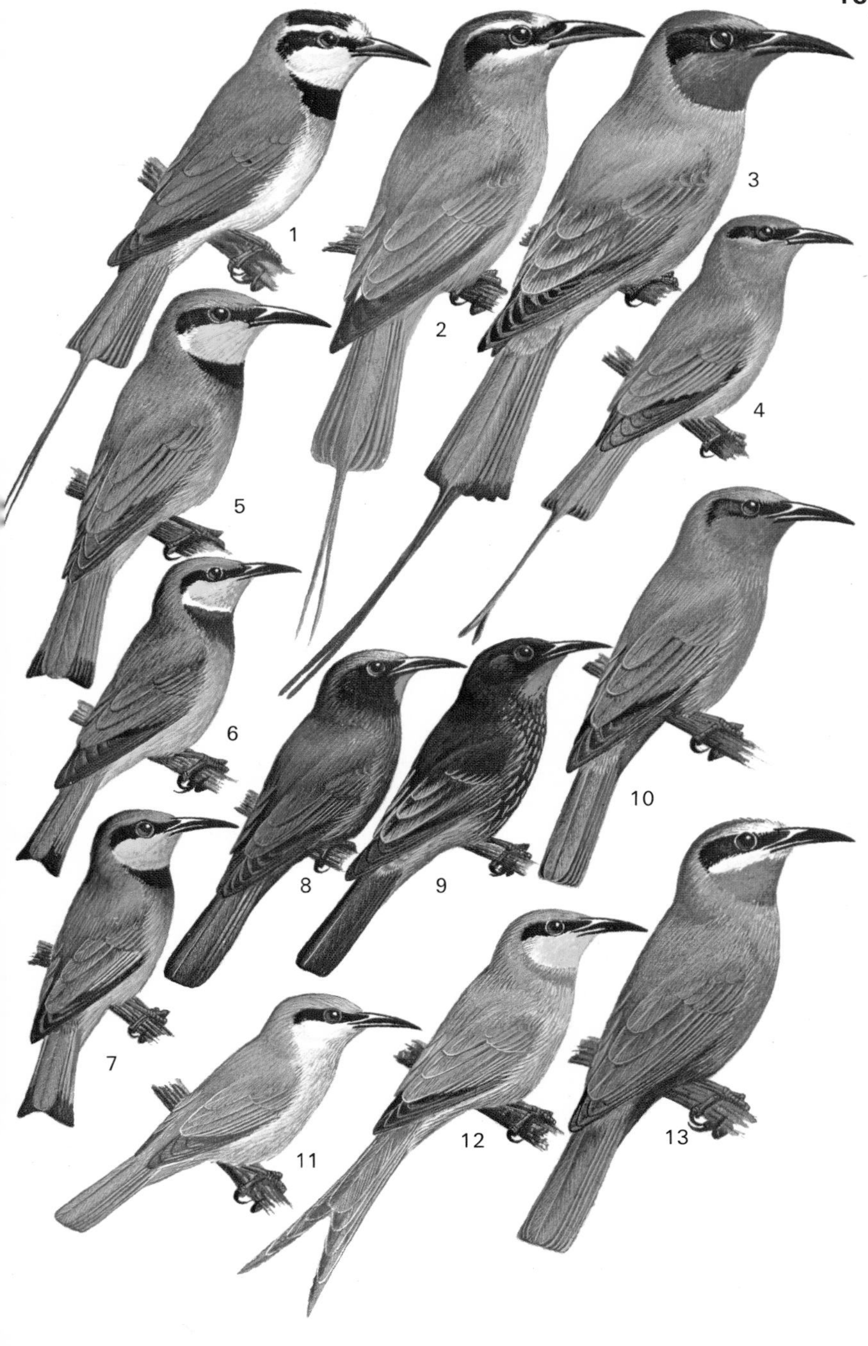
1
2
3
4
5
6
7
8
9
10
11
12
13

Plate 19   **HORNBILLS**

1 **WATTLED BLACK HORNBILL** *Ceratogyma atrata*   page 139
Large; blue face and throat wattles; ♂ all black; ♀ with rufous-brown head.

2 **BLACK AND WHITE CASQUED HORNBILL**   140
Bycanistes subcylindricus
White wing patch; parti-coloured casque.

3 **WHITE-TAILED HORNBILL** *Bycanistes sharpii*   139
Tail white except for black central feathers; dark patch on side of bill.

4 **TRUMPETER HORNBILL** *Bycanistes bucinator*   140
White breast and abdomen.

5 **SILVERY-CHEEKED HORNBILL** *Bycanistes brevis*   140
Wings black; casque pale.

6 **RED-BILLED HORNBILL** *Tockus erythrochynchus*   137
Red bill; white spots on wing coverts.

7 **WHITE-CRESTED HORNBILL** *Tropicranus albocristatus*   139
Very long graduated tail; white crest.

8 **YELLOW-BILLED HORNBILL** *Tockus flavirostris*   138
Banana-yellow bill; white spots on wing coverts and tail.

9 **CROWNED HORNBILL** *Tockus alboterminatus*   138
Dull red bill; white tips to outer tail feathers.

10 **VON DER DECKEN'S HORNBILL** *Tockus deckeni*   137
Wing coverts black, unspotted; bill of ♂ red with ivory tip; bill of ♀ black.

11 **HEMPRICH'S HORNBILL** *Tockus hemprichii*   138
Bill dusky red; outer pair tail feathers black, next two pairs white; frequents cliffs.

12 **GREY HORNBILL** *Tockus nasutus*   136
Ivory-white stripe on side of bill; throat and chest grey.

13 **GROUND HORNBILL** *Bucorvus leadbeateri*   141
Black with white primaries; red face and throat wattles; terrestrial, in distance resembles a domestic turkey.

14 **ABYSSINIAN GROUND HORNBILL**   141
Bucorvus abyssinicus
Wattles blue or blue and red; casque open in front.

Plate 20   O W L S   A N D   N I G H T J A R S

Plate 21   **SWIFTS**

1 WHITE-RUMPED SWIFT *Apus caffer*   page 119
Rump white; tail deeply forked and outer tail feathers strongly attenuated.

2 LITTLE SWIFT *Apus affinis*   119
Rump white; tail square; nests on buildings and under bridges.

3 HORUS SWIFT *Apus horus*   119
Rump white; tail forked but outer tail feathers not strongly attenuated; throat very white.

4 MOTTLED-THROATED SPINETAIL   120
Telacanthura ussheri
White rump and white patch on abdomen; throat mottled.

5 PALM SWIFT *Cypsiurus parvus*   120
Slim build; uniform greyish-brown; tail deeply forked and outer tail feathers slender and attenuated.

6 BOEHM'S SPINETAIL *Neafrapus boehmi*   120
Very small; tail very short; white rump; flight bat-like and erratic.

7 CASSIN'S SPINETAIL *Chaetura cassini*   121
Short tail; narrow white rump band; belly white.

8 SABINE'S SPINETAIL *Chaetura sabini*   120
Long white tail-coverts extend to end of tail; a forest species.

9 NYANZA SWIFT *Apus niansae*   118
Dark rump; forked tail; associated with cliffs.

10 SCARCE SWIFT *Apus myoptilus*   118
Dark greyish-brown with greyish throat; tail deeply forked; dark rump.

11 ALPINE SWIFT *Apus melba*   117
Large; underparts white with brown chest band.

12 MOTTLED SWIFT *Apus aequatorialis*   117
Large; pale edgings to feathers of underparts impart a mottled appearance; throat whitish.

Plate 22   BARBETS

Plate 23   HONEYGUIDES, WOODPECKERS, BROADBILL AND PITTA

Plate 24

LARKS, PIPITS, WAGTAILS AND LONGCLAWS

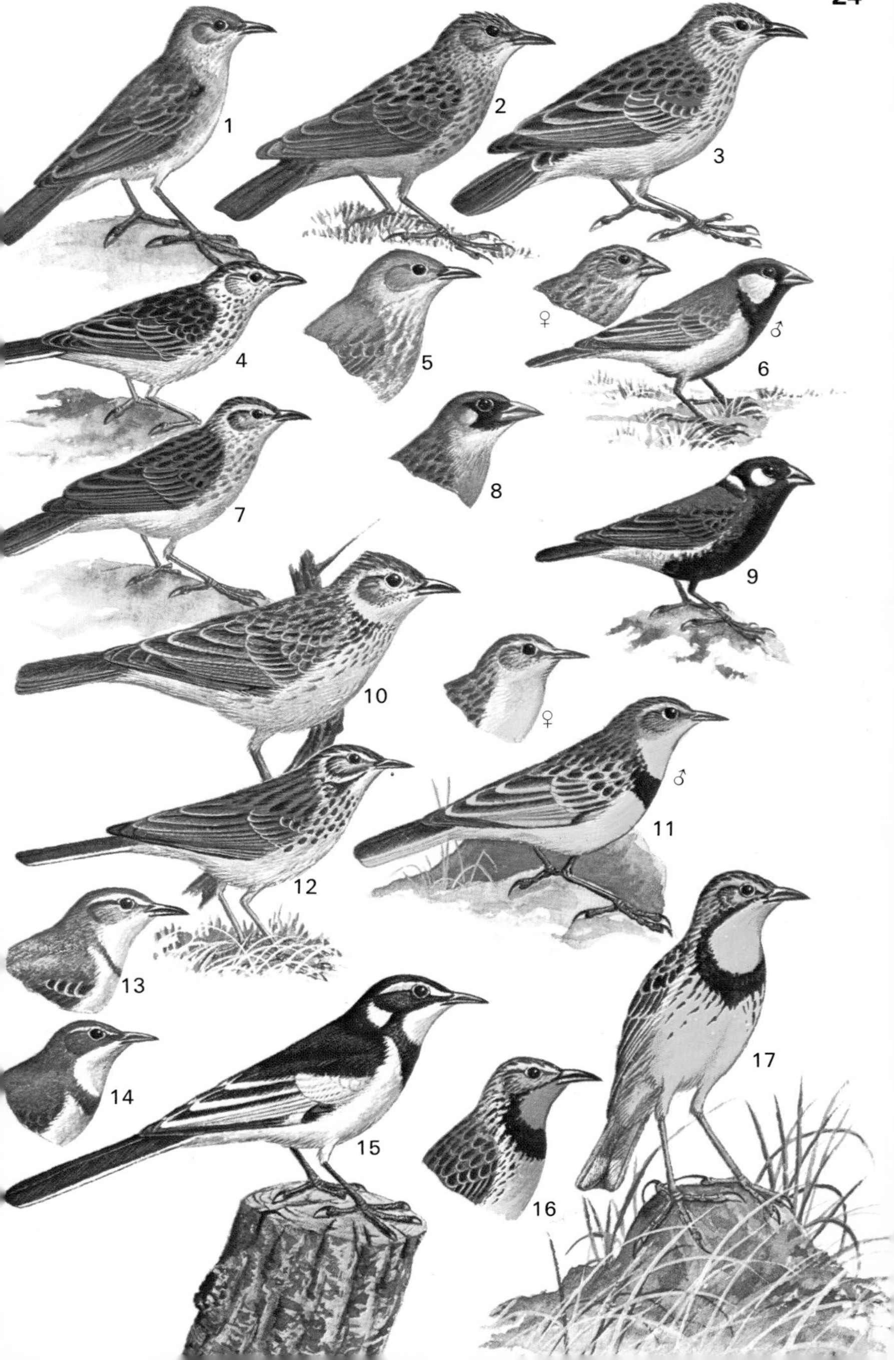
1
2
3
4
5
♀
♂
6
7
8
9
10
♀
♂
11
12
13
14
15
16
17

Plate 26   **BULBULS AND BABBLERS**

Plate 27   **THRUSHES, WHEATEARS, CHATS AND ALLIES (1)**

Plate 28 THRUSHES, WHEATEARS, CHATS AND ALLIES (2)

Plate 29   **FLYCATCHERS**

Plate 30   **WARBLERS (1)**

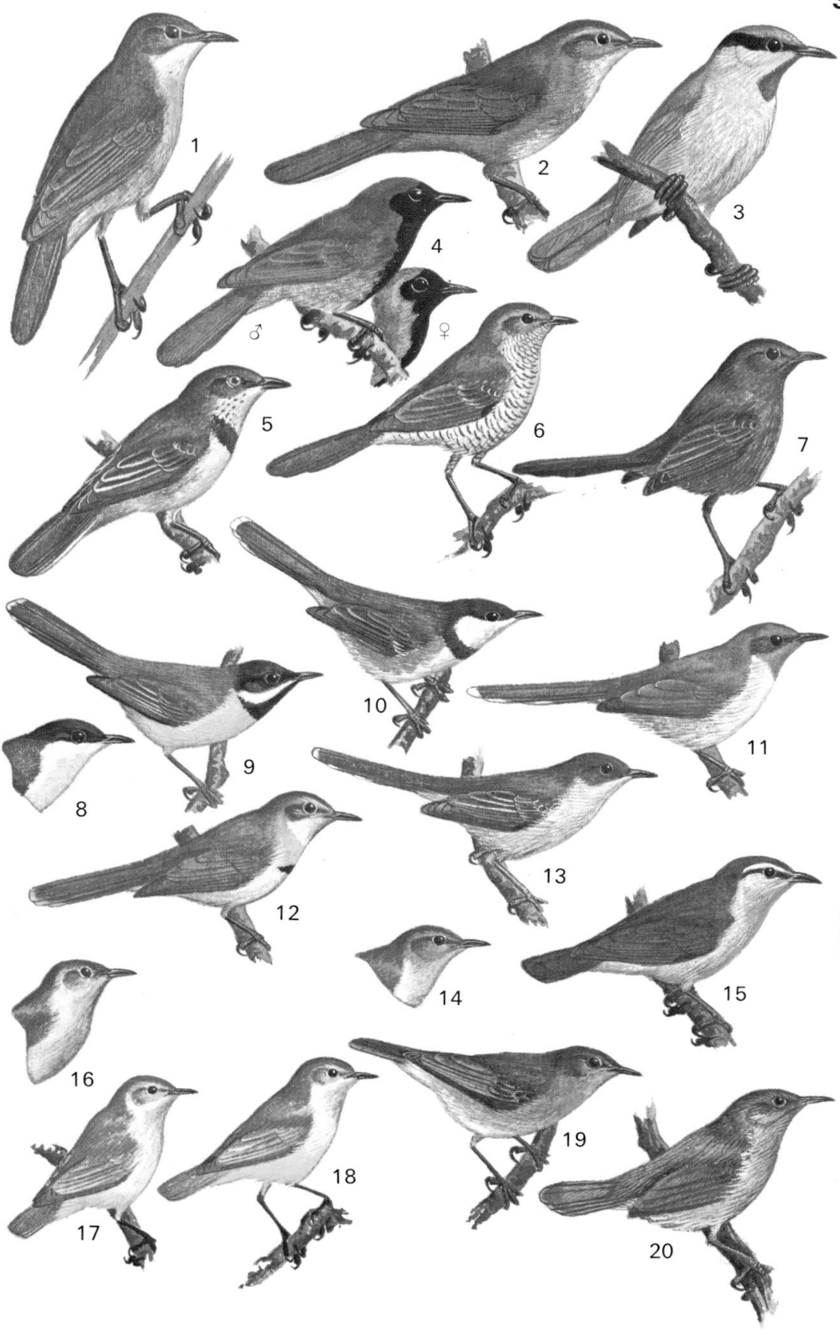
1
2
3
4
♂
♀
5
6
7
8
9
10
11
12
13
14
15
16
17
18
19
20

Plate 31

WARBLERS (2)

Plate 32   CUCKOO SHRIKES, HELMET SHRIKES AND SHRIKES

Plate 33 **SHRIKES**

Plate 34 **SUNBIRDS (1)**

Plate 35   **S U N B I R D S (2)**

1 LITTLE PURPLE-BANDED SUNBIRD   page 334
Nectarinia bifasciata
Small sized; similar to Mariqua Sunbird but much smaller.

2 MARIQUA SUNBIRD *Nectarinia mariquensis*   334
Medium sized; maroon breast band. ♀ greyish with buff eye-stripe;
dusky streaks on breast.

3 BEAUTIFUL SUNBIRD *Nectarinia pulchella*   339
3a.   Long central tail feathers; scarlet breast patch bordered yellow.
♀ whitish eye-stripe; yellowish-white below with trace of streaking on
chest.
3b.   In race found mainly east of Rift Valley the belly is black, not
metallic green.

4 VARIABLE SUNBIRD *Nectarinia venusta*   331
♂ plumage metallic blue-green; broad purplish chest patch. Belly colour varies in different regions and may be yellow or white, red or
orange: see text. ♀ greyish; yellowish-white below, unstreaked.

5 SUPERB SUNBIRD *Nectarinia superba*   336
Large size; heavy bill; belly deep maroon-red; ♀ under tail-coverts
orange.

6 BLUE-THROATED BROWN SUNBIRD   329
Nectarinia cyanolaema
Dark metallic blue crown and throat; ♀ pale stripe above and below
eye.

7 COPPER SUNBIRD *Nectarinia cuprea*   336
Copper-red mantle and chest; ♀ olive-brown, yellowish below.

8 SCARLET-TUFTED MALACHITE SUNBIRD   337
Nectarinia johnstoni
Very long tail; red pectoral tufts; occurs alpine zone of mountains;
♀ dark brown with red pectoral tufts.

9 MALACHITE SUNBIRD *Nectarinia famosa*   336
Emerald green plumage; long tail feathers; yellow pectoral tufts. ♀
brownish-grey; below yellowish, unstreaked.

10 PURPLE-BREASTED SUNBIRD   339
Nectarinia purpureiventris
Very long central tail feathers; short bill; rainbow plumage. ♀ olive
green with grey head.

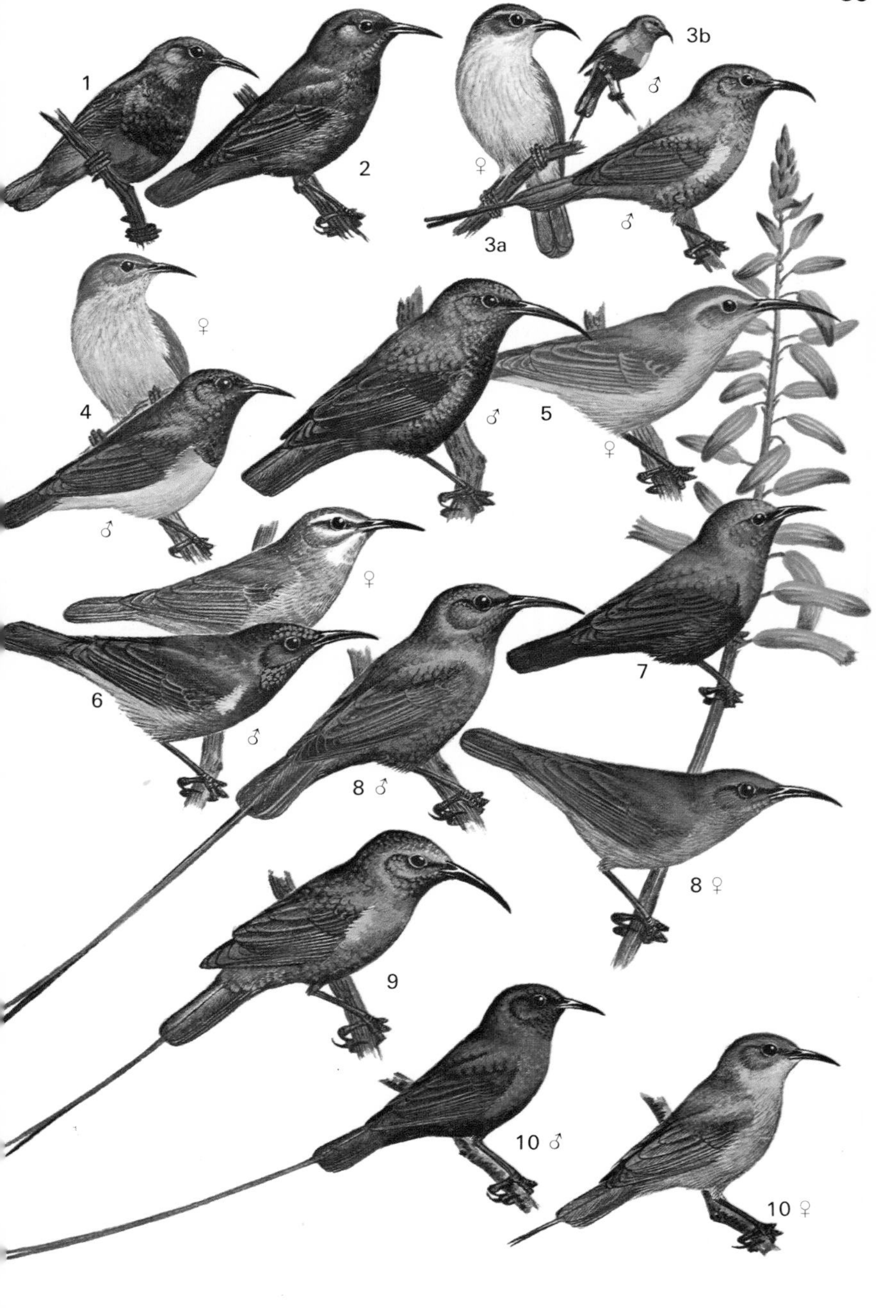
1
2
3b
♂
♀
3a
♂
♀
4
♂
5
♀
♂
♀
7
6
♂
8 ♂
8 ♀
9
10 ♂
10 ♀

Plate 36   **SUNBIRDS (3)**

35

1 **GOLDEN-WINGED SUNBIRD** *Nectarinia reichenowi*   page 338
   Long central tail feathers; wings and tail edged golden yellow. ♀
   yellowish below; wings and tail edged yellow.

2 **KENYA VIOLET-BACKED SUNBIRD**   342
   Anthreptes orientalis
   White breast; violet-blue upperparts and tail; ♀ grey-brown with pale
   eye-stripe and violet-blue tail.

3 **BRONZE SUNBIRD** *Nectarinia kilimensis*   337
   Long central tail feathers; metallic bronze green; black belly. ♀ yellowish below with dusky streaks.

4 **COLLARED SUNBIRD** *Anthreptes collaris*   343
   Metallic yellowish-green; narrow violet breast band. ♀ Similar to ♂ but
   throat greyish or yellowish.

5 **TACAZZE SUNBIRD** *Nectarinia tacazze*   338
   Long central tail feathers; metallic violet-bronze and black belly; ♀
   whitish streak on each side of throat; below greyish, unstreaked.

6 **PYGMY LONG-TAILED SUNBIRD** *Anthreptes platura*   343
   Long central tail feathers; yellow belly. ♀ pale greyish and yellow; short
   tail.

7 **MOUSE-COLOURED SUNBIRD** *Nectarinia veroxii*   336
   Greyish plumage; orange pectoral tufts.

8 **ANCHIETA'S SUNBIRD** *Anthreptes anchietae*   341
   Sexes similar; scarlet breast stripe; brown upperparts.

9 **OLIVE SUNBIRD** *Nectarinia olivacea*   328
   No metallic plumage; yellow pectoral tufts.

10 **GREY-CHINNED SUNBIRD** *Anthreptes tephrolaema*   341
   Grey chin; short bill. ♀ non-metallic olive-green.

11 **PLAIN-BACKED SUNBIRD** *Anthreptes reichenowi*   340
   Metallic blue-black on forehead and throat; ♀ green and yellow without metallic plumage.

12 **AMANI SUNBIRD** *Anthreptes pallidigaster*   341
   White belly; dark throat. ♀ greyish, non-metallic.

13 **BANDED GREEN SUNBIRD** *Anthreptes rubritorques* 342
   Greyish below; narrow red chest band in ♂.

Plate 37   TITS, WHITE-EYES, FINCHES AND BUNTINGS

Plate 38   SPOTTED CREEPER AND WAXBILLS (1)

Plate 39   **WAXBILLS (2)**

Plate 40   **WHYDAHS AND WAXBILLS (3)**

Plate 41   **WEAVERS (1)**

1 **SLENDER-BILLED WEAVER** *Ploceus pelzelni*   page 364
   Black face; bill slender; ♀ lacks black on face.

2 **LITTLE WEAVER** *Ploceus luteolus*   364
   Black face; relatively thick bill; ♀ lacks black on face.

3 **GROSBEAK WEAVER** *Amblyospiza albifrons*   363
   Blackish-brown; in some races with brown head; heavy bill; white wing
   and forehead patches. ♀ rusty-brown, paler below with dusky streaks
   on breast.

4 **HOLUB'S GOLDEN WEAVER** *Ploceus xanthops*   365
   Large thickset greenish-yellow weaver; brighter yellow below with
   orange wash on chest.

5 **VIEILLOT'S BLACK WEAVER** *Ploceus nigerrimus*   369
   All black plumage; pale yellow eye; ♀ dusky olive.

6 **GOLDEN WEAVER** *Ploceus subaureus*   365
   Chestnut wash on head; eye pale red.

7 **REICHENOW'S WEAVER** *Ploceus baglafecht reichenowi*   363
   Black mantle; front half of crown yellow; sides of face black; ♀ crown
   completely black.

8 **TAVETA GOLDEN WEAVER** *Ploceus castaneiceps*   366
   Chestnut patch on nape.

9 **GOLDEN PALM WEAVER** *Ploceus bojeri*   365
   Bright orange head; dark eye.

10 **ORANGE WEAVER** *Ploceus aurantius*   365
   Orange-yellow head and underparts; pale bill.

11 **NORTHERN BROWN-THROATED WEAVER**   366
   Ploceus castanops
   Chestnut-brown face; white eye.

12 **NORTHERN MASKED WEAVER** *Ploceus taeniopterus*   366
   Black face bordered by chestnut.

13 **MASKED WEAVER** *Ploceus intermedius*   367
   Front half of crown black.

14 **SPEKE'S WEAVER** *Ploceus spekei*   368
   Yellow crown; mottled black and yellow mantle.

15 **VITELLINE MASKED WEAVER** *Ploceus velatus*   367
   Very narrow black frontal band.

Plate 42   **WEAVERS (2)**

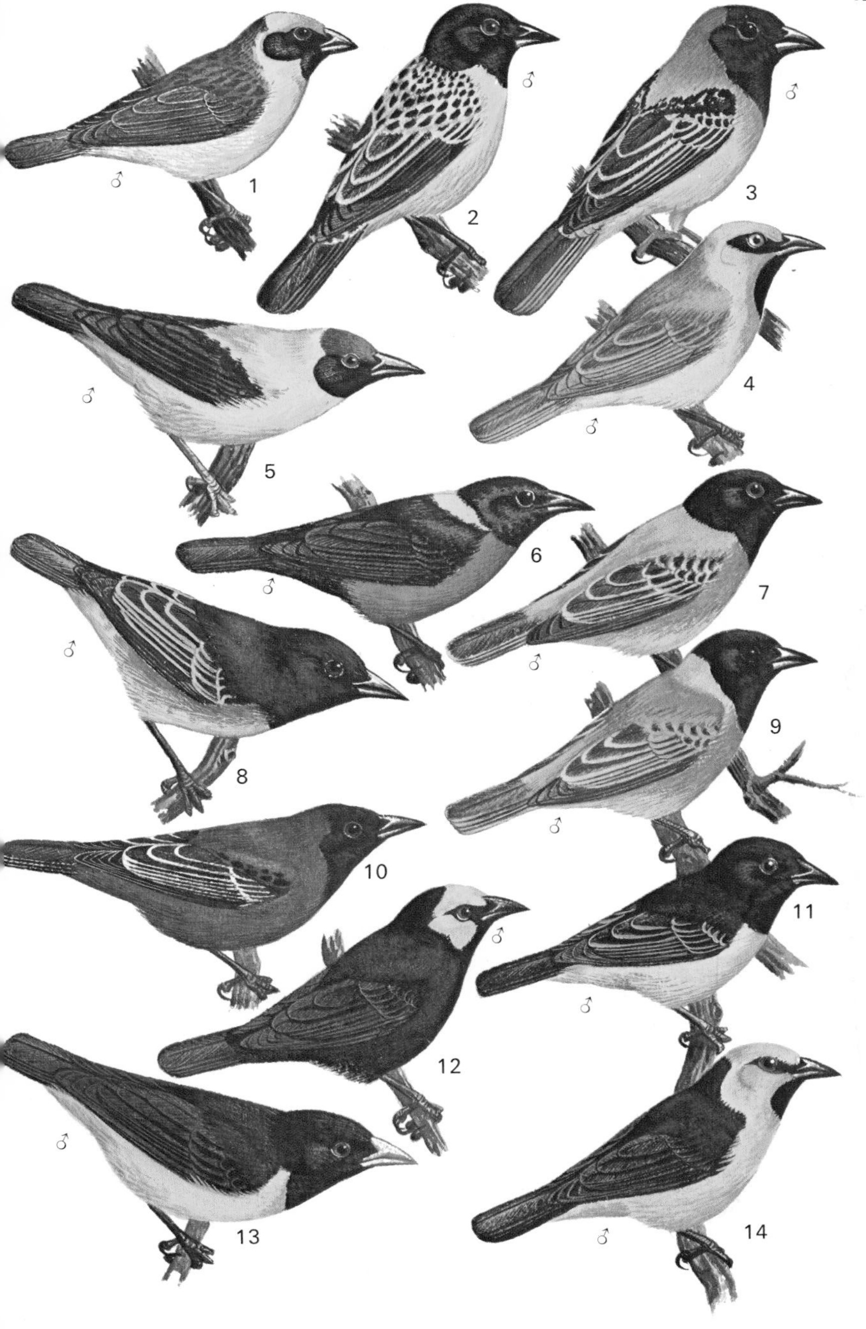
1
2
3
4
5
6
7
8
9
10
11
12
13
14

Plate 43   **WEAVERS (3)**

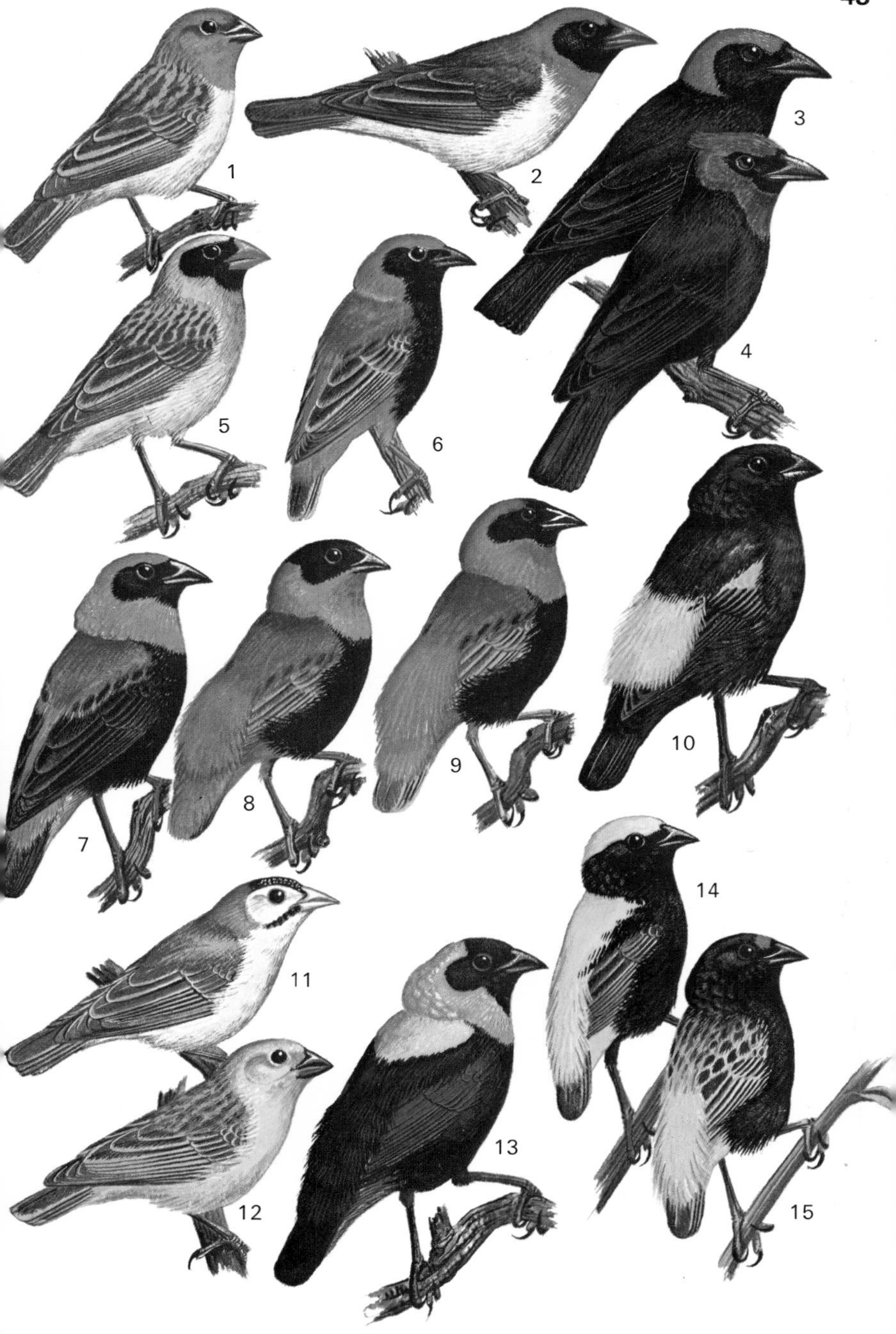
1
2
3
4
5
6
7
8
9
10
11
12
13
14
15

Plate 44   **WEAVERS (4)**

1   **WHITE-BROWED SPARROW WEAVER**
    Plocepasser mahali   page 381
    White eye-stripe; white rump.

2   **GREY-HEADED SOCIAL WEAVER**   *Pseudonigrita arnaudi*   382
    Short tail; pale grey cap.

3   **BLACK-CAPPED SOCIAL WEAVER**   382
    Pseudonigrita cabanisi
    Black cap; black tail.

4   **YELLOW-SPOTTED PETRONIA**   *Petronia xanthosterna*   385
    Mantle grey, unstreaked; pale yellow spot on throat.

5   **RUFOUS-TAILED WEAVER**   *Histurgops ruficauda*   382
    Cinnamon-rufous wings and tail.

6   **RED-BILLED BUFFALO WEAVER**   *Bubalornis niger*   380
    Large; black; pink bill.

7   **WHITE-HEADED BUFFALO WEAVER**   381
    Dinemellia dinemelli
    7a, 7b.   Large; red rump and under tail-coverts; white head.

8   **YELLOW-THROATED PETRONIA**   384
    Petronia superciliaris
    Mantle streaked; yellow throat spot.

9   **CHESTNUT SPARROW**   *Passer eminibey*   384
    Small; chestnut head, mantle and underparts; ♀ greyish-brown,
    streaked on mantle.

10 **PARROT-BILLED SPARROW**   *Passer gongonensis*   383
    Larger than similar Grey-headed Sparrow; heavy bill.

11 **RUFOUS SPARROW**   *Passer motitensis*   385
    Streaked mantle; white cheeks; throat black; ♀ has grey throat.

12 **GREY-HEADED SPARROW**   *Passer griseus*   383
    Head grey; mantle tawny brown; unstreaked.

13 **SOMALI SPARROW**   *Passer castanopterus*   383
    Crown chestnut; cheeks and underparts washed yellow.

Plate 45   **WEAVERS (5)**

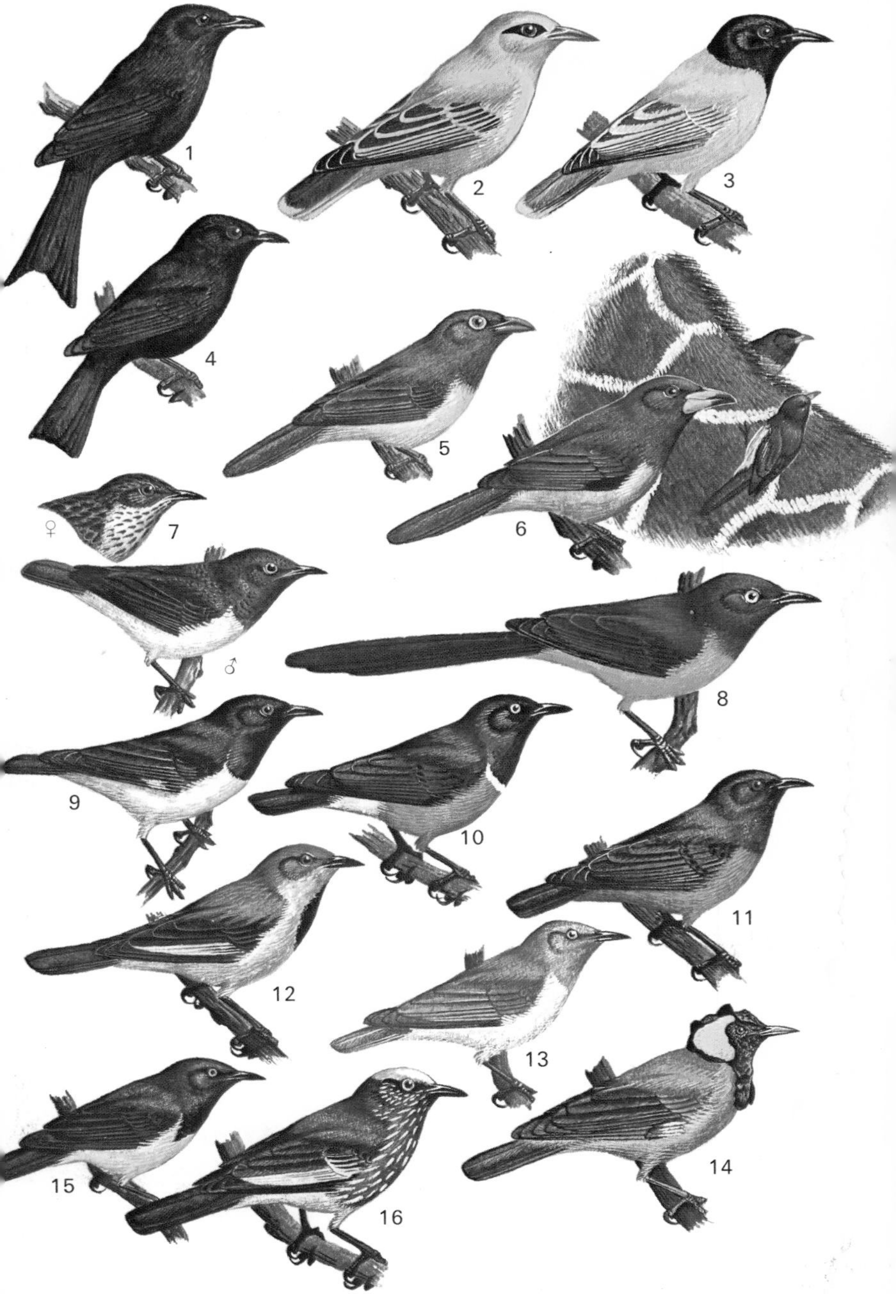
1
2
3
4
5
6
♀ 7
♂
8
9
10
11
12
13
14
15
16

Plate 47 **STARLINGS (2)**

Plate 48   C R O W S   A N D   R A V E N S

tawny buff with a black band across chest; throat white. A rare dry bush country species known from north-eastern Kenya, eastern Ethiopia and Somalia; very local and uncommon. The Singing Bush Lark *(M. cantillans)*, 5in, 13cm, has outer pairs of tail feathers white; a fawn-coloured bird with rufous wings. It indulges in a song flight in circles above its nesting ground. Williams' Bush Lark *(M. williamsi)*, 5in, 13cm, also has white outer tail feathers; above dark vinous-brown or dark vinous-grey with narrow pale tips to the feathers; below whitish with heavy rufous and dark brown mottling and spotting on the chest and flanks; bill heavy. This is a rare bird known at present from three localities in Kenya; these are Mt Marsabit, the Dida Galgalla desert and black lava desert 30 miles east of Isiolo, all localities in the Northern Frontier Province. The even rarer Friedmann's Bush Lark *(M. pulpa)*, 5in, 13cm, is similar to the Singing Bush Lark but with a heavier bill and much redder, black streaked plumage; known from northern and eastern Kenya (Tsavo National Park) and southern Ethiopia.

REDWING BUSH LARK   *Mirafra hypermetra*   Plate 24

Identification. 9in, 23cm. Similar to the Rufous-naped Lark but larger, with a longer tail and with contrasting patches of black streaks on each side of the foreneck. It perches on the tops of small bushes more frequently than that species.

Voice. A loud two-note whistle and a brief whistled song.

Distribution and Habitat. Local and uncommon resident in the southern Sudan, Ethiopia, southern Somalia, northern Uganda, Kenya and north-eastern Tanzania. Occurs in grassy open country where there are bushes and in dry bush country.

Allied Species. The Red Somali Lark *(M. sharpei)*, 9in, 23cm, is similar to the Redwing Bush Lark but is bright cinnamon-red above with white edgings to the feathers; below pale buffy-white with cinnamon streaking and spotting on lower neck and chest. Known only from a few localities in northern Somalia.

FLAPPET LARK   *Mirafra rufocinnamomea*   Plate 24

Identification. 5in, 13cm. This is a lark which varies greatly in general colour: it may be dark reddish-brown, earth-brown or bright cinnamon, the feathers mottled black and edged whitish; outer tail feathers pale rufous-buff; below tawny rufous, spotted black on the chest. The species attracts attention during its mating display flights when it produces a loud 'brrrrr, brrrrr, brrrrr, brrrrr', sound high in the air.

Voice. A soft two note 'tooee, toee'.

Distribution and Habitat. Local resident from the Sudan and southern

Ethiopia south through East and Central Africa. Frequents open bush country and plains where there is some bush cover.

NORTHERN WHITE-TAILED LARK
Mirafra albicauda   Plate 24

Identification. 5in, 13cm. A rather thickset, heavy-billed lark with dark upperparts and rufous edged wings; below with dense mottling on the chest; outer two pairs tail feathers pure white, very conspicuous in flight. Dark upperparts and white outer tail feathers are best field characters.
Voice. A sweet musical song uttered on the wing as the bird flies in circles above its nesting ground.
Distribution and Habitat. Widespread but local in East Africa, from the southern Sudan through Uganda, Kenya and northern Tanzania. Frequents open grasslands and mixed grass and bush, usually on black cotton soils. A secretive bird, terrestrial in habits, keeping to long grass from which it can be flushed. Rarely perches on bushes.

FAWN-COLOURED LARK   *Mirafra africanoides*   Plate 24

Identification. 5½in, 14cm. Upperparts rufous tawny with broad blackish streaking and a pronounced creamy-white eye-stripe; below pale buff, streaked brown on chest; outer webs and tips of outer tail feathers white. Frequently perches in trees and bushes.
Voice. A rather brief series of whistled notes uttered from a perch.
Distribution and Habitat. A local resident in East and Central Africa, commoner in the north of its range. Inhabits dry bush country on sand. In the field looks like a diminutive Rufous-naped Lark but with a relatively longer tail.

PINK-BREASTED LARK   *Mirafra poecilosterna*   Plate 24

Identification. 6in, 15cm. A rather slim, relatively long-tailed lark which habitually perches on small trees and bushes. Upperparts fawn-brown, greyer on the crown; wings and tail ashy-brown; below rufous-white with deeper rufous-pink mottling on chest and flanks.
Voice. Song a soft trill, uttered from a perch on bush or tree. Call note a thin 'tweeet' often repeated several times.
Distribution and Habitat. Widespread in dry bush country throughout the southern Sudan, southern Ethiopia, southern Somalia, northern Uganda, Kenya and north-eastern Tanzania.
Allied Species. Gillett's Lark *(M. gilletti)*, 5½in, 14cm, is similar in general

appearance to the Pink-breasted Lark but is more chestnut-brown above, the rump is grey and there are short chestnut streaks on the chest. Occurs in dry bush country in eastern Ethiopia and Somalia; local and uncommon.

RED-CAPPED LARK *Calandrella cinerea* Plate 24

Identification. 5½in, 14cm. A warm-brown lark with white underparts and a conspicuous chestnut-red cap and chestnut patch each side of the chest. Occurs in pairs or flocks.

Voice. A short twittering flock call or a two note 'tee, twee' when the bird rises.

Distribution and Habitat. Local resident and partial migrant throughout most of East and Central Africa. Locally common in many parts of Kenya, Uganda and Zambia. Frequents open plains, ploughed fields, cultivation, airfields and country after grass fires have passed.

Allied Species. The Short-toed Lark *(C. rufescens)*, 5in, 13cm, is a mottled greyish lark with a moderately heavy bill, heavy streaks on the chest and without rufous in wings. Normally in flocks. A very local species known from the Athi Plains, Kenya, eastern Ethiopia and Somalia. Occurs on open plains and dry open bush country.

MASKED LARK *Aethocorys personata* Plate 24

Identification. 5½–6in, 14–15cm. Upperparts, wings and tail uniform ash-brown; tail with pale cinnamon edges to outer feathers; bill large and heavy, pink; black patch in front of and below eyes and black patch on each side of chin; throat white; chest grey merging to warm vinous brown on belly and under tail-coverts. Best field characters are black face mask and pink bill.

Voice. A series of liquid, far-carrying notes, not unlike those of Short-tailed Lark.

Distribution and Habitat. Very local and uncommon, recorded from northern and southern Ethiopia and the Northern Frontier Province of Kenya. Most frequent in the black lava desert of the Dida Galgalla, on Mt Marsabit and in the Isiolo district.

Allied Species. The Short-tailed Lark *(Pseudalaemon fremantlii)*, 5½in, 14cm, is a short-tailed lark with much the appearance of a European Wood Lark. Upperparts grey to pinkish-grey, mottled and streaked blackish-brown; distinct white eye stripe and Y-shaped black marking below eye; bill long and heavy for size of bird; below white with dark patch on each side of chest; rufous wash on chest and flanks, overlaid on chest with short blackish streaks. Known from northern Somalia, southern Ethiopia, Kenya and north-eastern Tanzania; inhabits open plains, very local and uncommon.

The Crested Lark *(Galerida cristata)*, 6½in, 16½cm, is a rather plump sandy-coloured lark with a distinctive upstanding crest; brownish streaks on back and chest. The very similar Thekla Lark *(G. theklae)*, 6½in, 16½cm, is greyer, less sandy, and has bold short blackish streaks on chest. The Crested Lark occurs mainly in sandy areas, the Thekla Lark occurs mainly in black lava desert. The Crested Lark occurs locally from West Africa across the Sudan to Ethiopia and Somalia, south to northern Uganda and northern Kenya. The Thekla Lark occurs in Ethiopia, Somalia and northern Kenya. The Sun Lark *(G. modesta)*, 5½in, 14cm, has a very short crest; upperparts heavily streaked giving a dusky appearance; below, throat white merging to pale brown on chest and belly; black streaks on chest. Occurs very locally in the Sudan and northern Uganda.

FISCHER'S SPARROW LARK   *Eremopterix leucopareia*   **Plate 24**
Identification. 4½in, 11½cm. The sparrow larks are characterised by their heavy finch-like bills and blackish belly; usually very gregarious. The present species has a rufous-tinged crown edged dark brown; remainder upperparts greyish-brown; cheeks whitish; below, throat and very broad stripe down centre of belly blackish-brown, remainder underparts buffish-white. The ♀ lacks the distinctive head pattern and is greyish-brown with a pale eyestripe.
Voice. A low 'tweet, ees' flock call. A brief warbling song when nesting, uttered from the ground.
Allied Species. The Chestnut-backed Sparrow Lark *(E. leucotis)*, 5in, 13cm, has the upperparts chestnut, feathers edged white; head and neck black with ear-coverts and band across hind-neck white; the ♀ lacks black on head and neck. This is a plains and open thorn scrub bird found locally in East and Central Africa **(Plate 24)**. The White-fronted Sparrow Lark *(E. nigriceps)*, 4½in, 11½cm, has a black head with a white frontal patch; rest of upperparts pale brownish-grey. ♀ lacks black on head. Occurs in the Sudan, Ethiopia and Somalia in sandy semi-desert country.

CHESTNUT-HEADED SPARROW LARK
Eremopterix signata
Identification. 4½in, 11½cm. Similar to Fischer's Sparrow Lark but ♂ has the crown chestnut-brown with a white patch in the centre. It is a gregarious species, often in large flocks when visiting waterholes. ♀ lacks the chestnut and white head pattern having a greyish head with an indistinct eyestripe.
Voice. Various 'tsssp' type flock calls. Sings from the ground.
Distribution and Habitat. Occurs in the south-eastern Sudan, Ethiopia, Somalia and northern and eastern Kenya. Found in sandy semi-desert country and open bush areas.

SWALLOWS and MARTINS: Hirundinidae

Swallows and their allies are a well-marked group of birds which capture their insect food on the wing. They bear a superficial resemblance to swifts, but wing formation differs in being less slender and scythe-like. Build slim and flight graceful, less direct and rapid than swifts. Many species possess long and slender outer rectrices; feet small; bill short with wide gape.

AFRICAN SAND MARTIN   *Riparia paludicola*   **Plate 25**

Identification. 4½in, 11½cm. A uniformly coloured little martin with upperparts, throat and breast earth-brown, belly white; tail slightly forked. Gregarious, often near water.
Voice. Weak twittering notes.
Distribution and Habitat. Widely distributed resident and partial migrant East and Central Africa. Often in large loose flocks and associated with related species. Most numerous in vicinity of rivers, lakes and swamps.
Allied Species. The European Sand Martin *(R. riparia)*, 4½in, 11½cm, has earth-brown upperparts; below white with a brown chest band; tail slightly forked. Common winter visitor and passage migrant in East and Central Africa, less common in the south.

BANDED MARTIN   *Riparia cincta*   **Plate 25**

Identification. 6½in, 16½cm. Tail square or slightly forked; upperparts dark brown with white short streak on each side of the forehead; below white with brown band across chest. The European Sand Martin is smaller, has a forked tail and lacks the white forehead streaks.
Voice. A silent species; sometimes utters a brief twitter.
Distribution and Habitat. Widespread resident and local migrant in East and Central Africa. Usually in pairs or small parties; favours open grasslands, mixed grass and bush and the vicinity of water.
Allied Species. The European House Martin *(Delichon urbica)*, 5in, 13cm, is blue-black above with a contrasting white rump; tail forked; underparts white. This is a winter visitor in small numbers to East and Central Africa. The Mascarene Martin *(Phedina borbonica)*, 5in, 13cm, is sooty brown above, finely streaked with black; wings and tail blackish, the tail forked; underparts white, throat and belly streaked dark brown; sides of neck and flanks sooty. Occurs as a non-breeding visitor from Madagascar to Malawi, Zambia and Pemba Island, Tanzania between March and October.

AFRICAN ROCK MARTIN   *Hirundo fuligula*   **Plate 25**

Identification. 5in, 13cm. Uniform tawny-brown, slightly paler below with an ill-defined slightly rufous throat; tail slightly forked with a round white spot towards the ends of the rectrices, conspicuous when tail is spread in flight.
Voice. Various twittering notes.
Distribution and Habitat. Local resident widely distributed in small numbers in East and Central Africa. Frequents human habitations, cliffs and rocky outcrops and below road bridges.

ANGOLA SWALLOW   *Hirundo angolensis*   **Plate 25**

Identification. 6in, 15cm. Upperparts blue-black with a chestnut forehead patch; below, throat and chest chestnut edged by a blue-black band, more or less broken; remainder of underparts ashy-brown; tail forked and outer rectrices moderately elongated. The European Swallow has longer outer tail feathers and belly is white or white with a rufous wash.
Voice. Rapid twittering calls.
Distribution and Habitat. A locally common resident in East Africa, south to Malawi and Zambia. It occurs in the vicinity of human habitations and bridges, and near surface water; often in large flocks.
Allied Species. The European Swallow *(H. rustica)*, 6½–7½in, 16½—19cm, has very elongated outer tail feathers; above, including rump, blue-black; forehead and throat chestnut; blue-black band across chest; remainder underparts creamy-white, sometimes with rufous wash. An abundant winter visitor and passage migrant in East and Central Africa. Often in very large flocks.

BLUE SWALLOW   *Hirundo atrocaerulea*   **Plate 25**

Identification. 8in, 20cm. Entire plumage glossy blue-black; outer tail feathers very long and slender.
Voice. Typical swallow-type twittering.
Distribution and Habitat. A very local and uncommon swallow found in western Kenya, Uganda, the southern highlands of Tanzania and Central Africa; an intra-African migrant. Frequents open grasslands and mixed bush and grass; hawks low over the grass, often settling on isolated bushes and even on grass stems; not gregarious.
Allied Species. The Pearl-breasted Swallow *(H. dimidiata)*, 6in, 15cm, has uniform violet-blue-black upperparts without rufous on crown or rump; tail forked and outer rectrices long, no white spots; below white with grey wash on chest. Recorded from south-western Tanzania and Central Africa. Occurs in open grassland and bush and also in vicinity of water.

WIRE-TAILED SWALLOW   *Hirundo smithii*   **Plate 25**

Identification. 6in, 15cm. Outer tail feathers long and wire thin; upperparts glossy purplish-black with a rufous crown; below white. Easily distinguished from other black-backed swallows by its chestnut crown and very slender tail streamers.
Voice. A soft twittering warble.
Distribution and Habitat. Widely but locally distributed through East and Central Africa; partial migrant in some areas. Not usually gregarious and normally in pairs. Occurs around human habitations and bridges and along rivers and lakes.

ETHIOPIAN SWALLOW   *Hirundo aethiopica*   **Plate 25**

Identification. 5½in, 14cm. Above glossy blue-black with chestnut forehead patch; below creamy white, sometimes with slight tinge of rufous on throat; small black patch on each side of the chest; tail forked and outer rectrices elongated. Its best field characters are its pale throat and black chest patches.
Voice. Weak twittering calls.
Distribution and Habitat. It occurs locally in Ethiopia, the Sudan and Somalia southwards through Uganda and Kenya to north-eastern Tanzania. Found in open grasslands, areas of mixed bush and grass and also open woodlands. Most frequent along the Kenya coast where it nests in caves in the sea cliffs.
Allied Species. The White-tailed Swallow *(H. megaensis)*, 6in, 15cm, is a rare species confined to a few localities in southern Ethiopia. Upperparts glossy steel-blue; tail white with dusky tips, forked and outer rectrices elongated; underparts white. The white tail is very conspicuous in flight.

MOSQUE SWALLOW   *Hirundo senegalensis*   **Plate 25**

Identification. 9in, 23cm. A large heavy-looking swallow with elongated tail streamers; upperparts blue-black with contrasting rufous rump; underparts, throat white merging to rufous on breast, belly and under tail-coverts. Occurs in pairs. In lowland areas often associated with baobab trees; in highland areas of East Africa found in vicinity of isolated juniper trees.
Voice. A distinct metallic 'peeeeep;' often calls on the wing. Song a low, slow twitter.
Distribution and Habitat. Local resident and partial migrant in most areas of East and Central Africa. Occurs in localities from sea level to over 8,000ft, 2,440m. Inhabits open park-type country, cultivation where there are large isolated trees and bush and coastal scrub where there are baobab trees.

RED-RUMPED SWALLOW *Hirundo daurica* **Plate 25**

Identification. 7in, 18cm. Very similar to Mosque Swallow but much smaller with black under tail-coverts, not red. The black under tail-coverts are a good field character. Ear-coverts rufous.
Voice. Various twittering calls.
Distribution and Habitat. Local resident East Africa south to Malawi and Zambia; a migrant in some areas. Frequents the vicinity of human dwellings, open grasslands and sugarcane cultivation.

RUFOUS-CHESTED SWALLOW *Hirundo semirufa* **Plate 25**

Identification. 7½in, 19cm. Very similar to the Red-rumped Swallow from which it may be distinguished in having the lores, a line under the eyes and the ear-coverts glossy blue-black, not rufous. The tail streamers are also longer and more slender than in the Red-rumped Swallow. It is usually found in pairs but associates freely with other swallows.
Voice. A very high-pitched twittering call.
Distribution and Habitat. A local resident and partial migrant in the southern Sudan, Uganda and western Kenya. Occurs near water, over sugarcane cultivation and in open grasslands.

STRIPED SWALLOW *Hirundo abyssinica* **Plate 25**

Identification. 7in, 18cm. Easily recognised by its heavily black streaked underparts and chestnut crown and rump; outer tail feathers thin and elongated.
Voice. Squeaky metallic notes, not unlike a violin being tuned; also a brief warbling song.
Distribution and Habitat. Widely distributed throughout East and Central Africa in suitable localities; a resident and local migrant. May be encountered anywhere outside forest areas and often associated with human habitations and bridges.
Allied Species. The Larger Striped Swallow *(H. cucullata)*, 8in, 20cm, is similar to the Striped Swallow but is larger, the underparts are creamy white with thin black streaks and the crown and nape are chestnut streaked blue-black. It is a southern species known from southern Tanzania and Central Africa.

GREY-RUMPED SWALLOW *Hirundo griseopyga* **Plate 25**

Identification. 6½in, 16½cm, is a slim swallow with the mantle, wings and tail glossy blue-black; crown, rump and upper tail-coverts ash-grey; underparts white with a slight rufous wash on throat and chest.

Voice. Weak twittering notes.

Distribution and Habitat. Local resident and partial migrant from the Sudan and Ethiopia southwards to Central Africa. Open grasslands and swamps are its favoured habitats.

Allied Species. Andrew's Swallow *(H. andrewi)*, 6½in, 16½cm, is known only from Lake Naivasha in the Rift Valley, Kenya, where it occurs in migrating flocks of other swallows during early April. The location of its breeding grounds is unknown. It is similar to the Grey-rumped Swallow but has the underparts ash-grey with a darker patch on each side of the chest.

BLACK ROUGHWING SWALLOW
Psalidoprocne holomelaena   Plate 25

Identification. 7–7½in, 18–19cm. Entire plumage black with an oily greenish tinge; tail very long and deeply forked; under wing-coverts and axillaries ash-brown or whitish. Occurs in small loose flocks, perching on dead trees and hawking backwards and forwards along forest roads and glades.

Voice. Usually silent, but sometimes utters a weak twittering call.

Distribution and Habitat. Widespread local resident and partial migrant in East and Central Africa. Usually seen in small parties. Most frequent in highland areas where it inhabits forests and wooded areas.

WHITE-HEADED ROUGHWING SWALLOW
Psalidoprocne albiceps   Plate 25

Identification. 7in, 18cm. A black roughwing with a deeply forked tail and a very conspicuous white head in the ♂. The ♀ has a dark head but some white on the chin and sometimes a little white on the crown.

Voice. Weak twittering call notes.

Distribution and Habitat. Local resident and partial migrant Uganda, western and central Kenya, Tanzania, Malawi and Zambia. Occurs mainly in forested and well wooded localities.

WAGTAILS and PIPITS: Motacillidae

This is a group of graceful, slender terrestrial birds which run and walk. The pipits are generally brown above and usually streaked; they resemble larks but are more slender and have a different and more upright carriage, and their bills are slender. Wagtails have long tails and strikingly marked patterns, often with considerable yellow. They fall into two groups, those which occur singly or in pairs on or near water, and those which occur in flocks and are associated with cattle and herds of other domestic animals which disturb insects upon which the wagtails feed.

AFRICAN PIED WAGTAIL   *Motacilla aguimp*   **Plate 24**

Identification. 8in, 20cm. A large black and white wagtail associated with human habitations. Upperparts black with a white band over eye and a triangular white patch on each side of the neck. Below white with a black breast band; white stripe down sides of wings and outer tail feathers white.
Voice. Typical wagtail 'tsssp;' song not unlike that of a canary.
Distribution and Habitat. Widely distributed over most of the Ethiopian region and common in East and Central Africa. Closely associated with human dwellings but also occurs on sand bars in rivers, along lake margins and sometimes along rocky streams. A very tame and confiding bird.
Allied Species. The European White Wagtail *(M. alba)*, 6in, 15cm, has pale grey upperparts and a black throat in spring plumage; a white throat in winter. It is a common winter visitor to the Sudan and Ethiopia, uncommon in northern Uganda and Kenya. It occurs in flocks, sometimes associated with yellow wagtails on migration.

WELLS' or CAPE WAGTAIL   *Motacilla capensis*   **Plate 24**

Identification. 6in, 15cm. This species has smokey-grey upperparts and whitish underparts; a narrow black bar across chest. It looks like a small edition of the African Pied Wagtail but without that species' white bar along the wing.
Voice. A loud liquid 'tssp.'
Distribution and Habitat. It is an uncommon resident in East Africa, Zambia and southwards but not in Malawi. Frequents streams, the edges of swamps and pools and lake margins. Normally found in pairs or in family parties.

MOUNTAIN WAGTAIL   *Motacilla clara*   **Plate 24**

Identification. 6½in, 16½cm. This is easily the most graceful of the African wagtails. It is a pale blue-grey species, very slim and with a long tail, and with a narrow black chest band. It is nearly always associated with fast running rocky streams.
Voice. A loud metallic 'tsssp;' also a soft warbling song.
Distribution and Habitat. Local resident over much of East and Central Africa where there are rocky streams.
Allied Species. The European Grey Wagtail (M. cinerea), 7in, 18cm, is an

uncommon winter visitor to East Africa. It is similar in build to the Mountain Wagtail and also occurs along rocky streams but may be distinguished by the pale yellow on its belly whilst the Mountain Wagtail is white below. A number of grey- and yellow-headed races of the Yellow, Black, and Blue-headed Wagtails *(M. flava)*, 6½in, 16½cm, are common winter visitors and passage migrants in East and Central Africa.

RICHARD'S PIPIT   *Anthus novaeseelandiae*   **Plate 24**

Identification. 6in, 15cm. A slim, long-legged pipit with much white on two outer pairs tail feathers; upperparts tawny boldly streaked blackish; white stripe over eye; below pale buff with dark brown streaks on breast; hind claw longer than hind toe. This is the commonest of the open country pipits in East and Central Africa.

Voice. A sharp 'tweep' or 'tsseep, tsseep.' A brief, often repeated song when breeding.

Distribution and Habitat. Common resident and partial migrant throughout the greater part of the Ethiopian Region in suitable localities. Locally common in many parts of East and Central Africa. Occurs on open plains, grazing land and semi-desert country, and in the vicinity of inland waters. Occurs in pairs, single birds or family parties, not in flocks.

Allied Species. The Long-billed Pipit *(A. similis)*, 7in, 18cm, is found locally in East and Central Africa, being most frequent in Brachystegia woodland in southern Tanzania and Zambia. In the north of its range it occurs on grassy slopes where there are rocky or gravel outcrops. It differs from Richard's Pipit in having the upperparts indistinctly streaked, lacks white in the outer rectrices, has unstreaked flanks and the hind claw shorter than the hind toe. The Plain-backed Pipit *(A. leucophrys)*, 6½in, 16½cm, has the upperparts dark earth-brown or dark rusty-brown without darker streaking; no white in tail; below warm rufous or buffy-brown with a few indistinct streaks or spots on chest. It is found on open plains in Ethiopia and the Sudan, south through Uganda, Kenya and Tanzania to Malawi and Zambia; locally common. The very similar Sandy Plain-backed Pipit *(A. vaalensis)*, 6½in, 16½cm, is a paler more sandy bird with just a trace of indistinct streaking on chest. There are also differences in structure of flight feathers between the two but this is not a field character. It is a very local and uncommon bird in East and Central Africa. The Malindi Pipit *(A. melindae)*, 6in, 15cm, is a rare species found in coastal districts of Kenya and Tanzania; it resembles an olive-brown Richard's Pipit but has grey patches in outer tail feathers, not white. The Striped Pipit *(A. lineiventris)*, 6½in, 16½cm, is olive-brown above with dark streaking; wing-coverts, flight and tail feathers edged green; below buff with close dark streaks; outer tail feathers partly white. Inhabits rocky hills with scattered bush and scrub in southern Kenya, Tanzania and Central Africa.

The Sokoke Pipit *(A. sokokensis)*, 5½in, 14cm, has unusual habits for a pipit, living on the ground in glades and open forest in the coastal forests of Kenya and Tanzania. It is warm buff with heavy black streaking above; below yellowish-white with black streaks on chest and flanks. The Little Tawny Pipit *(A. caffer)*, 4½in, 11cm, is a very small species, tawny-brown with heavy dark streaking on upperparts and chest; outer tail feathers white on outer edges and tips. Found in acacia and Brachystegia woodland in East and Central Africa; very local and uncommon. The similar Short-tailed Pipit *(A. brachyurus)*, 4½in, 11cm, is very dark above with olive-brown streaking; below whitish with heavy streaking on chest and flanks. Known from western Uganda, north-western and southern Tanzania and Zambia. Inhabits mixed acacia grasslands and dambos. The European Tree Pipit *(A. trivialis)*, 6in, 15cm, is a common winter visitor and passage migrant in East and Central Africa. It is best identified in its winter quarters by its habitat, woodland and forest; it perches in trees readily. Upperparts black streaked, below creamy-buff boldly streaked black on breast and flanks. The Red-throated Pipit *(A. cervinus)*, 5½in, 14cm, is another winter visitor from the north. It is an open country pipit, often in loose flocks and frequently associated with flocks of Yellow Wagtails. It has streaked upperparts and a rufous-buff or rusty-red throat; heavily streaked black on underparts.

GOLDEN PIPIT   *Tmetothylacus tenellus*   Plate 24

Identification. 6in, 15cm. Upperparts pale olive-green with dusky centres to the feathers giving a slightly mottled appearance; below bright canary yellow with a black chest band; wings and tail bright canary yellow. When observed perched the bird appears as a rather yellowish-green pipit with no marked field character, but as soon as it takes wing its entire appearance changes, when it becomes a strikingly yellow bird. The ♀ is much paler and duller than the ♂. This species is remarkable among passerine birds in having the lower third of the tibia bare, as if it were a wading bird, whereas in fact it is an arid dry bush country species.

Voice. Utters a series of weak flute-like whistles, otherwise silent.

Distribution and Habitat. Local resident from Ethiopia and Somalia south through Kenya to north-eastern Tanzania. Occurs in dry bush country. It is sometimes abundant in the dry country north of the Tana River in Kenya. Usually seen singly, in pairs or in family parties.

YELLOW-THROATED LONGCLAW

Macronyx croceus   **Plate 24**

Identification. 8in, 20cm. The Longclaws are a group of large robust pipits with yellow or red on the underparts. The present species has the underparts bright yellow with a black chest band; above warm brown with dark streaking. The closely related Pangani Longclaw has the throat bright orange-yellow, a streaked chest band and yellow confined to the centre of the breast.

Voice. A rather drawn-out whistle 'tuewhee,' uttered over and over again.

Distribution and Habitat. Local resident, sometimes common, through East and Central Africa. It inhabits open woodland, grass country where there are bushes, cultivation and in southern Tanzania and Central Africa dambos in Brachystegia woodland.

Allied Species. Fulleborn's Longclaw *(M. fulleborni)*, 8in, 20cm, differs from the Yellow-throated Longclaw in having the yellow of the breast suffused with buff and the flanks brownish-buff. It occurs in the highlands of southern Tanzania, Malawi and Zambia. Its habitat is montane grasslands with scattered bushes. Sharpe's Longclaw *(M. sharpei)*, 6½in, 16½cm, is smaller than related species, warm brown above with dark streaking, pale yellow below with a band of black streaks across the chest. It occurs on short grassland in the highlands of Kenya. The Pangani Longclaw *(M. aurantii-gula)*, 7½in, 19cm, has a bright orange-yellow throat, a band of streaks across the chest and the yellow of the underparts confined to the centre of the breast; flanks streaked brown. It is a local resident in central and eastern Kenya and north-eastern Tanzania in grassy bush country. The Abyssinian Longclaw *(M. flavicollis)*, 7in, 18cm, is more dusky above than the Yellow-throated Longclaw; below, throat deep orange-buff enclosed by a band of mottled black markings; rest of underparts brownish-buff. A bird of the high mountain plateaux of Ethiopia, inhabiting moorland.

ROSY-BREASTED LONGCLAW   *Macronyx ameliae*   **Plate 24**

Identification. 7in, 18cm. Upperparts pale rusty-brown with black streaking; below, throat and breast bright salmon-red; a broad black collar across chest and curving upwards to base of bill. The ♀ is much paler below with pale salmon-red confined to a wash over the throat and belly.

Voice. A plaintive whistle 'chuit, chuit.'

Distribution and Habitat. It occurs in western and central Kenya and Tanzania, south through Central Africa. Found on open grassy plains and often in the vicinity of dams and other surface water.

Allied Species. Grimwood's Longclaw *(M. grimwoodi)*, 8½in, 22cm, resembles a larger and paler edition of the Rosy-breasted Longclaw. It is found in Angola and in north-western Zambia at Mwinilunga. It frequents marshy grasslands in areas where the Rosy-breasted Longclaw is also found.

CUCKOO SHRIKES: Campephagidae

The Cuckoo Shrikes are a group of medium-sized, shrike-like birds inhabiting forests and woodlands. In some species sexes are very dissimilar, the ♂♂ being black, the ♀♀ yellow, white and olive-grey. In the hand cuckoo shrikes may always be identified by their stiff pointed feather shafts of lower back and rump; these give the impression of spines amongst the feathers when brushed upwards.

BLACK CUCKOO SHRIKE   *Campephaga sulphurata*   **Plate 32**

Identification. 8in, 20cm. ♂ entirely black with a bluish-green gloss; small yellow gape wattles. These yellow gape wattles help to distinguish the Black Cuckoo Shrike from other black plumaged birds such as Square-tailed Drongo and Black Flycatcher. Some ♂ Black Cuckoo Shrikes have a small yellow patch on the shoulders. ♀ olive-brown to olive-grey above, barred dusky; wings and tail edged yellow and white; underparts barred white, yellow and black. Rather inconspicuous birds, usually in pairs, and often members of mixed bird parties. Restless and always on the move, feeding on caterpillars from foliage of trees and bushes.
Voice. Usually silent, but sometimes utters a soft low trill.
Distribution and Habitat. Widely distributed resident in East and Central Africa. Inhabits forest margins, woodlands, especially acacia woodland, bush country and coastal scrub.
Allied Species. The Purple-throated Cuckoo Shrike *(C. quiscalina)*, 8½in, 22cm, is a heavier looking bird, glossy blue-black with a purple throat and yellow gape. ♀ olive-green above with an ash-grey head; throat greyish-white; remainder underparts greenish yellow with indistinct narrow dusky barring. A widely distributed bird found in southern Sudan, Uganda, Kenya and Tanzania to northern Zambia. The Red-shouldered Cuckoo Shrike *(C. phoenicea)*, 8in, 20cm, is very similar to the Black Cuckoo shrike but both sexes may be distinguished by having a scarlet patch on the wing shoulders. Occurs in forests of western Kenya and Uganda, the Sudan and Ethiopia. Occurs alongside the Black Cuckoo Shrike in western Kenya. Petit's Cuckoo Shrike *(C. petiti)*, 7½in, 19cm, is blue-black; yellow gape wattles large and conspicuous in field. ♀ wholly bright canary-yellow below with some black chevron markings on chest and breast; above yellowish-olive, barred dusky, yellower on rump; tail dusky-olive, broadly tipped yellow on three outer

pairs feathers. ♂ differs from Black Cuckoo Shrike in having larger gape wattles and wash on inner webs of flight feathers, noticeable when bird flies, is grey, not yellow. The yellow underparts of the ♀ are quite different from the mottled white, black and yellow underparts of the ♀ Black Cuckoo Shrike. Petit's Cuckoo Shrike is a rain forest species found locally in Uganda and western Kenya.

WHITE-BREASTED CUCKOO SHRIKE
Coracina pectoralis   **Plate 32**

Identification. 10in, 25cm. A pale blue-grey bird with a white breast and belly; flight feathers and outer tail feathers black. ♀ has grey of face and throat paler than in ♂. In habits and flight it looks like a grey and white oriole.
Voice. A soft double whistle and a drawn-out trill.
Distribution and Habitat. Ranges from the Sudan and Ethiopia southwards to Central Africa. Very uncommon Uganda and Kenya but becomes more numerous in southern Tanzania and Central Africa. Found in savannah woodland in the north and in Brachystegia in the south.

GREY CUCKOO SHRIKE   *Coracina caesia*   **Plate 32**

Identification. 9in, 23cm. A uniformly coloured blue-grey bird with darker grey wings and tail; the ♂ has a blackish patch in front of eye. Immature barred black and grey above and below. A forest tree-tops bird, often a member of mixed bird parties; usually seen in pairs.
Voice. Not a vocal species but sometimes produces an oriole-like whistle of two or three notes.
Distribution and Habitat. Local resident in southern Sudan, Ethiopia, eastern Uganda, Kenya, Tanzania and Malawi. Inhabits evergreen and mountain forests, mainly in the highlands.

BULBULS: Pycnonotidae

The Bulbuls are a group of thrush-like birds of plain green, yellow, grey and brown plumage; tarsus very short; arboreal in habits and most species are inhabitants of forest and woodland; food mainly fruits with some insects; many species are outstanding songsters.

YELLOW-VENTED BULBUL *Pycnonotus barbatus* Plate 26

Identification. 7in, 18cm. A common garden bird throughout much of East and Central Africa. Upperparts greyish-brown, blackish or dark brown on head and chin, merging to brown on throat and chest; breast and belly whitish, under tail-coverts yellow. The head appears slightly crested when nape feathers are raised; the yellow under tail-coverts are conspicuous. Upon alighting the bird has the habit of half raising its wings and uttering a brief warbling song.

Voice. A rapid, brief song 'too, de de, de, che, che' and a scolding alarm call.

Distribution and Habitat. A common and widely distributed species found throughout the greater part of the Ethiopian Region, including East and Central Africa. Occurs as a garden bird, in old cultivation, woodland, coastal scrub, open forest and in secondary growth, especially lantana thickets; one of the commonest African birds.

Allied Species. The Little Grey Greenbul *(Andropadus gracilis)*, 6½in, 16½cm, is dark olive-green above, head darker and greyer with a faint whitish eye-ring; lower rump tinged yellow; tail olive-brown; below, throat grey, chest olive grey; breast and belly olive-brown to yellowish in centre of belly. A forest species found in Uganda and western Kenya. The Cameroun Sombre Greenbul *(A. curvirostris)*, 7in, 18cm, is very similar to the Little Grey Greenbul but has a heavier and longer bill. Again a forest species known from Uganda and western Kenya. Ansorge's Greenbul *(A. ansorgei)*, 6½in, 16½cm, differs from the Little Grey Greenbul in its more extensively yellow belly. It also is found in forests of Uganda and western Kenya. The Slender-billed Greenbul *(Stelgidillas gracilirostris)*, 6½in, 16½cm, is dull olive-green above, grey below with a paler throat. It is a forest species known from southern Sudan, Uganda, western Kenya and western Tanzania. The Little Greenbul *(Andropadus virens)*, 6½in, 16½cm, is very like a smaller edition of the Cameroun Sombre Greenbul but has a shorter and much broader bill. It occurs in southern Sudan, Uganda, Kenya, Tanzania, Malawi and Zambia; another forest species.

YELLOW-WHISKERED GREENBUL
Andropadus latirostris Plate 26

Identification. 7in, 18cm. Upperparts dark olive; below paler olive to yellowish in centre of belly; two conspicuous yellow streaks from base of bill on each side of the throat. In life this bird appears very dark in the forest undergrowth, but may be identified always at close quarters by the yellow stripes on each side of the throat.

Voice. A series of high and low whistles; song a series of 8–10 notes repeated over and over again.

Distribution and Habitat. Common in forests of southern Sudan, southwards through Uganda to eastern Kenya highlands, southwards to northern and western Tanzania. One of the commonest forest birds in Uganda and western Kenya.

ZANZIBAR SOMBRE GREENBUL
Andropadus importunus   Plate 26

Identification. 7in, 18cm. Olive green above and on wings and tail; paler below and tinged yellowish in centre of belly. Eye creamy-white – its best field character.
Voice. Call note a metallic 'clink;' also a cheerful warbling song.
Distribution and Habitat. This is a common bird in coastal scrub and forest in Kenya and Tanzania; also Zanzibar and Zambia.

OLIVE-BREASTED MOUNTAIN GREENBUL
Andropadus tephrolaemus   Plate 26

Identification. 7in, 18cm. This is a green bulbul with a clear grey head and throat and a white eye-ring; yellowish in centre of belly.
Voice. Produces a variety of clucking noises and has a sustained thrush-like song.
Distribution and Habitat. Inhabits mountain and highland forests in Uganda and Kenya. Found in undergrowth, in the foliage of smaller trees and amongst creepers.
Allied Species. The similar Mountain Greenbul *(A. nigriceps)*, 7in, 18cm, is found in mountain forests in Tanzania, Malawi and Zambia. The northern race from Kilimanjaro and Mt Meru, northern Tanzania, has a blackish crown; other races possess grey crowns and are best distinguished from the Olive-bellied Mountain Greenbul by lacking yellow in centre of belly. Shelley's Greenbul *(A. masukuensis)*, 6in, 15cm, is uniform olive-green, darker on mantle. It occurs in mountain forest in western Kenya, Tanzania and Malawi. The Stripe-cheeked Greenbul *(A. milanjensis)*, 7in, 18cm, is also olive-green in colour with the ear-coverts striped grey and white. It is found in highland forests of Tanzania and Malawi. The Honeyguide Green-bul *(Baeopogon indicator)*, 8in, 20cm, is dark olive-green above with grey cheeks and underparts; belly and under tail-coverts buff; three outer pairs rectrices mainly white. A forest treetop species which has a close resemblance to a honeyguide in life. Known from the southern Sudan, western Kenya and Uganda, mainly in the west. The Spotted Greenbul *(Ixonotus guttatus)*, 6in, 15cm, is greenish-grey above and white below, with conspicuous white spots

on the upperparts. It is a forest treetops species usually found in small parties. Occurs in southern Sudan and western Uganda.

YELLOW-THROATED LEAFLOVE
Pyrrhurus flavicollis **Plate 26**

Identification. 7in, 18cm. Above dark olive-grey; below, throat creamy-yellow, remainder underparts pale dull yellowish-olive.
Voice. Utters a scolding chatter and mewing calls.
Distribution and Habitat. Occurs locally in Uganda, western Kenya and western Tanzania. Frequents forests, secondary growth and gardens. A common bird at Entebbe, Uganda, especially in the botanical gardens.
Allied Species. The Yellow-bellied Greenbul *(Chlorocichla flaviventris)*, 8½in, 22cm, is deep olive-brown above, buffy-yellow below. It is widely distributed in the eastern half of Kenya and through Tanzania to Central Africa. Inhabits forests, woodlands with heavy undergrowth and coastal scrub. The Joyful Greenbul *(C. laetissima)*, 8½in, 22cm, with golden-green upperparts, wings and tail and bright yellow underparts occurs in rain forests in southern Sudan, Uganda, western Kenya and north-western Zambia. It draws attention by its loud chattering calls and thrush-like song. The White-tailed Greenbul *(Thescelocichla leucopleura)*, 8½in, 22cm, is dark olive-grey above, feathers of crown with darker edges giving a scaly appearance; below, throat and chest mottled pale olive and whitish, breast and belly yellowish white; tail with broad white tips with exception of central rectrices. This species occurs in swamp forest and is almost always associated with oil palms. Draws attention by its loud babbler-like calls. In East Africa recorded from western Uganda. The Leaflove *(Pyrrhurus scandens)*, 8in, 20cm, is a forest treetop species, greyish-brown on upperparts, whitish below; wings and tail pale cinnamon-rufous. Has habit of flirting wings and tail which appear almost translucent. Found in southern Sudan, Uganda and western Tanzania.

NORTHERN BROWNBUL   *Phyllastrephus strepitans*   **Plate 26**

Identification. 6½in, 16½cm. A rather slim, russet-brown bulbul with a dark rufous rump and upper tail coverts; below warm brown, whitish on throat and centre of belly.
Voice. Clear chattering call notes.
Distribution and Habitat. Ranges from the southern Sudan, southern Ethiopia and Somalia, through Kenya and eastern Tanzania. Inhabits bush country, riverine thickets and coastal scrub. Often in small parties and feeds on or near the ground in thick cover.
Allied Species. The very similar Brownbul *(Ph. terrestris)*, 7in, 18cm, has an

olive-brown back, white throat, greyish chest and flanks, a creamy-white belly and yellow eyes. It occurs in coastal areas of Kenya and Tanzania to Malawi and southwards. A skulker in thick scrub, coastal bush and wooded areas where there is dense undergrowth. The Grey-olive Greenbul *(Ph. cerviniventris)*, 7in, 18cm, is greyish-green above, the head greyer and the tail earth-brown; below pale greyish to whitish in centre of belly. Occurs in forest undergrowth in Uganda, western and central Kenya south to Malawi and Zambia.

FISCHER'S GREENBUL   *Phyllastrephus fischeri*   **Plate 26**

Identification. 6½in, 16½cm. A uniformly coloured species, greyish-olive above, wings and tail slightly tinged rufous, paler yellowish-olive below to brown on under tail coverts; throat whitish. Two races of *Ph. fischeri* are now generally considered to be distinct species. These are *Ph. f. placidus* which is greener above and slightly greyer below, and *Ph. f. cabanisi* which is darker above and yellower below.

Voice. A series of short notes, 'trip, trip, trip, trip;' song a series of flute-like whistles.

Distribution and Habitat. The nominate race occurs in coastal areas of East Africa from Somalia southwards. *Ph. f. placidus* is found in inland districts of Kenya, Tanzania and Malawi, and *Ph. f. cabanisi* occurs in western Kenya, Uganda south to Zambia. Fischer's Greenbul inhabits woodland and scrub areas and also forest undergrowth.

Allied Species. Xavier's Greenbul *(Ph. xavieri)*, 6½in, 16½cm, is bright olive-green above, bright yellow below. It occurs in forest undergrowth in western Uganda. Alongside it is another almost identical species the Icterine Greenbul *(Ph. icterinus)*, 6in, 15cm, which differs only in its slightly smaller size. It also occurs in the forests of western Uganda. The White-throated Greenbul *(Ph. albigularis)*, 6in, 15cm, has the upperparts and wings olive-green, crown with dark centres to feathers giving scaly appearance, below throat white merging to greyish on chest and white on belly with pale yellow streaks; tail russet-brown with green edgings to outer feathers. An uncommon forest bird known from southern Sudan and Uganda. The somewhat similar Yellow-streaked Greenbul *(Ph. flavostriatus)*, 7½in, 19cm, is olive-green above with a grey head; throat greyish-white to very pale grey on the breast and belly, streaked pale yellow; wings and tail green. Occurs locally in Uganda, south-eastern Kenya, eastern and western Tanzania and Malawi and Zambia. A forest undergrowth species. The Smaller Yellow-streaked Greenbul *(Ph. debilis)*, 5in, 13cm, is similar but very much smaller. It occurs in south-eastern Kenya, eastern Tanzania and southern Tanzania. Inhabits forest and wooded country, usually in undergrowth.

BRISTLEBILL   *Bleda syndactyla*   **Plate 26**

Identification. 8½in, 21½cm. A large, thickset bulbul, olive-green above, bright yellow below with a chestnut-red tail and a bare blue patch around eyes. Bill of ♂ larger and more hooked than that of ♀.
Voice. A monotonous 'chr, chr, chr, chr, chr' and a sharp 'pritt-pritt.'
Distribution and Habitat. A local resident in moist forests in southern Sudan, Uganda and western Kenya. Inhabits the undergrowth and small trees in dense forest.
Allied Species. The Green-tailed Bristlebill *(B. eximia)*, 7½in, 19cm, has a green tail with yellow tips to the outer pairs of rectrices. It occurs in forests of southern Sudan and in western and southern Uganda.

RED-TAILED GREENBUL   *Tricophorus calurus*   **Plate 26**

Identification. 7in, 18cm. A rather thickset, stocky species. Dark olive-green above, a bright chestnut-red tail, yellow belly and a very conspicuous white throat which is often puffed out and is the bird's most distinctive field character. Another greenbul is called the White-throated Greenbul, but its white throat is not a conspicuous field character.
Voice. A long drawn-out 'teeeeeep' and a brief warbling song.
Distribution and Habitat. A West African species which extends eastwards to Uganda. It is a forest bird, locally common, and on account of its white throat and red tail readily identifiable in the field.

NICATOR   *Nicator chloris*   **Plate 26**

Identification. 8½in, 21½cm. Upperparts bright olive-green, below grey, yellow under tail-coverts; conspicuous yellow spots on the wing and tips of tail feathers yellow. Inhabits forests and thick woodland and scrub, skulking amongst creepers and foliage. Ranges from southern Sudan, Uganda, Kenya and southwards to Central Africa.
Voice. Harsh guttural notes and a loud 'zokh;' also utters deep liquid notes not unlike those of an oriole.
Distribution and Habitat. A forest and thick woodland species found in southern Sudan, Uganda, western and coastal Kenya, Tanzania and Central Africa. Usually in dense forest canopy or creepers where it would be overlooked were it not for its calls.
Allied Species. The Yellow-throated Nicator *(N. vireo)*, 5½in, 14cm, is like a miniature Nicator but has a yellow patch on the throat. It occurs both in undergrowth and amongst the branches of forest trees in western Uganda.

HELMET SHRIKES: Prionopidae

A group of medium sized shrike-like birds with hooked bills. One of their main characteristics is their extreme sociability, being found always in small flocks, even during the nesting season. Flight graceful and butterfly-like. Calls also distinctive, a loud communal chattering and bill-snapping. In many species feathers of forehead project forwards and there is a fleshy wattle around the eye.

STRAIGHT-CRESTED HELMET SHRIKE
Prionops plumata **Plate 32**

Identification. 8in, 20cm. A distinctively patterned black and white bird with lemon-yellow eye wattles: crown blue-grey with whitish bristly feathers of forehead directed forwards; underparts white, feet orange. Always in small compact flocks which draw attention to themselves by their chattering and bill-snapping. Usually very tame and fearless of humans.
Voice. A chattering call, interspersed with occasional flute-like notes and bill snapping.
Distribution and Habitat. Widely distributed from Uganda, southern Ethiopia and Kenya south to Central Africa. Inhabits bush country, acacia woodlands and open Brachystegia woodland.

CURLY-CRESTED HELMET SHRIKE
Prionops cristata **Plate 32**

Identification. 8in, 20cm. Often considered to be conspecific with the Straight-crested Helmet Shrike but the ranges of these two birds appear to overlap in the Lake Baringo area, Kenya. Distinguished by its striking crest of long curly white feathers. It may possess or lack a white bar along the wing.
Voice. Chattering calls and bill snapping.
Distribution and Habitat. Local resident in the southern Sudan, northern Uganda, Ethiopia, north-western Kenya. It frequents areas of bush country, acacia woodland along rivers and scrub.
Allied Species. The Grey-crested Helmet Shrike *(P. poliolopha)*, 9in, 23cm, lacks the yellow eye wattles and is larger, with a lax grey occipital crest and a black patch on each side of the chest. It is a very uncommon bush-country bird in central districts of southern Kenya and northern Tanzania. It is not uncommon in the Loliondo district of northern Tanzania, where mixed flocks of Grey-crested and Straight-crested Helmet Shrikes occur.

RETZ'S RED-BILLED SHRIKE *Prionops retzii* Plate 32

Identification. 8in, 20cm. A rather thickset grey-brown helmet shrike with sharply contrasting dark breast and white abdomen, and white-tipped tail; bill, eye wattles and feet red; crest of erect feathers on forehead. Always in small flocks and often associated with parties of wood hoopoes.

Voice. Noisy chattering interspersed with soft whistles; also a sharp double alarm call.

Distribution and Habitat. Ranges from southern Somalia, south through Kenya and Tanzania to Malawi, Zambia and Rhodesia. Inhabits open forest and woodland areas, especially riverine acacias, Brachystegia and coastal scrub.

Allied Species. The Chestnut-fronted Shrike *(P. scopifrons)*, 7in, 18cm, is grey above with a curious pad of velvet-like chestnut bristles on the forehead; tail tipped white; below slate-grey to white on abdomen. An uncommon local resident in woodland, especially Brachystegia, in eastern districts of Kenya and Tanzania. The Red-billed Shrike *(P. caniceps)*, 7in, 18cm, is a thickset forest-treetops helmet shrike, always in small parties. Back, wings and tail black with an oily dark green sheen; head pale blue with a large triangular black patch on throat; chest greyish-white, breast and belly rich rufous; bill crimson-red; eye wattle flesh-coloured; feet orange-red. In East Africa occurs in forests of western Uganda, mainly the Bwamba forest in Toro. The red bill contrasting with the pale blue head is noticeable in the field.

WHITE-CROWNED SHRIKE *Eurocephalus ruppelli* Plate 32

Identification. 9in, 23cm. Dry thornbush country species. Mantle dusky brown with contrasting white crown and rump; a wide black patch behind eye; below white with a brown patch on each side of the breast. Immature has crown brown and upperparts barred. Found always in small parties. Field appearance distinctive, white crown and rump being very conspicuous; remarkable for its stiff, gliding flight between trees on rigid wings. Has a slight resemblance to a White-headed Buffalo Weaver but lacks the red rump characteristic of that species.

Voice. A harsh 'kaa, kaa, kaa' and various chattering and whistling call notes.

Distribution and Habitat. Local resident Ethiopia, Somalia and Sudan, south through northern Uganda, Kenya and Tanzania. A typical bird of acacia bush country; common locally in Kenya.

SHRIKES: LANIIDAE

Conspicuously coloured medium-sized birds with strong hooked bills. Some species, members of the genus *Lanius*, perch on vantage points from which they can pounce on their prey. The remainder, the genera *Nilaus, Malaconotus, Tchagra, Laniarius, Dryoscopus, Rhodophoneus* etc. mostly feed among foliage of trees and bushes. It is probable that these two groups are not related very closely. Call notes usually harsh but songs sometimes surprisingly musical.

NORTHERN BRUBRU   *Nilaus afer*   Plate 32

Identification. 5in, 13cm. A striking black and white bird with chestnut flanks; white stripe over eye extending to nape. Active in trees and bushes, searching foliage for insect food. Calls frequently. The southern race, *N. a. nigritemporalis*, from central Tanzania southwards, is sometimes considered a full species. It lacks the white stripe over the eye in the ♂, and the ♀ has a short eye-stripe which does not extend to the nape; also black streaking and barring on throat and breast.
Voice. A loud prolonged 'keeeeeeeeeerr' and a three to five note clear whistle.
Distribution and Habitat. Widely distributed over much of East and Central Africa. Frequents bush, scrub and woodland country. In East Africa much attracted to flowering acacia trees where it feeds on the many insects which visit the blossoms.

BLACK-BACKED PUFFBACK   *Dryoscopus cubla*   Plate 33

Identification. 6in, 15cm. ♂ above glossy blue-black with conspicuous rump patch of downy white feathers; wing-coverts and flight feathers edged white; underparts white, slightly greyish on breast and flanks. ♀ and immature have duller upperparts; rump grey and a short white streak above the eye. In life the rump feathers are often puffed out when they are very noticeable. Hunts insects and larvae amongst foliage of trees in manner of a warbler. Usually found in pairs and often members of mixed bird parties.
Voice. A loud, harsh 'chik, weeooo – chik, weeoo' frequently repeated; sometimes a double clicking note followed by a clear whistle. Often produces a loud 'brrrrrrp' with wings when flying from branch to branch.
Distribution and Habitat. Widely distributed resident Uganda and Kenya (except in extreme north) south through Tanzania to Malawi, Zambia and Rhodesia. Inhabits forested areas, woodland, thicket, gardens, scrub and acacia country.

Allied Species. Pringle's Puffback *(D. pringlii)*, 5in, 13cm, is the smallest of the puffback shrikes with a glossy black head, mantle and tail; outer tail feathers edged and tipped white; rump and underparts greyish-white; heavy black bill with a yellow base to the mandible. A bird of arid bush country in south-eastern Ethiopia, southern Somalia and eastern Kenya. The Puffback Shrike *(D. gambensis)*, 7in, 18cm, has a much duller black mantle, pale buffy-grey scapulars and edgings to flight feathers and a grey rump; below pale grey. ♀ brown above with a grey rump; below pale tawny buff. A forest treetop species found in East Africa south to northern Tanzania, common in Uganda and Kenya. The Zanzibar Puffback *(D. affinis)*, 6in, 15cm, has the crown, mantle, wings and tail glossy black; lower back, rump and underparts white; no white edging to flight feathers. ♀ has white streak from nostrils to over eye. The Black-backed Puffback has white edgings to wings and its white rump and underparts are tinged grey. Occurs in woodland and forest along the Kenya and Tanzania coast, on Zanzibar Island and in the forests of western Uganda. The Pink-footed Puffback *(D. angolensis)*, 6in, 15cm, ♂ has the crown and upper back dark slate-grey; mantle, wings and tail ash-grey; rump and underparts pale grey; feet pink. The ♀ has the crown and upper back pale grey; mantle, wings and tail olive-brown and rump greyish brown; below rufous-buff, centre of belly white and legs pink. A forest tree-top species found in southern Sudan, Uganda, western Kenya and western Tanzania. Usually in pairs.

BLACK-HEADED TCHAGRA   *Tchagra senegala*   **Plate 33**

Identification. 8in, 20cm. A brown bush shrike with striking chestnut-red wings, a black crown and a buffy-white eye stripe; tail black with white tips. Usually seen as it dives from cover into a bush, when red wings and white tipped black tail are noticeable.

Voice. A series of clear piping whistles and a churring alarm call. Has courtship flight, mounting sharply into air with crackling wings, then floating down in a spiral uttering a clear piping.

Distribution and Habitat. Common resident over most of East and Central Africa. Inhabits desert scrub, bush, wooded areas, gardens and neglected cultivation, undergrowth and scrub along rivers and mixed grass and bush.

Allied Species. The Brown-headed Tchagra *(T. australis)*, 7½in, 19cm, is very similar to the Black-headed Tchagra but has the crown brown, not black. Ranges from southern Sudan, Uganda and Kenya south through Tanzania to Central Africa. Frequents scrub, woodland and undergrowth.

THREE-STREAKED TCHAGRA   *Tchagra jamesi*   **Plate 33**

Identification. 6½in, 16½cm. An ashy-grey bush shrike with rufous wings and a white-tipped dark tail; narrow black streak down centre of crown and black streak on each side of head; underparts pale grey, whiter on throat and belly. Eye colour remarkable, the iris being brown with eight silver dots arranged around pupil.
Voice. A loud trill on a descending scale.
Distribution and Habitat. Occurs in arid bush country of Somalia, southern Ethiopia, south-eastern Sudan, eastern Uganda and south through Kenya to north-eastern Tanzania. Local and uncommon.

BLACKCAP TCHAGRA   *Tchagra minuta*   **Plate 33**

Identification. 6in, 15cm. Upperparts chestnut-red with a contrasting all-black cap; broken black V on mantle; tail black with buffy-white tips; below warm buff to white on throat. ♀ has a white streak from base of bill to over eye.
Voice. A harsh 'klop' and various bleating calls; also a flute-like song.
Distribution and Habitat. Local resident over much of East and Central Africa with possible exception of Somalia. Inhabits dense undergrowth of all kinds but is very partial to stands of elephant grass and sugarcane cultivation.

ROSY-PATCHED SHRIKE   *Rhodophoneus cruentus*   **Plate 33**

Identification. 9in, 23cm. A rather slim, long-tailed shrike with the general appearance of a babbler; above pale pinkish-brown with a very conspicuous rosy-red rump; tail with broad white tips to outer feathers; below white with a rosy red patch from throat to breast; flanks and under tail-coverts buff. The ♀ has a black gorget across the chest and a rosy-red patch from the gorget down centre of belly. Favours acacia bushes and often settles and runs on the ground. The red rump-patch is very striking in flight.
Voice. Various brief piping whistles; song very melodious, more thrush than shrike-like, four, five or six notes frequently repeated.
Distribution and Habitat. Local resident, usually uncommon, in southern Sudan, Ethiopia, Somalia southwards through Kenya to northern Tanzania. Inhabits open bush country and arid scrub.
Allied Species. The Red-naped Bush Shrike *(Laniarius ruficeps)*, 6½in, 16½cm. Mantle grey, wings and tail black; crown black (grey in ♀) with a bright orange-red patch on the hind crown and nape; underparts white. Ranges from southern and eastern Ethiopia to Somalia and through eastern and north-eastern coastal Kenya. Inhabits dense arid bush country; a skulker and difficult to observe; the red nape patch is noticeable in field.

LUHDER'S BUSH SHRIKE   *Laniarius luhderi*   Plate 33

Identification. 7in, 18cm. Upperparts, wings and tail black; crown chestnut-orange; white bar along wing; below, throat and breast orange-rufous, belly white.
Voice. A liquid 'chee-oo-ch, chee,' perhaps uttered by a pair of birds.
Distribution and Habitat. Forests of southern Sudan, Uganda, western Kenya and western Tanzania. Inhabits thick cover near forest or undergrowth in forest; shy and not often seen.

TROPICAL BOUBOU   *Laniarius ferrugineus*   Plate 33

Identification. 9in, 23cm. Upperparts, wings and tail glossy black, with or without a white wing-bar; below white with a pink flush. Immature barred tawny on upperparts. Always found in pairs, skulking in undergrowth, thick bush, creepers and thick foliage of trees. Draws attention by its clear bell-like whistles.
Voice. Varied and remarkable duet between ♂ and ♀; one utters three rapid clear bell-like whistles, answered immediately with a croaking 'kweee.' This second call is uttered so instantaneously that the entire call seems made by one bird. The notes vary very much and most localities seem to have their own variety of whistles and croak. The species also makes a harsh churring call.
Distribution and Habitat. Widely distributed throughout suitable areas of Ethiopian Region, including East and Central Africa. Inhabits thick cover in forest, woodland, riverine thickets, gardens, bush, and coastal scrub. Sometimes feeds on the ground in thick cover. Well known in gardens in towns, where it has the popular name of 'bell bird.'

BLACK-HEADED GONOLEK   *Laniarius erythrogaster*   Plate 32

Identification. 8in, 20cm. Upperparts jet-black; underparts bright red, under tail-coverts buff. Immature barred buff and black below. A beautiful and unmistakable bird, rather skulking in habits, keeping to dense bush and such-like cover.
Voice. A clear, two-note whistle 'wee-oooo' frequently repeated; also a harsher rasping call.
Distribution and Habitat. Local resident, sometimes common, in southern Sudan, Ethiopia, Uganda, western Kenya and north-western Tanzania. Occurs in dense bush, especially near water, thick tangled vegetation and neglected cultivation. It is a common bird around Entebbe and in the Ruwenzori National Park, Uganda, and Kisumu, western Kenya, where it is a conspicuous species in gardens.

Allied Species. The closely allied Crimson-breasted Boubou *(L. atrococ-cineus)*, 8in, 20cm, differs in having a white wing bar. It inhabits dense acacia bush in Zambia and Rhodesia. The Yellow-crowned Gonolek *(L. mufum-biri)*, 8in, 20cm, differs from the Black-headed Gonolek in having the crown and nape golden-yellow, white tips to the wing coverts and a less heavy bill. It inhabits dense papyrus beds. It is known from two localities in Uganda, the Kazinga Channel in the Ruwenzori National Park and papyrus swamps in south-western Kigezi; in Kenya it is recorded from papyrus swamps near Kisumu.

SLATE-COLOURED BOUBOU *Laniarius funebris* Plate 33

Identification. 7in, 18cm. Entire plumage dark slate-grey to blackish on head, wings and tail. Immature with indistinct tawny barring on upperparts. Skulking in habits, keeping to thick cover; found in pairs. In the field, except in a good light, it appears as a completely black bird.

Voice. ♂ and ♀ duet, one of pair uttering three or four bell-like notes followed immediately by the second bird giving a double croak. Also has various other whistles and churring notes and a harsh 'krrrr' alarm call.

Distribution and Habitat. Widespread resident, usually below 5,000ft, 1,530m, in southern Sudan, Ethiopia, Somalia, south through Uganda and Kenya to southern Tanzania. Inhabits dry bush country, keeping to thickets and stands of Salvadora bushes; also in coastal scrub and woodland where thick cover exists.

Allied Species. Fulleborn's Black Boubou *(L. fulleborni)*, 7½in, 19cm. Entire plumage dark slaty black; ♀ has olive wash over chest to belly; immature olive-grey above, dark olive below. This is a mountain forest species, found in pairs, known from mountain ranges in eastern Tanzania from the Usambara Mts southwards to the Nyika Plateau in Malawi and eastern Zambia. The Sooty Boubou *(L. leucorhynchus)*, 8in, 20cm, is an entirely sooty-black bird with long black rump feathers. Adults have a black bill, immatures a whitish bill. A skulker in dense forest undergrowth but draws attention by its clear whistles. Occurs in rain forest in the Sudan and Uganda. The very similar Mountain Sooty Boubou *(L. poensis)*, 7in, 18cm, is also entirely black with a more glossy mantle tinged greenish; tail rather short; ♀ similar but duller, less glossy. This is a mountain forest species known from western and south-western Uganda. Its call is a low, bell-like whistle. Quite common in higher forest on the Ruwenzori Mts and in the Impenetrable Forest, south-western Kigezi, Uganda.

GREY-HEADED BUSH SHRIKE *Malaconotus blanchoti* Plate 33

Identification. 10in, 25cm. A large, heavily-built bush shrike with a massive hooked black bill; crown and nape grey; remainder upperparts, wings and tail bright green with yellow spots on tips of secondaries and tail feathers; below bright yellow, washed orange-chestnut on chest. Immature similar but with horn coloured bill. Usually found singly or in pairs; often in foliage of large acacia trees.

Voice. A loud two or three note whistle; sometimes utters a curious rattling chatter.

Distribution and Habitat. Local and generally uncommon in East and Central Africa. Inhabits all types of woodland but in East Africa favours stands of acacia trees near water.

Allied Species. The Fiery-breasted Bush Shrike *(M. cruentus)*, 10in, 25cm, crown, nape and mantle blue-grey; rest of upperparts olive green; wing coverts and secondaries mainly black with yellow tips; tail green with black subterminal band and yellow tips; forehead and stripe over eye greyish-white; underparts bright yellow, throat and breast with strong crimson wash; under tail coverts orange-rufous. In East Africa it is known from the Bwamba Forest, western Uganda. Lagden's Bush Shrike *(M. lagdeni)*, 8½in, 21½cm, is similar to the Grey-headed Bush Shrike but has wing-coverts and inner secondaries black; below, yellow with orange stripe from throat down centre of breast. A very rare mountain forest species known in East Africa from forests of western Uganda. The Blackcap Bush Shrike *(Malaconotus alius)*, 9in, 23cm, is known only from the Uluguru Mts forest in eastern Tanzania. It is glossy blue-black on the crown, nape and ear coverts; rest upperparts, wings and tail dark green; below sulphur yellow with an olive wash on chest and flanks. Occurs in forest tree-tops.

SULPHUR-BREASTED BUSH SHRIKE
Malaconotus sulphureopectus Plate 33

Identification. 7in, 18cm. Rather a slim-looking shrike, pale grey above with bright yellowish-green wings and tail; forehead and stripe over eye bright yellow; below yellow with bright orange wash on chest, merging to yellow on belly. A very striking bird found in pairs in acacia woodland.

Voice. A loud piping whistle of ten or twelve notes.

Distribution and Habitat. Local and generally rather uncommon in East and Central Africa. Inhabits the foliage of acacia trees, riverine forest, clumps of thickly foliaged trees, bush and coastal scrub. Rather skulking in its habits and easy to overlook unless one hears its piping call.

Allied Species. The Grey Bush Shrike *(Malaconotus bocagei)*, 6in, 15cm, has the crown and upper mantle black; lower back, rump and wings olive grey; tail black with narrow white tips; forehead and stripe over eye white; below white with buff wash on chest and breast. A forest species which gathers much of its insect food from branches and clumps of moss high in the tree-tops. In East Africa known from Uganda and western Kenya.

DOHERTY'S BUSH SHRIKE *Malaconotus dohertyi* **Plate 33**

Identification. 7in, 18cm. Bright green above with a crimson-red forehead and throat, followed by a broad black breast band and a yellow belly. Immature with less red on forehead and barred black above. A skulking species found in forest undergrowth.
Voice. A series of clear bell-like whistles 'kwik, kwik kwik' and various flute-like notes.
Distribution and Habitat. Local resident in forests of the Kenya highlands; in Uganda found in the Mt Elgon forests and forests in the south-west.

FOUR-COLOURED BUSH SHRIKE
Malaconotus quadricolor **Plate 33**

Identification. 7in, 18cm. A skulking species of great beauty, bright green above with a yellow forehead and eye-stripe; bright red throat and black chest band; belly rich yellow washed with orange-red; tail dusky green.
Voice. Loud clear bell-like whistles, the origin of which is difficult to locate in dense bush.
Distribution and Habitat. A not uncommon resident in coastal and south-eastern Kenya, south through eastern Tanzania to Malawi and Rhodesia. Owing to its shy and skulking habits it is often overlooked. It inhabits thick coastal scrub, dense riverine thickets and bush.
Allied Species. The Gorgeous Bush Shrike *(M. viridis)*, 7in, 18cm, differs from the Four-coloured Bush Shrike in having the forehead and eye-stripe cinnamon-brown and yellow; chest-band black; throat and band across breast below black chest collar scarlet; belly and flanks green with a central chocolate-brown stripe; under tail coverts maroon-red. In the area covered known only from extreme north-western Zambia. Rare and little-known, in forest.

BLACK-FRONTED BUSH SHRIKE
Malaconotus nigrifrons **Plate 33**

Identification. 7in, 18cm. Crown and upper back blue-grey, a black forehead (absent in ♀ and immature) and a wide black stripe through the eye; underparts extremely variable, four main colour phases exist: rich orange-yellow, bright scarlet, salmon-pink and blackish-green. The orange-yellow phase is the most usual and the blackish-green phase is the rarest. Lower back, wings and tail green.

Voice. A loud whistle 'who-koo' and various harsh scolding calls.

Distribution and Habitat. A local and uncommon species in western and central Kenya, south through Tanzania to Central Africa. Mainly a bird of mountain or high level forest; frequents tree-top foliage and creepers; often a member of mixed bird parties.

Allied Species. The Multicoloured Bush Shrike *(M. multicolor)*, 7in, 18cm, is closely related to the Black-fronted Bush Shrike and may be con-specific. It differs mainly in having a green or black tail with broad yellow tips. It occurs in three colour phases, a scarlet-breasted, an orange-breasted and a black-breasted form. Occurs in forests of western Uganda where it also inhabits the tree tops and the masses of creepers hanging from the trees.

YELLOW-BILLED SHRIKE *Corvinella corvina* Plate 33

Identification. 12in, 30½cm; tail 7in, 18cm. A drab brownish-buff shrike, paler on the underparts, with narrow black streaking above and below; dark brown ear-coverts; bill clear chrome-yellow; wings conspicuously cinnamon-rufous in flight.

Voice. An often repeated 'scis-scis.'

Distribution and Habitat. Local and uncommon resident in Sudan, northern and eastern Uganda and western Kenya. Normally frequents acacia wood-lands and bush, especially near water and where there is a lush undergrowth. Sometimes in pairs, otherwise small groups are the rule. Hunts prey in typical shrike fashion, from a vantage point.

MAGPIE SHRIKE *Lanius melanoleucus* Plate 32

Identification. 14–15in, 35½–38cm. A very large black shrike with a long tail; white patch on each side of the mantle and a white wing-bar; rump grey. A most conspicuous bird which settles on the tops of bushes; occurs in pairs or family parties.

Voice. A loud warbling two-note call, repeated several times; also a harsh rasping call-note.

Distribution and Habitat. Local resident, widely but locally distributed in extreme south-western Kenya, Tanzania and Central Africa. Inhabits open country with scattered bush, neglected cultivation and acacia scrub and woodland. It specially favours black cotton-soil with scattered whistling acacias in parts of Tanzania.

Allied Species. Souza's Shrike *(L. souzae)*, 6½in, 16½cm, is a grey-capped shrike with a barred brown mantle; scapulars white, forming a conspicuous V on the back; ear-coverts black; tail narrow, brown with white tip; underparts greyish white. An open woodlands species found in western and south-western Tanzania, Zambia and Malawi. Emin's Shrike *(L. gubernator)*, 6½in, 16½cm, is a red-backed shrike with a grey head and a broad black forehead-band and eye-stripe; below tawny, white on throat and belly. Looks like a European Red-backed Shrike but has rump and upper tail-coverts chestnut, not grey. Found in savannah country in northern Uganda and southern Sudan. The well known European Red-backed Shrike and the Red-tailed Shrike are winter visitors to East and Central Africa; the former extending southwards to Central Africa, the latter extending southwards to northern Tanzania.

FISCAL SHRIKE   *Lanius collaris*   Plate 32

Identification. 9in, 23cm. Above black with a conspicuous white V patch on back; rump grey; below white; ♀ with chestnut patch on flanks; tail long and graduated, black broadly tipped white. Immature barred black and tawny above and lightly barred grey and white below. One of the commonest and best-known East African birds, being common even in townships; often seen perched on telegraph wires.
Voice. A rather sharp, drawn-out 'cheeeeeeeee;' alarm call a clear whistle.
Distribution and Habitat. Widespread but local resident, often common, throughout much of East and Central Africa. Inhabits cultivated areas, the vicinity of human habitations, lightly wooded country and the edges of dambos.
Allied Species. Mackinnon's Grey Shrike *(L. mackinnoni)*, 9in, 23cm, is very like the Fiscal Shrike but has upperparts grey instead of black and with a white stripe over the eye. A local and uncommon resident in Uganda, western Kenya and north-western and central Tanzania. It frequents wooded country, forest margins and glades and cultivation near forests. The well known European species Lesser Grey Shrike *(L. minor)*, is a winter visitor and passage migrant to East and Central Africa, and the Nubian Shrike *(L. nubicus)* and Woodchat Shrike *(L. senator)* winter in the northern parts of East Africa.

LONG-TAILED FISCAL   *Lanius cabanisi*   Plate 32

Identification. 12in, 30½cm. Upperparts black, merging to grey on lower back and rump; white wing-bar; tail very long, completely black; underparts white; ♀ with small chestnut patch on flanks. Immature tawny above, lightly

barred black. Commonly seen in small parties; birds perch close together on a single bush, raising, lowering and swinging tails in pendulum fashion.
Voice. A variety of harsh scolding calls and a clear whistle.
Distribution and Habitat. Local resident southern Somalia, eastern and central Kenya and eastern Tanzania. Inhabits coastal open low scrub and grassland with scattered bushes and open plains. Common in coastal districts of Kenya and on the Athi Plains, central Kenya.
Allied Species. The Grey-backed Fiscal *(L. excubitorius)*, 10in, 25cm, has upperparts pale grey; forehead and broad streak through eye black; tail white with broad black tip; underparts white. Immature lightly barred black and tawny. Like the Long-tailed Fiscal this species sometimes collects in small parties and is given to noisy chattering and tail waving. It occurs in southern Sudan, Ethiopia, Uganda, western half of Kenya and western Tanzania in bush and in acacia woodland.

TAITA FISCAL *Lanius dorsalis* Plate 32

Identification. 8in, 20cm. Crown and nape shining black; mantle blue-grey; tail black with white tips; white wing bar; underparts white. Immature tawny above with fine black barring; white below with some barring.
Voice. Various churring notes and a flute-like whistle.
Distribution and Habitat. Local resident thornbush country in southern Sudan, southern Ethiopia and southern Somalia, south to eastern Uganda and Kenya to north-eastern Tanzania. Has the habit of perching at the very top of acacia trees when it can be mistaken for a Pygmy Falcon.
Allied Species. The Somali Fiscal *(Lanius somalicus)*, 8in, 20cm, differs from the Taita Fiscal mainly in having broad white tips to the secondaries so that in flight the wings appear black and white. It occurs in Somalia, eastern Ethiopia and northern Kenya.

THRUSHES, WHEATEARS, CHATS and allies: Turdidae

A group of relatively long-legged birds of upright stance; eyes inclined to be large and bills usually pointed and slender; juvenile plumages spotted. Many species spend much time on the ground and feed mainly upon insects.

STONECHAT *Saxicola torquata* Plate 27

Identification. 5in, 13cm. The Stonechats resident in Africa are races of the well known European bird. ♂ has distinctive black head and throat, a conspicuous white half-collar, a white rump and a small white wing patch; a patch of deep chestnut on the chest; ♀ tawny-brown with white wing-patch; cinnamon brown below. Immature spotted buff above and on chest. Flight jerky, perches on top of bushes, fences and on telegraph wires. ♂ of Ethiopian race has no chestnut on chest.

Voice. A scolding 'tsk, tsk, tsk' and a softer clicking note; song a rather rapid warble.

Distribution and Habitat. Local resident, often common, in localities above 3,000ft, 914m, in East Africa, at lower levels in Central Africa. Very adaptable, frequents mountain moorlands, cultivation, grassland with scattered bush and lush marshy areas.

Allied Species. The European Whinchat *(S. rubetra)*, 5in, 12.5cm, is a winter visitor to East and Central Africa.

SCHALOW'S WHEATEAR   *Oenanthe lugubris*   Plate 27

Identification. 6in, 15cm. Crown greyish-white; mantle, face and throat black, rump and basal half of tail pale cinnamon, apical half of tail and wings black; breast and belly white. Northern Somalia birds have the rump and basal half of tail feathers white. ♀ sooty-brown above and on throat and chest; rest of underparts dusky-white; rump and base of tail cinnamon as in ♂.

Voice. A sharp 'chack,' sometimes repeated, but normally rather silent birds.

Distribution and Habitat. Highlands of Ethiopia, Somalia, Kenya and northern Tanzania. Frequents vicinity of inland cliffs and rocky outcrops. Common in the Rift Valley of Kenya.

Allied Species. The following European wheatears are winter visitors and passage migrants to East Africa: Common Wheatear *(Oe. oenanthe)*, Isabelline Wheatear *(Oe. isabellina)*, Pied Wheatear *(Oe. leucomela)* and Desert Wheatear *(Oe. deserti)*.

CAPPED WHEATEAR   *Oenanthe pileata*   Plate 27

Identification. 6½in, 16½cm. Upperparts russet-brown with a white rump; crown, sides of neck and ear coverts black; forehead and stripe over eye white; underparts white, a broad black band across chest; flanks rufous. Upright stance very marked; broad black chest band the best field character. Upperparts and chest spotted in immature.

Voice. One of the best African bird mimics, imitating the calls and songs of many other species and other sounds. It has its own brief warbling song which is constantly repeated, and which is often uttered during display flight.

Distribution and Habitat. Widely distributed but local from Kenya and eastern Uganda southwards to Central Africa. In some areas a partial migrant. Frequents open country from alpine moorlands and short cropped grasslands to coastal flats. It is much attracted to grasslands which have been burnt.

Allied Species. The Red-breasted Wheatear *(Oe. bottae)*, 8in, 20cm, is russet brown above with a white patch at base of tail; below russet, whiter on throat and belly. A large and thickset wheatear found in rocky moorland in the Ethiopian highlands. Heuglin's Wheatear *(Oe. heuglini)*, 5½in, 14cm, is very similar but darker and much smaller. It is a rare bird found in rocky dry country in the Sudan, northern Ethiopia and north-western Kenya. The Somali Wheatear *(Oe. phillipsi)*, 5½in, 14cm, is pale blue-grey above with forehead, stripe over eye and rump white; sides of face, throat and chest black; remainder underparts white. ♀ similar but duller. Occurs in central and northern Somalia and the Ogaden region, Ethiopia. Inhabits dry rocky scrub and bush country.

RED-TAILED or FAMILIAR CHAT
Cercomela familiaris **Plate 27**

Identification. 6in, 15cm. A slimly built greyish-brown chat with a rich rufous rump and rufous lateral tail feathers; paler brown below. An active and confiding little bird, often alighting on the ground. European bird-watchers seeing it for the first time are reminded of a ♀ black redstart.

Voice. A series of whistles and a three-note alarm call.

Distribution and Habitat. Very local and uncommon resident in Kenya and Uganda, becoming commoner southwards in Tanzania and Central Africa. Frequents many types of country from arid bush and rocky hillsides to lowland cultivated areas, but most frequent on rocky outcrops in Brachystegia woodland.

Allied Species. The Brown-tailed Rock Chat *(C. scotocerca)*, 5in, 13cm, is uniformly ashy-brown with a brown tail. It is associated with rocky areas in dry bush country in the Sudan, Ethiopia, Somalia and northern Kenya. The Black-tailed Rock Chat *(C. melanura)*, 5½in, 14cm, is uniformly ash-grey with a bronzy-black tail. It occurs in arid rocky country in the Sudan, Ethiopia and Somalia.

HILL or MOUNTAIN CHAT *Pinarochroa sordida* **Plate 27**

Identification. 6½in, 16½cm. A stocky species with the build of an English robin, dull greyish-brown, paler on the belly; tail feathers mainly white. White in tail conspicuous when bird flies.

Voice. Various soft metallic calls but usually silent.

Distribution and Habitat. Alpine zone in mountains in Ethiopia, Kenya and northern Tanzania. It is common on Mt Kenya and the Aberdare range in Kenya.

ANTEATER CHAT   *Myrmecocichla aethiops*   **Plate 27**

Identification. 8in, 20cm. A thickset brownish-black bird having something of the appearance of a starling, with a white patch in the wings, formed by the white bases of flight feathers and to be seen only when the bird is flying. Often common along road verges; tame and confiding.

Voice. Various piping and whistling calls and an attractive whistling song. Some individual birds mimic other birds' calls.

Distribution and Habitat. A common species in the highlands of Kenya; also recorded from Darfur and Kordofan in the Sudan. Inhabits open country with scattered bush and trees and also acacia woodland.

Allied Species. The Sooty Chat *(M. nigra)*, 7in, 18cm, has the flight feathers entirely black. ♂ glossy black with a white shoulder patch; ♀ and immature sooty-brown without white shoulders. A local resident in more or less open country in the Sudan, Uganda, western Kenya, western Tanzania and Zambia; often associated with termite hills upon which it likes to perch.

CLIFFCHAT   *Thamnolea cinnamomeiventris*   **Plate 27**

Identification. 8in, 20cm. ♂ a striking bird with back, head, wings, tail and chest glossy black; white wing shoulders; rump and belly chestnut-red; ♀ is grey above and on chest and lacks white wing shoulders; rump and belly chestnut-red.

Voice. A clear double whistle and a warbling song.

Distribution and Habitat. Widespread in East and Central Africa but local. Confined to rocky cliffs, hillsides where there are rocky outcrops, quarries and ruins. Usually in pairs.

Allied Species. The White-crowned Cliffchat *(Th. coronata)*, 8in, 20cm, differs from the Cliffchat in having the crown white in the ♂. Known from the Darfur, Kordofan and Nuba areas in the Sudan. A bird of rocky gorges and cliffs. The White-winged Cliffchat *(Th. semirufa)*, is similar to the Cliffchat and is the same size but lacks white on the wing shoulders; instead both sexes have the basal half of the primaries white. Known from the highlands of Ethiopia in rocky places. The White-headed Black Chat, often called Arnott's Chat, *(Th. arnotti)*, 7in, 18cm, is a thickset black and white chat inhabiting Brachystegia and mopane woodland in Tanzania and Central Africa. ♂ glossy black with white crown and white wing patch; ♀ also has white wing patch but is all black above, throat and chest white, belly black. Immature like ♀ but throat usually black. Conspicuous birds in Brachystegia woodlands, in pairs or family parties; feeds largely on ground but perches freely. The White-shouldered Black Chat *(Pentholaea albifrons)*, 5in, 13cm, occurs in savannah woodland in the Sudan, Ethiopia and northern Uganda. Adult ♂ black with white forecrown and white patch on wing shoulders; ♀ lacks white in plumage. Less terrestrial than most related species, perching freely and often. The Little Rock Thrush *(Monticola rufocinerea)*, 6in, 15cm, is a bird of forested or wooded ravines from Somalia and Ethiopia south through eastern Uganda, Kenya and northern Tanzania. It is ashy-brown with a rufous rump and tail; typically a bird of juniper forest. Its general appearance and habit of constantly flicking its tail suggests a large redstart rather than a rock thrush. The Angola Rock Thrush *(M. angolensis)*, 6½in, 16½cm, is a typical bird of open Brachystegia woodland, found in Tanzania, Malawi, Zambia and Rhodesia. It is mottled blue-grey and black on upperparts, grey on throat and rufous on belly. Three well-known European migrants and winter visitors are European Rock Thrush *(M. saxatilis)*, European Redstart *(Phoenicurus phoenicurus)* and Rufous Warbler *(Agrobates galactotes)*.

RED-BACKED SCRUB ROBIN   *Erythropygia leucophrys*   Plate 28

Identification. 6in, 15cm. Rufous-brown above, paler on rump; distinct white eye stripe; tail bright rufous with black subterminal band and narrow white tips to all but central tail feathers; below white to tawny on flanks and dark streaking on throat and breast. Immature mottled black and tawny above. The White-winged Scrub Robin *(Erythrina leucoptera)* which has more white edgings on wings, broader white tail tips and greyish streaking on chest, is now considered to be conspecific.

Voice. Alarm call of several harsh scolding notes: a clear warbling song, variable and apparently ventriloquial.

Distribution and Habitat. Local resident over much of East and Central Africa. Inhabits bush country, open woodlands with undergrowth, and dense scrub.

Allied Species. The Brown-backed Scrub Robin *(Erythropygia hartlaubi)*, 6in, 15cm, is dark brown above with a rufous tail, the apical third of which is black; white stripe over eye and white spots on wing coverts; below whitish to buff on flanks and under tail coverts; indistinct dusky streaking on chest. Occurs in western Uganda to central Kenya. Inhabits elephant grass and thick undergrowth, often along rivers and the margins of forests.

EASTERN BEARDED SCRUB ROBIN
Erythropygia quadrivirgata   **Plate 28**

Identification. 6½in, 16½cm. Upperparts rufous-brown; black streak on each side of the crown, immediately above white eye-stripe; tail black with white tips; below white, tawny-buff on chest and flanks. Immature mottled on upperparts.

Voice. Utters loud clear whistles; also a sustained warbling song.

Distribution and Habitat. Ranges from Somalia south through eastern Kenya and Tanzania to Malawi, Zambia and Rhodesia. Inhabits coastal scrub and bush and woodland undergrowth; shy and elusive.

Allied Species. The Bearded Scrub Robin *(E. barbata)*, 6½in, 16½cm, differs in having paler streaks on sides of crown and white outer tail feathers. It occurs in Brachystegia woodland, scrub and riverine forest from south-western Tanzania to Malawi and Zambia. Coll's Forest Robin *(E. leuco-sticta)*, 6½in, 16½cm, is brown above with a rufous rump and mainly black tail; white eye-stripes above and below eye, bordered by black stripes; below buffy-white, rufous on flanks. A bird of forest undergrowth, in East Africa known from the Bwamba Forest, western Uganda.

SPOTTED MORNING WARBLER   *Cichladusa guttata*   **Plate 28**

Identification. 6½in, 16½cm. A lightly built thrush-like bird, dull rufous-brown with a conspicuous cinnamon-red tail; below buff-white heavily spotted with black. Shy and skulking, disappearing into thick cover when disturbed, when its red tail suggests a robin chat.

Voice. An extremely variable, clear whistling song; bird most vocal in early morning and at dusk; also mimics the calls and songs of many other birds. Alarm notes harsh and scolding.

Distribution and Habitat. Local resident southern Sudan, southern Ethiopia and Somalia, south through Uganda and Kenya to central Tanzania. Inhabits dry bush country, especially thickets of Salvadora bushes along dry river beds, palm tree scrub and dense coastal bush. Relatively shy and retiring and usually seen as it disappears into thick scrub, when its rufous tail is conspicuous. Feeds largely on the ground, often in shade of bushes and palm scrub. It is a common bird of the semi-desert areas of northern Kenya.

MORNING WARBLER   *Cichladusa arquata*   **Plate 28**

Identification. 8in, 20cm. This is a larger edition of the Spotted Morning Warbler with unspotted buff underparts but with a narrow black neck band.

Voice. Has a fine clear warbling song; also utters various clucking notes not

unlike those of a nightingale. Also a mimic of other birds' calls and songs.
Distribution and Habitat. A local resident, usually below 2,500ft, 760m, in
south-western Uganda, Kenya and south to Central Africa. Occurs in scrub
in the immediate vicinity of palm trees.

FIRE-CRESTED ALETHE   *Alethe castanea*   Plate 28

Identification. 7in, 18cm. Upperparts warm dark brown, crown with an
orange streak down centre; underparts white, greyish on chest and flanks.
Voice. Various soft clucking notes.
Distribution and Habitat. In East Africa occurs in the forests of western and
southern Uganda. A forest undergrowth species, in evidence near foraging
swarms of safari ants.
Allied Species. The White-chested Alethe *(A. fulleborni)*, 7½in, 19cm, is a
stocky species, russet-brown above, with white underparts and a russet-olive
patch on each side of the chest. It occurs in mountain forest in north-eastern,
eastern and southern Tanzania, and in Malawi and eastern Zambia.

BROWN-CHESTED ALETHE   *Alethe poliocephala*   Plate 28

Identification. 6in, 15cm. Alethes are long-legged, thrush-like birds which
inhabit forest undergrowth; they are most in evidence near safari ant parties,
preying on the insects escaping from the ants. The present species is warm
russet-brown above, with a whitish stripe from bill to above eye; below,
throat white, chest brownish-buff, paler on flanks.
Voice. A repeated two or three note whistle.
Distribution and Habitat. Widespread in Uganda, westwards to Mount
Kenya and in western and south-western Tanzania. Inhabits forest and
mountain forest; shy and elusive.
Allied Species. The Red-throated Alethe *(Alethe poliophrys)*, 6½in, 16½cm,
may be distinguished by its deep rufous throat-patch. It occurs in the mountain forest and bamboo zones of western Uganda.

EQUATORIAL AKALAT   *Sheppardia aequatorialis*   Plate 28

Identification. 5in, 13cm. A plump robin-like bird, olive-brown above with
russet-brown rump and tail; below bright orange-brown on throat, chest and
flanks, whitish in centre of belly.
Voice. A series of croaking, frog-like calls.
Distribution and Habitat. Found in Uganda, southern Sudan and western
Kenya. Inhabits the undergrowth of forests; shy and not often seen although
not uncommon.

Allied Species. The Akalat *(S. cyornithopsis)*, 5in, 13cm, is a much rarer bird, found in western Uganda forests. It differs from the Equatorial Akalat in having orange-brown confined to chest; flanks olive-brown to grey, belly and under tail coverts white. The East Coast Akalat *(S. gunningi)*, 5in, 13cm, is bright yellowish-buff below and has slate-coloured wings. It occurs in coastal forests of Kenya and Tanzania. Sharpe's Akalat *(S. sharpei)*, 5in, 13cm, is olivaceous-buff on throat, breast and flanks and wings are olive-brown. Found in mountain forests in western Tanzania. The White-bellied Akalat *(Cossyphicula roberti)*, 5in, 13cm, is olive-brown above; upper tail-coverts and tail bright orange-rufous except central rectrices which are black; below throat and chest orange-buff, belly white. In East Africa known only from the Impenetrable-Kayonza Forest, south-western Uganda.

FOREST ROBIN   *Stiphrornis erythrothorax*   Plate 28

Identification. 4½in, 11½cm. Another olive-brown robin-like bird with a russet-brown tail; throat, chest and breast bright chrome-orange; belly white.
Voice. Usually a croaking churr, but also produces a clear, soft warbling song.
Distribution and Habitat. Widespread and locally not uncommon in forests of southern Sudan and Uganda, but very shy and not often observed. Inhabits dense cover of forest undergrowth.

WHITE-STARRED BUSH ROBIN   *Pogonocichla stellata*   Plate 28

Identification. 6in, 15cm. A robin-like forest bird, brilliantly golden-yellow below with a slate-blue head and an olive-green mantle; a small white spot in front of each eye and a silvery white spot bordered with black at the base of the throat; tail yellow and black. Juvenile olive-green spotted dull yellow; immature green above with few yellow spots, below pale mottled green. In East Africa typically a bird of bamboo forest. Often perches on ground to feed on ants; much in evidence when safari ants are present.
Voice. A rather harsh 'tssst' or 'tsssp' and a two-note call. Song a high pitched flute-like whistle.
Distribution and Habitat. A local resident through much of East and Central Africa. Inhabits forested areas, favouring bamboo and mixed bamboo and montane forest.

ROBIN CHAT   *Cossypha caffra*   Plate 28

Identification. 6½in, 16½cm. A rather small robin chat with the habits of an English robin: often seen in gardens. Has well-marked white eye-stripe; may be recognised by orange-rufous throat and chest and contrasting grey belly. The White-browed Robin Chat also has a white eye-stripe but its underparts are entirely rufous. Usually shy and retiring, but becomes tame and confiding in gardens where it is protected. Feeds largely on the ground, where it progresses by hopping, often raises and lowers the tail.

Voice. An outstanding warbling song; also a mimic of other birds' calls and songs.

Distribution and Habitat. A widespread resident in East and Central Africa in forests, wooded and scrub areas; most frequent in localities above 5,000ft, 1,530m.

Allied Species. The Olive-flanked Robin Chat *(Alethe anomala)*, 6in, 15cm, is brown above with a grey forehead and eye-stripe; tail russet; below, throat white, chest to belly grey, flanks olive-brown. It occurs in mountain forest in south-western Tanzania, Malawi and eastern Zambia. The Iringa Alethe *(A. lowei)*, 5in, 13cm, is dark olive-brown above, pale dull brown below to white on belly. It is known only from mountain forest in the Njombe area, southern Tanzania. The Usambara Alethe *(A. montana)*, 5in, 12.5cm, is similar with a russet streak from the bill to above the eye; below olive-grey, white on centre of throat, breast and abdomen. It is known only from the Usambara Mountains forest in north-eastern Tanzania. Archer's Robin Chat *(Cossypha archeri)*, 6in, 15cm, is chestnut brown above with a chestnut tail; white eye-stripe; sides of face blackish; underparts orange-brown to buffy white in centre of belly. In East Africa known from the Ruwenzori Mts and mountain forest in Kigezi, western Uganda.

GREY-WINGED ROBIN CHAT   *Cossypha polioptera*   Plate 28

Identification. 6in, 15cm. Crown grey bordered on each side by a black streak with a white eye-streak immediately below; back olive-brown; rump, tail and underparts orange-rufous; wings grey to olive-brown.

Voice. A subdued warbling song and various clucking notes.

Distribution and Habitat. Occurs in forest undergrowth in the southern Sudan, Uganda, western Kenya and north-western Tanzania.

Allied Species. The very similar Rufous-cheeked Robin Chat *(C. bocagei)*, 5½in, 14cm, differs in having the white eye-stripe partly concealed and no black edging to grey crown. It occurs in wet forests in northern Zambia.

RED-CAPPED ROBIN CHAT   *Cossypha natalensis*   Plate 28

Identification. 6½in, 16½cm. Centre of back and wings blue-grey; central tail feathers dark brown; remainder of plumage rich orange-rufous.

Voice. Has a loud warbling song and is an outstanding mimic of the songs and calls of other birds.

Distribution and Habitat. Widely distributed in East and Central Africa. Frequents dense forest undergrowth, woodlands and coastal scrub; partially migratory in some areas. A shy, skulking species which would be overlooked were it not for its loud song and calls.

BLUE-SHOULDERED ROBIN CHAT

Cossypha cyanocampter   **Plate 28**

Identification. 6½in, 16½cm. Thrush-like but smaller and with relatively long tail. Upperparts black on crown to dark slate on mantle; wings blackish with clear blue shoulders; white stripe over eye; below orange-buff, paler in centre of belly; tail rufous with blackish central rectrices.

Voice. A sustained warbling song of high quality; clucking notes.

Distribution and Habitat. Occurs in the forests of Uganda, southern Sudan and western Kenya. Inhabits undergrowth of forests and thick cover along rivers.

WHITE-BROWED ROBIN CHAT   *Cossypha heuglini*   **Plate 28**

Identification. 8in, 20cm. Thrush-like but with relatively longer tail. Above olive-grey; crown and sides of face black with conspicuous white eye-stripe; below bright orange-rufous; tail rufous except central rectrices which are olive-brown. Immature spotted and mottled tawny-buff on underparts. A bird of thick undergrowth, feeding mainly on the ground; usually shy; occurs in gardens. The Robin Chat also has a white eye-stripe but is smaller and only the throat and chest are rufous, belly grey.

Voice. A loud, purring 'pip, ir, ee' and song a series of sustained flute-like whistles of great beauty; sings especially at dusk and again at dawn. Singing birds difficult to locate and bird may be ventriloquial. Often mimics other birds' calls, such as Red-chested and Black Cuckoos.

Distribution and Habitat. A locally common resident over much of East and Central Africa. Frequents scrub along forest margins, woodland where there is thick undergrowth, gardens and coastal bush.

RUPPELL'S ROBIN CHAT   *Cossypha semirufa*   **Plate 28**

Identification. 7in, 18cm. Closely resembles White-browed Robin Chat but smaller with a greyer mantle and central tail feathers black, not olive-brown.

Voice. A sustained warbling song and a three-note whistle; also mimics voices and songs of many other birds.

Distribution and Habitat. Ranges from the Ethiopian highlands to highland forest in Kenya and northern Tanzania. Inhabits dense upland and montane forest where there is abundant undergrowth.

SNOWY-HEADED ROBIN CHAT   *Cossypha niveicapilla*   **Plate 28**

Identification. 8½in, 22cm. Easily recognised by its black mantle, white crown and orange-rufous underparts.

Voice. A loud and sustained warbling song interspersed with louder notes; also an outstanding mimic.

Distribution and Habitat. A West African forest species which ranges to southern Sudan, Uganda, western Kenya and north-western Tanzania. Inhabits dense forest and margins of swamp forest, keeping to the undergrowth and forest floor. Shy and elusive.

Allied Species. The Spot-throat *(Modulatrix stictigula)*, 5½in, 14cm, is a small thrush-like bird, dark olive-brown above with a dark chestnut tail; below, throat and chest buffy-white with black spots; flanks chestnut-brown, belly white. A very local and uncommon species known from montane forest in eastern and south-western Tanzania and in Malawi. The Dappled Spot-throat *(M. orostruthus)*, 5½in, 14cm, was previously classified amongst the bulbuls. It is brownish-olive above with a dark chestnut-brown tail; below olive-white, the chest and upper breast mottled dark olive-green; flanks dark olive. A rare and shy species known from montane forest in north-eastern Tanzania. The Red-tailed Ant-Thrush *(Neocossyphus rufus)*, 8in, 20cm, is dark rufous-brown above, paler and redder on the rump, tail, wings and underparts; tail relatively long. Occurs in forests in western Uganda, eastern Kenya and north-eastern Tanzania including Zanzibar. Inhabits coastal scrub and dense woodland and forests. The White-tailed Ant-Thrush *(Neocossyphus poensis)*, 8in, 20cm, is darker on the upperparts; below, throat sooty-brown, remainder underparts dusky-chestnut; three outermost tail feathers with broad white tips. In East Africa known from the forests of western Uganda and the Kakamega Forest, western Kenya. The Rufous Flycatcher-Thrush *(Stizorhina fraseri)*, 7in, 18cm, was previously classified amongst the flycatchers. It is an all chestnut-brown bird, very similar to a Red-tailed Ant-Thrush from which it differs in its smaller size, relatively shorter tail and shorter and very much wider bill. It occurs in the southern Sudan to western and southern Uganda. Inhabits rain forests. The White-throated Robin *(Irania gutturalis)*, 6½in, 16½cm, is a winter visitor to East Africa as far south as northern Tanzania, coming from Asia Minor. It resembles the Robin Chat but with a black tail; above grey with a white stripe over eye; sides of face and neck black with a white stripe down centre of throat; breast and flanks rufous, belly white. Inhabits dense scrub along dry river beds in arid bush country; shy and skulking. The Nightingale *(Luscinia megarhynchos)* and the Thrush Nightingale or Sprosser *(Luscinia luscinia)* are also winter visitors to East Africa.

AFRICAN THRUSH *Turdus pelios*   Plate 27

Identification. 9in, 23cm. A pale, washed-out-looking thrush, brownish-grey above with a pale ashy-grey chest; throat streaked ash-brown; breast and abdomen whitish, tinged cinnamon-buff on flanks. In general appearance very like a Kurrichane Thrush but grey on chest, not pale buff.
Voice. A clear, loud, typical thrush song, and a two-note whistle.
Distribution and Habitat. Widespread in East Africa but not in central or eastern Kenya. Inhabits forested and wooded localities, and in Uganda a common garden bird.

OLIVE THRUSH *Turdus olivaceus*   Plate 27

Identification. 9in, 23cm. Some authorities recognise the northern populations of this bird as a distinct species, *T. abyssinicus*. Upperparts dark olive-brown, below paler on the throat and breast with dusky streaks on throat; belly bright rufous; bill and feet orange. Immature has dusky spotted underparts.
Voice. Typical scolding thrush-type call-notes and a loud, usually brief song.
Distribution and Habitat. Local resident in East and Central Africa, south to Cape Province, South Africa. Inhabits forests and well-wooded areas, dense scrub, cultivation where there are trees and bush and also well-treed gardens. A common garden bird in the Kenya highlands.
Allied Species. The Kurrichane Thrush *(T. libonyanus)*, 9½in, 24cm, is a pale edition of the Olive Thrush with a white throat streaked only on the sides and with a white belly. It occurs in cultivated and woodland areas, often in drier localities than those favoured by the Olive Thrush. It is a locally common resident in Tanzania and Central Africa. The Ground-scraper Thrush *(T. litsipsirupa)*, 8½in, 21½cm, is a rather thickset thrush with a shortish tail and bearing a resemblance to a European mistle thrush. Above brownish-grey, below pale buff with heavy black spots. An orange-buff patch in the wings, conspicuous when the bird is flying. A locally common resident on the high plateau of Ethiopia, appearing again in the Brachystegia woodland and open scrub in Tanzania and Central Africa. The similar Spotted Ground Thrush *(T. guttata)*, 8½in, 21½cm, is a slimmer bird distinguished by the white spotting on its wing-coverts. It is a rare species known from coastal forests in Kenya and Tanzania and mountain forest in Malawi.

BARE-EYED THRUSH   *Turdus tephronotus*   Plate 27

Identification. 8½in, 21½cm. A pale ashy-grey thrush with an orange-rufous breast and belly and an area of bare yellow skin around the eyes; bill orange-yellow.
Voice. A wild, sustained thrush-type song.
Distribution and Habitat. Ranges from Somalia and Ethiopia south through central and eastern Kenya to eastern Tanzania. Inhabits arid bush country and coastal scrub.

ABYSSINIAN GROUND THRUSH   *Turdus piaggiae*   Plate 27

Identification. 7½in, 19cm. A stocky orange-rufous thrush with forehead orange-brown; white ring around eye and white spots on wing coverts; below orange-rufous, white in centre of belly.
Voice. A three- or four-note liquid whistle, and a prolonged song.
Distribution and Habitat. Highland forest in Ethiopia, Uganda, Kenya and northern Tanzania. Inhabits montane forest, especially where intermixed with bamboo. Feeds mainly on the ground.
Allied Species. The Orange Ground Thrush *(T. gurneyi)*, 7½in, 19cm, is a less rufous bird being olive-brown on upperparts and crown; white eye-ring incomplete; below bright orange-rufous, white in centre of abdomen. Found in mountain forests from Mt Kenya, Kenya southwards through Tanzania to Malawi where it occurs on the Nyika plateau. Local and uncommon.

BABBLERS, CHATTERERS and allies: Turdoididae

The babblers, chatterers and related species are an ill-defined group of thrush-like birds. Some species – babblers and chatterers – occur in noisy parties in bush and thorn-scrub country. The Illadopsis group and the hill babblers are forest species, more or less solitary and shy. Plumages are usually dull grey, brown, olive or rufous; wings rounded.

ARROW-MARKED BABBLER   *Turdoides jardinei*   Plate 26

Identification. 9in, 23cm. Stocky birds which occur in noisy parties. General colour greyish-brown, paler below with white arrow-shaped tips to the feathers of throat and breast; eye conspicuously yellow or orange. The similar Black-lored Babbler has bluish-white eyes.
Voice. A succession of chattering, bubbling call-notes which draw attention to the birds.

Distribution and Habitat. Locally common resident Uganda and southern Kenya, south through Tanzania to Malawi, Zambia and southwards. Frequents rank bush, the edges of papyrus swamps, rank grass and bush, sugar cultivation and where there is undergrowth in woodlands and along riverine forest. Babblers have a typical 'follow my leader' method of progression, one leaving cover for the next patch of bush with low direct flight, followed in rapid succession by remainder of the party.

Allied Species. The Northern Pied Babbler *(T. hypoleuca)*, 9½in, 24cm, has the underparts white with a dark patch on each side of the chest. It occurs in acacia bush and woodland in southern Kenya and in northern and north-eastern Tanzania. The Brown Babbler *(T. plebeja)*, 9in, 23cm, is a dark, greyish-brown species with a whitish chin, yellow eyes and very small whitish points on breast feathers. It occurs in bush savannah in Uganda and western Kenya. The White-rumped Babbler *(T. leucopygia)*, 8½in, 21½cm, is grey-brown with a more or less well-developed white rump. It occurs in Ethiopia, in southern Tanzania and in Central Africa in scrub country, woodland and acacia belts. Hinde's Pied Babbler *(T. hindei)*, 8in, 20cm, is sooty-brown with patches of white feathers of varying extent appearing on the head and body and giving the appearance of a semi-albino. A very uncommon species from central Kenya, known from the Fort Hall and Machakos districts.

BLACK-LORED BABBLER *Turdoides melanops* Plate 26

Identification. 9in, 23cm. Plumage greyish-brown, similar to the Arrow-marked Babbler but with black lores and a bluish-white eye.
Voice. A succession of bubbling and chattering calls.
Distribution and Habitat. A local resident in Uganda and Kenya, south to central Tanzania. Inhabits acacia bush and woodland, often near water, and papyrus and reed-beds.

SCALY BABBLER *Turdoides squamulata* Plate 26

Identification. 8½in, 21½cm. A stocky greyish bird with a relatively long tail and bright orange eyes. Distinguished from related Arrow-marked Babbler by white chin and black lores and ear-coverts. The similar Black-lored Babbler has bluish-white eyes and pale ear-coverts.
Voice. Various harsh babbling calls. Birds move in small flocks through thick scrub and draw attention to themselves by their grating call-notes.
Distribution and Habitat. The Scaly Babbler has a restricted distribution, found in coastal southern Somalia, coastal Kenya and inland to Garissa along the Tana River and in north-eastern Tanzania. Keeps to thick cover; uncommon and local.

Allied Species. The Dusky Babbler *(T. tenebrosa)*, 8½in, 21½cm, is dark olive-brown with a grey forehead; throat and chest with black streaks and olive edging to feathers giving a scaly appearance. An uncommon and local species recorded from eastern Ethiopia and southern Sudan. Inhabits thick vegetation near water. The Capuchin Babbler *(T. atripennis)*, 8in, 20cm, has the upperparts and underparts dark chestnut-brown, the wings and tail darker; head and throat grey. A West African forest species which is known from the Bwamba Forest, western Uganda. Unlike the other species it occurs in dense forest undergrowth and in swamp forest.

RUFOUS CHATTERER   *Argya rubiginosa*   **Plate 26**

Identification. 7½in, 19cm. A gregarious bird seen in small flocks in thick undergrowth and thorn thickets; cinnamon-rufous in colour, slightly darker on upperparts; bill yellow, eyes pale yellow. Like its allies it draws attention to itself by its noisy chattering.
Voice. A variety of chattering and bubbling calls and a plaintive whistle, not unlike that of the Blue-naped Mousebird.
Distribution and Habitat. Local resident southern Sudan, central and southern Ethiopia, southern Somalia, south through eastern Uganda and Kenya to Tanzania. Frequents thick bush and tangled cover in arid or semi-arid areas. Locally common in coastal bush in Kenya and Tanzania.
Allied Species. The Scaly Chatterer *(Argya aylmeri)*, 7in, 18cm, resembles an ash-brown edition of the Rufous Chatterer. It occurs in dry bush country in Somalia, Kenya and Tanzania.

HILL BABBLER   *Alcippe abyssinica*   **Plate 26**

Identification. 5in, 13cm. The Hill Babbler looks and behaves like a large thickset warbler. The back, wings and tail are olive-rufous; head and underparts grey. The southern Tanzania, Zambia and Malawi race has black streaks on the throat; the western Uganda race has a black crown.
Voice. A clear two-note whistle, various clucking sounds and a melodious warbling song.
Distribution and Habitat. Widespread in East Africa south to Malawi and Zambia. Inhabits forests where it forages in the foliage of trees and amongst hanging creepers.
Allied Species. Mountain Illadopsis *(Malacocincla pyrrhopterus)*, 5½in, 14cm. The Illadopsis group are rather small, relatively plump thrush-like birds with shortish tails, rounded wings and long legs, which live on the forest floor. All are drab plumaged in greys, browns and white; solitary and shy. The present species may be recognised by its grey throat and breast; above

dark rufous tinged olive-brown, greyer on crown. In East Africa known from the highlands of Uganda and western Kenya. Lives on the forest floor amongst dense undergrowth; shy and seldom seen. The Brown Illadopsis *(M. fulvescens)*, 6in, 15cm, occurs in pairs in the forests of Uganda, western Kenya and western Tanzania. It is tawny brown with a whitish throat. The Pale-breasted Illadopsis *(M. rufipennis)*, 5½in, 14cm, has a whitish throat and abdomen; rest of plumage tawny-brown. Occurs in the forests of Uganda, western Kenya and north-eastern Tanzania. The Scaly-breasted Illadopsis *(M. albipectus)*, 5½in, 14cm, also has a white throat and belly, but pale chest feathers edged blackish giving a scaly appearance. Found in Uganda and western Kenya forests. The Grey-chested Illadopsis *(M. polio-thorax)*, 6½in, 16½cm, is dark rufous-chestnut above, grey below. It occurs in the Kakamega Forest and Mount Elgon in western Kenya, and the Ruwenzori range and the highland forests of south-western Kigezi in Uganda.

WARBLERS: Sylviidae

A large family of small, active insectivorous birds of slim build; related to thrushes and flycatchers but bills slender and juvenile plumages unspotted. Many species, especially among the 'leaf-warblers,' *Phylloscopus*, and the Fan-tailed Warblers, *Cisticola*, lack distinctive markings and may appear confusingly alike. Voice, behaviour, habitat and distribution are important in their identification.

CINNAMON BRACKEN WARBLER
Bradypterus cinnamomeus   **Plate 30**

Identification. 5½in, 14cm. A skulking forest undergrowth warbler, bright rufous, with short rounded wings and a long, broad tail; paler below. Presence usually revealed by bird's loud call-notes or when it flushes from undergrowth when disturbed.

Voice. Usual call a harsh, rasping 'cheee, cheee;' song a loud clear warble uttered from dense herbage near ground.

Distribution and Habitat. Local resident through most of the highland areas of East Africa south to Malawi and Zambia. Occurs in or near mountain forest in thick tangled undergrowth, bush, bracken and bamboo. In East Africa found on mountains up to 12,500ft, 3,800m, and higher.

Allied Species. The Evergreen Forest Warbler *(B. mariae)*, 5in, 13cm, also frequents dense mountain forest undergrowth. Its general appearance is dull and dingy brown, paler on the throat. It occurs locally in central and southern Kenya highlands, Tanzania, Malawi and the Nyika plateau in Zambia. The Little Rush Warbler *(B. baboecala)*, 4½in, 11½cm, is olive-brown above, whitish below with some blackish streaks on foreneck and chest; flanks olive-brown. Inhabits dense waterside vegetation locally throughout East and Central Africa. Draws attention to itself by the sharp 'brrr-brrr-brrr' sound produced by rapid wing movements as it flits about reed beds. Grauer's Rush Warbler *(B. graueri)*, 5in, 13cm, is similar but larger. In East Africa known from forested swamps in south-western Uganda. The White-winged Rush Warbler *(B. carpalis)*, occurs in reed and papyrus beds near Kisumu, Kenya and in western and southern Uganda. It is dark brown above, below white with heavy V-shaped black marks on throat; wing shoulders white. The Bamboo Warbler *(B. alfredi)*, 5½in, 14cm, is olive-brown above; below white with grey mottling on centre of neck and chest, flanks and under tail coverts grey. Inhabits dense undergrowth on forest margins; occurs in western Uganda and western Tanzania. The Broad-tailed Warbler *(Schoenicola platyura)*, 6½in, 16½cm; tail 3½in, 9cm, is a small russet-brown warbler with buffy-white underparts and a long and very broad black tail. It draws attention by its distinctive call, a loud 'whist, whist' followed by a rattle. Inhabits tall lush grasslands, especially marsh hollows and vegetation along streams and marshes. Tail very conspicuous when bird is flushed. Widely distributed in East and Central Africa but very local. The European Sedge Warbler *(Acrocephalus schoenobaenus)*, 5in, 13cm, with a conspicuous cream-coloured eye-stripe and streaked mantle is a common winter visitor in East and Central Africa. Other European migrants include the following: Marsh Warbler *(A. palustris)*, Reed Warbler *(A. scirpaceus)*, Great Reed Warbler *(A. arundinaceus)*, Icterine Warbler *(Hippolais icterina)*, Olive-tree Warbler *(H. olivetorum)*, Upcher's Warbler *(H. languida)*, Olivaceous Warbler *(H. pallida)*, Barred Warbler *(Sylvia nisoria)*, Orphean Warbler *(S. hortensis)*, Garden Warbler *(S. borin)*, Blackcap *(S. atricapilla)*, Whitethroat *(S. communis)*, Willow Warbler *(Phylloscopus trochilus)*, Chiffchaff *(P. collybita)*, Wood Warbler *(P. sibilatrix)*.

GREATER SWAMP WARBLER   *Acrocephalus rufescens*   Plate 30

Identification. 6½in, 16½cm. A uniformly olive-brown or olive-grey warbler with a graduated tail; underparts slightly paler; gape deep orange. Found almost always in papyrus beds by or over water.

Voice. Various loud chattering and scolding calls – a very vocal bird; also has a clear warbling song.

Distribution and Habitat. Widespread in East and Central Africa in suitable habitats. Inhabits dense papyrus beds, drawing attention by its constant calls and song. Abundant at Lake Naivasha, Kenya.

Allied Species. The Lesser Swamp Warbler *(A. gracilirostris)*, 5½in, 14cm, is more russet-brown on the back and whiter below. It also has a wide range in East and Central Africa, in both reed and papyrus beds. The Yellow Swamp Warbler *(Calamonastides gracilirostris)*, 5½in, 14cm, is olive-green above with a rusty rump; below yellow with brownish flanks. It occurs in swamps around Lake George in western Uganda. The African Reed Warbler *(Acrocephalus baeticatus)*, 4½in, 11½cm, is pale brown on the upperparts, below buff, white in centre of abdomen. Found very locally in East and Central Africa; in addition to swamps it also occurs in thick bush and scrub, gardens, mangrove swamps and coastal thickets. The Yellow Flycatcher-Warbler *(Chloropeta natalensis)*, 5in, 13cm, is a yellow-breasted green warbler with a broad flycatcher-like bill; crown olive-brown. Local resident in East and Central Africa, usually inhabits thick herbage often near forest margins. The Mountain Yellow Flycatcher-Warbler *(C. similis)*, 5in, 13cm, is uniformly green above without a brown crown. It occurs in thick undergrowth at the edges of montane forest in East Africa.

AFRICAN MOUSTACHED WARBLER
Melocichla mentalis   **Plate 31**

Identification. 7½in, 19cm. A very large, heavy-looking bird for a warbler; at first sight might be mistaken for a bulbul. Upperparts warm dark brown, forehead and ear-coverts chestnut-brown; white stripe over eye; cheeks and throat white with a distinct black malar stripe; breast to under tail-coverts pale russet-brown.
Voice. A rasping 'te-te-te-te' and a rapid warbling song.
Distribution and Habitat. Widespread but local in East and Central Africa. Inhabits ranks grass and mixed grass and bush.

BROWN WOODLAND WARBLER
Phylloscopus umbrovirens   **Plate 30**

Identification. 4in, 10cm. The Woodland Warblers are related closely to the Willow Warblers which they resemble in habits and appearance. Upperparts tawny-brown with wings and tail edged bright green; below white with a tawny wash on throat and flanks. The immature is yellowish below. Arboreal, hunting its food among branches and foliage of trees and bushes.
Voice. A tinkling, warbling song, not unlike that of a Willow Warbler but clearer. Also utters a series of short trills and a two-note call 'tee, teewe.'
Distribution and Habitat. Local resident highlands Ethiopia and Somalia, south through highlands of Uganda, Kenya and northern Tanzania to the Uluguru Mts. Inhabits forested and woodland country.

Allied Species. The Yellow-throated Woodland Warbler *(Ph. ruficapilla)*, 3½in, 9cm, has a russet-green head and green back; below throat bright greenish-yellow, grey on chest and flanks, belly creamy-white. It occurs in forests on the Teita Hills, south-eastern Kenya and in mountain forests in Tanzania. The Uganda Woodland Warbler *(Ph. budongoensis)*, 4in, 10cm, has green upperparts and a white stripe over the eye, above a black streak through eye; below white, tinged greenish on flanks. Occurs in the forests of Uganda and western Kenya.

RED-FACED WOODLAND WARBLER
Phylloscopus laetus   **Plate 30**

Identification. 3½in, 9cm. A small leaf warbler with bright green upperparts, wings and tail; forehead, stripe over eye, face and throat rufous-buff; belly white.
Voice. A low warbling song; a double note call, 'tssp-tssp.'
Distribution and Habitat. Mountain forest in western and south-western Uganda. Active little birds, often in small parties, in foliage of forest trees and in bamboos.

NOTE ON THE CISTICOLA WARBLERS

The Cisticolas are a large genus of brown-plumaged warblers with either streaked or unmarked upperparts; in most species the tail feathers have black subterminal patch and white tip. Some are difficult to identify in the field without specialized knowledge; anyone wishing to study this group is advised to consult H. Lynes' 'Review of the Genus Cisticola,' *Ibis* Supplement, 1930.

SINGING CISTICOLA   *Cisticola cantans*   **Plate 31**

Identification. 5½in, 14cm. Upperparts and crown unstreaked. Mantle brown to greyish-brown, crown rufous; below white with buff wash on breast.
Voice. A loud 'tsss, wip, tsss, wip' repeated over and over again; also a brief, clear warbling song of four or five notes.
Distribution and Habitat. Common resident through East and Central Africa. Frequents rank grass and other herbage and often found in rank secondary vegetation in neglected cultivation and forestry plantations.
Allied Species. The Red-faced Cisticola *(C. erythrops)*, 5½in, 9cm, is similar to the Singing Cisticola but mantle is greyer; forehead, eye-stripe and sides of face russet; edges of flight feathers russet; below creamy-buff, paler on throat and centre of belly. Widespread but very local in East and Central Africa. Inhabits thick scrub and bush, especially lush vegetation along forest mar-

gins; rather shy and skulking. The Rock-living Cisticola *(C. emini)*, 5in, 13cm, is similar to the Singing Cisticola but has a bright chestnut crown, the chin white and the rest of the underparts warm buff. Inhabits rocky outcrops; very uncommon and local in East and Central Africa. The Black-lored Cisticola *(C. nigriloris)*, 6in, 15cm, has the mantle dusky earth-brown, the crown and nape chestnut, the lores black; below, buffy-cream, the breast and flanks dusky. Occurs in the highlands of southern Tanzania and Malawi, inhabits grass and bush on hillsides. The Whistling Cisticola *(C. lateralis)*, 5½in, 14cm, has the crown and mantle sooty-brown, below creamy-white, dusky on flanks. In East Africa occurs in the southern Sudan and in Uganda; inhabits moist and boggy areas in savannah woodland where there is an abundance of lush vegetation. The Trilling Cisticola *(C. woosnami)*, 5in, 13cm, differs from the Whistling Cisticola in having the crown dull chestnut and a finer bill. It occurs in Uganda and Tanzania to Central Africa, occurs in savannah and Brachystegia woodland.

HUNTER'S CISTICOLA   *Cisticola hunteri*   Plate 31

Identification. 5½in, 14cm. A dark-looking cisticola found in highland areas over 6,000ft, 1,830m, which draws attention by its habit of dueting. Two, three or more birds will gather together and start singing in duet. Upperparts dark brown, slightly russet on the head, with ill-defined streaking; below grey, paler on the throat.
Voice. The species sings in duet, a loud, clear babbling warble.
Distribution and Habitat. Occurs in localities over 6,000ft, 1,830m, in the Kenya highlands, on Mt Elgon in Uganda and in northern Tanzania. Inhabits scrub and bush, often along forest margins and in glades; occurs up to at least 13,000ft, 3,060m.
Allied Species. Chubb's Cisticola *(C. chubbi)*, 5½in, 14cm, resembles Hunter's Cisticola and also indulges in dueting; it differs in having paler upperparts and a russet cap. Occurs in western Kenya, Uganda and north-western Tanzania; found alongside *C. hunteri* on Mt Elgon. Inhabits forest glades and margins, and thick herbage along streams and rivers.

RATTLING CISTICOLA   *Cisticola chiniana*   Plate 31

Identification. 5in, 13cm. Mantle streaked dusky on brown or greyish-brown; crown dark rufous brown, more or less streaked dusky brown. A characteristic bird of thorn-bush and Brachystegia scrub. In pairs or family parties. Draws attention by its harsh scolding call-notes.
Voice. A loud, scolding 'chaaaaaa, chaaaaaaaa.'
Distribution and Habitat. Common resident locally in suitable areas East and

Central Africa. In East Africa it is a common and typical bird of thornbush country; further south it is common in Brachystegia and open woodland.
Allied Species. The Ashy Cisticola *(C. cinereola)*, 5½in, 14cm, is a rather pale grey cisticola with narrow dark streaking on crown and upperparts; below creamy white. Found in dry bush country in areas of rank grass; occurs in eastern and southern Kenya and north-eastern Tanzania. The Wailing Cisticola *(C. lais)*, 5½in, 14cm, differs from the Rattling Cisticola in having the top of the head deep chestnut brown, streaked dusky; it occurs in montane grasslands in southern Tanzania and Central Africa. Lynes' Cisticola *(C. distincta)*, 6in, 15cm, is very similar but is larger. It occurs in grass and bush on rocky hillsides in eastern Uganda and Kenya.

WINDING CISTICOLA   *Cisticola galactotes*   **Plate 31**

Identification. 5in, 13cm, is rather slim, brown above with heavy black streaking with a rufous crown; conspicuous rufous edging to wing feathers; underparts buffy-white.
Voice. A sustained trill.
Distribution and Habitat. Locally common in East and Central Africa in suitable habitats. Frequents swamps, marshes, lush grasslands and grassland-bush, often near water.
Allied Species. Carruther's Cisticola *(C. carruthersi)*, 5in, 13cm, is very similar but top of head chestnut, mantle darker and wing edges brown not rufous. Inhabits papyrus swamps in Uganda and western Kenya.

TINKLING CISTICOLA   *Cisticola tinniens*   **Plate 31**

Identification. 5in, 13cm. A rather slim cisticola with a rather long tail. Above, very heavily and broadly streaked black so that mantle sometimes appears blackish; crown, edges of wing feathers and edges of blackish tail feathers bright rufous; below buffy white.
Voice. A far-carrying tinkling whistle.
Distribution and Habitat. Found in the central highlands of Kenya, where it inhabits the rank vegetation at the margins of swamps, dams and streams, usually over 7,000ft, 2,140m.

STOUT CISTICOLA   *Cisticola robusta*   **Plate 31**

Identification. 5½–6½in, 14–16½cm. ♂ larger than ♀. A rather thickset cisticola with brownish-grey mantle and bright rufous crown, both heavily streaked with black; below buffy-white. Heavy streaking and rufous crown conspicuous in field.

Voice. A distinctive piping whistle.

Distribution and Habitat. Widely distributed but local in East and Central Africa. Inhabits mixed grass-bush country and lush herbage along swamp and marsh margins.

Allied Species. The Aberdare Cisticola *(C. aberdare)*, 6in, 15cm, is very similar to the Stout Cisticola but with broader and darker streaking on upperparts and tail very dark. It occurs at high altitudes in the western highlands of Kenya. The Croaking Cisticola *(C. natalensis)*, 5½in, 14cm, looks like a pale edition of the Stout Cisticola without a rufous cap. Found locally in grasslands in East and Central Africa.

TINY CISTICOLA *Cisticola nana*   Plate 31

Identification. 3½in, 9cm. This is a very small, short-tailed species, greyish-brown above without streaking and with a rufous crown; below pale buff.

Voice. A far-carrying tinkling whistle.

Distribution and Habitat. Ranges from eastern and central Kenya south to northern and central Tanzania. Inhabits mixed grassland and bush, and savannah woodland.

Allied Species. The Foxy Cisticola *(C. troglodytes)*, 4in, 10cm, is also rather short tailed; easily recognised by its uniform bright rufous-brown back and buff underparts. Found in mixed grass and bush in northern Uganda and north-western Kenya.

PECTORAL-PATCH CISTICOLA *Cisticola brunnescens* Plate 31

Identification. 3½in, 9cm. Stumpy-tailed species with upperparts streaked black; top of head buff; below buffy-white with a dusky patch on each side of the chest. Frequents open grasslands where conspicuous when indulging in jerky display flights high in the air during the breeding season.

Voice. High-pitched 'zeet, zeet, zeet' call uttered in flight.

Distribution and Habitat. Locally common resident through East and Central Africa. Inhabits open grasslands, with or without scattered bushes.

Allied Species. Zitting Cisticola *(C. juncidis)*, 4in, 10cm, has a slightly longer tail than the Pectoral-patch Cisticola. Above brown with blackish streaking; rump rufous; tail with subterminal black spots above and below and tip white. Local and generally uncommon East and Central Africa in grasslands and mixed grass and bush. The Desert Cisticola *(C. aridula)*, 4in, 10cm, is much paler and tail carries black spots only on the underside and without white tips. East Africa south to central Tanzania; occurs in grasslands and arid areas.

WING-SNAPPING CISTICOLA   *Cisticola ayresii*   **Plate 31**

Identification. 3½in, 9cm. A tiny, stumpy-tailed cisticola with heavily streaked crown and upperparts; below, whitish with a slight tawny wash; rump rufous. Differs from the Pectoral-patch Cisticola in lacking dusky streaks on each side of the chest. In Kenya a bird of short highland grasslands, usually over 8,000ft, 2,440m, but at lower altitudes elsewhere.
Voice. Indulges in display flights over nesting grounds during which it utters shrill whistling song accompanied by loud wing-snapping.
Distribution and Habitat. Locally distributed in the highlands of Kenya, southern and western Uganda to southern Tanzania and Central Africa. Inhabits open grasslands and short grassy plains.

TAWNY-FLANKED PRINIA   *Prinia subflava*   **Plate 31**

Identification. 5in, 13cm. A uniform tawny-brown, slim warbler with a long graduated tail and a conspicuous pale eye-stripe. Actions jerky, frequently raising and lowering the tail.
Voice. A loud, churring 'chee, cheer' often repeated, and a short piping song.
Distribution and Habitat. Common and widespread through most of East and Central Africa. Frequents rank grass and other herbage, scrub along streams, edges of forests, regenerating bush and scrub in old cultivation, plantations and gardens.
Allied Species. The Pale Prinia *(P. somalica)*, 4½in, 11¼cm, differs from the Tawny-flanked Prinia in being pale ashy-grey above, creamy white below; pale eye streak. Occurs in Somalia, southern Ethiopia, and eastern and south-eastern Kenya in dry thorn-bush country.

WHITE-CHINNED PRINIA   *Prinia leucopogon*   **Plate 31**

Identification. 5½in, 14cm. A grey warbler with a long slender tail; white or buffy-white on throat, grey breast, buff abdomen.
Voice. A sharp two-note call; also has a quavering, warbling song.
Distribution and Habitat. Forest areas and adjacent secondary growth in Uganda, western Kenya and north-western Tanzania. In pairs or small parties in dense undergrowth or other lush vegetation along forest margins and glades and in neglected cultivation near forest. ♂ often raises tail high over back; white chin conspicuous in field.

BANDED PRINIA *Prinia bairdii*   Plate 31

Identification. 4½in, 11½cm. Upperparts, wings and tail brownish-black, wings spotted and tail tipped with white; below, throat black, chest and flanks boldly barred black and white; abdomen white; eye yellow.

Voice. A shrill, rapid 'plee-plee-plee-plee.'

Distribution and Habitat. A local and generally uncommon forest bird found in southern Sudan, Uganda and western Kenya. Inhabits dense forest undergrowth, often feeding on or just above the ground.

REDWING WARBLER *Prinia erythroptera*   Plate 31

Identification. 5½in, 14cm. A rather Prinia-like warbler with greyish-brown upperparts and head, a long slender tail with dark subterminal ends and white tips, chestnut-brown wings and creamy underparts, pale tawny on flanks, belly and under tail-coverts. In non-breeding dress mantle vinous-brown.

Voice. A twittering 'tee-tee-tee'.

Distribution and Habitat. Widely distributed in East and Central Africa but very local and generally not common. Inhabits rank grass and herbage in savannah woodland in the north and Brachystegia woodland in the south of its range.

BLACK-COLLARED APALIS *Apalis pulchra*   Plate 30

Identification. 5in, 13cm. The Apalis warblers, which are well represented in East and Central Africa, are of slim build with long narrow, strongly graduated tails; plumage may be mainly brown, grey or green. Many species have a black bar or collar across base of neck or chest. Most are forest dwellers, either in undergrowth or in tree-tops. The Black-collared Apalis has grey upperparts; below white with a black chest band and rufous flanks and belly. Tail frequently raised over back and wagged from side to side. Usually frequents forest undergrowth or bush, often near water.

Voice. A brief loud warbling song; call a double 'cheewee, cheewee.'

Distribution and Habitat. Local resident mountain and highland forests of southern Sudan, Uganda and Kenya. A common species in the forests of western Kenya and in the Mpanga forest in western Uganda.

Allied Species. The Collared Apalis *(A. ruwenzorii)*, 4in, 10cm, has pale grey upperparts; below, rufous-buff on throat, breast and flanks and a grey chest band. Occurs in mountain forest in western and south-western Uganda. The Bar-throated Apalis *(A. thoracica)*, 4½in, 11½cm, has grey upperparts, brownish on head; below white with grey band across lower neck; belly yellow. Some races have yellow wash on underparts and head. Occurs in forests in south-eastern Kenya south to Central Africa.

BLACK-THROATED APALIS *Apalis jacksoni* **Plate 30**

Identification. 4½in, 11½cm. Black throat and contrasting yellow breast and white neck streak render identification easy; crown grey, mantle bright green. Immature paler and duller.

Voice. A loud and distinct churring call.

Distribution and Habitat. A local and uncommon resident in highland forests in southern Sudan, Uganda and western and central Kenya, and north-western Tanzania. Frequents both forest treetops and the undergrowth; seen usually in pairs.

Allied Species. The Masked Apalis *(A. binotata)*, 4in, 10cm, is green above with green wings and tail; crown and face grey; breast and abdomen white, greenish on flanks; throat and chest black with a white patch on each side of the neck. A forest species known from highland forest locally in Uganda and Mt Elgon, western Kenya. The Black-capped Apalis *(A. nigriceps)*, 4in, 10cm, is one of the most beautiful African warblers: above, bright green with a jet black crown and face and a bright yellow collar on the hind-neck; below white with a black crescent on the lower throat. A forest treetops species in some western and southern Uganda forests. The White-winged Apalis *(A. chariessa)*, 4½in, 11¼cm, is a rare and little-known species recorded from the Tana River forests in Kenya, the Uluguru Mts forests in Tanzania and from Malawi. Upperparts, face, wings and tail and a patch on lower neck glossy blue black; edges of secondaries white, forming a wing patch, and tips of tail white; below, throat white, chest to belly bright yellow washed rufous on chest. ♀ has face and neck patch grey not black.

BLACK-BREASTED APALIS *Apalis flavida* **Plate 30**

Identification. 4½in, 11½cm. The widely accepted name 'black-breasted' is unfortunate as species has only a small black patch in centre of chest and in the Somalia race there is no black on the underparts at all. Upperparts green, merging to grey on forehead; below white with broad yellowish band across chest with black patch or spot in centre. Immature paler and greener.

Voice. A two-note soft churr and a brief warbling song.

Distribution and Habitat. A widely distributed resident in East and Central Africa. Frequents a variety of habitats from forest margins and woodland to bush, thorn scrub and acacia woodland.

Allied Species. The Green-tailed Apalis *(Apalis caniceps)*, 4in, 10cm, is green-backed with a grey crown; wings and tail green; below white with broad greenish-yellow chest patch. Occurs in woodland and savannah country in Uganda, western and eastern Kenya and eastern and southern Tanzania. Often in small flocks in woodland trees, behaving like white-eyes.

CHESTNUT-THROATED APALIS
Apalis porphyrolaema **Plate 30**

Identification. 5in, 13cm. Upperparts, wings and tail ash-grey; pale tips to tail feathers; below, chestnut-red patch on chin and upper throat, grey on lower throat, breast and flanks, white in centre of belly.

Voice. A single shrill 'tsssp' note.

Distribution and Habitat. Highland forest of western and south-western Uganda, western and central Kenya and north-eastern Tanzania. Feeds mainly in the tree-tops.

Allied Species. The Grey Apalis *(A. cinerea)*, 5in, 13cm, upperparts grey to ashy-grey on crown and face; three outer tail feathers mainly white; underparts creamy-white. A forest treetop and undergrowth species known from southern Sudan, Uganda to central Kenya and north-eastern Tanzania. The Brown-headed Apalis *(A. alticola)*, 5in, 13cm, is very similar to the Grey Apalis but head is browner and tail feathers grey not white. Occurs locally in mountain forest in Tanzania, Malawi and Zambia.

BLACK-HEADED APALIS *Apalis melanocephala* **Plate 30**

Identification. 5½in, 14cm. Upperparts dusky-grey to blackish-brown with a black or a dark-brown crown; below creamy-white; tail long, grey with whitish tips.

Voice. A sharp 'territ-territ,' often repeated; also a brief trill.

Distribution and Habitat. Occurs in both montane and coastal forests in Kenya, Tanzania, Malawi and Zambia. Mainly a bird of the treetops and foliage.

Allied Species. The Black-backed Apalis *(A. rufogularis)*, 4½in, 11½cm, has ♂ upperparts blackish, below creamy-white; outer four pairs tail feathers white. ♀ uniform dark grey above; below greyish white, throat and breast orange-buff; four outer pairs tail feathers white. Previously the ♂ and ♀ of this Apalis were incorrectly designated as separate species. A treetop species found in Uganda and western Kenya.

RED-FACED APALIS *Apalis rufifrons* **Plate 30**

Identification. 4½in, 11½cm. A pale ash-brown apalis with a black, white-tipped tail; forehead rufous; below white with buff-tinged flanks and sometimes indistinct blackish mottling on chest. Cocks its tail up at right angles and also waves it from side to side.

Voice. A clear chirping song.

Distribution and Habitat. Ranges from Somalia and eastern Ethiopia south through eastern Kenya to north-eastern Tanzania. A bird of desert scrub and bush; usually in pairs, low down in bushes. Their tails are nearly always in motion.

Allied Species. The Karamoja Apalis *(A. karamojae)*, 4½in, 11½cm, occurs in acacia bush and scrub in eastern Uganda and in northern Tanzania, south of Lake Victoria. Upperparts pale ash-grey, tail black, underparts creamy white; outer tail feathers white. The Buff-bellied Warbler *(Phyllolais pulchella)*, 3½in, 9cm, is a tiny Apalis-like warbler, pale greyish-brown, underparts pale yellowish buff with no distinctive markings. Usually in pairs in the tops of acacia trees. Locally not uncommon in East Africa south to northern Tanzania. **(Plate 30.)**

GREY-CAPPED WARBLER   *Eminia lepida*   Plate 30

Identification. 6in, 15cm. A large thickset warbler with appearance suggesting a small bulbul. Above bright green, including wings and tail; crown grey encircled by a black band; underparts pale grey with conspicuous dark chestnut patch in centre of throat. Immature duller. A skulking bird keeping to dense thickets often near water.

Voice. Extremely variable; various loud trills and clear whistles; often mimics other birds.

Distribution and Habitat. Widely distributed resident southern Sudan, Uganda, western and central Kenya and northern Tanzania. Inhabits thick scrub and forest undergrowth and dense vegetation along streams and rivers; not uncommon in gardens at Entebbe, Uganda.

BLACK-FACED RUFOUS WARBLER
Bathmocercus rufus   Plate 30

Identification. 5in, 13cm. A rather thickset warbler with a medium long tail; ♂ has upperparts, wings, tail and sides of breast bright foxy-red; forehead, face, throat, chest and streak down breast black. ♀ resembles ♂ in pattern but is olive-grey instead of foxy-red.

Voice. A constant 'tss-pt, tss-pt, tss-pt.'

Distribution and Habitat. Ranges from the southern Sudan through Uganda to western Kenya; inhabits dense forest undergrowth.

Allied Species. Mrs Moreau's Warbler *(Scepomycter winifredae)*, 6in, 15cm, is a thickset warbler with a very restricted distribution, confined to highland forest on the Uluguru Mts, eastern Tanzania. Head, chin and throat chestnut-red, remainder of plumage olive brown; tail of medium length. Inhabits the undergrowth and forest floor in dense montane forest. The Red-capped Forest Warbler *(Artisornis metopias)*, 4in, 10cm, resembles an Apalis but has a rather short tail; crown, cheeks and hind neck chestnut-brown, mantle olive-brown, wings and tail greyer; below, chin to belly white, flanks olive-brown. A bird of forest undergrowth in montane forest from north-eastern to southern Tanzania. The Red-winged Grey Warbler *(Drymocichla incana)*, 5in, 13cm, is pale grey with underparts slightly paler; basal three-quarters of primaries tawny-rufous. A rather uncommon bird, in East Africa known from the southern Sudan and north-western Uganda. Occurs in savannah woodland where there is rank grass and herbage.

GREY-BACKED CAMAROPTERA
Camaroptera brevicaudata   Plate 30

Identification. 4in, 10cm. A plump, rather short-tailed warbler with head, mantle and underparts grey, contrasting with green wings. A skulking species inhabiting thick cover.
Voice. A drawn-out bleating call 'squeeeee' frequently repeated, which draws attention to the bird in spite of its skulking habits.
Distribution and Habitat. A common species over much of East and Central Africa found in both highland and lowland forest, woodland and scrub.
Allied Species. The Green-backed Camaroptera *(C. brachyura)*, 4in, 10cm, differs in having the mantle green, not grey. It may be conspecific with the grey-backed species. Found in coastal scrub and forest in coastal districts of Kenya and Tanzania. The Yellow-browed Camaroptera *(C. superciliaris)*, 4in, 10cm, is bright green including wings and tail; eye-stripe and face bright yellow; below white, greenish on flanks, undertail coverts bright yellow. In forests of western Uganda, in undergrowth and foliage of small trees. The Olive-green Camaroptera *(C. chloronota)*, 3½in, 9cm, has upperparts dull olive-green; below greyish-white with chest and flanks dusky buff. Forest undergrowth in Uganda and western Kenya.

GREY WREN WARBLER   *Camaroptera simplex*   Plate 30

Identification. 5in, 13cm. A dark grey bush warbler with a rather long tail which is constantly cocked up and down. Underparts have a trace of pale barring across belly. Immature paler.
Voice. A loud metallic clicking or bleating call 'tk, tk' repeated over and over again.

Distribution and Habitat. Common local resident from Ethiopia and Somalia south through Uganda, Kenya and Tanzania to Zambia. Inhabits dry bush and acacia country and in south of range thickets in Brachystegia woodland.

BARRED WREN WARBLER   *Camaroptera stierlingi*   Plate 30

Identification. 5in, 13cm. Upperparts olive-brown; wing-coverts tipped white; underparts whitish with dark brown barring.
Voice. A shrill trilling call.
Distribution and Habitat. A local resident in central and south-western Tanzania to Malawi, Zambia and southwards. Inhabits brush and thickets in Brachystegia woodland.

YELLOW-BELLIED EREMOMELA
Eremomela icteropygialis   Plate 30

Identification. 3½in, 9cm. A short-tailed warbler with pale grey upperparts, throat and breast and contrasting pale yellow belly. Mouse-coloured Penduline Tits resemble the Yellow-bellied Eremomela at first glance but lack contrasting yellow belly and bill is much shorter.
Voice. A weak, plaintive 'tsee, tsee.'
Distribution and Habitat. Widespread resident over much of East and Central Africa in wooded country and dry bush country. Usually in pairs or family parties.

YELLOW-VENTED EREMOMELA
Eremomela flavicrissalis   Plate 30

Identification. 3in, 8cm. Very similar to Yellow-bellied Eremomela but smaller and with a white belly, yellow confined to lower belly.
Voice. Weak 'tsssp' calls.
Distribution and Habitat. Occurs in Somalia and in northern and eastern Kenya in semi-desert bush. Found in eastern Kenya alongside the Yellow-bellied Eremomela in several places.
Allied Species. The Green-cap Eremomela *(E. scotops)*, 4in, 10cm, has grey upperparts and a green cap; below yellow, white on chin. A bird of open bush and Brachystegia woodland. It occurs locally in Uganda and in western and central Kenya, becoming common in Brachystegia woodland in Tanzania, Malawi, Zambia and southwards. The Green-backed Eremomela *(E. canescens)*, 4in, 10cm, has the head pale grey and the rest of the upperparts bright yellowish-green; black streak through eye to ear-coverts; below, throat and chest white, breast to under tail-coverts bright pale yellow. It occurs in

savannah woodland in the Sudan, Ethiopia, Uganda and western Kenya. The Brown-crowned Eremomela *(E. badiceps)*, 4in, 10cm, has the mantle grey, the forehead and crown bright chestnut and a black streak through eye to ear-coverts; below, throat creamy-white, a black band across chest and whitish below, flanked grey. It is a rain forest species known in East Africa only from the Bwamba Forest, western Uganda. The very similar Turner's Eremomela *(E. turneri)*, 4in, 10cm, differs in having the chestnut on the crown restricted to the forehead. It is found in the Kakamega Forest, western Kenya.

WHITE-BROWED CROMBEC *Sylvietta leucophrys* Plate 31

Identification. 3in, 8cm. The Crombecs are plump little warblers with such short tails that they appear almost tailless in the field. The present species has a green back, wings and tail; crown and stripe through eye russet-brown; a broad white streak above eye; below greyish-white; under tail-coverts greenish-yellow.

Voice. A brief soft trill.

Distribution and Habitat. Mountain and high level forest in central and western Kenya, Uganda and western Tanzania. Frequents dense undergrowth of forest and margins of forest; white eye-stripe very conspicuous in field.

Allied Species. The Green Crombec *(Sylvietta virens)*, 2½in, 7cm, is a dull, dark greenish-grey species with greyish-white underparts, washed brownish-buff on chest and throat. Occurs locally in forest undergrowth in Uganda and in the Kakamega Forest, western Kenya. In some ways resembles a Grey-backed Camaroptera but is smaller with a very much shorter tail.

CROMBEC *Sylvietta brachyura* Plate 31

Identification. 3in, 8cm. Plump little warbler with an extremely short tail; silvery grey above with a pale eye-stripe; dusky streak through eye; below rufous merging to white on throat and abdomen. Usually in pairs, climbing amongst branches of thorn trees and bushes in a manner reminiscent of a nuthatch.

Voice. A sharp, two-note 'tic, tic' and a brief warbling song.

Distribution and Habitat. Local resident, often common, in Sudan, Ethiopia, Somalia and through Uganda and Kenya to northern Tanzania. Inhabits dry bush, coastal scrub and acacia woodland.

RED-FACED CROMBEC *Sylvietta whytii* Plate 31

Identification. 4in, 10cm. Is a larger species, lacks the dusky eye-streak and has more extensive and darker rufous underparts.
Voice. Various 'tsssp' type calls.
Distribution and Habitat. It occurs locally over a wide area of East and Central Africa and inhabits bush, acacia woodland and Brachystegia scrub and woodland.
Allied Species. The Long-billed Crombec *(S. rufescens)*, 4in, 10cm, is similar to the Red-faced Crombec but has a longer, decurved bill, and the ear-coverts grey not rufous. It occurs in Zambia, Malawi and Rhodesia. The Somali Long-billed Crombec *(S. isabellina)*, occurs in arid bush country in Ethiopia, Somalia and northern and eastern Kenya. It differs from the Red-faced Crombec in having a longer bill and the underparts isabelline-grey, paler on the throat. The Red-capped Crombec *(S. ruficapilla)*, 4in, 10cm, is pale grey above with a pale rufous forehead and the ear-coverts and patch on upper chest chestnut, remainder underparts whitish. It occurs in Brachystegia woodland and thickets in Zambia and Malawi.

BANDED TIT-WARBLER *Parisoma bohmi* Plate 30

Identification. 4½in, 11½cm. A rather plump little bird, tit or warbler-like in its appearance and habits; upperparts grey; tail blackish, edged white on outer feathers; below white with indistinct dusky spotting on throat and a black band across chest; flanks tawny-rufous, eye yellow.
Voice. A short trilling song, often repeated, and loud double-note call 'tik-wirra, tik-wirra.'
Distribution and Habitat. Northern and eastern Kenya, south to central Tanzania. Found in acacia woodland and bush in drier areas.
Allied Species. The Grey Tit-Warbler *(P. plumbeum)*, 4½in, 11½cm, differs in lacking the black chest-band and tawny flanks and has the outer tail feathers white. It also resembles the Ashy Flycatcher except for its white outer tail feathers. It has a wide range in East Africa, inhabiting wooded country and bush. The Brown Tit-Warbler *(P. lugens)*, 4½in, 11½cm, is a dark smoky-brown, warbler-like bird with a whitish belly; outer tail feathers edged and tipped with white. Occurs locally in Kenya and Tanzania, favouring acacia woodland and savannah woodland. The Yellow-bellied Hyliota *(Hyliota flavigaster)*, previously classified among the flycatchers, is 5in, 13cm, iridescent blue-black above with a white wing stripe and bright tawny-yellow underparts. ♀ grey above. Inhabits wooded areas, keeping to the foliage of small trees; actions similar to those of a tit. Occurs in Uganda, Kenya and Ethiopia, south to Zambia and Malawi. The Southern Hyliota *(H. aus-*

tralis), 5in, 13cm, is dull velvety black above, not glossy blue-black; ♀ brownish-grey on upperparts. Occurs in western Kenya to western Uganda, south to Malawi and Zambia. The Yellow Longbill *(Macrosphenus flavicans)*, 5in, 13cm, is rather short-tailed with a straight long bill; above olive-green, slightly darker on head; below, throat dusky-white merging to silky lemon-yellow on belly to golden-yellow on flanks. Occurs in forest undergrowth in Uganda. The Grey Longbill *(M. concolor)*, 5in, 13cm, is similar but has the underparts dull olive-grey. In both species feathers of lower back and flanks very long, giving the birds a puffed out appearance. It occurs in forest undergrowth in western Uganda. The Greenbul Warbler *(Suaheliornis kretschmeri)*, also known as Suaheli Longbill, 6in, 15cm, is generally dull green with pale greyish-white underparts with a yellow wash; bill long and straight. It occurs in forest undergrowth in north-eastern, eastern and south-eastern Tanzania. In the field, except for its straight bill, it looks very much like a greenbul with which, in the past, it has been classified.

GREEN HYLIA   *Hylia prasina*   Plate 30

Identification. 4½in, 11½cm. A dark olive-green bird with a broad greenish-yellow stripe over the eye; wings and tail green; below whitish olive-grey; bill short and slightly curved. This is a bird of uncertain status, previously classified among the sunbirds.
Voice. A harsh, grating 'grr-grr' quite unlike any sunbird call; also a loud warbling song with high notes.
Distribution and Habitat. Occurs in southern Sudan, Uganda and western Kenya. A locally common but shy forest bird, usually found in rank under-growth but sometimes a member of bird parties in treetops.

FLYCATCHERS: Muscicapidae

This is a large family of small or medium-sized birds, usually with flattened bills and well-developed bristles at gape; immature plumages spotted. Many species perch upright on some vantage point, such as a dead branch or wire fence, from which short erratic flights are made after their insect prey. Other species hunt insect food amongst foliage in the manner of warblers.

DUSKY FLYCATCHER   *Alseonax adustus*   Plate 29

Identification. 4in, 10cm. A small plump flycatcher with a rather short tail; dark sepia or greyish-brown with a pale chin and belly. Immature heavily spotted buffy-white above and on chest. Usually seen perched on a dead twig from which it makes short flights; very tame and confiding.

Voice. Usually silent, but sometimes utters a soft two-note call, or when at nest a weak chatter.

Distribution and Habitat. A widely distributed and common resident in East and Central Africa. In East Africa occurs in wooded and forest areas, also common in tree-shaded gardens. Further south it occurs both in evergreen forest and Brachystegia woodland.

Allied Species. The European Spotted Flycatcher *(Muscicapa striata)*, 5in, 13cm, is a winter visitor and passage migrant to East and Central Africa. It is larger and slimmer than the Dusky Flycatcher with a longer tail and a lightly streaked whitish breast. The European Pied and White-collared Flycatchers *(M. hypoleuca* and *M. albicollis)* are also winter visitors to East Africa. The Swamp Flycatcher *(Alseonax aquaticus)*, 5in, 13cm, is a thickset dark sepia-brown species with a conspicuous white throat and belly; broad sepia band across chest and upper breast. It occurs locally from southern Sudan, south-wards through Uganda and western Kenya to Zambia. It has a restricted habitat, being confined mainly to the margins of reed and papyrus beds in or near water. Boehm's Flycatcher *(Myopornis bohmi)*, 4½in, 11½cm, is brown, streaked with blackish above; below white with wedge-shaped black spotting on chest and flanks. It occurs in Brachystegia woodland in western and southern Tanzania and in Zambia. The Ashy Flycatcher *(Alseonax cinereus)*, 5in, 13cm, occurs locally in wooded country in East and Central Africa. It is rather slim, pale blue-grey above, whitish below with a wash of blue-grey on breast and flanks; a white streak above and below eye. The Yellow-footed Flycatcher *(A. seth-smithi)*, 3½in, 9cm, is dark slate with black wings and tail; below white; feet light yellow. In East Africa known only from western Uganda; inhabits roads and clearings in forest. Cassin's Grey Fly-catcher *(A. cassini)*, 5in, 13cm, is a thickset dark grey flycatcher with black wings and tail and a white belly. Occurs along forest streams and rivers in Uganda and in north-western Zambia. The Dusky Blue Flycatcher *(Pedilo-rhynchus comitatus)*, 4½in, 11½cm, also frequents forest streams and rivers in southern Sudan, western and southern Uganda. Upperparts rich bluish-slate with black wings and tail; below throat white, belly greyish-white, chest, upper breast and flanks bluish-slate. The Sooty Flycatcher *(Artomyias fuli-ginosa)*, 4in, 10cm, is dark sooty-brown, slightly paler below with some dusky streaking. A forest species constantly perching on bare branches of dead trees; flight more extended than most flycatchers and bird bears a close resemblance to a sand martin when in flight. It occurs from southern Sudan to Uganda. The Grey-throated Flycatcher *(Alseonax griseigularis)*, 4in, 10cm, is dark slaty-grey with wings also grey; tail black. Frequents forest undergrowth and sometimes banks of forest streams. Occurs in western and southern Uganda.

WHITE-EYED SLATY FLYCATCHER
Dioptrornis fischeri **Plate 29**

Identification. 6in, 15cm. Upperparts slate-grey, paler below; a conspicuous white ring around eye. Immature with whitish spots on upperparts. A plump-looking flycatcher recognised by its slaty-grey plumage and white eye-ring. Often alights on ground to pick up insects; very active at dusk, often observed on paths in wooded and forest areas in the manner of a robin chat.

Voice. Usually silent: most vocal in evening when utters a sharp sunbird-like 'tsssk' and a short descending trill.

Distribution and Habitat. Resident, locally common in highlands of East Africa south to Malawi and Zambia. Occurs in highland forest, forest margins and scrub, and in cultivation where there are trees. A common bird in the highlands of Kenya where it is well-known in gardens.

Allied Species. The Shrike Flycatcher *(Megabyas flammulatus)*, 6in, 15cm, occurs in the forests of western and southern Uganda and in the Kakamega Forest, western Kenya. ♂ black above with pure white rump and underparts; ♀ earth-brown above, below white with brown streaking. When perched both sexes wag the tail slowly up and down. The Black and White Flycatcher *(Bias musicus)*, 5in, 13cm, has black upperparts and chest and a white belly in the ♂; the ♀ is cinnamon-rufous with white and tawny underparts. Found in the forests of Uganda, Kenya and eastern Tanzania. The Forest Flycatcher *(Fraseria ocreata)*, 5½in, 14cm, is dark slate-grey above, below white with narrow grey concentric barring on chest and flanks. An uncommon forest species known from western Uganda.

SOUTH AFRICAN BLACK FLYCATCHER
Melaenornis pammelaina **Plate 29**

Identification. 8in, 20cm. Plumage entirely black with a bluish gloss. Immature with tawny spots. Behaves in the manner of a puff-backed shrike, searching foliage for insects. The Drongo is also all black but has a long forked tail, not rounded, and ruby-red not dark brown eyes; also a much heavier and hooked bill. The ♂ Black Cuckoo-Shrike also resembles a Black Flycatcher but may be distinguished by its yellow gape.

Voice. A low piping 'tweee, tweee, tweee, eeeeee.'

Distribution and Habitat. Sparsely distributed resident in Kenya, Tanzania, Malawi, Zambia and Rhodesia. Inhabits acacia and other woodlands and bush country. In Kenya not uncommon in the Tsavo National Park.

Allied Species. The Black Flycatcher *(M. edolioides)*, 7½in, 19cm, is a West African species which occurs in woodlands and cultivation in Uganda, western Kenya and north-western Tanzania. Its plumage is dull blackish-slate without the metallic blue gloss. The Yellow-eyed Black Flycatcher *(M. ardesiaca)*, 7in, 18cm, differs from the South African Black Flycatcher in its smaller size and bright yellow eye, the latter a good field character. It is a rare bird, in East Africa known only from the Impenetrable Forest, south western Uganda.

SILVERBIRD *Empidornis semipartitus* Plate 29

Identification. 7in, 18cm. A slim, rather long-tailed flycatcher, pale silvery-grey above and bright rufous below. Immature spotted pale buff on upper-parts and mottled with black below. Usually occurs in pairs. The silvery back and rufous underparts render identification easy.
Voice. Usually silent but the ♂ has a soft warbling song.
Distribution and Habitat. An uncommon and local resident in dry bush and acacia woodland in Ethiopia, Uganda, western Kenya and northern Tanzania. In Kenya it is locally common in the Lake Baringo area.

GREY FLYCATCHER *Bradornis microrhynchus* Plate 29

Identification. 5in, 13cm. Upperparts, wings and tail grey with dusky crown streaks; below pale grey merging to white on throat and abdomen. Generally resembles a plump Spotted Flycatcher but lacks that species' breast streaks. Usually encountered in pairs.
Voice. Normally silent, but sometimes utters a soft 'tsssp.'
Distribution and Habitat. Occurs in dry bush and savannah woodlands from Ethiopia and Somalia through Uganda and Kenya to southern Tanzania.
Allied Species. The Pale Flycatcher *(B. pallidus)*, 6in, 15cm, is similar to the Grey Flycatcher but is larger with a relatively longer tail and is pale brownish-grey in colour; no black streaks on crown. Locally common and widespread resident in East and Central Africa. Inhabits savannah woodland, acacia country, coastal scrub and cultivation.

CHIN-SPOT FLYCATCHER *Batis molitor* Plate 29

Identification. 4in, 10cm. A small, short-tailed, rather stumpy black, grey and white flycatcher. ♂ has black band across chest, ♀ has a chestnut band and also a chestnut patch on the throat. Immature resembles ♀ but has buff speckling above and on chest. Species differs from the Wattle-eyed Flycatchers in lacking red eye-wattles. Occurs in pairs, usually in acacia trees. In flight produces a sharp 'brrrrp' with wings. Chestnut throat-patch of ♀ conspicuous in field.

Voice. A clear squeaky 'chrr – chrr' and a louder double alarm call.

Distribution and Habitat. A common and widespread resident in East and Central Africa. Inhabits bush country and woodland, especially acacia, and also forest edges, cultivation and gardens.

Allied Species. The Cape Puff-back Flycatcher *(B. capensis)*, 4½in, 11½cm, is a forest species which occurs locally in extreme southern Kenya and in Tanzania, south to Central Africa. The ♂ has a very wide black chest band and the ♀ has the throat and chest rufous-brown. In the Ruwenzori Puff-back Flycatcher *(B. diops)*, 4½in, 11½cm, the sexes are alike, both ♂ and ♀ having a very broad black chest band. This species occurs in mountain forest in western and south-western Uganda. The Grey-headed Puff-back Flycatcher *(B. orientalis)*, 4in, 10cm, has a grey crown and a narrow black chestband; ♀ has a deep chestnut chest-band. It occurs in the Sudan, Ethiopia and Somalia, south to extreme northern Kenya. The Pygmy Puff-back Flycatcher *(B. perkeo)*, 3in, 8cm, is similar to the Grey-headed Puff-back Flycatcher but is much smaller and the ♀ has a pale tawny chest-band, not deep chestnut. It occurs in dry bush country in Ethiopia and Somalia south to Kenya. The Black-headed Puff-back Flycatcher *(B. minor)*, 4in, 10cm, has the crown black, not grey; ♀ with dark chestnut breast-band. Occurs in the Sudan, Ethiopia and Somalia southwards through eastern districts of Kenya and Tanzania.

BLACK-THROATED WATTLE-EYE   *Platysteira peltata*   Plate 29

Identification. 5in, 13cm. A conspicuous black and white flycatcher with bright scarlet wattles above eyes. ♂ white below with a narrow black band across chest; ♀ with throat and chest glossy black. Scarlet eye wattles are prominent in field and distinguish wattle-eyes from puff-back flycatchers. Occurs in pairs; habits tit-like, obtaining much of its insect food from foliage of trees and shrubs.

Voice. A series of short clear whistles.

Distribution and Habitat. Occurs in wooded areas of eastern Kenya, Tanzania and Central Africa.

Allied Species. The Wattle-eye Flycatcher *(P. cyanea)*, 5in, 13cm. Differs in having a conspicuous white wing bar and the ♀ has a deep chestnut throat and chest, not black. It occurs in woodlands and forests in Uganda, western Kenya and north-western Tanzania.

JAMESON'S WATTLE-EYE   *Dyaphorophyia jamesoni*   **Plate 29**

Identification. 3in, 8cm. A plump and very short-tailed flycatcher, glossy greenish-black above and on throat and chest; chestnut patch on each side of the neck; breast and belly pure white; large turquoise-blue eye wattles. ♀ slightly greyer on upperparts.

Voice. A sharp 'brrrp,' perhaps made with wings, and various clicking sounds.

Distribution and Habitat. Forests of southern Sudan, Uganda and western Kenya. Inhabits dense undergrowth; shy and not often seen, but draws attention by the sharp 'brrrp' it produces.

Allied Species. The Yellow-bellied Wattle-eye *(D. concreta)*, 3½in, 9cm, is olive-green above with a chestnut-yellow breast and belly; eye-wattle bright green. Occurs in forest undergrowth in western Kenya, western Uganda and the Kungwe-Mahare Mts, western Tanzania. The Chestnut Wattle-eye *(D. castanea)*, 4in, 10cm, is a thickset forest undergrowth flycatcher which appears to be almost tailless in the field. The ♂ has blackish upperparts; rump and underparts white with a very broad black breast-band. The ♀ has the crown and rump slate-grey, rest of upperparts, throat and breast bright chestnut; belly white; eye wattles purplish grey in both sexes. It occurs locally in forests of western Kenya, Uganda and north-western Tanzania. This wattle-eye has a very distinctive call, a sustained 'pop, pop, pop, pop' similar to a tinker-bird's calls.

CHESTNUT-CAP FLYCATCHER   *Erythrocercus mccallii*   **Plate 29**

Identification. 4in, 10cm. A tiny olive-brown flycatcher with a relatively long bright chestnut tail; crown chestnut with short white streaks; below, throat and chest tawny-brown to buffy-white on rest of underparts. Very active little birds found in small parties in the foliage of forest trees; constantly spreading their tails.

Voice. A high pitched 'tsssp' frequently repeated.

Distribution and Habitat. In East Africa known only from the forests of western Uganda; most frequent in the Budongo Forest.

Allied Species. Livingstone's Flycatcher *(E. livingstonei)*, 4in, 10cm, has the upperparts greenish-grey to yellowish-green; tail pale chestnut with black spots near the tips on the six central feathers; throat white to lemon-yellow on breast and belly. Very similar in habits to the Chestnut-cap Flycatcher. Occurs from southern Tanzania southwards to Malawi and Zambia. Inhabits woodlands.

LITTLE YELLOW FLYCATCHER
Chloropetella holochlora **Plate 29**

Identification. 3½in, 9cm. A tiny yellow flycatcher, greenish on the mantle, with a relatively long tail. Very similar in habits to the two previous species, very active in foliage of trees.

Voice. A plaintive 'zee, zee' rather like a Collared Sunbird's call.

Distribution and Habitat. Ranges from southern Somalia through coastal Kenya to eastern Tanzania. Inhabits woodland and forests in coastal districts.

BLUE FLYCATCHER *Erannornis longicauda* **Plate 29**

Identification. 5½in, 14cm. A very beautiful small blue flycatcher with a long graduated tail. Plumage cerulean blue, paler on throat and belly. Immature spotted buff on upperparts. Tame and confiding, readily identified by colour and habit of constantly fanning its tail.

Voice. A brief, sunbird-like twittering song.

Distribution and Habitat. A local resident in woodland and forest areas, in cultivation and in gardens; ranges from western Kenya, Uganda, western and north-eastern Tanzania, to Malawi and Zambia.

Allied Species. The White-tailed Blue Flycatcher *(E. albicauda)*, 5½in, 14cm, differs in having the three outer pairs of tail feathers white. It occurs in western Uganda and very locally in northern Tanzania. Inhabits forest margins, woodland and gardens. The Crested Flycatcher *(Trochocercus cyanomelas)*, 4½in, 11½cm, has the head and chest blue-black, the mantle bluish-slate; narrow white bands on wing; breast and abdomen white; no white on tail; crested. The ♀ is duller and greyer. The crested flycatchers draw attention by their restless behaviour, constantly flitting about and fanning and closing their tails. Local but widespread in East and Central Africa; inhabits forests, woodlands and dense coastal thickets. The White-tailed Crested Flycatcher *(T. albonotatus)*, 4in, 10cm, has a black head and crest and broad white tips to the tail feathers. It inhabits forested areas in western Kenya, Uganda and Tanzania. The Blue-headed Crested Flycatcher *(T. nitens)*, 4½in, 11½cm, has the upperparts, head and chest glossy blue-black; breast and abdomen grey, tail dark. It frequents the forests of western and southern Uganda. The Dusky Crested Flycatcher *(T. nigromitratus)*, 3½in, 9cm, is slate-grey with crown and crest dull black. It occurs in the Kakamega Forest, western Kenya and in forests in Uganda.

PARADISE FLYCATCHER *Terpsiphone viridis* **Plate 29**

Identification. ♂ 12–14in, 30–36cm; ♀ 8in, 20cm. Unmistakable: combination of very long tail and chestnut, black, grey and white plumage render species easy to identify. In some parts of its distribution, especially in eastern Kenya, a white phase of plumage in the adult ♂ is commoner than the normal chestnut phase. In this plumage the back, wings and tail are white, not chestnut. The ♀ which is much shorter tailed than the ♂, does not have a white plumage. Immature resembles ♀ but is duller.
Voice. Call note a sharp and loud two- or three-note whistle; song a loud and distinct warble.
Distribution and Habitat. A widespread and locally common resident throughout East Africa. In Central Africa mainly a summer migrant from September to March, but some birds resident throughout year. Inhabits wooded areas, forests, thick scrub, thornbush and acacia country, cultivation and gardens. The white phase is common in the Tsavo National Park, Kenya.

BLACK-HEADED PARADISE FLYCATCHER
Terpsiphone rufiventer **Plate 29**

Identification. 8–9in, 20–23cm. Head and neck glossy black with a bluish or violet wash; remainder of plumage rufous-chestnut; central tail feathers elongated in ♂ but not to the extent of the Paradise Flycatcher. ♀ lacks elongated central tail feathers and throat greyish. Immature similar but duller. Easily recognised by its rufous underparts.
Voice. A loud two- or three-note whistle.
Distribution and Habitat. In East Africa found in forests of western Uganda and north-western Tanzania; also in northern Zambia.

TITS: Paridae

The Tits are a group of small, rather plump birds of distinct structure and habits. They are extremely active and acrobatic when feeding, often hanging upside-down while searching for insects in foliage or on bark. They are often members of mixed bird parties.

GREY TIT *Parus afer* **Plate 37**

Identification. 4½in, 11½cm. Upperparts pale blue-grey, head and throat black; a broad white stripe from base of bill down sides of neck and a white patch on nape; belly greyish-white. The white streak down sides of neck is the best field character.

Voice. A harsh 'chiss, tch-tch-tch' and a single 'tseee.'

Distribution and Habitat. It is possible that East African population, *P. a. thruppi*, with a broken white stripe down sides of neck, should be considered a distinct species from the Central African birds with an unbroken white neck stripe. Local resident through East and Central Africa. In the northern half of its range it inhabits dry bush and acacia woodland, especially stands of acacias along rivers. In the south it is mainly a bird of Brachystegia woodland.

Allied Species. The White-backed Black Tit *(P. leuconotus)*, 5in, 13cm, is a little-known species found in high level wooded mountain valleys and gorges in Ethiopia. It is black with a blue gloss and a contrasting buffy-white mantle.

WHITE-BREASTED TIT   *Parus albiventris*   **Plate 37**

Identification. 5½in, 14cm. A black tit with a contrasting white belly; wing feathers and wing coverts edged white. In pairs or family parties; very active and always on the move.

Voice. A sharp 'tss, tseee' or 'tss, tss, tss, tee;' song a repeated warbling 'chee, chee, churr.'

Distribution and Habitat. Locally common resident southern Sudan, Uganda, Kenya and Tanzania. Inhabits acacia country, woodlands, forests and coastal bush.

Allied Species. The Cinnamon-breasted Tit *(P. rufiventris)*, 5½in, 14cm, resembles a greyish edition of the White-breasted Tit but with a rufous-cinnamon belly. It occurs in woodlands in Tanzania, Malawi, Zambia and Rhodesia. The Black Tit *(P. leucomelas)*, 5½in, 14cm, is glossy violet-black with contrasting white shoulders and white edgings to the flight feathers. It occurs very locally in bush, forest and woodland in Uganda, western Kenya, Tanzania, Malawi, Zambia and Rhodesia. The Southern Black Tit *(P. niger)*, 5½in, 14cm, has very narrow white edgings to wing feathers and appears completely black in the field, not black with white shoulders. It is found locally in scrub and woodland in Malawi, Zambia and Rhodesia. The Dusky Tit *(P. funereus)*, 5in, 13cm, is a common bird of forest tree-tops in western Kenya and Uganda. It is entirely dark slate-grey with bright red eyes. Usually in small flocks, often associated with mixed bird parties. The Stripe-breasted Tit *(P. fasciiventer)*, 4½in, 11½cm, is a grey-backed tit with a blackish head and chest and a blackish stripe down the centre of the breast. It is a mountain forest bird found on the Ruwenzori Mts and the forested mountains of south-western Uganda. The Red-throated Tit *(P. fringillinus)*, 4½in, 11½cm, is a grey-backed tit with pale rufous-buff underparts and a conspicuous rufous collar on hind neck; crown grey; wing feathers and tail edged white. The Cinnamon-breasted Tit has no rufous collar on hindneck. Inhabits acacia woodland and open plains with scattered trees and bush, in pairs or family parties. Local and uncommon in southern Kenya and northern Tanzania, most frequent in Masai country.

AFRICAN PENDULINE TIT *Remiz caroli* Plate 37

Identification. 2½in, 6½cm. A tiny, rather short-tailed grey bird with buff underparts, darker on the flanks. Bill very short and tapering and sharp. Occurs in pairs or small parties in bush country. Recalls an Eremomela warbler, but the latter has a yellow belly and a longer bill.
Voice. A squeaky two-note call, often repeated.
Distribution and Habitat. Local resident in small numbers in southern Uganda, Kenya, Tanzania, Malawi, Zambia and Rhodesia. Inhabits bush, scrub, stands of acacia and Brachystegia woodlands.

MOUSE-COLOURED PENDULINE TIT
Remiz musculus Plate 37

Identification. 2½in, 6½cm. A tiny short-tailed tit with a short, tapering sharp bill; above pale grey, below creamy-white with a slight tinge of buff on the belly. The closely related African Penduline Tit has a pale buff forehead and the underparts cinnamon-buff.
Voice. A high-pitched 'teep, teep' frequently repeated.
Distribution and Habitat. A very local species found in acacia bush and woodland in Kenya, northern Uganda, and north-eastern Tanzania. Usually in small flocks or sometimes pairs.

SPOTTED CREEPER: Salpornithidae

There is only one species in this family, the Spotted Creeper of Africa and Asia. A small tree-climbing bird with whitish or buff-spotted plumage. Woodpecker-like in actions but tail is not specialised for climbing and is rounded; held away from the bark when bird is climbing, thus resembling the actions of nuthatches.

SPOTTED CREEPER *Salpornis spilonota* Plate 38

Identification. 6in, 15cm. A small woodpecker-like bird with white spotted brown plumage and white spotted wings and tail; bill slender and decurved.

Habits similar to those of a European tree creeper but does not use its rounded tail as a support. Obtains its food from the bark of trees, flying to the base and climbing upwards. Usually seen singly or in pairs.

Voice. A shrill whistle of several notes run together and sometimes a single 'tseee' not unlike a tit's call.

Distribution and Habitat. An uncommon and local resident through East and Central Africa, more frequent in the south of its range. Inhabits park-like country, savannah and acacia woodland and in the south Brachystegia woodland. Very uncommon in Kenya and Uganda, more frequent in Zambia and Rhodesia.

SUNBIRDS: Nectariniidae

A distinct family of small birds with slender curved bills and, in most species, brilliant metallic plumage in the males. In some species male has a dull female-like non-breeding plumage. Some females are difficult to identify in the field and are best recognised by their associated males. Flight very erratic and rapid. Most species visit flowering trees, such as Erythrina, in which they may be observed at close quarters. The best way to see several of the rarer forest species is to wait in the vicinity of a flowering tree for the birds to appear.

LITTLE GREEN SUNBIRD *Nectarinia seimundi*   Plate 34

Identification. 3½in, 9cm. Sexes alike. A short-tailed all green sunbird without pectoral tufts; underparts slightly paler and yellower than head and mantle. Not metallic in any way.

Voice. Soft 'tsssp' call notes.

Distribution and Habits. In East Africa occurs in southern Sudan and Uganda. A forest species normally found in the tree-tops. Much attracted to Erythrina trees and to Loranthus flowers.

OLIVE SUNBIRD *Nectarinia olivacea*   Plate 36

Identification. 5–6in, 13–15cm. Sexes similar; in some races ♀♀ possess pectoral tufts as well as the ♂♂. A medium-sized, rather slim sunbird with non-metallic green plumage; above dusky olive-green, paler below, more or less tinged yellow, with yellow pectoral tufts. One of its field characters is its habit of constantly flicking its wings.

Voice. Two- or three-note 'tsssp' call; also a sustained warbling song.

Distribution and Habitat. Mainly a forest species but also occurs in dense coastal scrub. Ranges throughout East and Central Africa in suitable habitats.

BLUE-HEADED SUNBIRD   *Nectarinia alinae*   Plate 34

Identification. 5in, 13cm. Sexes similar. Crown, head, throat and chest metallic violet-blue; back orange-brown; belly sooty-black; pectoral tufts pale yellow, present in ♂ only; eyes red. The much commoner Green-headed Sunbird has the head and chest metallic green, the back olive-green and the belly grey.
Voice. A three- or four-note 'tchee, ttchee, ttchee' and a sustained warbling song.
Distribution and Habitat. A mountain forest sunbird found in the Ruwenzori range and in the Kigezi highland forests, Uganda. Much attracted to clumps of the parasite *Loranthus* growing in forest trees.

GREEN-HEADED SUNBIRD   *Nectarinia verticalis*   Plate 34

Identification. 5½in, 14cm. Sexes similar. A mainly non-metallic olive-green sunbird with a metallic green head and throat; mantle olive-green, breast and belly grey; pectoral tufts pale yellow present in ♂ only. ♀ resembles ♂ but has throat grey like remainder of underparts. Immature resembles ♀ but lacks metallic green crown and throat is dusky.
Voice. A double-note call 'tee-cheek, tee-cheek'; also a soft warbling song.
Distribution and Habitat. Local resident southern Sudan, Uganda, Kenya east to Mt Kenya, south through Tanzania to Malawi and Zambia. Inhabits evergreen forests, wooded areas and riverine forest and also cultivation and gardens near forest. Attracted to flowering Erythrina trees and low growing flowers such as Leonotis.
Allied Species. Bannerman's Sunbird *(N. bannermani)*, 5½in, 14cm, is a rare species in our area confined to evergreen forest in north-western Zambia. Differs from the Green-headed Sunbird in having head and throat metallic steely-blue; ♀ with only a trace of metallic colour on crown.

BLUE-THROATED BROWN SUNBIRD
Nectarinia cyanolaema   Plate 35

Identification. 5½in, 14cm. ♂ a dull-looking sooty-brown sunbird, paler on the belly; crown and throat patch dark metallic steel-blue; pectoral tufts pale yellow. ♀ olive above and on wings and tail; pale stripe above and below eye; chin whitish merging to pale brown on throat; remainder underparts whitish, mottled olive-grey on breast and flanks.

Voice. A harsh, repeated 'teep, teep, teep, teep.'

Distribution and Habitat. A common forest sunbird in southern Sudan, Uganda and also recorded from the Kakamega Forest, western Kenya. Keeps mainly to the tree-tops; attracted to flowering Nandi Flame trees and Erythrina trees.

GREEN-THROATED SUNBIRD   *Nectarinia rubescens*   Plate 34

Identification. 4½–5in, 11½–13cm. ♂ a square-tailed, velvety-black sunbird with a metallic green throat patch edged at bottom with metallic violet; crown metallic green, edged violet towards nape. ♀ dark olive-brown with yellowish-white streak above eye; below, whitish with heavy dusky-olive streaking on breast and flanks.

Voice. A loud and distinctive 'tssp-tee' not unlike call of Scarlet-chested Sunbird.

Distribution and Habitat. An uncommon and local species found in southern Sudan, Uganda, western Kenya and north-western Tanzania. A forest species keeping largely to the tree-tops; attracted to flowering Nandi Flame trees and Erythrinas.

AMETHYST SUNBIRD   *Nectarinia amethystina*   Plate 34

Identification. 4½–5in, 11½–13cm. ♂ a square-tailed, velvety black sunbird with a metallic green cap and a rosy-purple throat; ♀ olive-brown with whitish eye-stripe, heavily streaked olive-brown on whitish ground on breast and flanks; immature like ♀ but has black throat. ♀ Scarlet-chested Sunbird has no pale eye-stripe, is darker brown above and heavily mottled rather than streaked below.

Voice. A variety of loud 'cheep' or 'tsssp' calls and a loud warbling song.

Distribution and Habitat. Local resident and partial migrant southern Sudan, Kenya, Tanzania and Central Africa. A common species, often called the Black Sunbird, found in a variety of habitats from mountain forest to coastal scrub and mangrove swamps, savannah and Brachystegia woodland, bush country, cultivation and gardens.

SCARLET-CHESTED SUNBIRD   *Nectarinia senegalensis*   Plate 34

Identification. 6in, 15cm. ♂ a rather thickset, square-tailed velvety-brown or black sunbird with a metallic green cap, throat and moustache streak and a vivid scarlet chest; scarlet feathers of chest with narrow subterminal blue bars. ♀ dark brown above without an eye-stripe, below whitish, very heavily mottled and streaked dark brown; immature like ♀ but throat blackish. ♀

Amethyst Sunbird is olive-brown with a pale eye-stripe and is streaked below.

Voice. A variety of loud clear notes, the commonest of which is a descending 'tssp, teee, tee;' song a loud trilling warble.

Distribution and Habitat. Local resident and partial migrant in East and Central Africa. A common and conspicuous species found in a variety of habitats from forest margins, woodland, savannah and park-like country to bush, riverine acacias and cultivation; often visits gardens; specially attracted to flowering Leonotis.

HUNTER'S SUNBIRD *Nectarinia hunteri*   **Plate 34**

Identification. 5½in, 14cm. ♂ similar to Scarlet-chested Sunbird but differs in having a velvety-black chin and upper throat, a metallic violet rump and a violet patch on the wing shoulders. ♀ similar to ♀ Scarlet-chested Sunbird but paler.

Voice. A single or double 'tschee, tschee' repeated at about two-second intervals. Soft warbling song.

Distribution and Habitat. Hunter's Sunbird occurs in eastern Ethiopia, Somalia, northern and eastern Kenya and north-eastern Tanzania. It is found in arid bush country. Much attracted to flowering acacia trees and bushes and flowering Delonyx trees.

VARIABLE SUNBIRD *Nectarinia venusta*   **Plate 35**

Identification. 3½in, 9cm. ♂ bright metallic blue-green with broad purplish-blue throat and chest patch; breast and abdomen yellow, more or less washed orange (white in Somali and north-eastern Kenya race; orange-red in western Uganda and Zaire race); pectoral tufts yellow and orange-red. ♀ and immature olive-grey, whitish or yellowish-white below, unstreaked. The somewhat similar Collared Sunbird is metallic yellowish-green and lacks the broad purple chest patch.

Voice. Short 'tssp' calls and a longer churring call; song a soft warble.

Distribution and Habitat. Local resident and partial migrant over much of East and Central Africa. A common species in East African gardens. Inhabits bush country of all sorts, edges of forests, woodland, cultivation and rank vegetation near water. Attracted to flowers of orange Leonotis, Loranthus and to various flowering acacias.

Allied Species. The White-bellied Sunbird *(N. talatala)*, 4in, 10cm, is metallic green on upperparts with blue or gold reflections; throat metallic blue-green, fringed by blackish band; breast and belly white; pectoral tufts yellow. ♀ ashy-grey above, dusky-white below, unstreaked. Occurs in bush and woodland in southern Tanzania and Central Africa. The Angola White-bellied Sunbird *(N. oustaleti)*, 4in, 10cm, differs from the White-bellied Sunbird in having a violet band across the chest tipped with maroon; pectoral tufts yellow and orange. A rare woodland sunbird found in southern Tanzania and in Zambia.

EASTERN DOUBLE-COLLARED SUNBIRD
Nectarinia mediocris   **Plate 34**

Identification. 4in, 10cm. ♂ bright metallic green; upper tail-coverts blue or violet-blue; narrow violet-blue line at base of throat, followed by scarlet band across chest; belly olive, conspicuous yellow pectoral tufts. ♀ and immature dusky olive-green.

Voice. A clear, sharp 'tssp, tssp, tssp' frequently uttered; a clear warbling song.

Distribution and Habitat. Local resident highland areas over 5,000ft, 1,530m, in Kenya, Tanzania, Malawi and Zambia. A highlands sunbird frequenting montane forest, scrub and gardens; much attracted to flowers of red-hot-pokers and Leonotis.

Allied Species. The Tanzania, Malawi, Zambia, Rhodesia and Angola races of the Southern Double-collared Sunbird *(N. chalybea)*, 4in, 10cm, are found in Brachystegia woodland and scrub, and not in mountain forest. They are best recognised by pale wings, tail and non-metallic grey rump; upper tail-coverts variable and may be grey, metallic green or violet. It is possible that these birds constitute a full species and that the South African races of *N. chalybea*, which have metallic backs and rumps and violet upper tail-coverts, are conspecific with *N. mediocris*. The Greater Double-collared Sunbird *(N. afer)*, 5–5½in, 13–14cm, is metallic green on upperparts and throat to chest, with a broad red chest-band, yellow pectoral tufts and an olive-grey belly. ♀ uniform olive, paler in centre of belly. It inhabits montane forest and the alpine scrub zone; it occurs on the Ruwenzori range and in south-western Kigezi in Uganda, and the Nyika plateau in Malawi and Zambia.

NORTHERN DOUBLE-COLLARED SUNBIRD
Nectarinia preussi   **Plate 34**

Identification. 3½in, 9cm. ♂ a bright metallic green sunbird with a narrow purple chest-band followed by a very broad deep red breast-band; belly dark olive; upper tail-coverts violet; pectoral tufts yellow. ♀ uniform olive-green, paler on the belly. Except for its much smaller size and relatively shorter tail, very similar to Greater Double-collared Sunbird. The Eastern Double-collared Sunbird has a much narrower red breast-band and blue upper tail-coverts.

Voice. The usually soft sunbird 'tssp' and a warbling song.

Distribution and Habitat. Found in mountain forest, usually below 8,000ft, 2,440m, in the Kenya highlands, Mt Elgon and in western and south-western Uganda. Best identified by its small size and very wide red breast band.

OLIVE-BELLIED SUNBIRD *Nectarinia chloropygius* Plate 34

Identification. 4in, 10cm. ♂ a metallic-green sunbird with a broad scarlet breast-band, an olive belly, very large yellow pectoral tufts; upper tail-coverts green like the back. ♀ dark olive above and on wings; tail blackish; below bright greenish-yellow with olive streaking on throat, breast and flanks; chin whitish. Immature like ♀ but with dusky throat.

Voice. A weak 'tsp, tsp, tsp, tsp, tsp' and a sustained warbling song.

Distribution and Habitat. A locally common sunbird in Uganda and southern Sudan; also occurs in western Kenya (Kakamega Forest) and north-eastern Tanzania. Frequents forest, margins of forest and secondary growth and lush bush near swamps. Visits Erythrina trees.

Allied Species. The Tiny Sunbird *(N. minulla)*, 3in, 8cm, is a small edition of the Olive-bellied Sunbird; the ♂ has subterminal blue bars on feathers of red breast band and a darker olive belly; the ♀ differs only in smaller size. An uncommon forest species found in western Uganda.

LOVERIDGE'S SUNBIRD *Nectarinia loveridgei* Plate 34

Identification. 4½in, 11½cm. Rather a thickset sunbird with a relatively short tail. ♂ metallic green on upperparts and throat; narrow band metallic violet across chest; breast and belly yellowish olive with deep orange-red suffusion on breast; pectoral tufts yellow. ♀ olive above with slight metallic grey wash on crown and mantle; below yellowish-olive.

Voice. Loud 'tsssp' call notes and a warbling song.

Distribution and Habitat. Confined to mountain forest on the Uluguru Mountains, eastern Tanzania. Found only in forest and along forest margins.

Allied Species. Moreau's Sunbird *(N. moreaui)*, 4½in, 11½cm, differs from Loveridge's Sunbird in having deeper red breast suffusion and sides of the breast are yellow. The ♀ is yellower below and has a metallic greenish-grey wash on crown and mantle. Confined to mountain forest on the Nguru Mountains and mountains south of the Uluguru range (where only *N. loveridgei* is found).

REGAL SUNBIRD *Nectarinia regia* Plate 34

Identification. 4–4½in, 10–11½cm. ♂ metallic green with graduated black tail; narrow violet band across chest; breast and abdomen bright chrome yellow with scarlet band down centre of underparts to under tail-coverts; pectoral tufts yellow. ♀ uniform olive-green above, yellowish olive below; wings olive, tail blackish.

Voice. Loud, clear 'tsssp' calls and a rapid warbling song.

Distribution and Habitat. Inhabits mountain forest up to 12,000ft, 3,660m. Occurs on the Ruwenzori range in western Uganda and the forested mountains of south-western Uganda. Also found on the Kungwe-Mahare Mountains in western Tanzania. Visits flowers of the forest tree *Symphonia gabonensis* together with Purple-breasted Sunbird.

MARIQUA SUNBIRD *Nectarinia mariquensis* Plate 35

Identification. 5in, 13cm. ♂ metallic green on upperparts and throat, slightly coppery in tint, with a maroon breast band and black belly; no pectoral tufts. ♀ greyish-brown with pale buff eye-stripe; below yellowish-white with dusky streaks on breast and flanks; immature like ♀ but throat black. The Red-chested Sunbird resembles this species but has bluish-green upperparts, a deep red breast band and its central rectrices are elongated.

Voice. A clear, loud 'tssp, tssp' and a brief warbling song.

Distribution and Habitat. Local resident with restricted migratory movements Ethiopia, Somalia south through Uganda and Kenya to Central Africa. Mainly a bird of savannah woodlands, acacias, cultivated areas and arid scrub and bush country.

Allied Species. Shelley's Sunbird *(N. shelleyi)*, 4½in, 11½cm. ♂ is bright metallic green on upperparts and throat with a broad scarlet band across chest, not purple or maroon; wings and tail black; no pectoral tufts. ♀ olive above, yellowish-white below with olive mottling on chest and often with some feathers tipped dull red. This is a rare sunbird known from near Morogoro, Tanzania, Malawi and Zambia. Occurs mainly in Brachystegia woodland; much attracted to yellow- and red-flowered parasitic Loranthus growing in the trees.

LITTLE PURPLE-BANDED SUNBIRD
Nectarinia bifasciata Plate 35

Identification. 4in, 10cm. ♂ metallic bluish-green on upperparts and throat, a narrow purple band bordering throat followed by a wider band across chest; breast and belly black; no pectoral tufts. ♀ olive-grey above; below dusky

yellowish-white with olive streaking on chest and flanks. Immature similar to
♀ but with black throat.

Voice. Usual sunbird 'tsssp' calls.

Distribution and Habitat. A very local species in East and Central Africa,
most frequent in coastal districts of Kenya and Tanzania. It inhabits woodlands, coastal scrub and bush and gardens.

Allied Species. The Violet-breasted Sunbird *(N. chalcomela)*, 4½in, 11½cm, is
similar to the Little Purple-banded Sunbird and is also green with a black
belly, but has a broad band of deep violet-purple across chest, no maroon
band and no pectoral tufts. ♀ is paler below with a well-defined pale streak
behind eye. Occurs in Somalia and eastern districts of Kenya. The Pemba
Sunbird *(N. pembae)* is very similar but has a relatively shorter tail and the
green metallic plumage is much brighter. It is confined to the island of Pemba,
north of Zanzibar.

SHINING SUNBIRD   *Nectarinia habessinica*   Plate 34

Identification. 5in, 13cm. ♂ brilliant metallic green, often with golden sheen
on mantle and throat; crown metallic purple-blue; bright red breast-band,
yellow pectoral tufts, black belly. ♀ uniform pale grey with whitish eye-stripe;
wings and tail grey with pale edgings.

Voice. Rather harsh sunbird 'tsssps' and a sustained warbling song.

Distribution and Habitat. Local resident eastern Sudan, Ethiopia and Somalia south to north-eastern Uganda and northern Kenya. Inhabits dry thornbush country and juniper forest in northern Somalia. It is much attracted to
flowering aloes, salvias, flowering acacia trees and bushes and to fruiting
Salvadora bushes. The red breast-band, yellow tufts and black abdomen are
good field marks.

Allied Species. The Splendid Sunbird *(N. coccinigaster)*, 5½in, 14cm, is
similar to the Shining Sunbird but has a broader red breast-band suffused
with metallic violet, and the ♀ has indistinct greenish streaking on the chest.
It occurs in the southern Sudan and has been recorded from the north of West
Nile Province, Uganda. It inhabits savannah woodlands. The Orange-tufted
Sunbird *(N. bouvieri)*, 4in, 10cm, is a forest sunbird found in the southern
Sudan, Uganda, western Kenya, north-western Tanzania and north-western
Zambia. ♂ metallic green with a dark brown belly; forehead bluish-purple;
violet chest-band and maroon stripe below; pectoral tufts orange and yellow.
♀ olive above with a pale eye-streak; yellowish-olive below with indistinct
streaking on throat, chest and flanks. The Northern Orange-tufted Sunbird
(N. osea), 3½in, 9cm, occurs in the Sudan and in West Nile Province,
Uganda. ♂ metallic bluish-green with a violet-blue chest and black belly;
pectoral tufts orange and pale yellow. ♀ greyish-olive, paler below, not
streaked.

COPPER SUNBIRD *Nectarinia cuprea* Plate 35

Identification. 4in, 10cm. ♂ brilliant metallic copper with violet and red reflections; breast and abdomen black; no pectoral tufts. ♀ olive-brown above, dull yellowish below; wings olive-brown, tail black with grey tips to outer feathers. The non-breeding plumage of the ♂ resembles the ♀ but wings black and metallic wing coverts are retained.

Voice. A sharp but not very loud 'tsssp.'

Distribution and Habitat. Local resident and partial migrant Sudan, Ethiopia, Uganda, western Kenya south to Central Africa. Inhabits bush country, open savannah woodland, cultivation and gardens where there are trees and bushes. Much attracted to flowers of orange Leonotis.

MOUSE-COLOURED SUNBIRD *Nectarinia veroxii* Plate 36

Identification. 4½in, 11½cm. Sexes alike. A grey sunbird with slight bluish-green metallic wash on upperparts; below pale greyish-white; red and creamy-yellow pectoral tufts. Bird has habit of constantly flicking its wings, a habit also shared by Olive Sunbird.

Voice. A loud clear warbling song; call a rather drawn-out and plaintive 'teeeee.'

Distribution and Habitat. Ranges through coastal areas of southern Somalia, Kenya and Tanzania; also on Zanzibar Island. Inhabits dense coastal scrub, woodland and forest and also mangrove swamps.

SUPERB SUNBIRD *Nectarinia superba* Plate 35

Identification. 5½in, 14cm. A large, rather heavy-looking sunbird with a relatively short square tail and a long bill. ♂ metallic green above, bluer green on crown; wings and tail black; throat and chest metallic violet-blue; breast and abdomen deep maroon-red; no pectoral tufts. ♀ olive-green above with pale stripe over eye; below pale greenish-yellow, unstreaked; under tail-coverts orange.

Voice. A loud typical sunbird 'tsssp' and a brief warbling song.

Distribution and Habitat. Widespread but local and uncommon in Uganda; has been recorded Kakamega Forest, western Kenya. A forest treetop sunbird often attracted to flowering Erythrina trees near forest; also often visits banana cultivation to feed on nectar in flowers.

MALACHITE SUNBIRD *Nectarinia famosa* Plate 35

Identification. ♂ 9in, 23cm; ♀ 5in, 13cm. ♂ unmistakable, bright emerald green with long central tail feathers and yellow pectoral tufts, the latter conspicuous only when displaying. In non-breeding plumage pale brownish-grey but with long tail and green wing-coverts and rump. ♀ and immature brownish-grey above, paler, yellowish and unstreaked on underparts. ♀ Golden-winged Sunbird has yellow-edged wings and tail; ♀ Bronze Sunbird is lightly streaked olive below.

Voice. A rapid 'chiii' or a harsher 'chee, chee.' Song is a rapid jingling warble, often of short duration.

Distribution and Habitat. Local resident with restricted migrations, highland areas of southern Sudan, Ethiopia, south through highlands of Uganda, Kenya and Tanzania to the montane grasslands of Malawi and Zambia and the eastern border of Rhodesia. In East and Central Africa inhabits bushy moorlands over 5,000ft, 1,530m, montane grasslands where there are protea bushes, edges of forest and forest glades and montane scrub. In East Africa much attracted to the orange-flowered Leonotis and to flowering red-hot-pokers.

SCARLET-TUFTED MALACHITE SUNBIRD
Nectarinia johnstoni   **Plate 35**

Identification. ♂ 10–12in, 25–30cm; tail 6–8in, 16–20cm. ♀ 5½–6in, 14–15½cm. ♂ a brilliant metallic green sunbird with very long central tail feathers and bright red pectoral tufts. In non-breeding dress body feathers blackish-brown but long tail feathers retained. ♀ dark brown, paler in centre of belly, without elongated rectrices but with pectoral tufts. The Malachite Sunbird is smaller and with a shorter tail and only ♂ has yellow pectoral tufts.

Voice. Call note a sharp 'tssssk;' also has a jingling warbling song.

Distribution and Habitat. A species confined to alpine moorlands. In Kenya known from Mt Kenya and the Aberdare range; in Uganda on the Ruwenzori range and the Birunga volcanoes in south-western Kigezi; in Tanzania on Mount Kilimanjaro in the north and on the Livingstone range in the south; also on the Nyika plateau in Malawi and Zambia. Much attracted to flowering protea bushes and giant lobelias.

BRONZE SUNBIRD *Nectarinia kilimensis*   **Plate 36**

Identification. ♂ 9in, 23cm; ♀ 5½in, 14cm. ♂ a black-looking sunbird with long central tail feathers; in good light upperparts, head, throat and chest metallic bronze-green; belly black; no pectoral tufts. ♀ olive-grey with dark ear-coverts and underparts yellowish with olive streaking. Immature like ♀ but throat dusky. The ♂ Tacazze Sunbird is metallic violet, tinged bronze-green only on the head and ♀ is unstreaked pale grey below. ♀ Malachite Sunbird is yellowish below without streaks.

Voice. A very distinct, loud 'chee-choo, wee' usually uttered twice; also a brief warbling song.

Distribution and Habitat. Resident, locally common, in Uganda, the highlands of Kenya, Tanzania, Malawi, Zambia and eastern Rhodesia. In Uganda occurs as low as 2,500ft, 760m, but elsewhere it is a highlands bird, commonest between 5,000 and 7,000ft, 1,530–2,140m. Occurs in wooded areas, cultivation, gardens, near human habitations and in mountain scrub. Much attracted to flowering Erythrina trees. A common garden bird in Nairobi and Entebbe, East Africa.

TACAZZE SUNBIRD *Nectarinia tacazze* Plate 36

Identification. ♂ 9in, 23cm; ♀ 5½in, 14cm. ♂ a large, thickset sunbird with long central tail feathers; appears black, changing in good light to brilliant metallic violet, glossed copper or bronze on head; belly black; no pectoral tufts. ♀ dusky olive-grey, paler below with whitish streak down each side of throat. Immature like ♀ but with dusky throat. ♂ Bronze Sunbird appears blackish but metallic upperparts and breast coppery-green, not violet. ♀ Bronze Sunbird has yellowish underparts streaked with olive.

Voice. Loud single or double 'tssssp' and a sustained warbling song usually delivered from high in a tree.

Distribution and Habitat. Resident in mountain areas over 7,000ft, 2,140m, in Ethiopia, south-eastern Sudan, eastern Uganda, Kenya and northern Tanzania. Inhabits montane forests and marshy glades in forest, and in gardens and the vicinity of human habitations at high levels. Much attracted to the flowers of red-hot-pokers and often visits flowers in gardens. Common in the Kenya Highlands on both sides of the Rift Valley.

GOLDEN-WINGED SUNBIRD *Nectarinia reichenowi* Plate 36

Identification. ♂ 9in, 23cm; ♀ 6in, 15cm. ♂ unmistakable, brilliant metallic reddish-bronze and copper with bright yellow edgings to wings and tail; long central tail feathers; belly brownish-black. Non-breeding ♂ has most of the metallic body plumage replaced by dull black. ♀ olive above, yellowish below, also with yellow edges to wing and tail feathers. Immature like ♀ but underparts darker. Yellow-edged wings and tail distinguish species in all plumages.

Voice. A variety of liquid, clear 'tweep' and 'tsssp' calls and a warbling song.

Distribution and Habitat. Local resident highlands over 5,000ft, 1,530m, Mt Elgon, Uganda and the highlands of Kenya and northern Tanzania. Inhabits moorland, mountain bush and edges of forest: much attracted by stands of the bushy orange-flowered Leonotis. ♂♂ have a curious slow, zigzag display flight among bushes, when yellow wings and tail are very conspicuous.

PURPLE-BREASTED SUNBIRD
Nectarinia purpureiventris   **Plate 35**

Identification. ♂ 9–10in, 23–25½cm; tail 5½–7in, 14–17cm; ♀ 5in, 13cm. ♂ a long-tailed sunbird of rainbow hues, often called the Rainbow Sunbird. Crown and throat velvety metallic violet, hind neck metallic greenish-blue to violet-pink and golden-bronze on mantle; lower throat bronze-green to deep purplish-violet on rest of underparts. Non-breeding ♂ has body plumage dull greenish-grey but retains metallic wing-coverts and rump feathers and long tail streamers. ♀ olive-green with grey head, paler on throat and rest of underparts; central tail feathers extend 1½cm beyond rest.
Voice. A relatively weak but typical sunbird 'tsssp;' ♂ has a soft but rapid warbling song.
Distribution and Habitat. In East Africa known only from forests on the Ruwenzori range and the Impenetrable-Kayonza forests, south-western Kigezi, Uganda. This is a forest tree-tops sunbird which, unlike other species, only rarely descends to feed at flowers near the ground. It favours the globular red flowers of a tree, *Symphonia gabonensis*: these flowers from the ground look like red berries, nearly an inch across, growing along the branches. The Regal and Blue-headed Sunbirds also feed at these blossoms. Seen in silhouette the long tail and relative small body and bill are distinctive.

RED-CHESTED SUNBIRD   *Nectarinia erythrocerca*   **Plate 34**

Identification. ♂ 5½–6in, 14–15cm; tail 2½in, 6½cm; ♀ 4½in, 11½cm. ♂ a metallic bluish-green sunbird with a deep red chest band and a black belly; central tail feathers elongated about ¾in, 2cm beyond rest; no pectoral tufts. ♀ darkish olive-brown above; no pale eye-stripe; below dull yellowish-white with dark mottling on neck and chest.
Voice. A sharp sunbird-type 'tsssp' or 'tink, tink.'
Distribution and Habitat. Locally common western Kenya, Uganda, the southern Sudan, and north-western Tanzania. This is a common sunbird in Uganda, most frequent in the vicinity of water. Often occurs in gardens and parks where attracted by flowers.

BEAUTIFUL SUNBIRD   *Nectarinia pulchella*   **Plate 35**

Identification. ♂ 6in, 15cm; ♀ 4½in, 11½cm. ♂ a small long-tailed sunbird, shining metallic green with a scarlet breast-patch bordered on each side by yellow. Belly entirely black in race found east of the Rift Valley, metallic green in race west of Rift Valley, except near Kisumu, Kenya, where black-bellied birds are found. ♂ in non-breeding plumage drab grey, whitish below with retained metallic wing-coverts, rump and tail. ♀ ashy-grey with whitish eye-stripe; below yellowish-white with trace of streaking on breast. Immature like ♀ but throat blackish.

Voice. A sharp clear 'tsp' and a soft warbling song.

Distribution and Habitat. Local resident with restricted migratory movements from the Sudan, Ethiopia and Somalia southwards through Uganda and Kenya to southern Tanzania, but not in coastal districts. Inhabits bush country, savannah and open woodlands and stands of acacias. Especially attracted to flowering acacias and aloes.

Allied Species. The Smaller Black-bellied Sunbird *(N. nectarinioides)*, ♂ 4½in, 11½cm; ♀ 3½in, 9cm; is the smallest of the long-tailed sunbirds; central tail feathers extend 1½–2cm beyond rest. Plumage metallic green with a bright red breast-band, sometimes with a trace of yellow at edges, and a black belly. The ♀ is olive-grey with indistinct dusky-olive streaking on throat, chest and flanks. The Black-bellied race of Beautiful Sunbird is larger and has a yellow patch on each side of the red breast-band. It is a local and uncommon resident in eastern districts of Kenya and north-eastern Tanzania. Most frequent along the Tana River in Kenya. Inhabits arid bush country and most in evidence in acacias bordering rivers or dry river beds, where it feeds at the orange and yellow flowers of Loranthus parasitic on the acacias.

GREY-HEADED SUNBIRD *Anthreptes axillaris* Plate 34

Identification. 4–4½in, 10–11½cm. Sexes similar. A bright green warbler-like sunbird with a pale grey head; small white eye-ring; bill only slightly decurved; eyes orange-red, bill horn-coloured; orange-red pectoral tufts in the ♂, absent in ♀.

Voice. A high-pitched 'peeet,' but usually silent.

Distribution and Habitat. A forest tree-top species found locally in Uganda, most frequent in western districts. Feeds on spiders, insects and insect larvae captured among foliage in manner of a warbler, seldom visiting flowers.

PLAIN-BACKED SUNBIRD *Anthreptes reichenowi* Plate 36

Identification. 4in, 10cm. ♂ non-metallic green, paler and yellower on belly, with a metallic dark blue forehead and throat and lemon-yellow pectoral tufts. The ♀ lacks the dark blue forehead and throat patches and has no pectoral tufts.

Voice. A double 'peet, peet' and a soft warbling song.

Distribution and Habitat. A rare sunbird found locally in coastal forests of Kenya and Tanzania. Occurs both in undergrowth and in the treetops. Most frequent in the Sokoke Forest, Kenya.

AMANI SUNBIRD   *Anthreptes pallidigaster*   Plate 36

Identification. 3in, 8cm. A tiny, rather thickset sunbird with a relatively short tail. ♂ upperparts and throat metallic dark bottle-green with violet patch in centre of throat; breast and abdomen white; red pectoral tufts. ♀ grey above with slight metallic wash, below greyish-white, tinged yellow in centre of belly; no pectoral tufts.
Voice. Very weak 'tssss' calls and a soft warbling song of short duration.
Distribution and Habitat. A very uncommon and local sunbird known from the Sokoke-Arabuku forests on the Kenya coast and the forests of the eastern Usambara Mountains, north-eastern Tanzania. A bird of the treetops, warbler-like in its feeding habits.

ANCHIETA'S SUNBIRD   *Anthreptes anchietae*   Plate 36

Identification. 4in, 10cm. Sexes similar. Upperparts dark sooty-brown, forehead, throat and chest metallic dark blue; centre of breast and belly scarlet, bordered on each side by yellow; abdomen pale grey, under tail-coverts red.
Voice. A plaintive single note 'tee' or 'teee,' often repeated; also a weak warbling song.
Distribution and Habitat. Local and uncommon in south-western and southern Tanzania, Malawi and Zambia. Occurs in Brachystegia woodlands. Sometimes associates with mixed bird parties; warbler-like in feeding habits, less attracted to flowering trees than many sunbirds.

GREY-CHINNED SUNBIRD   *Anthreptes tephrolaema*   Plate 36

Identification. 3½in, 9cm. A thickset stumpy sunbird with a rather short tail. ♂ upperparts metallic golden-green; rump and upper tail coverts non-metallic olive-green; wings and tail dark olive-brown; below, chin grey, throat and chest metallic green with a narrow dull orange band across chest; remainder underparts olive-grey, paler on belly; pectoral tufts yellow. ♀ uniform olive-green, paler below; no pectoral tufts. This sunbird is placed as a race of the Gambian *A. rectirostris* by some but it is unlikely that the two are conspecific.
Voice. A weak, zosterops-like 'zeet, zeet,' frequently repeated.
Distribution and Habitat. A forest tree-top sunbird found locally in the southern Sudan, Uganda and western Kenya. Often associates with Apalis warblers, tits and other tree-top species. Visits fruiting fig trees and other fruiting trees and feeds to some extent on fruit.

BANDED GREEN SUNBIRD   *Anthreptes rubritorques*   **Plate 36**

Identification. 3½in, 9cm. Similar to the Grey-chinned Sunbird but differs in having the chin and throat grey with a narrow scarlet band across chest; greyish olive on breast and flanks, yellowish-white in centre of belly; pectoral tufts chrome yellow. ♀ lightly metallic green above, dull yellowish-olive below.

Voice. Weak 'teeep, teeep' calls and a brief warbling song.

Distribution and Habitat. A rare sunbird with a very restricted distribution in the forests of the eastern Usambara Mts and the Nguru Mts, north-eastern Tanzania. Inhabits forest tree-tops; sometimes visits flowering Erythrina trees at edge of forest.

KENYA VIOLET-BACKED SUNBIRD
Anthreptes orientalis   **Plate 36**

Identification. 4½in, 11½cm. ♂ metallic violet-blue above and on tail and chin; wings grey; underparts white with yellow pectoral tufts; some metallic green feathers on wing shoulders and rump. The ♀ grey above with white streak above eye; tail violet black; wings grey, underparts white; no pectoral tufts. The Violet-backed Sunbird is larger and greyish below in the ♂, yellowish on belly in ♀.

Voice. A high-pitched but not very loud chirping call and a sharper 'teep;' a soft warbling song.

Distribution and Habitat. Locally common resident southern Sudan, north-eastern Uganda, northern and eastern Kenya and north-eastern and central districts of Tanzania. Inhabits arid and semi-dry bush country; especially attracted to flowering acacia trees and bushes and parasitic Loranthus.

Allied Species. The Violet-backed Sunbird *(A. longuemarei)*, 5in, 13cm, is larger and greyish below in the ♂, yellow on breast and abdomen in ♀. It is a West African species which occurs eastwards to Uganda, western Kenya, western Tanzania, Malawi, Zambia and Rhodesia. Found in savannah woodland and bush country. The Uluguru Violet-backed Sunbird *(A. neglectus)*, 5in, 13cm, is dusky brownish-grey below; blackish non-metallic collar on hindneck. Unlike the other two species the ♀ resembles the ♂ in plumage but lacks the metallic violet chin; grey below, bright yellow on abdomen. This is a forest sunbird with a very restricted distribution, recorded from the Tana River and Taita Hills in Kenya and the forests on the eastern Usambara Mts, Nguru and Uluguru Mountains in north-eastern Tanzania. A forest sunbird which keeps largely to the tree-tops.

COLLARED SUNBIRD *Anthreptes collaris* **Plate 36**

Identification. 3½in, 9cm. A tiny thickset sunbird with a short tail. ♂ metallic yellowish-green above and on throat; a narrow violet band across chest; rest of underparts yellow, slightly greenish on flanks; pectoral tufts yellow. ♀ and immature are also metallic green on upperparts but not on the throat; throat and chest olive-yellow, breast and abdomen bright yellow; no pectoral tufts. The ♂ Variable Sunbird resembles this species but has the plumage metallic blue-green and has an extensive violet chest patch.
Voice. A weak 'tsssp' frequently uttered and a soft warbling song.
Distribution and Habitat. Widely distributed and locally common in East and Central Africa. Inhabits forests, woodland, scrub, bush country and in coastal districts common in coastal scrub and also mangrove swamps; often visits gardens.

PYGMY LONG-TAILED SUNBIRD *Anthreptes platura* **Plate 36**

Identification. ♂ 6½–7in, 16–18cm; tail 3½–4in, 9–10cm; ♀ 3in, 8cm. ♂ a metallic golden-green sunbird with a bright yellow breast and abdomen and very long spatulate-tipped central tail feathers; bill very short for a sunbird. ♀ pale grey above, pale yellow below; tail feathers not elongated. ♂ in non-breeding dress moults long tail feathers and body plumage and resembles ♀ except for metallic wing coverts.
Voice. A warbler-like 'teep, teep;' song a soft warbling trill.
Distribution and Habitat. Local, but not uncommon in some areas. Found in northern Uganda and in north-western Kenya where it appears to be a visitor in the breeding season, arriving in August and departing north in February. It also occurs in the Sudan, Ethiopia and Somalia. Inhabits arid thorn-bush and acacia woodland, especially along dry river beds where it is attracted to flowering acacias and fruiting Salvadora bushes.

WHITE-EYES: Zosteropidae

A group of small green or yellowish-green warbler-like birds with conspicuous white rings around their eyes. Gregarious, in flocks even during the nesting season. Often associated with mixed bird parties. The classification of these birds is still unsatisfactory; different populations vary greatly and the status of some races and species is uncertain.

YELLOW WHITE-EYE *Zosterops senegalensis* **Plate 37**

Identification. 4in, 10cm. The bird in East Africa known previously as the Green White-eye is now lumped with *Z. senegalensis*. Plumage variable, powdery yellowish-green to green above, below bright yellow to greenish-yellow; best recognised by its narrow white eye-ring.

Voice. Various peeping flock calls; song a series of soft warbling notes.

Distribution and Habitat. Local resident and partial migrant over much of East and Central Africa. Inhabits a variety of habitats from open thornbush country, acacia and savannah woodland tò Brachystegia woodland, cultivation, forests and gardens.

KIKUYU WHITE-EYE *Zosterops kikuyuensis* Plate 37

Identification. 4½in, 11½cm. Upperparts bright green with a broad yellow forehead; white eye-ring large and conspicuous; below, yellow on throat and centre of breast, merging to yellowish green on flanks. Immature duller and darker. Yellow White-eye smaller with narrow white eye-ring and very yellow below. Gregarious.

Voice. High pitched piping flock calls; song a soft clear warble.

Distribution and Habitat. A local resident highland areas of southern half of Kenya to highlands of northern Tanzania – Mt Hanang, Ngorongoro, Longido, Oldeani and Ufiome. In Kenya very common in forests of Aberdare Mts and Mt Kenya, and in forest around Nairobi. Inhabits highland forests, bamboos and gardens.

BROAD-RINGED WHITE-EYE *Zosterops eurycricotus* Plate 37

Identification. 4½in, 11½cm. A deep green white-eye with a very large and conspicuous white eye-ring; below olive-yellow, yellower on throat and abdomen. The Kikuyu White-eye differs in having a broad yellow forehead and being yellower below.

Voice. High pitched plaintive 'tsssp, tsssp' and a brief warbling song.

Distribution and Habitat. Mountain forest in northern Tanzania, including Mt Meru and Kilimanjaro.

Allied Species. The Taita White-eye *(Z. silvanus)*, 4½in, 11½cm, is another species with a very large white eye-ring but has the breast, abdomen and flanks grey. It occurs in forests on the Taita Hills, south-eastern Kenya. The Pale White-eye *(Z. pallidus)* has a small white eye-ring and a pale grey belly, often yellowish in centre. It occurs in the forests of Mt Kulal, northern Kenya, and on the Pare Mts, north-eastern Tanzania.

BUNTINGS: Emberizidae

Mainly ground-feeding, finch-like birds found singly, in pairs or in small parties. Distinguished from finches by bill structure, the cutting edge of the upper mandible being Sinuate (wavy-edged).

GOLDEN-BREASTED BUNTING   *Emberiza flaviventris*   **Plate 37**

Identification. 6in, 15cm. Best recognised by rufous back, white-tipped wing-coverts and golden-rufous breast; crown and sides of face black with a white stripe down centre of crown and a white band on each side of the face; white tips to two outer pairs of tail feathers conspicuous when bird flies. Immature duller with buff streak on crown.

Voice. A trilling 'zizi, zizi' and a bubbling song 'tee, wee-cheee-te-tweee' repeated over and over again.

Distribution and Habitat. Resident, widespread and locally common in East and Central Africa. Inhabits dry forest and woodlands, scrub and acacia country. Usually seen singly or in pairs.

Allied Species. The Somali Golden-breasted Bunting *(E. poliopleura)*, 5½in, 14cm, differs in having the feathers of the upperparts margined white and with more white on the underparts, giving the bird a generally brighter appearance. Occurs in dry acacia scrub in south-eastern Sudan, north-eastern Uganda, Ethiopia, Somalia and Kenya to northern Tanzania. Cabanis's Yellow Bunting *(E. cabanisi)*, 6½in, 16½cm, has upperparts grey and brown with distinct black streaks; crown black with or without a white stripe down centre; white stripe over each ear; sides of face black; double white wing-bar; underparts mainly yellow. The similar Golden-breasted Bunting has a rufous back. Occurs in wooded and bush country in western Uganda and in Tanzania south to Central Africa. The Brown-rumped Bunting *(E. forbesi)*, 6in, 15cm, has a black crown with three white streaks and a chestnut-brown back and rump. Occurs in dry bush country in northern Uganda and the Sudan. The European Ortolan Bunting *(E. hortulana)*, 5in, 13cm, is an uncommon winter visitor to East Africa, south to northern Kenya.

CINNAMON-BREASTED ROCK BUNTING
Emberiza tahapisi   **Plate 37**

Identification. 5½in, 14cm. A slim, reddish-brown bunting with crown, sides of face, throat and chest black; white streak down centre of crown and white streaks above and below eye. ♀ has crown dark tawny, streaked black and is greyish on throat and chest. Immature like ♀ but duller.

Voice. A drawn-out two note call 'tee, eeee;' song a bubbling 'chi, chi – cheeee, che, che' often repeated.

Distribution and Habitat. Local but not uncommon in East and Central Africa. Inhabits rocky, stony ground and hillsides where there is scattered bush and short grass; also frequents Brachystegia and mopane woodland. Usually tame and confiding. Feeds mainly on the ground.

Allied Species. The House Bunting *(E. striolata)*, 5in, 13cm, is similar but has the throat grey, streaked with black; rufous-brown on chest and belly. Frequents arid rocky country in northern East Africa, south to north-eastern Uganda and north-western Kenya.

FINCHES: Fringillidae

The finches are thick-billed seed-eating birds which resemble weavers but have nine visible primaries only, not ten. Nests open and cup-shaped, unlike those of weavers.

YELLOW-FRONTED CANARY   *Serinus mozambicus*   **Plate 37**

Identification. 4½in, 11½cm. Upperparts olive-green with dusky streaks; forehead and streak above eye bright yellow; rump bright yellow, contrasting with rest of upperparts; below yellow with a dark moustache stripe separating yellow cheeks from yellow chin.

Voice. Single or double 'tsssp' calls; song of the usual canary type.

Distribution and Habitat. Occurs locally through East and Central Africa. Inhabits woodlands and scrub and is often associated with baobab trees in East African coastal districts.

Allied Species. The White-bellied Canary *(S. dorsostriatus)*, 5in, 13cm, is a greenish-yellow canary with dark streaks on the upperparts; relatively long forked tail; yellow throat and chest, white belly. Bill relatively small; ♀ duller. Locally common in bush country in Uganda, Kenya and northern Tanzania. Small bill and white belly conspicuous in field. The Grosbeak Canary *(S. donaldsoni)*, 5½in, 14cm, is a heavy billed canary, green with dark streaks and a very bright chrome-yellow rump; yellow eye-stripe; bright yellow underparts. ♀ ash-brown with dark streaks and bright yellow rump; below yellowish-white with dark streaks on chest and flanks. Inhabits semi-desert country of Somalia and eastern Kenya as far south as Voi. The Kenya Grosbeak Canary *(S. buchanani)*, 6in, 15cm, has a very heavy pinkish bill; above green with dark streaking, below greenish-yellow, not bright yellow; ♀ similar but streaked on chest. Occurs in arid bush country in southern Kenya south to central Tanzania. The Yellow-crowned Canary *(S. flavivertex)*, 5in, 13cm, is a high altitude species usually found in localities over 6,500ft, 1,980m. ♂ crown golden-yellow; back green streaked with black; rump yellowish-green; wings dusky with two conspicuous yellow bars; tail strongly forked, black edged with yellow; below greenish-yellow to white in centre of belly. ♀ duller and more heavily streaked below. Occurs in highlands of East and Central Africa.

YELLOW-RUMPED SEED-EATER   *Serinus atrogularis*   Plate 37

Identification. 4in, 10cm. A tawny-grey seed-eater with whitish underparts and a bright lemon-yellow rump which contrasts strongly with remainder upperparts when bird is in flight. Occurs in pairs or in small flocks.
Voice. Usual canary-type song and double 'tsssp' calls.
Distribution and Habitat. Local resident, often common, in East and Central Africa. Inhabits most types of woodlands, cultivation, open bush, grasslands and park-like country.
Allied Species. The White-rumped Seed-eater *(S. leucopygius)*, 4in, 10cm, differs in having a white rump. It occurs in the Sudan, Ethiopia, south to northern Uganda, in grasslands and savannah woodlands.

BRIMSTONE CANARY   *Serinus sulphuratus*   Plate 37

Identification. 6in, 15cm. A thickset greenish-yellow canary with a stout horn-grey bill and bright yellow underparts; greenish-yellow rump; sexes similar. Immature duller.
Voice. Rather harsh chirping calls and a varied but typical canary song.
Distribution and Habitat. Local resident Uganda and Kenya southwards to Central Africa. Inhabits scattered bush in open country, mountain moorland, riverine thickets and vegetation near water, cultivation and gardens. Less gregarious than most canaries, usually in pairs or small parties.
Allied Species. The Black-faced Canary *(S. capistratus)*, 5in, 13cm, resembles a small Brimstone Canary but with a black forehead band and dark grey face and chin. Occurs in Zambia and western Uganda. The Papyrus Canary *(S. koliensis)*, 4½in, 11½cm, is similar but with a very small bill. It is known from western Kenya and central and southern Uganda. Usually associated with papyrus swamps.

AFRICAN CITRIL   *Serinus citrinelloides*   Plate 37

Identification. 4½in, 11½cm. ♂ with or without a narrow black frontal band; yellow stripe over eye; upperparts yellowish-green narrowly streaked black;

face and throat black; below yellow with a little light streaking on chest and flanks. The ♀ lacks the black face.

Voice. Soft cheeping calls and a sustained whistling song.

Distribution and Habitat. Widespread but local in East and Central Africa. Inhabits woodlands, forest margins, savannah woodlands, cultivation and gardens.

Allied Species. The Black-headed Siskin *(S. nigriceps)*, 4½in, 11½cm, is olive green with a dull black head and neck; ♀ has head olive-green washed black on crown and throat. A high altitude species confined to northern and central Ethiopia. The Warsanglia Linnet *(Warsanglia johannis)*, 5in, 13cm, is a dusky grey linnet-like bird with a white forehead and stripe over eye; rump and flanks chestnut; rest of underparts greyish-white. Known only from the Eregavo area of northern Somalia.

STREAKY SEED-EATER *Serinus striolatus* **Plate 37**

Identification. 6in, 15cm. Tawny-brown with dark streaked upperparts and crown; whitish eye stripe; below tawny white or buff, streaked dark brown on throat, breast and flanks; immature duller. A common species best recognised by streaky plumage, the rump being the same colour as rest of upperparts and the conspicuous white eye stripe.

Voice. A high-pitched three-note call and a bubbling canary type song.

Distribution and Habitat. Common resident highlands Ethiopia, Kenya, Uganda, northern Tanzania and the highlands of Malawi and Zambia. Inhabits moorland bush, forest margins, grass and scrub, cultivation and gardens. A very common bird in the highlands of Kenya.

Allied Species. The Streaky-headed Seed-eater *(S. gularis)*, 5½in, 14cm, is a grey seed-eater with crown streaked black, ash-brown and white; white stripe over eye; below white, streaked on chest and flanks. A common bird in Brachystegia woodland in Tanzania and Central Africa, also in open woodland in Ethiopia, the southern Sudan, Uganda and western Kenya. The Black-eared Seed-eater *(S. mennelli)*, 5½in, 14cm, is similar but with sides of face black. A local species found in Brachystegia woodland in Malawi, Zambia and Rhodesia. Reichard's Seed-eater *(S. reichardi)* is similar to the Streaky-headed Seed-eater but has heavier streaking on underparts. Occurs in Brachystegia woodland in Zambia. The Brown-rumped Seed-eater *(S. tristriatus)*, 5in, 13cm, is ashy-brown, lightly streaked black on head; below whitish. Found in the highlands of Ethiopia and northern Somalia; inhabits scrub and forest margins.

THICK-BILLED SEED-EATER *Serinus burtoni* **Plate 37**

Identification. 7in, 18cm. A large, heavily-built seedeater with a thick bill; upperparts dark brown with indistinct blackish streaking; small white patch on forehead; wings and tail edged green; below brownish-grey, mottled on chest, paler on belly.
Voice. Silent, unobtusive birds; sometimes utter a soft 'pleet;' song a brief soft warble.
Distribution and Habitat. A bird of highland forest and bush in the vicinity of forest. Occurs in the highlands of Kenya, Uganda and Tanzania; shy and elusive and often overlooked.

ORIOLE FINCH *Linurgus olivaceus* **Plate 37**

Identification. 5in, 13cm. ♂ golden yellow or greenish-yellow with an orange bill and a black head and throat. ♀ greenish-yellow and lacks the black on head and throat. The orange bill is conspicuous in the field.
Voice. Silent birds, sometimes utter a soft 'tsssp' call.
Distribution and Habitat. Highland forests in Kenya, eastern and western Uganda, and from north-eastern to south-western Tanzania. Much attracted to stinging nettles when these plants are seeding.
Allied Species. The Golden-winged Grosbeak (*Rhynchostruthus socotranus*), 6in, 15cm, is a heavy greenfinch-like bird, brown with a black head, throat and chest; edges of secondaries and tail feathers with broad yellow edging; below pale grey, whitish on belly; bill large and heavy. Known only from the juniper forests of northern Somalia and Socotra Island. Feeds amongst the foliage of juniper branches; very uncommon and elusive.

WAXBILLS: Estrildidae

A large family of small, ground-feeding seed-eating birds. Nest structure distinctive, not woven but a domed structure of grass stems and tops. The newly hatched young have patterns of dark spots on the palate and tongue.

PETERS' TWINSPOT *Hypargos niveoguttatus* **Plate 38**

Identification. 5in, 13cm. A handsome black, crimson, brown and grey waxbill with round white spots on the belly. ♂ crown greyish-brown, mantle, wings and wing-coverts russet-brown; hindneck, rump, face, throat and chest crimson; tail black with crimson wash; breast and belly black with round white spots. ♀ paler and has chin to chest deep buff with crimson wash; breast and belly grey, spotted with white.

Voice. A weak rather squeaky tril, but birds usually silent.

Distribution and Habitat. Widespread and sometimes common eastern Kenya and Tanzania, but skulking in habits and not often seen. Most frequent in coastal areas. Inhabits dense scrub, bush, coastal thickets and heavy undergrowth bordering streams.

Allied Species. The Brown Twinspot *(Clytospiza monteiri)*, 5in, 13cm, has the head grey, back and wings brown, rump crimson, tail blackish; below crimson streak down centre of throat in ♂, white streak in ♀; breast and abdomen pale chestnut with round white spots. Found in forest undergrowth, dense scrub and elephant grass near forest. An uncommon and local bird found in Uganda and the southern Sudan. The Dusky Firefinch *(Lagonosticta cinerovinacea)*, 4½in, 11½cm, is brownish-grey above and on chest; rump deep maroon-red; tail black; breast and abdomen black with maroon red flanks speckled with white. A rare bird of highland forest undergrowth, known from south-western Uganda.

GREEN-BACKED TWINSPOT   *Mandingoa nitidula*   Plate 38

Identification. 3½in, 9cm. A bright green waxbill with a blackish breast and belly heavily marked with round white spots. ♂ has the face and chin tomato-red. ♀ with face green or with at most a wash of red.

Voice. Usually silent; a squeaky two note call.

Distribution and Habitat. Very local and inconspicuous little bird found in Ethiopia and Sudan southwards through Uganda and Kenya to Central Africa. Inhabits dense undergrowth of forests, thickets and heavy vegetation along streams.

ABYSSINIAN CRIMSONWING   *Cryptospiza salvadorii*   Plate 38

Identification. 4½in, 11½cm. Sexes alike. Head, nape, upper back and underparts greyish-olive; back, rump, flanks and wing-coverts crimson-red; bill leaden grey. Best distinguished from Red-faced Crimsonwing by lack of eye patch.

Voice. A soft 'teeeep.'

Distribution and Habitat. Locally common in highland forest and bamboo zone in Ethiopia, Kenya, Uganda and north-eastern Tanzania. Inhabits undergrowth of forest and bamboo; often seen on forest tracks feeding on small seeds or picking up grit. Common on Mt Kenya and Aberdare Mountains, Kenya.

RED-FACED CRIMSONWING *Crytospiza reichenovii* Plate 38

Identification. 4½in, 11½cm. Plumage olive with crimson-red on the back, rump, wing-coverts and flanks; ♂ with a crimson-red patch round eye; bill leaden grey. ♀ similar to ♂ but has pale olive eye patch.

Voice. A high pitched 'tzeeet.'

Distribution and Habitat. Locally common in highland forest and bamboo in Uganda and Tanzania. Inhabits dense undergrowth, usually in pairs or family groups; sometimes seen on forest paths in early morning or late evening. Red eye patch of ♂ conspicuous in field.

DUSKY CRIMSONWING *Cryptospiza jacksoni* Plate 38

Identification. 4½in, 11½cm. Sexes alike. Dark grey with crown, face, mantle, rump, flanks and wing coverts crimson; bill leaden grey. Easily distinguished from other species by dark grey and crimson plumage.

Voice. Usually silent; call note a soft 'tzeek.'

Distribution and Habitat. Forests of the Ruwenzori range and highland forest in Kigezi, Uganda. Inhabits dense undergrowth and bamboo, rarely apparent but sometimes seen on road margins through forest. Most frequent in the Impenetrable Forest, south-western Uganda.

SHELLEY'S CRIMSONWING *Cryptospiza shelleyi* Plate 38

Identification. 5in, 13cm. ♂ differs from other crimsonwings in having a red bill. Crown, cheeks, mantle and rump bright maroon-crimson; below, throat and breast pale olive, belly deep pinkish-olive. ♀ differs in having pale olive head and a black and red bill.

Voice. A series of rapid twittering notes, not unlike the call of some small sunbird.

Distribution and Habitat. A rare and seldom seen species found in the mountain forests of western and south-western Uganda. Inhabits dense forest undergrowth; less frequently seen along road margins than related species.

BLACK-BELLIED SEED-CRACKER *Pirenestes ostrinus* Plate 38

Identification. 6in, 15cm. ♂ head, chest, flanks, rump and central tail feathers crimson-red; rest of plumage black; bill blue-grey; legs yellowish. ♀ resembles ♂ but black plumage replaced by brown. ♂ distinguished from Red-headed Bluebill by its all grey bill, yellowish legs and crimson-washed tail; ♀ lacks white spots on underparts and is brown not dark grey.

Voice. A soft tinkling call note, but birds usually silent.

Distribution and Habitat. Found locally, but everywhere uncommon, in Uganda and in the Kakamega Forest, western Kenya. Inhabits dense forest undergrowth, especially the margins of forests and in glades; also in dense scrub and secondary growth near water.

Allied Species. Rothschild's Seed-cracker *(P. rothschildi)*, $5\frac{1}{2}$in, 14cm, differs only in smaller size and smaller bill (width of lower mandible at base $\frac{7}{16}$–$\frac{1}{2}$in, 12–13mm, against $\frac{9}{16}$–$\frac{11}{16}$in, 14–17mm). A rare bird known from western Uganda in forest undergrowth. The Large-billed Seed-cracker *(P. maximus)*, $6\frac{1}{2}$in, $16\frac{1}{2}$cm differs in having a larger and heavier bill, $\frac{11}{16}$–$\frac{3}{4}$in, 18–19mm, wide at base of lower mandible. Recorded from western and north-western Uganda; frequents dense thickets in savannah woodland and edges of forest. The Lesser Seed-cracker *(P. minor)*, 5in, 13cm, is an earth-brown species with the front half of crown, face, throat, chest, rump and central tail feathers crimson. ♀ has less red on the head and underparts. Found in Malawi, eastern and southern Tanzania. Inhabits dense scrub along wooded streams. The closely related Urungu Seed-cracker *(P. frommi)*, 5in, 13cm, has a larger and heavier bill ($\frac{17}{32}$–$\frac{5}{8}$in, $13\frac{1}{2}$–16mm, width at base of lower mandible, against $\frac{3}{8}$–$\frac{15}{32}$in, 9–12mm, in Lesser Seed-cracker). Found in the Uluguru Mts and south-western Tanzania and in Zambia; inhabits rank undergrowth in forests.

GREY-HEADED NEGRO FINCH *Nigrita canicapilla* Plate 38

Identification. 5in, 13cm. Upperparts grey; forehead, face, wings, tail and underparts black; white spots on wing coverts. Black underparts and grey mantle best field characters.

Voice. A soft three-note whistle.

Distribution and Habitat. Local and usually uncommon in Uganda, western, central and southern Kenya and northern Tanzania. Inhabits forest and woodlands, usually seen along margins or in forest glades; frequents both the foliage of trees and the undergrowth.

Allied Species. The Pale-fronted Negro Finch *(N. luteifrons)*, 4in, 10cm, lacks the white spots on the wings and has a buffy-grey not black forehead; ♀ grey, not black, on underparts. Known from the Bwamba Forest, western Uganda; frequents tree foliage. The Chestnut Negro Finch *(N. bicolor)*, 4in, 10cm, has the forehead and underparts deep maroon-chestnut; mantle sooty-brown. Occurs in forests in Uganda and western Kenya. The White-breasted Negro Finch *(N. fusconota)*, 4in, 10cm, has white underparts, a pale brown back and a black head, rump and tail. It is found in the Kakamega Forest, western Kenya and in Uganda. May be observed in either the foliage of tall forest trees or in the undergrowth.

JAMESON'S HYLIA-FINCH   *Parmoptila rubrifrons*   Plate 39

Identification. 3½in, 9cm. A small, rather tit-like little bird with a slender bill for a waxbill. Inhabits tree foliage. Upperparts olive-brown; forehead red; face and underparts chestnut; ♀ paler, buffy-white below mottled darker.
Voice. A weak 'zee' call note.
Distribution and Habitat. In East Africa recorded in forests of western and south-western Uganda. Inhabits foliage, mainly in trees. Several birds often perch alongside one another in the manner of waxbills.

RED-HEADED BLUEBILL   *Spermophaga ruficapilla*   Plate 38

Identification. 6in, 15cm. A large black and red waxbill inhabiting forest undergrowth. ♂ head, chest, flanks and upper tail coverts bright crimson-red; rest of plumage black; bill heavy, metallic blue to pink along cutting edges; feet dark horn. ♀ black replaced by dark grey and with round white spots on the breast and belly. In the Usambara Mts, N.E. Tanzania race the ♂ is grey not black. The Black-bellied Seedcracker has a differently shaped blue-grey bill and yellowish legs; the ♀ is brown and red and has no white spots on underparts.
Voice. A series of barely audible clinking notes.
Distribution and Habitat. Locally not uncommon in southern Sudan, Uganda, western Kenya and northern and western Tanzania. Inhabits dense forest undergrowth; sometimes comes to the forest edge to bask in sun, especially following heavy rain storms.
Allied Species. Grant's Bluebill *(S. poliogenys)*, 5½in, 14cm, resembles the Red-headed Bluebill but red much brighter and on crown red confined to forehead; ♀ has top and sides of head grey; chin to breast red; remainder underparts grey with round white spots. A rare and seldom seen species recorded from the Bwamba Forest, western Uganda.

WHITE-COLLARED OLIVEBACK   *Nesocharis ansorgei*   Plate 38

Identification. 4in, 10cm. A small waxbill with habits of a warbler, searching in foliage of forest trees and undergrowth for insect food. Upperparts bright golden-olive; head and throat black; collar on hind neck grey; collar between neck and chest white; breast golden-olive, belly grey. ♀ has less pronounced grey collar on hind neck.
Voice. A soft sunbird-like 'tsssp.'
Distribution and Habitat. An extremely local and uncommon bird in the forests of western Uganda. Found in pairs in foliage of trees, often along forest margins; sometimes members of mixed bird parties. The golden-olive back and white throat band are distinctive.

GREY-HEADED OLIVEBACK *Nesocharis capistrata* Plate 38

Identification. 4½in, 11½cm. Top of head and nape grey, mantle and tail olive green; cheeks white; throat and line around cheeks black; rest of underparts grey to golden-yellow on flanks. This is another waxbill with warbler-like habits, searching foliage for insect food.
Voice. Soft 'tsssp' calls but normally silent.
Distribution and Habitat. Another very uncommon species, known from north-western Uganda and southern Sudan. It frequents forest margins, savannah bush and woodland.

GREEN-WINGED PYTILIA *Pytilia melba* Plate 39

Identification. 5in, 13cm. Also known as the Melba Finch. A red-billed, green, finch-like bird with a red face, throat, rump and tail; head grey; breast golden-orange. ♀ and immature lack red on face and throat and are vermiculated grey and white below. Shy, usually in pairs or family parties. When disturbed the birds dive into the nearest thicket, leaving a fleeting impression of a green bird with a red rump and tail.
Voice. Usually silent, but sometimes utters weak chirping calls.
Distribution and Habitat. Local, sometimes common, resident through East and Central Africa. Inhabits bush country, coastal thickets, thorn scrub, neglected cultivation and rank grass and bush.
Allied Species. The Red-winged Pytilia *(P. phoenicoptera)*, 5in, 13cm, is a red-billed grey finch-like bird with the wings, tail and rump deep red; flanks vermiculated grey and white. A very uncommon species found in dense thickets in mixed grass and bush savannah in the Sudan, northern Uganda and north-western Kenya. The Orange-winged Pytilia *(P. afra)*, 5in, 13cm, is another red-billed finch-like species with forehead, face, chin, rump and tail feathers crimson-red; edges of flight feathers and wing coverts orange-red; crown and mantle olive green. Distinguished from the Green-winged Pytilia by its grey throat and orange-edged wings. Widely distributed in East Africa but everywhere uncommon. Skulking in habits, in thick bush and thickets in savannah country.

YELLOW-BELLIED WAXBILL *Estrilda melanotis* Plate 40

Identification. 3½in, 9cm. A tiny greenish waxbill with a buff belly, black tail and crimson rump; bill colour distinctive and a good field character, upper mandible black, lower mandible red; sexes alike; immature duller. Southern birds have a black face mask. Usually in small flocks in lush undergrowth.
Voice. A weak 'swee, swee.'

Distribution and Habitat. Local resident through most of East and Central Africa. Occurs in rank herbage along forest margins and streams and in grassy areas in wooded and forest country.

Allied Species. The Fawn-breasted Waxbill *(E. paludicola)*, 4½in, 11½cm, is a pale brown waxbill with a greyish head, red bill and red rump; below creamy-white with a strong pink wash on the belly. A local species found in western Kenya, Uganda, Tanzania and Central Africa; occurs in swampy grasslands and bush, woodland and forest margins. General pale appearance, pinkish belly and red bill are best field characters.

BLACK-CROWNED WAXBILL   *Estrilda nonnula*   Plate 40

Identification. 4in, 10cm. A small black-capped waxbill with vermiculated grey upperparts, red rump and flanks and whitish underparts to pale grey below tail; bill black and red. The Black-headed Waxbill has black on abdomen and under tail coverts.
Voice. Weak twittering calls.
Distribution and Habitat. Locally common in western Kenya, Uganda and north-western Tanzania. Found in flocks in neglected cultivation, open bush, forest margins and in tall grass and lush vegetation near water.

BLACK-HEADED WAXBILL   *Estrilda atricapilla*   Plate 40

Identification. 4in, 10cm. A small vermiculated greyish waxbill with a black cap and tail; red rump and flanks and black under tail coverts. Underparts, chin and breast greyish-white, merging to black on belly and under tail coverts; bill black and red. The very similar Black-crowned Waxbill is whiter on the face and underparts and pale grey on under tail coverts.
Voice. Weak 'teep' calls.
Distribution and Habitat. Locally not uncommon in the Kenya Highlands and western and southern Uganda. Inhabits forested areas, most frequent along margins of forest, in glades and along forest tracks where there is an abundance of grasses. Occurs in small flocks.

CRIMSON-RUMPED WAXBILL   *Estrilda rhodopyga*   Plate 40

Identification. 4in, 10cm. A small brown waxbill with a slaty-grey bill, a crimson streak through the eye and crimson rump; tail feathers edged crimson; underparts buffy-brown.
Voice. Weak 'tssp' calls.
Distribution and Habitat. Locally common over much of East Africa and

south to Malawi. Favours marshy areas where there is a lush growth of grasses, forest margins and open grasslands.

Allied Species. The Black-rumped Waxbill *(E. troglodytes)*, 3½in, 9cm, is easily distinguished from the Crimson-rumped and Common Waxbills by its black rump and tail. It occurs in open savannah woodland and bush in southern Sudan and north-western Uganda.

COMMON WAXBILL   *Estrilda astrild*   Plate 40

Identification. 4in, 10cm. A pale brown waxbill with a conspicuous vivid red bill and a red streak through the eye; brown, not red, on the rump and tail; red in centre of belly. Immature duller with dusky bill.

Voice. Constant weak twittering flock calls.

Distribution and Habitat. Resident, often abundant, through East and Central Africa. Occurs in flocks in lush grasslands, neglected cultivation and rank grass and bush, often near water.

BLACK-FACED WAXBILL   *Estrilda erythronotos*   Plate 40

Identification. 5in, 13cm. A small, relatively long-tailed waxbill with black face, ear-coverts and throat; general colour pale pinkish grey with blackish vermiculations; rump and tail-coverts red; below pinkish grey with indistinct barring, washed red on flanks, blackish on belly and under tail-coverts; ♀ paler below. The closely related Black-cheeked Waxbill has little or no black on the throat and under tail-coverts are pale grey, not black.

Voice. A series of soft liquid 'tssssps.'

Distribution and Habitat. Locally not uncommon in acacia woodland and arid thornbush country of Kenya, southern Uganda, northern half of Tanzania and Zambia. Frequents acacia trees and bushes, feeding on blossoms and insects attracted to the flowers. Usually in pairs or small family groups.

Allied Species. The Black-cheeked Waxbill *(E. charmosyna)*, 5in, 13cm, differs in having little or no black on the chin and throat; below pale pinkish-grey narrowly and indistinctly barred with grey. This species has often been considered as conspecific with the Black-faced Waxbill, but the two exist side by side in several localities in Kenya and northern Tanzania. The Black-cheeked Waxbill also occurs in acacia woodland and scrub and is known from Kenya and north-central Tanzania.

LAVENDER WAXBILL   *Estrilda perreini*   Plate 40

Identification. 4½in, 11½cm. A blue-grey waxbill with a red rump, a black stripe through the eye, a black chin and a black tail.

Voice. Soft 'tsssp' calls, but normally silent.
Distribution and Habitat. An uncommon and local waxbill of woodland and bush with tall grass, found in western and south-western Tanzania and in Central Africa.

PURPLE GRENADIER *Uraeginthus ianthinogaster* Plate 40

Identification. 5½in, 14cm. A rich cinnamon-rufous waxbill with red bill, a black tail and conspicuous cobalt blue on the lower back, rump, belly and face; ♀ paler with less blue in plumage.
Voice. A weak chirping note.
Distribution and Habitat. Occurs locally in dry thorn scrub and bushy areas from southern Sudan, Ethiopia and Somalia south through northern Uganda, Kenya to northern Tanzania.

RED-CHEEKED CORDON-BLEU *Uraeginthus bengalus* Plate 39

Identification. 5in, 13cm. ♂ easily recognised: a mainly azure blue waxbill with crimson cheek patches; ♀ and immature duller and lacking crimson on face. In pairs or family parties; tame and confiding.
Voice. Weak, squeaking call note and a three note song 'ts, ts, tseee' repeated over and over again.
Distribution and Habitat. Widespread in East Africa south to northern Tanzania and in Zambia. Found in thornbush and acacia country, wooded savannah, neglected cultivation, edges of forest and in gardens and around human habitations. Feeds largely on the ground.
Allied Species. The Southern Cordon-bleu *(U. angolensis)*, 5in, 13cm, differs in having no red on the cheeks which are blue. It occurs in bush country and woodland in the southern half of Tanzania and in Central Africa.

BLUE CAPPED CORDON-BLEU
Uraeginthus cyanocephalus Plate 39

Identification. 5in, 13cm. Easily distinguished from the Red-cheeked Cordon-bleu by its blue, not fawn-brown crown and lack of red cheek patches. In the ♂ the entire head is blue.
Voice. A weak squeaking call.
Distribution and Habitat. Occurs in dry bush country of southern Somalia, Kenya and Tanzania. Rather local and much less common than the Red-cheeked Cordon-bleu.

RED-BILLED FIREFINCH   *Lagonosticta senegala*   **Plate 39**

Identification. $3\frac{1}{2}$in, 9cm. A small pinkish-red waxbill with a distinct rosy-red and grey bill. ♀ and immature browner and duller. The African and Jameson's Firefinches have blue-grey bills. Feeds mainly on the ground. It is a common species well known as the 'animated plum,' a not inappropriate name.

Voice. A weak 'tweet, tweet;' does not appear to trill like the African Firefinch.

Distribution and Habitat. A common resident in suitable localities throughout East and Central Africa. Usually seen feeding on the ground near human dwellings; also in scrub, thickets and riverine undergrowth.

Allied Species. The Black-faced Firefinch *(L. larvata)*, $4\frac{1}{2}$in, $11\frac{1}{2}$cm, is brownish-grey with the crown, rump, tail and chest maroon red; sides of face, chin and throat black; the ♀ is paler and lacks the black face. Occurs in tall grass savannah in northern Uganda and the southern Sudan. The Bar-breasted Firefinch *(L. rufopicta)*, 4in, 10cm, is a small reddish waxbill with a red bill, dark brown back and crimson upper tail coverts; chin to breast vinous-crimson with broken white bars across the chest. Found in open savannah bush and around human habitations in north-western Uganda and southern Sudan.

AFRICAN FIREFINCH   *Lagonosticta rubricata*   **Plate 39**

Identification. $4\frac{1}{2}$in, $11\frac{1}{2}$cm. Small, deep red and brown finch-like birds, the ♀ and immature paler and greyer. Best distinguished from Red-billed Firefinch by blue-grey bill and blackish under tail-coverts. Occurs in pairs and feeds largely on the ground. Much less common in gardens than the Red-billed Firefinch.

Voice. A bell-like trill, followed by several chirping notes.

Distribution and Habitat. Widely distributed but local in East and Central Africa. Inhabits thick lush bush and rank grass, forest margins, thick bush along streams and overgrown cultivation.

Allied Species. The very closely related Jameson's Firefinch *(L. jamesoni)*, $4\frac{1}{2}$in, $11\frac{1}{2}$cm, also has a blue-grey bill but is paler above, washed with rose-pink. It inhabits more arid areas than the African Firefinch, favouring thickets in dry thornbush country. The Black-bellied Firefinch *(L. rara)*, 5in, 13cm, has the head, upperparts, chest and flanks vinous-red; breast and abdomen black; bill black, lower mandible pink. ♀ has vinous-buff underparts. Similar to a large African Firefinch but has black extending on to breast. Occurs locally in Uganda and western Kenya, inhabiting mixed grass and bush country and thick vegetation along streams.

ZEBRA WAXBILL *Amandava subflava* **Plate 40**

Identification. 3½in, 9cm. May be recognised by its yellow or orange-yellow underparts with olive barred flanks; above, brown with a red stripe above eye and red under tail-coverts. Occurs in flocks.

Voice. Chirping 'zeeet' calls.

Distribution and Habitat. Occurs locally in open grasslands, often in marshy places, from Uganda and Kenya south to Central Africa.

QUAILFINCH *Ortygospiza atricollis* **Plate 39**

Identification. 3in, 8cm. Tiny short-tailed waxbills found in swampy depressions in open plains country. ♂ forehead, face and chin black; rest upperparts greyish-brown; chest, breast and flanks barred brown and white; centre of lower breast orange-brown; belly white; tail very short, outer feathers white-tipped; bill bright red and black. ♀ duller, has chin white and black on head replaced by grey.

Voice. Metallic chirping calls made on the wing.

Distribution and Habitat. Widespread but local in East and Central Africa. Inhabits open plains country especially in the vicinity of swamps and marshes and the margins of pools. Birds perch always on the ground, flushing from underfoot; usually in pairs or small groups. Metallic call notes in flight draw attention.

Allied Species. The Locust Finch *(O. locustella)*, 3in, 8cm, has the same habits and habitat preferences as the Quailfinch. General plumage blackish with white dots; face, throat and breast red; ♀ whitish below. A very uncommon and local species found in southern Tanzania and Zambia.

CUT-THROAT *Amadina fasciata* **Plate 39**

Identification. 4½in, 11½cm. A small finch-like bird of speckled brown appearance, paler below with a rufous belly; ♂ with very conspicuous red band on throat. Immature resembles ♀. Gregarious in small flocks and often associated with cordon-bleus and other waxbills.

Voice. Sparrow-like chirping calls.

Distribution and Habitat. Local resident and partial migrant through East and Central Africa. Inhabits dry thornbush and acacia country; often noticed around waterholes and dams. Common in the arid northern districts of Kenya.

SILVERBILL *Euodice malabarica* **Plate 39**

Identification. 4in, 10cm. A pale ashy-brown seed-eater with flight feathers, rump and tail black; throat and chest ashy-buff, breast and abdomen white; bill pale blue-grey. Gregarious, in small flocks.
Voice. Soft double notes and a longer weak trill.
Distribution and Habitat. Locally common in arid bush country in East Africa south to northern Tanzania.

GREY-HEADED SILVERBILL *Odontospiza caniceps* **Plate 39**

Identification. 4½in, 11½cm. A seed-eater with a vinous-pink back, conspicuous white rump and black wings and tail; head grey, sides of face and throat speckled with white; breast and belly vinous-brown.
Voice. High pitched weak trill.
Distribution and Habitat. A very local and uncommon bird of dry bush country with a wide range in East Africa. The contrasting pinkish-brown back, white rump and black tail are good field characters. Gregarious in small flocks. Most frequent in the Dodoma district of Tanzania and in southern Kenya.

BRONZE MANNIKIN *Lonchura cucullata* **Plate 39**

Identification. 3½in, 9cm. Tame, gregarious little birds feeding on grass seeds and on the ground like sparrows. Above dusky with oily-green gloss, darker on head, throat and breast; rump and flanks vermiculated black and white; belly white; bill pale blue-grey. The immature is brown with a black tail.
Voice. A sharp low 'tik, tik.'
Distribution and Habitat. A common resident in East and Central Africa. Found in bush country, coastal scrub, cultivation, grasslands, edges of swamps and lakes and around human habitations.

BLACK AND WHITE MANNIKIN *Lonchura poensis* **Plate 39**

Identification. 4in, 10cm. Rather thickset, heavy billed seed-eater with upperparts, head, throat and chest glossy black; breast and abdomen white, barred black on flanks. Gregarious, feeding on seeding grasses in small flocks. The Bronze Mannikin differs in having a greyish-brown mantle; the Rufousbacked Mannikin, which may be conspecific, has a bright chestnut back.
Voice. Various subdued chirping calls.
Distribution and Habitat. Locally common in Uganda, western Kenya and north-western Tanzania. Frequents grassy margins and glades of forests and in savannah woodland.

RUFOUS-BACKED MANNIKIN   *Lonchura nigriceps*   **Plate 39**

Identification. 3½in, 9cm. Similar to the Black and White Mannikin but with mantle bright chestnut. Head, throat and chest black, rest of underparts white.
Voice. Various chirping calls.
Distribution and Habitat. Occurs in scrub, edges of forest and mixed bush and grass from southern Somalia, south through eastern and central Kenya and Tanzania to Central Africa.

MAGPIE MANNIKIN   *Lonchura fringilloides*   **Plate 39**

Identification. 5in, 13cm. Resembles a large edition of the Black and White Mannikin, but has the mantle brown with black centres to the feathers and white shaft streaks; head and throat black, breast and belly white.
Voice. Soft chirping calls but usually silent.
Distribution and Habitat. Widespread in East and Central Africa but everywhere very uncommon and local; perhaps most frequent in north-eastern Tanzania. Found in lush bush and grass, often at forest margins; frequently in the foliage of mango trees.

WEAVERS, SPARROWS, WHYDAHS and allies: Ploceidae

This is one of the largest bird families in Africa. Most but not all are seed-eaters with short heavy bills. They resemble true finches in general appearance but have ten, not nine primaries. Finches build open nests; weavers and allies weave domed structures with a side, top or bottom entrance. Many species are highly gregarious, nesting in colonies. In some species the males have a female-like non-breeding plumage. The Whydahs and Indigo Birds are parasitic in their nesting habits.

PIN-TAILED WHYDAH   *Vidua macroura*   **Plate 40**

Identification. ♂ 12–13in, 30–33cm; ♀ 4½in, 11½cm. A red-billed, black and white whydah with a long narrow black tail. ♀ and immature streaky and sparrow-like with a buff stripe down centre of crown and a pink bill. ♂ in non-breeding dress like ♀ but larger with much white in the wings. Flight erratic and jerky; has characteristic display flight, the ♂ hovering and 'dancing' in the air over the ♀ perched below.
Voice. Various chirping calls and a sustained twittering song.
Distribution and Habitat. Widely distributed in East and Central Africa. Inhabits all types of grasslands, light bush and scrub and also found in

cultivation. Usually in small parties, the ♂♂ greatly outnumbered by ♀♀ and immature birds.

STRAW-TAILED WHYDAH   *Vidua fischeri*   Plate 40

Identification. ♂ 11in, 28cm; ♀ 4in, 10cm. ♂ unmistakable, a small black and cream coloured whydah with two central pairs of tail feathers pale yellow, very thin and elongated, resembling straws. ♀ and ♂ in non-breeding plumage sparrow-like, streaked above, with a reddish-brown crown; bill red. Immature like ♀ but duller and bill dusky. Found in pairs or small flocks. ♂ has remarkable display; settling above ♀ it flaps wings, at the same time holding on by its feet to prevent itself from flying.
Voice. A sharp 'tssp' and a brief three- or four-note song, repeated over and over again.
Distribution and Habitat. Local resident Ethiopia and Somalia south to Kenya and Tanzania. Inhabits dry bush and scrub country.

STEEL-BLUE WHYDAH   *Vidua hypocherina*   Plate 40

Identification. ♂ 12in, 30cm; ♀ 4in, 10cm. ♂ entire plumage glossy bluish or purplish-black; central tail feathers greatly lengthened, slender, widening towards ends. ♀ and immature resemble ♀ Pin-tailed Whydah but white below, not buff; bill in all plumages greyish-white.
Voice. Chirping calls and a sustained soft warbling song.
Distribution and Habitat. An uncommon and local species in dry bush country in Ethiopia, Somalia, northern Uganda, northern and eastern Kenya and northern Tanzania.

PARADISE WHYDAH   *Steganura paradisaea*   Plate 40

Identification. ♂ 15–16in, 38–41cm; ♀ 5in, 13cm. ♂ unmistakable, recognised by its black, chestnut and buff plumage and remarkable tail. Perches frequently on tops of acacia trees and flies in a curious undulating, jerky manner. Non-breeding ♂ and ♀ sparrow-like with black bill and a broad whitish stripe down centre of crown. Immature dull tawny-brown with white belly.
Voice. A rather shrill, metallic 'teeet' call, but usually silent.
Distribution and Habitat. Local resident in suitable localities through East and Central Africa but not common. Inhabits bush and acacia country and savannah woodlands.
Allied Species. The Broad-tailed Paradise Whydah *(S. orientalis)*, ♂ 14in, 35cm; ♀ 5in, 13cm, differs in having the central tail feathers broad along entire length, not tapering to a point. It occurs in the Sudan, Ethiopia,

Kenya, Tanzania and locally in Central Africa. It occurs in acacia bush and woodland and savannah woodland.

INDIGO-BIRD *Hypochera chalybeata* Plate 40

Identification. 4½in, 11½cm. ♂ glossy blue or purplish-black with a white or pinkish-white bill and orange-pink legs. ♀ and ♂ in non-breeding dress and immature plumage sparrow-like, upperparts brown with dark streaks; crown dark brown with a broad buff stripe down centre; buff streak over eye; below dusky-buff, whiter on belly. Several other species of Indigo-birds have been described but their status is controversial and most are not identifiable in the field.
Voice. Sharp 'tk tk' calls; also imitates calls of Red-billed Firefinch.
Distribution and Habitat. Locally distributed over much of East Africa and in Zambia. Inhabits cultivated areas, gardens, open woodland and bush. The white bill and orange-pink legs are conspicuous in the field.
Allied Species. The White-footed Indigo-bird *(H. funerea)*, 4½in, 11½cm, may be distinguished by its white bill and its white or mauve-tinged white legs. It occurs in dry bush country in East and Central Africa. The Variable Indigo-bird *(H. amauropteryx)*, 4½in, 11½cm, has a pink or reddish bill and orange or pink legs. It occurs in coastal districts of Kenya, in central and south-western Tanzania and in Central Africa. Inhabits bush country and woodland.

GROSBEAK WEAVER *Amblyospiza albifrons* Plate 41

Identification. 7in, 18cm. A large, heavy swamp-haunting weaver with a thick bill. Male slate-black with white patch on forehead and white wing-patch; southern and western races rusty-brown on head. ♀ and immature rusty-brown with dark streaked underparts. Often seen perched on bulrushes in swamps and marshes; occurs in small parties.
Voice. A short low whistle and a brief bubbling song.
Distribution and Habitat. Local resident and partial migrant through East and Central Africa, but uncommon in far south. Inhabits swamps and dense vegetation near water and swamp forests; visits cultivation.

REICHENOW'S WEAVER *Ploceus baglafecht reichenowi* Plate 41

Identification. 6in, 15cm. Upperparts black; ♂ with front half of crown rich golden-yellow; ear-coverts black; ♀ has crown and ear-coverts black; under-parts in both sexes bright yellow. Immature like ♀ but upperparts dusky-olive with dark streaks. Usually in pairs or small parties, not gregarious. The

Black-necked Weaver has a black mantle, but face yellow and ♂ has a black throat-patch.

Voice. A sparrow-like chirp and a brief chattering song.

Distribution and Habitat. Local resident highlands over 4,000ft, 1,220m, southern Ethiopia, Kenya west to Mt Elgon and northern Tanzania. Inhabits edges of forests, moorland scrub, wooded areas, cultivation and the vicinity of human habitations.

Allied Races. Nominate Baglafecht Weaver is a green-backed, yellow-breasted species with a golden-yellow forehead and black ear-coverts; belly white. Occurs in Ethiopia and northern Uganda. It frequents lush bush, margins of forest and lush grass near water. Stuhlmann's Weaver *(P. b. stuhlmanni)* has the crown and face black in both ♂ and ♀; rest upperparts, wings and tail green, mantle with black streaks; below bright yellow. Locally common central Uganda southwards to southern Tanzania. A closely related race occurs in highland forests in Malawi and Zambia.

Allied Species. Bertram's Weaver *(Ploceus bertrandi)*, 6in, 15cm, has a yellow crown and yellowish-green underparts, wings and tail; nape patch, face and chin black; below yellow. ♀ has the crown black. An uncommon and very local bird in the highlands of eastern and southern Tanzania, from the Nguru and Uluguru Mts southwards. Favours vegetation along mountain streams and hillsides with mixed grass, bush and trees.

LITTLE WEAVER　　*Ploceus luteolus*　　　　　　　　Plate 41

Identification. 4½in, 11½cm. A small yellow weaver, greenish on the back, with a black face, forecrown and throat; ♀ and immature lack black face and are paler.

Voice. Soft 'tsssp' notes.

Distribution and Habitat. Local resident acacia woodland and scrub in East Africa south to northern Tanzania. Not gregarious, normally seen in pairs or family parties.

SLENDER-BILLED WEAVER　　*Ploceus pelzelni*　　　　Plate 41

Identification. 4½in, 11½cm. A small yellow weaver, green on mantle, with a black face, forehead and throat and a slender black bill. ♀ bright yellow with a greenish back, no black on face. The Little Weaver has a shorter and more stubby bill and a different habitat – acacia woodlands.

Voice. Subdued chattering calls, but relatively quiet for a weaver.

Distribution and Habitat. Locally common in western Kenya, Uganda and northern Tanzania around Lake Victoria. Inhabits lake shore vegetation, swamps and swamp forest. Common at Entebbe, where often seen in gardens. Slender black bill conspicuous in field.

GOLDEN WEAVER *Ploceus subaureus* **Plate 41**

Identification. 6in, 15cm. ♂ a yellow weaver, slightly greenish on the mantle, with a pale chestnut wash on head and throat; eye pale red. ♀ green above with very indistinct olive streaks; below yellow, paler on the belly; eye pale red. The Golden Palm Weaver has a brilliant orange head and blackish-brown eyes.

Voice. Various chattering calls.

Distribution and Habitat. Locally distributed central and eastern Kenya and in Tanzania, including Zanzibar. Commonest in coastal areas where often exists alongside Golden Palm Weaver. Gregarious. Inhabits coconut plantations, coastal scrub and bush, along rivers and in cultivation where there are trees.

HOLUB'S GOLDEN WEAVER *Ploceus xanthops* **Plate 41**

Identification. 7in, 18cm. A large thickset greenish-yellow weaver, brighter yellow below and washed orange on throat and upper breast. ♀ and immature slightly paler and duller than ♂; eyes pale creamy-yellow. Found singly, in pairs or in small parties, not gregarious.

Voice. A harsh sparrow-like chirping call.

Distribution and Habitat. Local resident East and Central Africa. Inhabits a variety of country where there is plenty of rank vegetation, including cultivation and gardens, woodlands, the vicinity of swamps and marshes.

ORANGE WEAVER *Ploceus aurantius* **Plate 41**

Identification. 5in, 13cm. A brilliant orange-yellow weaver with a greenish-yellow back and golden rump; wings and tail blackish-olive; bill horn coloured, not black. ♀ unstreaked green above, below white with greenish wash on throat and chest; bill pale horn.

Voice. Usual chattering weaver calls.

Distribution and Habitat. Found locally in Uganda, western Kenya and north-western Tanzania, mainly around Lake Victoria and in nearby swamps. Inhabits reed beds, papyrus, and lush lake shore vegetation; gregarious, often associated with other species of weaver.

GOLDEN PALM WEAVER *Ploceus bojeri* **Plate 41**

Identification. 6in, 15cm. An entirely yellow weaver with a bright orange head; chestnut wash on chest. ♀ unstreaked greenish-yellow, below yellow; eyes dark brown. Gregarious but sometimes encountered in single pairs.

Voice. A low-pitched weaver chattering.
Distribution and Habitat. Local resident southern Somalia, south through eastern Kenya to north-eastern Tanzania. A common species and one of the most noticeable weavers on the Kenya coast, breeding in small colonies in coconut palms and in bushes in coastal scrub.

TAVETA GOLDEN WEAVER *Ploceus castaneiceps* Plate 41

Identification. 5½in, 14cm. ♂ a bright yellow weaver with a greenish-yellow back and greenish wings and tail; chestnut patch on nape and chestnut wash on chest; ♀ yellowish-olive with dusky streaks on mantle; yellowish stripe above eye; below pale buffy-yellow.
Voice. A constant low chattering.
Distribution and Habitat. An extremely local species but often common where it does occur. Found in south-eastern Kenya and north-eastern Tanzania. Abundant around camps and park lodges in the Amboseli National Park, Kenya. Inhabits open acacia woodland where there is bushy undergrowth, and lush vegetation in the vicinity of water.

NORTHERN BROWN-THROATED WEAVER
Ploceus castanops Plate 41

Identification. 5½in, 14cm. ♂ a bright golden-yellow weaver with a green back; forehead, front half of face and throat rich chestnut; eye white. ♀ olive-buff with dusky streaking on mantle; below yellowish-buff.
Voice. Various subdued chattering calls.
Distribution and Habitat. Found locally in southern Sudan, Uganda and along the shores of Lake Victoria in western Kenya. Frequents papyrus and reed beds and other waterside vegetation. Not uncommon along the Kazinga Channel in the Ruwenzori National Park, Uganda. Usually gregarious in small flocks, sometimes associated with Yellow-collared and Golden-backed Weavers.

NORTHERN MASKED WEAVER *Ploceus taeniopterus* Plate 41

Identification. ♂ with a black face mask and yellow underparts; relatively little black on face, extensive chestnut on head and throat. ♀ olive-buff above, streaked blackish; below pale yellowish-buff.
Voice. Usual weaver chattering.
Distribution and Habitat. Local resident in Sudan, Uganda and at Lake Baringo in the Rift Valley, Kenya. Frequents swamps and the lush vegetation along swamps and lake shores.

MASKED WEAVER *Ploceus intermedius* Plate 41

Identification. 5½in, 14cm. A mainly yellow weaver with an olive-green, indistinctly streaked mantle; face and front half of crown black. The closely related Vitelline Masked Weaver has the black on the crown restricted to a very narrow frontal band. ♀, ♂ in non-breeding dress and immature lack black on head, upperparts more olive and a yellow stripe over eye; below yellowish to white on abdomen. Gregarious, breeding in dense colonies; nest construction spherical with a short spout entrance. The Vitelline Masked Weaver is less gregarious and its onion-shaped nest, constructed of blades of grass, has a large bottom-side entrance and no spout.
Voice. The usual chattering weaver calls at nesting colonies but less noisy than many other weavers.
Distribution and Habitat. Local resident, with restricted spasmodic migrations during non-breeding season. Occurs southern Sudan, Ethiopia, Somalia, south through Uganda, Kenya and Tanzania to Central Africa. In north of range generally a bird of dry thornbush country but also occurs in acacia woodland and savannah; in the south it is largely confined to the vicinity of water.

VITELLINE MASKED WEAVER *Ploceus velatus* Plate 41

Identification. 5½in, 14cm. ♂ closely resembles Masked Weaver but crown mainly chestnut with a very narrow black frontal-band. ♀, ♂ in non-breeding dress and immature olive-yellow above, streaked dusky on mantle; below yellowish. Much less gregarious than Masked Weaver and pairs often nest alone. Nest contruction is a good field character for distinguishing these two weavers – see under Masked Weaver.
Voice. Soft chattering calls and a 'tsssp' call note.
Distribution and Habitat. Local resident and partial migrant during non-breeding season in Sudan, Ethiopia, Somalia and southwards through Uganda, Kenya and Tanzania to Central Africa. This is one of the common dry country weavers in Kenya.
Allied Species. The Tanzania Masked Weaver *(P. reichardi)*, 5½in, 14cm, resembles the Vitelline Masked Weever but has a broad black band on the forehead and chestnut flanks; the ♀ is indistinctly streaked above. A very local and uncommon species found in southern Tanzania, usually in the vicinity of swamps and water. Heuglin's Masked Weaver *(P. heuglini)*, 5½in, 14cm, has a black face mask but the crown is yellow; mantle yellowish-green without streaking. ♀ has black-streaked olive upperparts, below yellow with buff wash on breast. Found in savannah bush and woodland, often at waterholes, in eastern and central Uganda and in western Kenya.

SPEKE'S WEAVER *Ploceus spekei* **Plate 41**

Identification. 6in, 15cm. A thickset yellow weaver with a dusky mottled back, a yellow crown and a black face and chin. ♀ and immature upperparts olive-brown, slightly mottled; below white, washed yellowish-buff on throat and breast. Gregarious, breeds in colonies, often in acacia trees and in swamps.

Voice. Usual weaver chatter at nesting colonies, and a sharp 'teep.'

Distribution and Habitat. Local resident and partial migrant Somalia, Ethiopia, south through Kenya to north-eastern Tanzania. Inhabits lightly wooded areas, cultivation, riverine acacias, swamps and vicinity of buildings and houses. A common bird in the eastern highlands of Kenya, including Nairobi.

Allied Species. Fox's Weaver *(P. spekeoides)*, 6in, 15cm, is a rare and very local weaver found in north-western to central Uganda in or near swamps. It is a yellow weaver with a black face and chin, yellow crown and dusky mottled back; similar to Speke's Weaver but with a conspicuous yellow rump and shorter tail; ♀ olive-yellow above with dusky streaks; rump yellow; underparts yellowish.

BLACK-HEADED WEAVER *Ploceus cucullatus* **Plate 42**

Identification. 7in, 18cm. A thickset black-headed yellow weaver with chestnut hind crown and nape; broad yellow collar on hind neck; mantle marked black on yellow with a yellow V; below, throat black, remainder underparts yellow, washed rufous on breast and flanks. Layard's Black-headed Weaver, now considered conspecific, has head and nape completely black with no chestnut on crown or nape. ♀ and immature olive-brown above, indistinctly streaked; yellowish-white below. Gregarious, breeding in colonies in trees or palms, often alongside human dwellings. It is frequently associated with Vieillot's Black Weaver and mixed colonies are not uncommon.

Voice. A noisy chatter at nesting colonies.

Distribution and Habitat. Local resident, often abundant, Sudan, Ethiopia, Uganda and western Kenya. Occurs in forested and cultivated areas, nesting nearly always in vicinity of human habitations. Very common in many parts of Uganda.

LAYARD'S BLACK-HEADED WEAVER
Ploceus cucullatus nigriceps **Plate 42**

Identification. 6½in, 16½cm. Now considered to be conspecific with Black-headed Weaver. A black-headed, yellow and black weaver without chestnut on hind crown or nape; upperparts mottled black and yellow but without the yellow V. ♀ and immature brownish-grey with indistinct streaking; below dull yellowish-white. Gregarious, nesting in colonies. This species and the Golden Palm Weaver are the two common weavers on the Kenya coast.

Voice. A loud chattering at nesting colonies; also a single harsh 'zeeet.'

Distribution and Habitat. Local resident southern Somalia south through Kenya and Tanzania to Central Africa. Frequents coastal bush, open woodland, vegetation near water and the vicinity of human dwellings.

VIEILLOT'S BLACK WEAVER   *Ploceus nigerrimus*   Plate 41

Identification. 7in, 18cm. ♂ entirely black with conspicuous creamy-white eye; ♀ and immature dusky-olive, streaked on upperparts, dull yellowish-white below.

Voice. A typical weaver chattering at nesting colonies.

Distribution and Habitat. Local resident southern Sudan, Uganda, western Kenya and western Tanzania. Inhabits forested and wooded areas and cultivation. Often associates with Black-headed Weavers.

Allied Species. Maxwell's Black Weaver *(P. albinucha)*, 5in, 13cm, is a relatively small all-black forest weaver with white eyes; smaller than Vieillot's Black Weaver and ♀ black, not olive with streaked upperparts. Half-concealed grey patch on nape. This is a rare tree-top weaver, in East Africa known only from the Bwamba Forest, western Uganda.

WEYNS' WEAVER   *Ploceus weynsi*   Plate 42

Identification. 6in, 15cm. A thickset weaver with black upperparts, head and chest; wings black with yellow edgings; tail dark olive; breast and abdomen yellow, flanks rich chestnut. ♀ and immature dark olive with indistinct dusky streaking; below whitish with olive wash on throat, chest and flanks; wings blackish-olive with pale yellow edgings; tail olive.

Voice. Rather soft chirping calls.

Distribution and Habitat. This is a rare and local forest weaver found in Uganda. It is most frequent near Entebbe where it occurs both in forest and in lush waterside vegetation. Often visits erythrina trees when these are in flower, for nectar.

CLARKE'S WEAVER   *Ploceus golandi*   Plate 42

Identification. 5in, 13cm. ♂ a black weaver with a bright yellow breast and abdomen; wings black, edged with yellow; rump and tail olive-green. ♀ bright green above with black streaks on mantle; wings black with yellow edgings; tail dark olive; underparts bright canary yellow, merging to buffy-white on belly.

Voice. A high pitched twittering.

Distribution and Habitat. A very rare and local weaver, known only from the Sokoke-Arabuku Forest on the Kenya coast. Found in small flocks in tree-tops in Brachystegia woodland; often associated with other birds in mixed bird parties.

YELLOW-BACKED WEAVER *Ploceus capitalis* Plate 42

Identification. 6in, 15cm. ♂ head and throat black; conspicuous yellow hind neck band and yellowish-green mantle; below, chestnut on breast and flanks, yellow on belly. The ♂ Golden-backed Weaver has black extending from crown to nape and entire mantle is bright yellow. ♀ and immature pale brown above, streaked dusky; below white, washed cinnamon on breast and flanks. Gregarious; nearly always near water, especially papyrus and reed beds or elephant grass.

Voice. Various churring call-notes, typical of weavers in flocks.

Distribution and Habitat. Local resident southern Sudan and western Ethiopia, Uganda, western Kenya and north-western Tanzania. Inhabits swamps and lake shore and adjacent cultivation and forest edge. A common bird around Lake Victoria where it nests in colonies in reed beds alongside the closely allied Golden-backed Weaver.

Allied Species. The Somali Yellow-backed Weaver *(P. dichrocephalus)*, differs in having the head and sides of face dusky chestnut; below chin and throat dusky saffron. A very uncommon and local species found in southern Ethiopia, southern Somalia and extreme north-eastern Kenya. Occurs in riverine acacia woodland and vegetation along rivers.

GOLDEN-BACKED WEAVER *Ploceus jacksoni* Plate 42

Identification. 6in, 15cm. ♂ a black-headed weaver with the black extending on to the nape; mantle bright golden-yellow; below bright chestnut to yellow in middle of belly. ♀ and immature olive-brown above with dusky streaking, below yellow to white on belly; eyes red. Gregarious, breeding in colonies over or near water.

Voice. Usual weaver type calls at nesting colonies.

Distribution and Habitat. Local resident south-eastern Sudan, Uganda, western and central Kenya south to central Tanzania. Frequents shores of lakes, swamps and larger rivers. Common locally on Lake Victoria and breeds alongside Yellow-backed Weaver.

CHESTNUT WEAVER *Ploceus rubiginosus* **Plate 42**

Identification. 6½in, 16½cm. ♂ very distinct, bright chestnut with black head and throat. ♀ and ♂ in non-breeding plumage sparrow-like, brownish-grey, streaked black above; below tawny-buff to white on throat and belly. Immature like ♀ but tinged rufous. Very gregarious, breeding in dense colonies in acacia trees.
Voice. Usual weaver type chattering calls at nesting colonies.
Distribution and Habitat. Local resident, partial migrant in non-breeding season, Ethiopia, southern Sudan, Somalia, south through north-eastern Uganda and Kenya to central Tanzania. Inhabits arid bush country and acacia woodlands, entering cultivation where wheat is grown.

COMPACT WEAVER *Ploceus pachyrhynchus* **Plate 42**

Identification. 5in, 13cm. A thickset, short-tailed Weaver with a heavy conical bill; upperparts dark olive with very indistinct dark mottling; forehead chestnut, merging to yellow on hind crown; wings dark brown; face and throat black; remainder underparts yellow to white on belly. ♀ like ♂ but crown blackish and a golden-yellow stripe over eye.
Voice. A rather harsh 'cheee,' followed by a series of double notes.
Distribution and Habitat. Locally common in Uganda, western Kenya and north-western Tanzania. Inhabits open park-like country and forest margins where there is long grass. Gregarious in small flocks in grasslands.

DARK-BACKED WEAVER *Ploceus bicolor* **Plate 42**

Identification. 6in, 15cm. Sexes similar. A thickset black and golden-yellow weaver with a bluish or greenish-white bill and red eyes. The race found along the Kenya-Tanzania coast has the head, upperparts, wings, and tail jet black and the breast and abdomen bright golden-yellow. Elsewhere the mantle is greyish, the wings and tail paler and the underparts less golden.
Voice. A double 'weet-weet' and various high pitched squeaky notes.
Distribution and Habitat. Locally distributed coastal and western Kenya, Uganda and Tanzania, south to Central Africa. Inhabits coastal forest and scrub, rain forest and heavy woodland. A tree-top species usually found in pairs; sometimes associated with mixed bird parties.

YELLOW-MANTLED WEAVER *Ploceus tricolor* **Plate 42**

Identification. 6in, 15cm. A black weaver with a bright yellow collar on the hind neck; breast and abdomen deep chestnut. ♀ has sooty-brown underparts, otherwise similar to ♂.

Voice. A sharp 'tssst' or 'chirr-it,' but usually silent.

Distribution and Habitat. A very uncommon and local forest weaver found in Uganda and in the Kakamega Forest, western Kenya. Habits woodpecker or tit-like, climbing about over branches of tall trees searching for insects. Usually in pairs or small family parties.

SPECTACLED WEAVER   *Ploceus ocularis*   Plate 42

Identification. 6in, 15cm. A green-backed weaver with yellowish-green wings and tail, yellow underparts and a black patch around the eye; ♂ has black chin, ♀ an orange-rufous chin. Occurs singly or in pairs, rather shy and skulking.

Voice. Usually a silent bird, sometimes calling weakly 'tss, tss, tss, tss, tss' or a single metallic 'peeeet.'

Distribution and Habitat. Local resident in small numbers through East and Central Africa. Inhabits forest, acacia woodland, riverine forest and rank vegetation near streams and lakes.

BLACK-NECKED WEAVER   *Ploceus nigricollis*   Plate 42

Identification. 6in, 15cm. Upperparts, wings and tail black, contrasting with bright yellow underparts. ♂ has crown and face yellow and chin black; ♀ has black crown and a yellow eye stripe; entire underparts yellow. Immature like ♀ but greenish above. Occurs usually in pairs; not gregarious, shy and retiring. Reichenow's Weaver is also black above but has sides of face black, not yellow.

Voice. A curious vibrating 'teeee, teeee.'

Distribution and Habitat. Uncommon local resident East Africa south to southern and central Tanzania. Found both in forests and in thick bush and scrub.

BLACK-BILLED WEAVER   *Ploceus melanogaster*   Plate 42

Identification. 5½in, 14cm. A black weaver with golden-yellow forecrown and cheeks; ♀ has forecrown, face and throat yellow.

Voice. A rather high pitched chirp, but usually silent.

Distribution and Habitat. An uncommon forest weaver found in Uganda and in western Kenya. Inhabits both treetops and dense undergrowth of forests; normally encountered in pairs.

Allied Species. The Strange Weaver *(P. alienus)*, 5½in, 14cm, has upperparts, wings and tail green, head and throat black; breast and abdomen yellow with a chestnut patch on chest. It occurs singly or in pairs in treetops and undergrowth of mountain forests in western and south-western Uganda. The Usambara Weaver *(P. nicolli)*, 5½in, 14cm, has brownish-black upperparts, wings and tail, head and throat dusky-olive, dull yellow on forehead; below yellow with chestnut patch on chest. This is another rare and very local forest weaver, known only from the Usambara Mts, north-eastern Tanzania. The Olive-headed Golden Weaver *(P. olivaceiceps)*, 5in, 13cm, has yellowish-green upperparts, head and throat, yellow underparts with a chestnut patch on the chest. A rare and local weaver found in Brachystegia woodland in south-western Tanzania.

BROWN-CAPPED WEAVER   *Ploceus insignis*   Plate 42

Identification. 5½in, 14cm. A black and yellow forest weaver, the ♂ with a bright chestnut cap. General colour bright yellow with black wings and tail, a black face and chin and a yellow stripe down the middle of the back. ♀ with the cap black, not chestnut.
Voice. Usually silent, but sometimes utters a sharp 'tssst.'
Distribution and Habitat. A local and uncommon forest species found in Uganda, central and western Kenya and northern and western Tanzania. Inhabits the treetops usually in pairs or family parties, searching the branches in the manner of a tit. The broad yellow stripe down the back and the male's chestnut crown are conspicuous in the field.

RED-HEADED MALIMBE   *Malimbus rubricollis*   Plate 43

Identification. 7in, 18cm. The malimbes are a group of black and red forest treetops weavers. Crown, nape and sides of neck bright scarlet red; remainder plumage black. ♀ resembles ♂ but has black forehead. Immature like adults but duller. The Crested Malimbe has a dark crimson-red crown and throat and a square crimson crest. Hunts insects among branches like a large tit; not gregarious, usually in pairs and often members of mixed bird parties in forest.
Voice. Low wheezy and chirping call notes, but usually silent.
Distribution and Habitat. Local resident forests southern Sudan, Uganda and western Kenya in the Kakamega Forest. Inhabits forest treetops and the vines and creepers hanging from forest trees.
Allied Species. Gray's Malimbe *(M. nitens)*, 6½in, 16½cm, is a black weaver with a deep red throat and chest and a bluish-white bill. Found in the Bwamba Forest, western Uganda. May be distinguished from the Crested and Red-headed Malimbes by less extensive red and a bluish-white, not black, bill. The Red-bellied Malimbe *(M. erythrogaster)*, 7in, 18cm, has a red crown, breast and abdomen. It also has been recorded from the Bwamba Forest, western Uganda.

CRESTED MALIMBE *Malimbus malimbicus* **Plate 43**

Identification. 7in, 18cm. A thickset black forest weaver with square-crested head and throat deep crimson-red. ♀ resembles ♂ but crest shorter; immature duller. The Red-headed Malimbe is black with orange-red or scarlet on the crown, not deep crimson, and its underparts are completely black. Inhabits treetops in forests, singly or in pairs. Not gregarious but often seen in mixed bird parties.

Voice. A low musical whistle and various short chirping calls.

Distribution and Habitat. A West African species which extends to western Uganda where it is resident and locally common in the rain forests. Relatively abundant in the Bwamba Forest, western Uganda.

RED-HEADED WEAVER *Anaplectes rubriceps* **Plate 43**

Identification. 6in, 15cm. Sometimes included in the genus *Malimbus*. ♂ recognised easily by bright red head, mantle and chest; bill pinkish-red; ♀ greyish with red or yellow edgings to wing and tail feathers; bill pale pink. Immature like ♀ but washed buff and bill dusky. Not gregarious; occurs singly, in pairs or in family parties.

Voice. Usually silent, but utters a high-pitched chatter at nest.

Distribution and Habitat. Widely distributed local resident through East and Central Africa. Found generally in savannah woodlands, scrub or Brachystegia woodlands. Frequents foliage of trees, creepers and bushes; mainly insectivorous.

CARDINAL QUELEA *Quelea cardinalis* **Plate 43**

Identification. 4in, 10cm. A small short-tailed sparrow-plumaged weaver with a crimson-red head and throat and a black bill. ♀ and immature lack red head. Occurs in loose colonies of a dozen or so pairs, and in larger flocks during the non-breeding season.

Voice. A soft 'zeet, zeet' call note.

Distribution and Habitat. Local resident, migratory during the non-breeding season, in southern Sudan, Ethiopia and Somalia south through Uganda, Kenya and Tanzania to Zambia. Inhabits open bush country where there is rank grass.

Allied Species. The Red-headed Quelea *(Q. erythrops)*, 5in, 13cm, is larger with a blackish-crimson throat and a relatively longer tail; bill black. This is a widely distributed species in East Africa south to Malawi and Zambia, but very local and often absent from apparently suitable habitats. Inhabits rank grasslands and marshes.

RED-BILLED QUELEA or SUDAN DIOCH
Quelea quelea **Plate 43**

Identification. 5in, 13cm. A streaky sparrow-like weaver with a pink-red bill and legs; ♂ in breeding dress has black face and is suffused pink on crown and breast. ♀, non-breeding ♂ and immature lack black face and pink suffusion. Extremely gregarious, sometimes in flocks numbering many hundreds of thousands of birds. The Cardinal and Red-headed Queleas are smaller with red heads and black bills.
Voice. A constant but low murmuration of chatter from flocks and breeding colonies.
Distribution and Habitat. Resident and spasmodic migrant through East and Central Africa. Inhabits dry thornbush country, scrub and acacia thickets, at times entering cultivation where it is very destructive to wheat crops.

YELLOW-CROWNED BISHOP   *Euplectes afer* **Plate 43**

Identification. 4in, 10cm. A black bishop weaver with a bright canary-yellow crown, back and rump; the long yellow feathers of the rump are puffed up during display. ♀ and immature sparrow-like, streaky, and in field best identified by association with adult ♂. The larger Yellow Bishop has a black crown.
Voice. A rather slowly uttered 'zeet, zeet;' ♂ often calls when flying in circles above swampy nesting ground.
Distribution and Habitat. Occurs widely in East and Central Africa but everywhere very local and usually uncommon. Inhabits areas of marshland and swamps where there is rank grass and sedge; nests in small scattered colonies.

WHITE-WINGED WIDOWBIRD   *Euplectes albonotatus* **Plate 45**

Identification. ♂ 7in, 18cm; ♀ 5in, 13cm. A black widowbird with a moderately long tail; white wing patch conspicuous in flight. ♀ and immature streaky, sparrow-like, best identified by associated ♂♂. ♂ non-breeding plumage like ♀ but white wing-patch retained. Gregarious, found in scattered colonies when nesting and in flocks when not breeding.
Voice. Various brief twittering notes.
Distribution and Habitat. Local resident and partial migrant through East and Central Africa. Inhabits rank tall grass and bush and grass, usually on dry ground but sometimes in swampy hollows; much attracted to dams in agricultural land; common in the Kenya Highlands. Often associates with Yellow Bishops and Red-collared Widowbirds.

RED-COLLARED WIDOWBIRD *Euplectes ardens* **Plate 45**

Identification. ♂ 11in, 28cm; ♀ 5in, 13cm. ♂ entire plumage black with crescent-shaped scarlet patch on upper breast. The Kilimanjaro, Kenya Highlands and Ethiopian Highlands race has the crown and nape scarlet. Some birds in Uganda, Tanzania and Central Africa, occurring alongside normal ♂♂, have the plumage entirely black without a red breast-patch. ♀, ♂ in non-breeding dress and immature streaked black and tawny on upperparts; below buff, washed yellowish on throat and chest. Breeds in loose colonies of scattered pairs; in flocks in non-breeding season and when feeding.

Voice. Various chirping calls and a metallic rasping song.

Distribution and Habitat. Local resident and partial migrant in East and Central Africa. Inhabits areas of rank grass and mixed grass and bush.

FAN-TAILED WIDOWBIRD *Euplectes axillaris* **Plate 45**

Identification. 6½in, 16½cm. Longer-tailed than the bishop weavers; black with orange-red shoulders and bluish-white bill; medium sized tail, often fanned. A very conspicuous bird when it perches on reeds or bushes or flies in display over breeding ground. ♀ and immatures sparrow-like, with shoulders black, edged with orange or buff. ♂ in non-breeding plumage resembles ♀ but retains orange-red shoulders.

Voice. Various twittering calls.

Distribution and Habitat. Local resident and partial migrant through East and Central Africa. Inhabits swamps and marshes and the edges of lakes and rivers where there is rank tall grass; also in sugar-cane cultivation.

YELLOW BISHOP *Euplectes capensis* **Plate 43**

Identification. 6in, 15cm. ♂ black with shoulders and rump bright yellow. ♀ and immature sparrow-like with an olive rump; ♂ in non-breeding plumage also sparrow-like but retains yellow rump. Not gregarious, usually in pairs or single.

Voice. A series of brief cheeping and twittering calls.

Distribution and Habitat. Local resident and partial migrant, often common, throughout East and Central Africa. It inhabits grassy bush country, savannah woodland, the edges of forest and woodland and overgrown neglected cultivation.

FIRE-FRONTED BISHOP *Euplectes diademata* **Plate 43**

Identification. 4in, 10cm. A black-breasted bishop with a red forehead and a bright chrome-yellow lower back and rump; wings and tail brown. ♀, non-breeding ♂ and immature sparrow-like and streaky, not identifiable in field except in association with adult ♂.
Voice. A sharp 'zeep, zeep.'
Distribution and Habitat. Occurs very locally in drier parts of southern Somalia, eastern Kenya and north-eastern Tanzania; inhabits areas of tall grass or marshy hollows in arid bush country. Moderately gregarious, nesting in small scattered colonies. Not uncommon in the Voi area of Tsavo National Park.

BLACK BISHOP *Euplectes gierowii* **Plate 43**

Identification. 6in, 15cm. A large black bishop weaver with an orange-red chest-band, nape and hind neck; mantle orange-red or yellow. ♀, non-breeding ♂ and immature sparrow-like, streaked dusky above, best recognised in field by size and by association with adult ♂.
Voice. Various subdued twittering calls.
Distribution and Habitat. A very local and generally uncommon species found from Uganda and Ethiopia south to northern Tanzania in the vicinity of Lake Victoria. Inhabits swampy areas of bush and tall grass, elephant grass, sugar-cane cultivation and margins of swamps. Not highly gregarious, but sometimes in small flocks.

BLACK-WINGED BISHOP *Euplectes hordeacea* **Plate 43**

Identification. 5½in, 14cm. A large red and black bishop with contrasting black wings and tail and buff or white under tail-coverts. ♀, non-breeding ♂ and immature buff with streaked mantle, black wings and tail and yellowish eye stripe. Black wings and tail distinguish this species from the smaller red bishops. In pairs or small loose flocks.
Voice. Various twittering calls but often silent.
Distribution and Habitat. Local resident and partial migrant through East and Central Africa. Inhabits lush grasslands with bushes, maize and sugar-cane fields and coastal scrub.

YELLOW-SHOULDERED WIDOWBIRD
Euplectes macrocercus **Plate 45**

Identification. ♂ 10–12in, 25–31cm; ♀ 5½in, 14cm. Sometimes considered to be conspecific with Yellow-mantled Widowbird. ♂ an all black, relatively long-tailed widowbird with canary-yellow shoulders. ♂ in non-breeding plumage streaky and sparrow-like, but retains yellow shoulders. ♀ and immature sparrowlike, best recognised by association with males.

Voice. A thin piping 'zee, zee, zee' or 'zeet.'

Distribution and Habitat. Locally not uncommon in Uganda and western Kenya. Inhabits areas of marshland with lush grass and scattered bush. Not specially gregarious, but sometimes in flocks at roosts and in smaller groups when feeding. Occurs alongside the Yellow-mantled Widowbird in several localities.

Allied Species. Hartlaub's Marsh Widowbird *(E. hartlaubi)*, ♂ 12–14in, 31–36cm; ♀ 6in, 15cm; is a heavy-looking black widowbird with orange-buff shoulders; ♀ sparrow-like. It frequents areas of extensive marsh with lush grass in Uganda and western Kenya south to Zambia. Everywhere uncommon and local. The Mountain Marsh Widowbird *(E. psammocromius)*, ♂ 20in, 51cm, ♀ 8in, 20cm; occurs in marshy valleys in the southern highlands of Tanzania and the highlands of Malawi and Zambia. The ♂ is black with a very long tail and yellow and buff shoulders; ♀ dusky and sparrow-like. The Long-tailed Widowbird is larger with an even longer tail and has red and buff shoulders.

YELLOW-MANTLED WIDOWBIRD
Euplectes macrourus   **Plate 45**

Identification. ♂ 10–12in, 25–31cm; ♀ 5½in, 14cm. Sometimes considered to be conspecific with the Yellow-shouldered Widowbird. ♂ a black widowbird with yellow shoulders and a yellow mantle. The non-breeding ♂ retains the yellow shoulders but not the yellow mantle. ♀ and immatures sparrowlike, not identifiable in field unless associated with adult ♂.

Voice. Various 'zeeting' calls, not unlike those of some cisticola warblers.

Distribution and Habitat. Locally not uncommon in Uganda, western Kenya, Tanzania and Zambia. Inhabits open grassy plains, marshes, bush and margins of swamps and lakes.

RED BISHOP   *Euplectes orix*   **Plate 43**

Identification. 4½in, 11½cm. One of the several species of bright red and black bishop weavers. ♂ distinguished by pale brown wings and tail, orange-red under tail coverts and black forehead. ♀, non-breeding ♂ and immature sparrow-like, streaky above. The Zanzibar Red Bishop is smaller with a scarlet crown and black underparts; the larger Black-winged Red Bishop has the wings and tail black. Not highly gregarious, but often in small flocks and breeds in loose scattered colonies. All ♂ bishop weavers are very conspicuous during the breeding season, making display flights over grass with rump feathers fluffed up.

Voice. Various twittering calls.

Distribution and Habitat. Local resident, migratory in non-breeding season, through East and Central Africa. Inhabits tall rank grass, sugar cane, maize cultivation, elephant grass and rank herbage near water. Wanders to open plains and short grass bush country after nesting.

ZANZIBAR RED BISHOP *Euplectes nigroventris* Plate 43

Identification. 4in, 10cm. A small black and red bishop distinguished by its brown wings and tail, red crown and completely black underparts. ♀, non-breeding ♂ and immature sparrow-like, streaked above and distinguished in field from Red Bishop only by smaller size. Usually in small flocks; breeds in small scattered colonies.

Voice. A sharp twittering call.

Distribution and Habitat. Local resident and partial migrant in southern Somalia, eastern Kenya, Zanzibar and Pemba islands and eastern Tanzania. Inhabits bush and scrub where there is an abundance of rank grass and herbage; common on the Kenya coast.

WEST NILE RED BISHOP *Euplectes franciscana* Plate 43

Identification. 4in, 10cm. ♂ a bright red bishop with crown, face and breast black; wings and tail brown; red upper tail-coverts very long extending to end of tail feathers. ♀, non-breeding ♂ and immature sparrow-like.

Voice. Various zeeting call notes.

Distribution and Habitat. Ranges from the Sudan to Ethiopia, south to Uganda and the Rift Valley, Kenya. A striking little bird, remarkable for its long rump and tail coverts. Common at Lake Baringo, Kenya. Occurs in open grasslands and reed beds along lake margins.

LONG-TAILED WIDOWBIRD *Euplectes progne* Plate 45

Identification. ♂ 24–30in, 61–76cm; ♀ 6in, 15cm. This is one of the most striking of African birds, jet black with a neck ruff, a tail 2ft, 60cm, or more long and bright red and buff shoulders. Flies slowly with slow jerky wing-beats and tail expanded, a few feet above nesting ground. ♀ and immature pale tawny buff, heavily streaked; ♂ in non-breeding dress like ♀ but larger and retains red shoulder patches. Forms flocks in non-breeding season when frequents and roosts in swamps and reedbeds.

Voice. A loud sharp chirping call.

Distribution and Habitat. Local resident in the highlands of central and western Kenya, over 6,000ft, 1,830m. Elsewhere found in the highlands of Angola and in South Africa. Frequents open high level grasslands and moorland, the vicinity of dams and marshes and cultivation. In Kenya common on the Kinangop plateau and in the Nanyuki district.

JACKSON'S WIDOWBIRD   *Euplectes jacksoni*   Plate 45

Identification. ♂ 13–14in, 33–36cm; ♀ 5½in, 14cm. ♂ entirely black with olive-brown shoulders and a long, thick decurved tail. ♀, non-breeding ♂ and immature sparrow-like, tawny streaked dark brown. When nesting, ♂♂ construct circular dancing rings on which they display by repeatedly springing two or more feet into the air.

Voice. A soft 'cheee' uttered during display, and a brief clicking song.

Distribution and Habitat. Local resident highlands over 5,000ft, 1,530m, in western and central Kenya and the Loliondo and Crater Highlands in northern Tanzania. Gregarious; found during breeding season in highland grasslands. Forms flocks in post breeding period, when it visits cultivated areas.

PARASITIC WEAVER   *Anomalospiza imberbis*   Plate 43

Identification. 4½in, 11½cm. A rather short-tailed greenish-yellow finch-like bird with indistinct dark mottling on upperparts and a black bill; ♀ more buffy in colour, less yellow. Has the appearance of some short-tailed canary with a heavy black bill.

Voice. Soft 'tsssp' calls.

Distribution and Habitat. Widely distributed in East and Central Africa but everywhere very local and uncommon. Inhabits open grasslands where it is parasitic upon grassland Cisticola warblers.

RED-BILLED BUFFALO WEAVER   *Bubalornis niger*   Plate 44

Identification. 10in, 25½cm. A very large thickset weaver, black except for white-margined flight feathers and white bases to body feathers; bill dull red to pinkish red; eye brown. ♀ and immature greyish-brown above, whitish below, streaked dusky. Gregarious, building large stick nests close together in baobab or acacia trees. In the White-billed Buffalo Weaver the ♀ is slaty-black above and below, very similar to the ♂; the bill is white or yellowish-white.

Voice. Very noisy birds, especially at nesting colonies, with a variety of loud, falsetto croaking and chattering calls.

Distribution and Habitat. Ranges from Somalia and eastern Ethiopia south-wards through Kenya and Tanzania to Central Africa and South Africa. Inhabits acacia woodland, savannah country especially where there are baobab trees, and thornbush country. Locally common in the Northern Frontier Province of Kenya and in the Tsavo National Park, Kenya.

Allied Species. The White-billed Buffalo Weaver *(B. albirostris)*, 10in, 25½cm. ♂ differs mainly in bill colour, white or yellowish-white; ♀ quite different from the Red-billed Buffalo Weaver, slaty black all over and similar to the ♂. Ranges from Sudan and western Ethiopia south to northern half of Uganda and western Kenya. Inhabits savannah woodlands and acacia country; also favours baobab trees for nesting.

WHITE-HEADED BUFFALO WEAVER
Dinemellia dinemelli   Plate 44

Identification. 9in, 23cm. A large heavy brown and white weaver, rather parrot-like in general appearance, with a most conspicuous orange-red rump and under tail-coverts; especially noticeable during flight. Usually seen in pairs or small flocks. Frequently feeds on the ground below acacia trees and often associated with Superb and Hildebrandt's Starlings.

Voice. A harsh, parrot-like call and a series of chattering notes.

Distribution and Habitat. Local resident Somalia, Ethiopia and Sudan south through Uganda and Kenya to Tanzania. Inhabits acacia woodlands, dry bush and thornbush scrub. One of the most noticeable birds in the dry thornbush country of Kenya.

WHITE-BROWED SPARROW WEAVER
Plocepasser mahali   Plate 44

Identification. 6in, 15cm. Also called the Stripe-breasted and Black-billed Sparrow Weaver. Upperparts light brown, darker on crown with broad white band above eyes and white rump; below white. Gregarious in small flocks and nesting colonies. Immature duller than adult.

Voice. Noisy birds, especially at nesting colonies, uttering a 'chuk, chuk' call and various loud chatterings; male's song not unlike that of Superb Starling.

Distribution and Habitat. Local resident, often common, through East and Central Africa. Found in dry bush and acacia country and in Central Africa in thorn scrub and mopane woodland. Locally very common in Northern Frontier Province, Kenya.

Allied Species. Donaldson-Smith's Sparrow Weaver *(P. donaldsoni)*, 6in, 15cm, is an uncommon bird of northern Kenya and south-western Ethiopia, inhabiting dry bush country and stands of acacia. It is buff-brown, paler below with a white rump. It is common in the vicinity of Isiolo, northern Kenya. The Chestnut-crowned Sparrow Weaver *(P. superciliosus)*, 6in, 15cm, is a pale brown sparrow-like bird with a chestnut crown; white stripe over eye and black stripe down each side of throat; two whitish wing bars; below greyish-white. A very silent and unobtrusive bird, found in small parties or pairs in bush and savannah woodland. Found in north-western Kenya, northern Uganda, Sudan and western Ethiopia.

RUFOUS-TAILED WEAVER *Histurgops ruficauda* Plate 44

Identification. 8½in, 22cm. Sexes alike. Upperparts greyish-brown with whitish edgings to feathers giving a scaly effect; wings dark brown with inner webs of flight feathers pale chestnut; tail pale chestnut except central feathers which are brown; underparts creamy-white mottled with brown; eye pale blue. Field appearance, a mottled brown buffalo weaver; rufous in wings and tail conspicuous in flight.
Voice. Harsh chattering calls, especially at nesting colonies.
Distribution and Habitat. Occurs locally in northern Tanzania; relatively common in Serengeti National Park. Inhabits open plains where there are groups of acacia trees. Often feeds on the ground, sometimes in company of starlings.

GREY-HEADED SOCIAL WEAVER
Pseudonigrita arnaudi Plate 44

Identification. 5in, 13cm. Sexes alike. A rather short-tailed greyish-brown weaver with a pale dove-grey cap. Immature browner and cap buff.
Voice. A short piping call and a rather squeaky chatter.
Distribution and Habitat. Local resident western and southern Sudan and southern Ethiopia, south through Uganda and Kenya to central Tanzania. Inhabits dry thornbush and acacia country; gregarious, nesting in scattered colonies.

BLACK-CAPPED SOCIAL WEAVER
Pseudonigrita cabanisi Plate 44

Identification. 5in, 13cm. Sexes alike. A pale brown weaver with a black crown and black tail; underparts white with black streak in centre of breast; bill greenish-white. Immature pale brown.
Voice. Subdued chattering calls.
Distribution and Habitat. A very local bird in northern and eastern Kenya, Ethiopia and north-eastern Tanzania. Inhabits dry bush country where there

are acacias in which it nests in colonies. This is a common bird in the Samburu Game Reserve, Kenya.

RUFOUS SPARROW   *Passer motitensis*   Plate 44

Identification. 5½in, 14cm. Typical sparrow; ♂ with black-streaked rufous back and unmarked rufous rump; crown grey, pale rufous stripe from eye to nape; black streak through eye to ear-coverts; cheeks white; chin and throat black; rest underparts whitish to grey on flanks. ♀ has throat grey. The Kenya race lacks the black eye stripe and has grey cheeks.
Voice. Typical sparrow chirping.
Distribution and Habitat. Local resident in the Sudan, Ethiopia and Somalia, Uganda, Kenya and northern Tanzania. Inhabits open thornbush country and cultivation; often near human habitations. Often feeds on the ground.
Allied Species. The Indian race of the House Sparrow *(P. domesticus)*, 5½in, 14cm, is an introduced species recorded from Mombasa, Kenya and Zanzibar. Present status unknown but no recent records.

SOMALI SPARROW   *Passer castanopterus*   Plate 44

Identification. 5in, 13cm. Differs from the Rufous Sparrow in having the top of the head tawny-rufous and the underparts and cheeks washed with yellow.
Voice. Typical sparrow chattering.
Distribution and Habitat. Local resident Somalia, Ethiopia and northern Kenya where it is most frequent in Turkana near Lodwar. In dry bush country, favouring old acacia trees growing along wadis.

GREY-HEADED SPARROW   *Passer griseus*   Plate 44

Identification. 6in, 15cm. Head grey; mantle tawny-brown without streaking; rump and shoulders bright rufous. Immature duller with trace of streaking on mantle.
Voice. Typical sparrow chirping.
Distribution and Habitat. Local resident over much of East Africa south to Malawi and Zambia. Usually associated with human dwellings, but also occurs in bush country and cultivation.

PARROT-BILLED SPARROW   *Passer gongonensis*   Plate 44

Identification. 7in, 18cm. General appearance a large edition of the Grey-headed Sparrow with a relatively much heavier bill. Head greyish, unstreaked tawny-brown mantle and rufous rump; below greyish; bill very large and heavy.

Voice. Typical sparrow chirping.

Distribution and Habitat. Central and southern Ethiopia and eastern Kenya. Inhabits open country with scattered trees and bushes; most frequent at the Kenya coast.

Allied Species. Swainson's Sparrow *(P. swainsonii)*, 6in, 15cm, is like a very dark edition of the Grey-headed Sparrow with a chestnut-brown lower back. Occurs from Port Sudan to Ethiopia and northern Somalia in bush and acacia country. The Swahili Sparrow *(P. suahelicus)*, 5½in, 14cm, differs from the Grey-headed Sparrow in having the head, nape and mantle the same colour, dusky grey. It occurs locally in open acacia and other woodland and bush country in southern Kenya and northern Tanzania.

CHESTNUT SPARROW   *Passer eminibey*   Plate 44

Identification. 4½in, 11½cm. ♂ uniform deep chestnut; wings and tail brown with pale edgings. ♀ and non-breeding ♂ earth-brown above with black streaking on mantle; pale rufous stripe over eye; underparts pale buffy-grey to whitish on belly. ♀♀ and non-breeding ♂♂ best identified by small size.

Voice. Subdued chirping.

Distribution and Habitat. Locally common in southern Sudan, Ethiopia, eastern Uganda, Kenya and northern Tanzania. Inhabits arid bush country; gregarious, often associated with Red-billed Queleas and other weavers.

YELLOW-SPOTTED PETRONIA   *Petronia xanthosterna* Plate 44

Identification. 6in, 15cm. A grey sparrow-like bird, unstreaked, with greyish-white underparts; pale yellow spot in centre of throat, not always noticeable in field; narrow white ring around eye; pale stripe above eye. Occurs in pairs or small flocks; feeds mainly on the ground.

Voice. Sparrow-like chirps but usually silent.

Distribution and Habitat. Occurs locally in the Sudan, Ethiopia and Somalia south through eastern Uganda, Kenya to north-eastern Tanzania. Found in arid bush country, open savannah woodland and cultivation where there are bushes and trees.

Allied Species. The Bush Petronia *(P. dentata)*, 5in, 13cm, is smaller and paler than the Yellow-spotted Petronia with a greyish crown and a pale russet-brown mantle. It occurs in the Sudan, Ethiopia, northern Uganda and north-western Kenya in arid bush country.

YELLOW-THROATED PETRONIA
Petronia superciliaris **Plate 44**

Identification. 6in, 15cm. Brownish-grey in general colour with heavy blackish streaking on upperparts; below greyish-white with a yellow spot in centre of throat.
Voice. Various chirping notes.
Distribution and Habitat. Locally common in woodland and bush country in Tanzania and Central Africa. Found in pairs or small parties.

SPECKLE-FRONTED WEAVER *Sporopipes frontalis* **Plate 43**

Identification. 5in, 13cm. A pale greyish-brown, sparrow-like bird with a bright rufous hind neck; crown and stripe on each side of throat black, speckled with tiny white spots; below greyish-white.
Voice. A liquid 'tsssk' and a finch-like twittering song.
Distribution and Habitat. Locally common in the drier areas of Kenya, Uganda and northern and central Tanzania; also in the Sudan and Ethiopia. Found in arid bush, woodland and marginal cultivation; gregarious or in pairs.

STARLINGS: Sturnidae

A group of medium-sized usually gregarious birds; many species possess brilliantly metallic plumage, greens, blues, purples and violet predominating. Most species are noisy and conspicuous.

REDWING STARLING *Onychognathus morio* **Plate 47**

Identification. 12in, 30cm. A thickset starling with a long tail, entire plumage glossy violet-black with flight feathers conspicuously rufous in flight. ♀ has head, neck and throat washed grey; eyes red. Immature sooty-black with little gloss. Occurs in pairs or flocks.
Voice. Loud, drawn-out whistles 'tee-jeeoooo' and shorter piping calls. Often calls on the wing.
Distribution and Habitat. Local resident through East and Central Africa. Occurs usually on rocky hills, cliffs and precipices, wooded and forested areas and in cultivation. In Nairobi, Kenya it is found on buildings in the city centre.
Allied Species. The Chestnut-wing Starling *(O. fulgidus)*, 11in, 28cm, is very similar to the Red-wing Starling in general appearance but differs in having

the sides of the face, chin and throat glossy green, not violet-black. It is a West African forest treetop starling known from forests in western Uganda and southern Sudan; uncommon and local.

SLENDER-BILLED CHESTNUT-WING STARLING
Onychognathus tenuirostris   **Plate 47**

Identification. 10in, 25cm. A slim blue-black starling with chestnut flight feathers; tail long; bill slender. ♀ differs from ♂ in having greyish head and chest.

Voice. Shrill liquid whistles and some chattering notes.

Distribution and Habitat. A high altitude species found both in montane forest and on alpine moorlands from Ethiopia south through Uganda, Kenya and Tanzania to Malawi and Zambia. Not uncommon alpine zone of Mt Kenya where birds search giant lobelias for snails. It is a more lightly built, slimmer bird than the Redwing Starling.

WALLER'S CHESTNUT-WING STARLING
Onychognathus walleri   **Plate 47**

Identification. 8in, 20cm. A thickset, relatively short-tailed blue-black starling with chestnut flight feathers; ♀ greyish on head. In pairs or small flocks in forest treetops.

Voice. Various liquid whistles.

Distribution and Habitat. This is another high-level forest species found in East Africa south to Malawi and Zambia. Occurs in mountain forest, usually above 5,000ft, 1,530m.

Allied Species. The Narrow-tailed Starling *(Poeoptera lugubris)*, 7in, 18cm, is a very slender blue-black starling with a long, graduated tail; ♀ greyer and with chestnut in the wing apparent in flight. A forest treetops starling known from the southern Sudan and forests in western Uganda. Stuhlmann's Starling *(Stilbopsar stuhlmanni)*, 6in, 15cm, is another small slender species, blue-black in ♂, ♀ grey with mainly chestnut flight feathers. Differs from the Narrow-tailed Starling in smaller size and thicker, shorter tail. Found in the forests of western Kenya and Uganda; also in southern Sudan. Kenrick's Starling *(Stilbopsar kenricki)*, 6in, 15cm, resembles Stuhlmann's Starling but is dull black without blue sheen. ♀ has chestnut in flight feathers. Found in mountain forests in Kenya and north-eastern Tanzania.

BRISTLE-CROWNED STARLING *Galeopsar salvadorii* **Plate 47**

Identification. 15–16in, 38–41cm. A large, very long-tailed blue-black starling with chestnut flight feathers and a rounded cushion of velvety-black feathers on the forehead; eyes red. ♀ similar but slightly greyish on head.

Voice. Various loud liquid whistles.

Distribution and Habitat. Ranges from Somalia and Ethiopia south to north-eastern Uganda and Kenya as far south as Lake Baringo and Isiolo. Inhabits inland cliffs and rocky gorges, in pairs or in small flocks. Much attracted to fruiting bushes of Salvadora persica. The velvety pompom on the forehead is very conspicuous in the field.

Allied Species. The White-billed Starling *(Pilorhinus albirostris)*, 10in, 25cm is a blue-black to violet-black starling with a square tail and a white bill. It is confined to rocky gorges and cliffs in northern and central Ethiopia. The white bill is conspicuous in the field. The Somali Chestnut-wing Starling *(Onychognathus blythii)* is very similar to the Redwing Starling but has a longer and more graduated tail. It measures 11in, 28cm. Confined to northern and north-eastern Ethiopia and northern Somalia; inhabits cliffs and rocky gorges.

PURPLE-HEADED GLOSSY STARLING
Lamprotornis purpureiceps   **Plate 47**

Identification. 7in, 18cm. A thickset, short-tailed, metallic green starling with a purple head and throat; eye dark brown; crown feathers short and velvety in texture. A forest treetop species, best identified by its short-tailed chunky appearance and its dark, not yellow, eye.

Voice. Various short, liquid whistles.

Distribution and Habitat. Local but not uncommon in the forests of western Uganda and south-eastern Sudan. Frequents fruiting fig trees, often in large flocks.

BLACK-BREASTED GLOSSY STARLING
Lamprotornis corruscus   **Plate 47**

Identification. 7in, 18cm. A rather slim, relatively long-tailed starling with dull metallic oily-green upperparts and chest; breast violet, merging to black on belly; eye bright orange.

Voice. Various harsh chattering and whistling calls.

Distribution and Habitat. Eastern and central districts of Kenya and eastern Tanzania; most frequent in coastal districts and along Tana River in Kenya. Frequents bush, open woodland and riverine forest. Often in large flocks when Salvadora bushes along the Tana are in fruit.

SPLENDID GLOSSY STARLING
Lamprotornis splendidus   **Plate 47**

Identification. 12in, 30cm. Mainly a forest treetop species, brilliantly metallic green and blue with a velvety-black band across the closed wing; tail violet-black, broadly tipped metallic blue-green; underparts, chin to belly metallic violet and coppery, the sides of chest and lower belly and under tail coverts metallic blue; eye creamy yellow. In flight the bird produces a loud swishing sound with its wings. Occurs in pairs or small flocks. Much attracted to fruiting fig trees.

Voice. Loud single or double guttural 'chark' or 'chark, chark' and a variety of liquid whistles.

Distribution and Habitat. A West African forest species which extends eastwards to southern Sudan, western Ethiopia, Uganda, western Kenya, western Tanzania and north-western Zambia. A partial migrant in some areas. Numerous in the forests of Uganda and common at Entebbe.

PURPLE GLOSSY STARLING   *Lamprotornis purpureus*   **Plate 47**

Identification. 10½in, 27cm. A thickset, brightly metallic bluish-green starling with violet-blue underparts; eye orange-yellow, conspicuously large. Violet-blue underparts and large orange-yellow eye distinguish it from the smaller Blue-eared Glossy Starling. The larger Splendid Glossy Starling has velvety-black bands across the closed wing and tail and a creamy eye.

Voice. Various chattering calls and soft whistles.

Distribution and Habitat. Locally not uncommon in Uganda, rarer in western Kenya; also occurs in the southern Sudan. Inhabits savannah woodlands, edges of forest and open bush country with scattered trees. Frequently gregarious in large flocks; feeds in trees and on the ground.

BRONZE-TAILED STARLING   *Lamprotornis chalcurus*   **Plate 47**

Identification. 8½in, 21½cm. A metallic bluish-green starling with deep violet-blue ear coverts; eye yellow; central tail feathers bronzy-violet or bronzy-blue. Similar to Blue-eared Glossy Starling in field and unless good view is obtained difficult to distinguish; best field characters are contrasting violet-blue ear coverts and violet-bronze central tail feathers.

Voice. Various musical whistles, but less vocal than Blue-eared Starling.

Distribution and Habitat. Ranges from southern Sudan to Uganda and western Kenya. Found usually in open savannah woodland and in bush country where there are scattered trees.

BLUE-EARED GLOSSY STARLING
Lamprotornis chalybaeus **Plate 47**

Identification. 9in, 23cm. A thickset metallic green starling, golden or bluish in some lights, with a bright orange-yellow eye. Throat and chest metallic green like upperparts, merging to metallic violet on belly. Ear-coverts bluish but not conspicuously so. Often perches and feeds on ground. Immature sooty-black with slight green gloss. Ruppell's Long-tailed Starling differs in having a white eye and a longer, graduated tail.
Voice. A variety of deep musical whistles and high-pitched chattering notes.
Distribution and Habitat. Common and widespread resident and partial migrant through greater part of East and Central Africa. Locally abundant in Kenya and Tanzania; found both in highlands and in lowland localities. Inhabits open park-like country, cultivation, the vicinity of human habitations and all kinds of woodlands.
Allied Species. The Lesser Blue-eared Starling *(L. chloropterus)*, 7in, 18cm, closely resembles a small edition of the Blue-eared Starling. It occurs mainly in woodland, especially in Brachystegia; gregarious. It has much the same distribution as the Blue-eared Starling but is much less common in the north of its range, becoming locally abundant in southern Tanzania and Central Africa. The Wedge-tailed Starling *(L. acuticaudus)*, 8in, 20cm, is similar to a Blue-eared Starling but has a more graduated, wedge-shaped tail and red eyes. Occurs in woodland in north-western Zambia.

RUPPELL'S LONG-TAILED STARLING
Lamprotornis purpuropterus **Plate 47**

Identification. 13–14in, 33–36cm. A brightly metallic violet-blue starling with the head and throat washed bronze; tail long and graduated; eyes creamy-white. Immature duller. Best recognised by long tail and creamy eye. Usually in pairs or small parties; often alights and feeds on the ground.
Voice. Various chattering calls and whistles.
Distribution and Habitat. Local resident and partial migrant southern Sudan, Ethiopia, south through Uganda and Kenya to Tanzania. Inhabits bush and acacia country, savannah and open woodland and cultivation.
Allied Species. Meve's Long-tailed Starling *(L. mevesii)*, 14in, 36cm, is a local resident, sometimes common, in mopane woodland in Malawi, Zambia and Rhodesia. It differs from Ruppell's Long-tailed Starling in having the head dark blue and violet without bronze sheen; rump metallic coppery-gold.

VIOLET-BACKED STARLING *Cinnyricinclus leucogaster* **Plate 46**

Identification. 6½in, 16½cm. Upperparts and throat brilliant violet-blue, changing in some lights to crimson-purple; breast and belly white; eyes yellow. ♀ and immature quite different with mottled brown upperparts, below white streaked and spotted dark brown. A bird of the tree-tops, rarely seen on the ground. Appears when trees, especially figs, are in full fruit, disappears when crop is over; very gregarious.

Voice. A soft twittering whistle of three or four notes.

Distribution and Habitat. Local resident and migrant throughout East and Central Africa. Frequents forested and wooded areas, open park-like country with scattered trees and gardens where there are fruiting trees; also in dry bush country where there are fig trees.

Allied Species. Sharpe's Starling *(Cinnyricinclus sharpii)*, 6½in, 16½cm, is another bird of the treetops in forest or wooded country, local in Uganda, Kenya and northern Tanzania. It resembles a ♂ Violet-backed Starling at a distance but upperparts and throat are dark metallic blue-black; below pale buff, washed rufous on the belly.

ABBOTT'S STARLING *Cinnyricinclus femoralis* **Plate 46**

Identification. 6½in, 16½cm. A rather stumpy-looking blue-black starling with a white breast and abdomen; eye yellow; sexes alike. The similar Sharpe's Starling has the breast and abdomen rufous-buff.

Voice. Various rather high-pitched whistles.

Distribution and Habitat. A local and very uncommon starling found in south-eastern Kenya and north-eastern Tanzania. Inhabits mountain forest, keeping to the treetops. Perhaps most frequent in forests on Mt Kilimanjaro, Tanzania, where it associates with another treetop species, Kenrick's Starling.

MAGPIE STARLING *Speculipastor bicolor* **Plate 46**

Identification. 7½in, 19cm. ♂, upperparts, head, chest, wings and tail bluish-black; white patch on flight feathers; breast and abdomen creamy-white; eye bright red. ♀ differs in having head and chest grey, not black.

Voice. Various shrill whistles.

Distribution and Habitat. Local and often of irregular appearance in northern arid districts of Kenya and north-eastern Uganda; also in southern Ethiopia and southern Somalia. Most frequent in Turkana district, Kenya where it is locally common, especially in those areas where large termite hills are a feature of the landscape.

WHITE-WINGED STARLING *Neocichla gutturalis* **Plate 46**

Identification. 8in, 20cm. A pale-looking greyish-brown starling with dark wings and tail and a white wing patch; below, pinkish-buff with a wide black streak on the throat. Found in small groups, nearly always in Brachystegia woodland. Not very starling-like in appearance; flight rather heavy, resembling that of helmet-shrikes.
Voice. Harsh, strident call notes.
Distribution and Habitat. A very local and uncommon bird found in central and south-western Tanzania and in the Luangwa Valley in Zambia. Inhabits Brachystegia (miombo) woodland, especially where the trees are well spaced and large. Feeds on the ground. White wing patches noticeable in flight.

FISCHER'S STARLING *Spreo fischeri* **Plate 46**

Identification. 7in, 18cm. A plump, short-tailed pale grey starling with a white belly and pale grey crown; eye pale cream. In shape and stance general appearance that of Superb Starling but quite different in colour.
Voice. Various whistles and chattering calls.
Distribution and Habitat. Local and generally uncommon in southern Ethiopia, southern Somalia, eastern Kenya and north-eastern Tanzania. Often settles and feeds on the ground. Common in the Tsavo National Park, Kenya.

WHITE-CROWNED STARLING *Spreo albicapillus* **Plate 46**

Identification. 9in, 23cm. An ashy-brown starling with a relatively long tail; crown and abdomen white and white streaks on breast. Feeds largely on the ground.
Voice. Chattering calls.
Distribution and Habitat. Local resident eastern Ethiopia, Somalia and at North Horr, Kenya. Inhabits acacia woodland, especially along dry river beds. Common in parts of northern Somalia.

HILDEBRANDT'S STARLING *Spreo hildebrandti* **Plate 46**

Identification. 7in, 18cm. Dark metallic violet-blue on upperparts, wings, tail, and chest; breast and belly rufous; under wing and under tail-coverts rufous; eye orange-red. The somewhat similar Superb Starling has a white band across breast and white under the wings and tail, and a cream coloured eye.
Voice. Various melodious whistles; song a series of drawn-out double whistles.

Distribution and Habitat. Local resident southern half of Kenya and northern Tanzania; commonest in the Ukamba country of Kenya. Inhabits bush and wooded savannah, riverine acacia belts and cultivation. Usually gregarious and like the Superb Starling commonly feeds on the ground.

Allied Species. Shelley's Starling *(S. shelleyi)*, 6½in, 16½cm, differs in having the breast and belly dark rufous-chocolate. It breeds in Ethiopia and Somalia and appears as a non-breeding migrant in eastern Kenya. It is common along the Tana River when the Salvadora bushes are in fruit. It inhabits acacia bordered dry river beds and thornbush country. The Chestnut-bellied Starling *(S. pulcher)*, 7in, 18cm, resembles a very dull plumaged Hildebrandt's Starling, greenish sooty-brown on the head and neck, dull green on mantle; below chestnut. It occurs in central and eastern Sudan and northern Ethiopia. Found in dry acacia and bush country.

SUPERB STARLING   *Spreo superbus*   Plate 46

Identification. 7in, 18cm. A plump short-tailed starling, metallic blue and green, head blackish; breast and belly bright rufous-chestnut; narrow white band across breast; under tail-coverts and below wings white; eyes pale yellowish-cream. Immature duller and eyes dark. Hildebrandt's and Shelley's Starlings also have rufous bellies but lack white breast-band and under tail-coverts, and below wings rufous. Feeds mainly on the ground, often below or near acacia trees.

Voice. Various chattering and whistling notes; song a sustained warbling. Sometimes mimics other bird calls.

Distribution and Habitat. Widespread resident and partial migrant, often common, Somalia and Ethiopia, south through Kenya and Uganda to southern Tanzania. Frequents thornbush and acacia country and the vicinity of human dwellings. Gregarious and usually tame and fearless of man.

GOLDEN-BREASTED STARLING   *Cosmopsarus regius*   Plate 46

Identification. 12–14in, 30–36cm. Slim with long graduated tail; brilliant green, blue and violet on upperparts and throat; below contrasting rich golden-yellow on breast, belly and under tail-coverts; eyes white. Immature much duller. The most beautiful of the East African starlings and the easiest to identify in the field. Normally occurs in small flocks or pairs; usually shy and wild.

Voice. Various loud whistling call notes.

Distribution and Habitat. Local resident and partial migrant Ethiopia and Somalia, south through eastern Kenya and northern half of eastern Tanzania. Inhabits dry bush and thornbush country; locally common in the Tsavo National Park, Kenya.

ASHY STARLING   *Cosmopsarus unicolor*   **Plate 47**

Identification. 12in, 30cm. Sexes alike. An entirely brownish-grey starling
with a long graduated tail; eye pale yellowish-cream. Trace of a greenish wash
on mantle.
Voice. Soft whistling calls.
Distribution and Habitat. Locally common in bush country, acacia woodland
and open park-like country with baobab trees in Tanzania. The pale creamy
eyes are conspicuous in the field. Occurs in pairs or small flocks.

WATTLED STARLING   *Creatophora cinerea*   **Plate 46**

Identification. 8½in, 21½cm. Gregarious pale grey starling with a prominent
whitish rump and black wings and tail. In breeding season the ♂ has the head
bare of feathers, the skin yellow and black, with a large fleshy black wattle on
forehead above bill and another smaller black wattle in centre of crown;
double large pendulent wattle on throat. In non-breeding season the wattles
disappear and head becomes feathered. ♀ retains head feathers but grows
two small wattles on throat. Immature resembles ♀ but browner.
Voice. A soft but rather squeaky whistle; less noisy than many species of
starling.
Distribution and Habitat. Widely distributed throughout East and Central
Africa. Extremely erratic in its appearances. Its movements appear to depend
on the availability of an abundance of insect life. It breeds in East Africa
where good rains have fallen and insects, often but not always grasshoppers
and locusts, are plentiful. It inhabits thornbush and acacia woodland, open
country, and especially pasture where it associates with horses, cattle and
sheep, running between the animals' feet and catching insects disturbed by
them.

RED-BILLED OXPECKER   *Buphagus erythorhynchus*   **Plate 46**

Identification. 7in, 18cm. Rather slim, ash-brown birds with thick red bills
and a yellow eye-ring wattle; associated with domestic stock and large game
animals (but not elephants), perching upon and climbing all over the animals
searching for food – ticks and bloodsucking flies.
Voice. A hissing 'tssssss' and a shrill chattering call, often uttered in flight.
Distribution and Habitat. Local resident and partial migrant from Somalia,
Ethiopia and the Sudan southwards through Kenya, Uganda and Tanzania
to Central Africa. Numerous in many parts of its range, especially where
there is an abundance of game animals. Frequents open plains country and
also bush and woodland, often found in cultivated areas where associated
with domestic stock.

YELLOW-BILLED OXPECKER   *Buphagus africanus*   Plate 46

Identification. 7½in, 19cm. Similar in general appearance to the Red-billed Oxpecker but with a much heavier chrome-yellow, red-tipped bill and a pale buff rump-patch; lacks eye-wattles.

Voice. Hissing and chattering calls.

Distribution and Habitat. Has a wide range through East and Central Africa but is a far less common species than the Red-billed Oxpecker. Both species occur alongside one another in the Northern Frontier Province of Kenya and elsewhere. Like the Red-billed Oxpecker it associates both with big game and with domestic animals.

ORIOLES: Oriolidae

A group of active, thrush-sized birds, usually of brilliant yellow plumage, inhabiting treetops in woodland and forest. Calls are loud, clear melodious whistles.

AFRICAN GOLDEN ORIOLE   *Oriolus auratus*   Plate 46

Identification. 9in, 23cm. ♂ bright yellow with black eye streak; wings black, broadly edged yellow on coverts and flight feathers; tail black and yellow; bill carmine. ♀ and immature yellowish-green with darker wings and tail; underparts yellow lightly streaked grey; eye streak dark grey. Flight rapid and direct, long undulations with upward sweep as it enters tree; shy, stays well concealed amongst foliage of tree-tops.

Voice. A clear melodious whistle 'weeka-wee-ooo' and other whistles and a mewing call.

Distribution and Habitat. Local resident and partial migrant through much of East and Central Africa, breeding in Tanzania and southwards. Frequents tall bushy woodland, open and riverine forest and Brachystegia woodland.

Allied Species. The European Golden Oriole *(Oriolus oriolus)*, 9in, 23cm, is a winter visitor and passage migrant to East and Central Africa. ♂ differs in having black wings without wide yellow edges; ♀ is pale grey below and lacks the dusky eye streak. Often abundant during April on migration along the Kenya coast. Inhabits bush, scrub, woodland and forest.

BLACK-HEADED ORIOLE   *Oriolus larvatus*   Plate 46

Identification. 9in, 23cm. A bright yellow oriole with a black head and throat; wing feathers primaries edged white, secondaries edged yellow ♂ and ♀

similar; immature greener with yellow streaks on head and throat. Normally in this species the tail is green and yellow, but the Kenya highlands forest race, *O. l. percivali*, has the central rectrices black centred.

Voice. A series of liquid melodious whistles.

Distribution and Habitat. Common resident and partial migrant throughout East and Central Africa. Inhabits acacia and other types of open woodland, scrub, coastal bush and highland forest. Keeps to treetops but less shy than the two golden orioles.

Allied Species. The Black-winged Oriole *(O. nigripennis)*, 9in, 23cm, is a lowland forest species in East Africa known from southern Sudan and the Bwamba Forest, western Uganda. Like the Kenya Highlands forest race of the Black-headed Oriole the central tail feathers are black; the primaries are black and the secondaries are edged broadly with yellow. The Western Black-headed Oriole *(O. brachyrhynchus)*, 8½in, 21½cm, is also found in lowland forests; it may be distinguished from the Black-winged Oriole by its green and yellow tail feathers, and from the Black-headed Oriole by its green-edged, not yellow-edged, secondaries. It occurs in southern Sudan, Uganda and western Kenya in the Kakamega Forest. The Black-headed Forest Oriole *(O. monacha)*, 9in, 23cm, occurs in juniper forest in the highlands of Ethiopia. Its secondaries are edged with green, the primaries with grey; there are no white tips to the primary feathers. The Green-headed Oriole *(O. chlorocephalus)*, 8½in, 22cm, is another yellow oriole but with the head and chest moss green, not black; wing feathers edged blue-grey; tail green with yellow tips to outer feathers. It occurs in mountain forest on the Usambara, Nguru and Uluguru Mountains, Tanzania, in mountain forest in southern Tanzania and in Malawi.

DRONGOS: Dicruridae

Medium-sized black shrike-like birds with hooked bills and more or less forked tails, the outer feathers curving outwards towards the tip, 'fish-tail' fashion. Feeding habits resemble those of some species of flycatchers – catching insects in flight and returning to same perch.

DRONGO *Dicrurus adsimilis* Plate 46

Identification. 9–10in, 23–25½cm. Plumage glossy black; tail forked and 'fish-tailed;' inner webs of flight feathers ashy imparting a pale wash to the wings when the bird flies; iris red. Immature has greyish tips to feathers of upper-parts and underparts. The ♂ Black Cuckoo Shrike is glossy black but lacks the forked tail, has a yellow gape and a dark brown eye. The South African Black Flycatcher is of slim build with an unforked tail, a small bill and dark brown eyes.

Voice. Most vocal at dawn and at dusk, relatively silent during the day. Has a great variety of harsh metallic call notes and clear whistles.

Distribution and Habitat. Common resident through most of East and Central Africa. Inhabits all kinds of woodland, acacia and thornbush country and semi-wooded scrub; at the coast favours coconut plantations.

Allied Species. The Velvet-mantled Drongo *(D. modestus)*, 9½–11in, 24–28cm, is all black with the tail noticeably long and strongly 'fish-tailed.' Feathers of mantle velvety in texture, not glossy. This is a forest species, usually seen perched on bare branches of tall forest trees. It ranges from southern Sudan to Uganda and western Kenya.

SQUARE-TAILED DRONGO   *Dicrurus ludwigii*   Plate 46

Identification. 7in, 18cm. A smaller bird than the Drongo with the tail relatively short and only slightly forked. Immature spotted buffy-grey on mantle and chest.

Voice. Normally silent during the day; various whistles.

Distribution and Habitat. Local but widely distributed in East Africa, commoner in Central Africa. Inhabits forests, dense woodland and Brachystegia woodland. In East Africa most frequent in western Kenya and north-eastern Tanzania.

CROWS and allies: Corvidae

Plumage of many species black or black and white. The largest of the perching birds; bills usually heavy with nostrils covered by forward-pointing bristles. Most species feed mainly on the ground; omnivorous.

PIED CROW   *Corvus albus*   Plate 48

Identification. 18in, 46cm. Black with a white breast and a white crescent on the hind neck; immature similar.

Voice. A deep guttural croak.

Distribution and Habitat. Widely but locally distributed throughout most of the Ethiopian Region. In East and Central Africa locally common; subject to erratic migrational movements. Inhabits open country, cultivation, refuse dumps, the vicinity of human habitations and margins of rivers, lakes and swamps, and the sea coast.

WHITE-NECKED RAVEN   *Corvus albicollis*   Plate 48

Identification. 22in, 56cm. A large, heavily-built raven, entirely black except for a crescent shaped white patch between the hind neck and the upper part of the mantle. Immature similar.
Voice. Typical deep raven croaks.
Distribution and Habitat. The White-necked Raven occurs locally through East and Central Africa, frequenting rocky hills and escarpments, inland cliffs and the vicinity of hunting camps; much attracted to neighbourhood of human dwellings where it acts as a scavenger.

THICK-BILLED RAVEN   *Corvus crassirostris*   Plate 48

Identification. 25in, 64cm. The Thick-billed Raven differs from the White-necked Raven in being larger, having a much larger and heavier bill, and in having a large white patch on the back of the head joined by a narrow white streak to a white crescent at the base of the hind neck. Immature similar.
Voice. Harsh and guttural croaks.
Distribution and Habitat. Confined to northern and central Ethiopia, where it takes the place of the White-necked Raven. It occurs in rocky hill country, on inland cliffs and near human habitations where it acts as a scavenger.

FAN-TAILED RAVEN   *Corvus rhipidurus*   Plate 48

Identification. 18in, 46cm. This is an all-black raven with an extremely short tail; immature similar to adult but duller and browner. Nostril bristles very long and fan shaped.
Voice. A shrill falsetto 'pruk.'
Distribution and Habitat. Northern districts of Kenya and Uganda, to the Sudan, Ethiopia and Somalia. Common in rocky hill country and the vicinity of inland cliffs; acts as a scavenger near human habitations and camps.

DWARF RAVEN   *Corvus edithae*   Plate 48

Identification. 18in, 46cm. An all black raven with a moderately long tail; closely resembles an all black Pied Crow. The Fan-tailed Raven has an extremely short tail and broad wings. The Dwarf Raven is sometimes classified as a race of the Brown-necked Raven of the Middle East. Its colonial nesting habits and call suggest that this is incorrect.

Voice. Very weak cawing and croaking notes.

Distribution and Habitat. Locally not uncommon in Ethiopia, Somalia and northern Kenya. Often gregarious, nesting in colonies in acacia trees, not on cliff faces like most ravens. Attracted to human encampments and settlements as a scavenger.

CAPE ROOK   *Corvus capensis*   **Plate 48**

Identification. 17in, 43cm. Entire plumage glossy black, tinged brown on the head; feathers of throat lax, bill very slender for a corvid. Resembles a European Rook but throat covered with long feathers.

Voice. A guttural, high-pitched 'kaaah.'

Distribution and Habitat. Local resident, sometimes common, in southern Sudan, Ethiopia and Somalia, south to Uganda, Kenya and northern Tanzania. In Zambia occurs in the Balovale district; widely distributed but uncommon in Rhodesia. Frequents open plains where there are scattered trees, cultivated and pasture land and sometimes lightly wooded areas.

INDIAN HOUSE CROW   *Corvus splendens*   **Plate 48**

Identification. 13in, 33cm. In general appearance resembles a large slender jackdaw. An introduced species now locally common in East Africa.

Voice. A series of rather soft caws.

Distribution. An introduced crow now abundant along the Kenya coast and in north-eastern Tanzania; also on Zanzibar Island and Port Sudan. Associated with man.

PIAPIAC   *Ptilostomus afer*   **Plate 48**

Identification. 14in, 35cm. A blackish-brown, long-tailed magpie-like bird found in flocks in the vicinity of borassus palms. The bill is black, or purplish-pink with a black tip; eye violet. Occurs in small flocks and feeds mainly on the ground. Often associates with cattle, elephants and other large animals, using them as animated perches and catching insects disturbed by them.

Voice. A deep piping call; alarm call a scolding chatter.

Distribution and Habitat. A West African species which extends to western and northern Uganda with one record in extreme western Kenya. Inhabits grasslands near borassus palms and pasture; very gregarious.

Allied Species. The Chough *(Pyrrhocorax pyrrhocorax)*, 13in, 33cm, velvety glossy black with purplish tinge and slender red bill and red legs, occurs rarely in the Simen district of northern Ethiopia. It frequents cliffs in mountain country.

ABYSSINIAN BUSH CROW *Zavattariornis stresemanni* Plate 48

Identification. 11in, 28cm. Upperparts grey, forehead and upper tail-coverts whitish; wings and tail black with slight gloss; below white, greyish on chest and flanks; bare skin around eye blue.

Voice. A high-pitched 'chek.'

Distribution and Habitat. Restricted to the Boran district of southern Ethiopia, most frequent near Yavello. Inhabits acacia bush and stunted woodland, normally in small parties. Rather starling-like in its habits.

Appendix

Institutions and Societies: The following Institutions and Societies are listed for the convenience of visitors who may wish to make contacts with local naturalists and to refer to ornithological collections and libraries.

Kenya: The National Museum, P.O. Box 40658, Nairobi. Extensive exhibition and research collections. The Belcher Ornithological Library and the Natural History Society's Library are housed in the museum.

The East Africa Natural History Society, c/o The National Museum, P.O. Box 40658, Nairobi.

Uganda: The Uganda Museum, Kampala. No extensive zoological collections at present.

The Uganda Society, Private Bag, Kampala. Small reference collections of birds are kept at the headquarters of the Queen Elizabeth National Park and the Murchison Falls National Park.

Tanzania: King George V Memorial Museum, P.O. Box 511, Dar es Salaam. A small exhibition collection of birds is being built up.

Zambia: Rhodes-Livingstone Museum, P.O. Box 124, Livingstone. Limited bird collections being built up.

Zambia Natural History Club, P.O. Box 844, Lusaka, Zambia.

Zimbabwe Rhodesia National Museum of Southern Rhodesia, P.O. Box 240. Bulawayo. Extensive exhibition and research bird collections and library facilities.

Rhodesian Ornithological Society, c/o P.O. Box 240, Bulawayo.

Bibliography. The following books are suggested for reference purposes:

ALEXANDER, W. B., *Birds of the Ocean*, New York and London.

ARCHER, G. F. and E. M. GODMAN, *Birds of British Somaliland and the Gulf of Aden*, 4 vols., London.

BANNERMAN, D. A., *The Birds of West and Equatorial Africa*, 8 vols., Edinburgh and London.

BATES, G. L., *Handbook of the Birds of West Africa*, London.

BENSON, C. W. and C. M. N. WHITE, *Checklist of the Birds of Northern Rhodesia*, Lusaka.

BENSON, C. W., *Checklist of the Birds of Nyasaland*, Blantyre.

BELCHER, C. F., *Birds of Nyasaland*, London.

CAVE, F. O. and J. D. MACDONALD, *Birds of the Sudan*, Edinburgh.

CHAPIN, J. P., *The Birds of the Belgian Congo*, 4 vols., New York.

DELACOUR, J. and PETER SCOTT, *The Waterfowl of the World*, 3 vols., London.

FRIEDMANN, H., *The Parasitic Cuckoos of Africa*, Washington.

FRIEDMANN, H., *The Honey-Guides*, Washington.

FRIEDMANN, H., *The Parasitic Weaverbirds*, Washington.

JACKSON, F. J., *The Birds of Kenya Colony and the Uganda Protectorate*, 3 vols., London and Edinburgh.

LYNES, H., 'Review of the genus Cisticola,' *Ibis*. ser. 12, vol. 6, supp., London.

PETERSON, R. T., G. MOUNTFORT and P. A. D. HOLLOM, *A Field Guide to the Birds of Britain and Europe*, London.

MACKWORTH-PRAED, C. W. and C. H. B. GRANT, *Birds of Eastern and North-eastern Africa*, 2 vols., London.

ROBERTS, A., *The Birds of South Africa*, revised edition by MCLACHLAN and LIVERSIDGE, London.

SCLATER, W. L., *Systema Avium Aethiopicarum*, London.

SMITHERS, REAY H. N., M. P. STUART IRWIN and M. PATERSON., *Checklist of the Birds of Zimbabwe Rhodesia*, Cambridge, England.

VAURIE, CHARLES, *The Birds of the Palearctic Fauna*, London.

Index

Numbers in **bold** type refer to plate numbers